Plato and the Body

SUNY series in Ancient Greek Philosophy

Anthony Preus, editor

Plato and the Body

Reconsidering Socratic Asceticism

Coleen P. Zoller

Cover art: Stavros Kotsireas, *The Refugees*, 1988. Reprinted with permission.

Published by State University of New York Press, Albany

© 2018 State University of New York

All rights reserved

No part of this book may be used or reproduced in any manner whatsoever without written permission. No part of this book may be stored in a retrieval system or transmitted in any form or by any means including electronic, electrostatic, magnetic tape, mechanical, photocopying, recording, or otherwise without the prior permission in writing of the publisher.

For information, contact State University of New York Press, Albany, NY
www.sunypress.edu

Library of Congress Cataloging-in-Publication Data

Names: Zoller, Coleen P.
Title: Plato and the body : reconsidering socratic asceticism / Coleen P. Zoller.
Description: Albany : State University of New York Press, [2018] | Series: SUNY series in ancient Greek philosophy | Includes bibliographical references and index.
Identifiers: LCCN 2017044461 | ISBN 9781438470818 (hardcover : alk. paper) | ISBN 9781438470825 (pbk. : alk. paper) | ISBN 9781438470832 (ebook)
Subjects: LCSH: Plato. | Asceticism. | Socrates.
Classification: LCC B398.A8 Z65 2018 | DDC 184—dc23
LC record available at https://lccn.loc.gov/2017044461

10 9 8 7 6 5 4 3 2 1

For Jeff Turner,
my Socratic interlocutor, mentor, and friend

Contents

Acknowledgments		ix
Chapter 1.	Interpreting Asceticism in Plato	1
Chapter 2.	Moderation and Training for Death in the *Phaedo*	25
Chapter 3.	Beauty, Education, and Erotic Ascent in the *Symposium* and *Phaedrus*	59
Chapter 4.	Health, Justice, and Peace in the *Republic* and *Gorgias*	105
Chapter 5.	Interpretative Possibilities for the Late Dialogues	169
Epilogue		185
Notes		189
Works Cited		219
Index		239

Acknowledgments

My greatest debt is to Jeff Turner, who graciously read innumerable drafts and shared incredibly insightful guidance at every stage of my project. I also wish to thank the following mentors, colleagues, students, and friends for helpful feedback as I developed my manuscript: Richard Patterson, Roslyn Weiss, Mitch Miller, William Johnson, Tony Long, Tom Chance, Ed Lee, Tarik Wareh, Amy Coplan, Carol Wayne White, Sarah Farrant, Alissa Packer, Rabbi Nina Mandel, James Powers-Black, Karla Bohmbach, Lynn Palermo, Brian Johnson, Emily Anderson, Tom Stanley, students in my Plato seminars at Susquehanna University, audiences at various conferences and colloquia, and my anonymous readers and the editors at SUNY Press. I am particularly grateful to Courtney Radel and Jessica Gilchrist for their work as summer research assistants and to Susquehanna University for the 2014–16 grants that made their research possible. And much gratitude to Courtney Radel for compiling the index. Finally, many thanks to pictorial artist Stavros Kotsireas for permission to use his etching "The Refugees" as cover art.

Some pages of already published work appear here. I would like to thank the following for permission to reprint this material: Cambridge Scholars Press for excerpts from Zoller (2007) in chapters 1, 2, and 3; University of Malta Press for excerpts from Zoller (2010) in chapters 1, 2, and 3; and Lexington Books for excerpts from Zoller (2009) in chapters 1 and 4.

Chapter 1

Interpreting Asceticism in Plato

1.1 Loving Wisdom and Living in a Body

Many commentators have assumed that Plato is responsible for originating the view that loving wisdom is incongruous with being embodied. For instance, many feminists are critical of what they call Plato's "somatophobia" and take his dualistic metaphysical worldview to be incompatible with feminism.[1] And at the opposite end of the political spectrum, Strauss also accuses Plato of ignoring the body, *erôs,* and nature.[2] However, we are missing something about his dialogues when we accuse Plato of beginning the tradition that suppresses the importance of the physical in the life of the philosopher or any human being. My primary aim in this project is to offer insight into Plato's nuanced attitude toward the physical universe in general, and human bodies in particular, because this pertains to his understanding of what philosophy is and what philosophers do. As Plato developed what we now call philosophy, he set a framework that involves analytical thought in addition to a particular kind of lifestyle. Yet, on account of a caricature of his views concerning the physical, Plato is often named as the originator of an embarrassing view of embodied life.

One of Plato's main goals is to use his character Socrates[3] as an exemplar of the philosopher's special and rare nature. He has Socrates call himself a philosopher (*Ap.* 29d, *Phd.* 61a); and in most of his dialogues, Plato demonstrates that by observing Socrates we can learn about the lifestyle that is conducive to inquiry. But Plato's Socrates is not a simple character; his peculiar words and deeds are not always easy to interpret. Among the many complex aspects of Plato's Socrates is his remarkable self-discipline, what the Greeks would call *askesis* (practice; training). His self-discipline is highlighted in the dialogues, dovetailing with his desire to pursue knowledge and do what he thinks is best. Socrates's conversations with his interlocutors sometimes tempt us to believe that doing the right thing is easy when one has knowledge of what is best. However, Plato's Socrates usually claims not to have any substantial knowledge (*Ap.* 21b-d). This leaves Plato's readers at a bit of a loss with respect to the exact nature of Socrates's self-discipline. Many Platonic dialogues aim at the vindication of Socrates and philosophy, both of which can be difficult to understand. My project focuses on cultivating a more refined conception of the ascetic lifestyle epitomized by Plato's Socrates in the *Phaedo, Symposium, Phaedrus, Gorgias,* and *Republic*.[4]

Who is Plato's Socrates? This book will remind us that he is a philosopher deeply engaged in worldly matters, who uses his body to enjoy eating (*Smp.* 220a) and drinking (*Smp.* 220a), to sleep peacefully (*Crt.* 44a; *Prt.* 310b-c; *Smp.* 223d), to have sexual intercourse, to create a family (*Ap.* 34d; *Crt.* 60a), to participate in democracy, serving his community as a gadfly, a soldier (*Smp.* 219e; *Chrm.* 153b-d), and a member of the Council (*Ap.* 32b-c), to stand up to tyranny (*Ap.* 32d-e), to look after his circle of friends, to walk daily to the agora, to stroll the outskirts of Athens and observe the beauty of nature (*Phdr.* 229a-b), to travel to Piraeus for a religious festival (*R.* 327a), to adore beautiful people (*Smp.* 212c, 216d, 218e; *Prt.* 309a-b, 316a; *Chrm.* 153d-154d, 155d), to flirt (*Phdr.* 234d, 237a-b, *Smp.* 213d, *Chrm.* 156a), to be in love with Alcibiades (*Grg.* 481d), to follow his erotic passion for ideas and virtues. Is this down-to-earth life consistent with his asceticism?

For the sake of uncovering Plato's vision of how human beings who want to be wise and good should be disposed toward the physical world and the human body, we must understand Plato's answers to the following questions: What attitudes and dispositions do wisdom lovers have? How exactly do philosophers care for the soul, and what treatment of the body does that psychic care[5] dictate? In what sorts of activities do philosophers participate? What do they value, and why? Or, to put it generally, what sort of lifestyle is entailed by the *askesis* of which Socrates is an exemplar? Plato's answers to these kinds of questions reflect his sense of the standards of philosophy. Here I will try to clarify Plato's account of these matters without being constrained by the need to conform to the interpretation of Platonism that became conventional, which is linked especially to the *Phaedo*. As Roochnik writes, "This dialogue gives voice to what is surely the most familiar characterization of Platonic philosophy: it is a quest for an 'otherworldly' wisdom, for a realm far above, and superior to, the earthly and mortal."[6] Like Roochnik, I challenge some of the fundamental assumptions about Plato made by those who espouse the most traditional interpretation of Platonic philosophy as otherworldly.[7]

In this introductory chapter, I will compare and contrast two interpretations of asceticism; briefly examine some consequences of misinterpreting Socratic asceticism, especially for women, people of color, the other animals, and nature itself; examine the analogical reasoning Plato relies on to advance innovative claims; consider the transformation of vernacular that arises out of Plato's use of analogical reasoning; call attention to Plato's use of pedagogical irony; and lay out the plan for the other chapters.

1.2 Two Interpretations of Socratic Asceticism

Conceiving of the soul as what animates the material stuff of the body causes Plato to consider the soul a human being's true self.[8] As a result, he is deeply concerned with how one ought to think of and treat the soul. Nevertheless, throughout the dialogues Plato makes clear that the question of how one should be disposed toward the soul is very much intertwined with the question of how one ought to handle the body, especially given that Plato's dialogues indicate that the largest aspect of the soul, the appetite, is charged with wanting what the human body needs to survive. Some of the appetite's pleasures come from restoration in the body, and although appetite belongs to the soul, the appetite in particular, and soul in general, could not be more essentially connected with the body. It is misguided to think the soul can be properly cared for while the body is renounced, and I will demonstrate that Plato does not make this mistake as some critics have thought.

A widespread and popular characterization of Plato assumes that his dualistic metaphysics requires the renunciation of all things physical, including the desires and needs of the human body. Plato variously describes the relation between the soul and the body as a prisoner in a cage (*Phd.* 82e3; *Cra.* 400c), a tomb (*Cra.* 400b; *Grg.* 493a), an oyster in its shell (*Phdr.* 250c6), a barnacle-covered sea-soaked creature (*R.* 611d–612a), an orbit shaken by a commotion (*Ti.* 43c-d), a person dressed in a costume to be stripped off (*Grg.* 524d), and the victim of a bad influence, maimed by the association (*R.* 611b). These metaphors vary in the degree to which they denounce the body, but they hold up the soul as more authentic than and superior to the body. However, I believe that a misinterpretation of the nature of Socrates's asceticism and his attitude toward the physical took hold when Neoplatonists such as Plotinus interpreted the Platonic dialogues with their own philosophical positions in mind, including the conviction that ethical-philosophical aspirations require treating matter as evil.[9] The view that matter is evil precipitates the austere treatment of the body and abhorrence of the physical world. These thinkers take the physical endeavors of life, such as sleeping, eating, being sexual, to be unimportant, detrimental in fact, to one who loves wisdom and goodness, and as a result, they roundly condemn the body. From this point of view, the way to contend with physically oriented desires in the soul is by attempting to eliminate them. According to Plotinus, the only situation better than not having to consider one's embodiment at all is that one experiences just enough physical illness to remind one why the body is the sort of despicable thing one is right to neglect.[10]

Neoplatonists regard the obliteration of the passions as the self-discipline appropriate for a philosopher. Plotinus held up "as an example to all who practised philosophy" a friend who ate only every other day, whose "renunciation and indifference to the needs of life" caused him to be "so gouty that he had to be carried in a chair," in addition to not being able to stretch out his hands.[11] Such injurious consequences of living an austere life do not disturb Plotinus at all; to him, all that matters is thought. Of Plotinus himself, Porphyry writes, "Even sleep he reduced by taking very little food, often not even a piece of bread, and by his continuous turning in contemplation to his intellect."[12] Conveying the view that it is a misfortune to be born into a body, Plotinus refused to have his likeness created by artists[13] and even rejected the notion of celebrating his own birthday (though he enthusiastically celebrated Plato's and Socrates's birthdays).[14] When Porphyry tells us that Plotinus refused medical treatments,[15] repudiated meat eating,[16] and slept and ate very little,[17] we might be tempted to think of Plotinus as a stern person, impervious to the needs and desires of the body. But when we learn that Plotinus was sickly,[18] with bad eyesight,[19] and had at age eight been shamed for his continuing desire to breastfeed,[20] it is no wonder that Porphyry begins *On the Life of Plotinus* with the following opening line: "Plotinus, the philosopher of our times, seemed ashamed of being in the body."[21] If the shame Porphyry discusses plays a role in Plotinus's thought, it is crucial not to assume automatically that Plato takes the human body as the epicenter of shame as well.

Given that Plotinus claims to be nothing more than an interpreter and continuator of Plato,[22] the important differences between Plato's views of embodiment and those of Plotinus were glossed over. Plotinus set the tone for subsequent readings of Plato by interpreting Plato in a way that was more in line with his own views, and thus began the legacy of interpreting Plato as a philosopher for whom the body is a source of shame. While the Neoplatonists were tempted to see their austere version of asceticism in Plato, in fact, careful consideration of the dialogues reveals a much more sophisticated conception of asceticism associated with Plato's Socrates.[23]

Before we explore whether or not Plato is the kind of ascetic his Neoplatonic and medieval Christian inheritors make him out to be, we must delve further into the meaning of asceticism. The Greek term *askesis* typically referred to athletic exercise. It is characteristic of Plato to make analogies between the body and the soul, and with respect to the issue of training, he was the first Western thinker to assert that human beings should pursue both the discipline that brings physical health as well as the kind that brings psychic health. Although some Indian and Chinese views of holistic medicine predate him by roughly 2,500 years, in the West Plato is the first proponent of holistic medicine despite merely sketching his view. We see this commitment to holistic medicine when he has Socrates say that, just as one part of the body cannot be treated successfully without treating the entire body, "one should not attempt to cure the body apart from the soul" (*Chrm.* 156c-e).[24]

This position is echoed also by Timaeus when he asserts the importance of not exercising the soul without the body or the body without the soul "so that each may be balanced by the other and so be sound" (*Ti.* 88b-c).[25] *Republic* 403d also comments on the relation between body and soul, suggesting that "a fit body doesn't by its own virtue make the soul good, but instead the opposite is true—a good soul by its own virtue makes the body as good as possible."[26] Yet, later in the *Republic*, Plato has Socrates say, "It's clear that [a person of understanding] will always cultivate the harmony of the body for the sake of the consonance of his soul" (591c-d). If we combine these notions, we arrive at Plato's theory of holistic medicine: a healthy soul facilitates physical health, and a healthy body reinforces the health of the soul.

It was common in Plato's time for individuals to employ physical trainers to assist them in their physical exercise. Having had his own psychic trainer (the historical Socrates), Plato wrote dialogues that exhort readers to engage in *askesis* that improves the condition of the soul, and Plato believes the care of the soul is not disconnected from the embodied life. As Peterson explains, "Care for the soul is a very practical matter of figuring out how you will conduct your life day to day. It is care for your dispositions and beliefs, your mental and emotional equipment out of which you act everyday. (Socrates does not mean that care for the soul is concern for some separable item stuck in the body, the tending of which is separate from concern for the activities of daily life.)"[27]

Unfortunately, the term *askesis* became increasingly identified with the austere view of psychic training maintained by the Neoplatonists and some medieval Christians. When the Christian version of *askesis* became primary, the Socratic/Platonic notion of *askesis,* a practice that is not linked to the austere rejection of pleasure and the physical, became secondary. As the original understanding of the term took a backseat to the Christian conception, discussing asceticism became a tricky business because of the potential for equivocation between these two dramatically different approaches to self-discipline.

Here I will contrast two interpretations of Plato's conception of *askesis,* which I refer to as "austere dualism" and "normative dualism."[28] Austere dualism denotes the interpretation of Plato that construes him as a strict metaphysical dualist whose contention that the physical world is not real leads him to renounce all things physical, especially the human body and its needs and the related desires in the soul's appetite. Having largely ignored the important role that the physical endeavors of daily life play in loving wisdom, austere dualist commentators interpret Plato's call for loving wisdom as a recommendation that one ought to renounce the physical entirely and withdraw from it as much as possible. This interpretation contends that Plato promotes the exclusively contemplative life as the philosophical ideal, while loathing the physical world and the human body.

At one end of the continuum of commentators who read Plato this way stands Plotinus, esteeming austere asceticism, and at the other end is Nietzsche, despising austere asceticism.[29] Nietzsche traces Christianity's self-denial back to Plato and loathes the "theoretical optimism" he thinks he sees in Plato, what he thinks of as a life-denying philosophy.[30] While I disagree with Nietzsche's interpretation of Plato as hostile to life, I concur with his appraisal that this austere strategy should not be venerated. Nevertheless, the austere dualist interpretation of Plato has long been conventional. Scholars who defend the traditional view include not only the Neoplatonist commentators, such as Plotinus, Olympiodorus, and Damascius, and Christian inheritors,[31] such as Clement of Alexandria, Gregory of Nazianzen, and his disciple Evagrius Ponticus, but also more recent commentators, including Nietzsche, Jowett, Archer-Hind, Stewart, Zeller, Grube, Collingwood, Hackforth, Bluck, A. E. Taylor, Dodds, Friedländer, Gosling, Guthrie, Gallop, Elshtain, C. C. W. Taylor, Hartsock, Dover, Bostock, Vernant, Rowe, Plumwood, Frede, Kahn, Nehamas, Lear, Robinson, Hadot, Griswold, Pakaluk, and Barney.[32] Part of my project will be to note misleading translation choices that operate on the presumption of austere dualism and, in turn, reinforce that interpretation.

In Roochnik's criticism of these interpreters, he says, "Such commentators take Plato to be a 'Platonist' who hates the sensible realm, and longs for the day when the soul will depart to 'the other place,' unencumbered by the nuisance of having a body."[33] Quite representative of the austere dualist interpretation, Pakaluk writes:

> Thinking is not something encouraged in the corporeal world, supported by it or aimed at by it. Rather, a true philosopher will engage in thinking *in spite of* the body, with its cares and distractions, and *in spite of* the corporeal world as a whole, with its business, wars, and absence of leisure. Thinking, then, is something alien to the world, and therefore its complete fulfillment is to be found, if at all, outside the world.[34]

And Griswold's view is arguably the most extreme illustration of the austere dualist interpretation. He writes:

> This leaves the world we actually inhabit an unlovable, even hateful, place. There would seem to be neither political nor philosophical reconciliation with the world (no scheme that explains the rationality of the world in a way that allows us to accept it as, perhaps forgive it for, being what it is). It is a tribute to Plato's artistry that so desperate a picture of the human condition could nonetheless have inspired so many for so long.[35]

I contest this austere interpretation, contending instead that in Plato's view philosophy was not "dangerously otherworldly,"[36] as austere dualist interpreters regularly posit.

Instead, I will demonstrate ample evidence that Plato should be read as a "normative dualist," to borrow Alison Jaggar's term.[37] The normative dualist version of asceticism prioritizes the soul over the body, but Plato does not loath the physical world and the human body just because he places the greatest value on the Forms and the soul. Jaggar uses this phrase in the course of critiquing thinkers who assume the physical basis of rationality is unimportant. As a normative dualist, Plato does hold the soul and its care as more dear than the body and its care, and feminists like Jaggar find this disappointing because they value the human body inherently. Platonism and feminism diverge here. Plato ranks Form over thing and soul before flesh, but he does so *without* denigrating the human body or nature itself, and this distinction is extremely important. On this view, philosophical asceticism is a practice that is *not* predicated upon disdain for the body in particular and the physical world in general.

It seems at times that Plato wishes the effort to be wise and good could be facilitated by never having been born in a human embodied state, but we should not assume that position entails fear of and loathing for the physical world or the human body. He is not satisfied by the finite realm of the physical, but he does not maintain that the physical is abhorrent or irrelevant. A philosopher loves the Forms, such as Beauty and Goodness, and will love the world to the extent that it has a share in and imitates the Forms. Indeed, Plato's philosophers have reason to love and be curious about the world, while they prioritize making their souls as wise and good as possible. Nehamas recognizes this when he writes that "beauty is not the exclusive property of the Forms. It is a feature of the world around us. . . . In a very serious sense, as the philosopher gains a vision of the Form of Beauty, he falls in love with the world itself."[38] As I will show, on account of this love Plato's philosophers use the flesh as a vehicle to embody the divine Forms in the physical world to the greatest extent possible.

1.3 A Brief Look at Some Consequences of Misinterpreting Socratic Asceticism

Some might suggest that misinterpreting Socratic asceticism is simply a scholarly problem with historical value but without consequence on the way human beings actually live their lives today. I disagree. How we interpret the asceticism Plato admires in his Socrates has been influential in shaping Western consideration of the human body. Getting this aspect of Platonic interpretation wrong is not just a scholarly problem. Through the Neoplatonic influence upon Christian thought, their austere account of asceticism steered the early Christian attitude toward embodiment, and as an outcome of Christianity's prominence, Western civilization has suffered from a very problematic relationship with embodiment. A host of problems have ensued. When we devalue the physical, we lessen concern for all that is linked with it—women, people of color, the other animals, and nature itself.

In this book I will uncover how carefully worked out Plato's views about the body and the soul are. His corpus contains an extensive number of substantial passages that discuss important issues about the body and the soul, and once we liberate our reading of those passages from the misleading approach that has been brought to them, we are able to use Plato's views as a resource on a variety of relevant issues. Let me comment briefly in this section on some examples of how Plato's view of the physical could be a resource for those working on assorted contemporary problems. As we shall see in this section, sundry concerns have been at stake while Plato's interpreters have been shaping civilization.

First, interpreting Plato's metaphysics has consequences for how we treat the natural world.[39] The austere dualist interpretation contends that Plato denounces all physical things, including nature itself. For instance, Plumwood claims that "Plato strongly devalues nature in virtually all its forms."[40] If Plumwood were correct, then Plato's way of thinking would be responsible for a tradition that has permitted the neglect and/or destruction of the physical environment and the other life forms in it. However, there is no evidence that Plato's metaphysical commitments preclude him from venerating the natural world in his dialogues. Instead, in Plato's dialogues we find interlocutors honoring nature.

For example, at *Timaeus* 77a-c Plato has Timaeus explain that without trees, plants, and seeds to protect and nourish us our bodies would "waste away and be depleted, and so to perish." And the beginning of the *Laws* is set with elderly gentlemen from Athens, Crete, and Sparta appreciating the trees and meadows that will refresh them along the route of their very long Cretan path (625b-c). The Athenian also praises pottery and weaving (both the skills and the natural materials they require, such as clay and wool) as "a gift from God to men" that protects people from being "intolerably poor" (*L.* 679a-b). More than once in the *Laws* Plato has the Athenian give a nod to the duty human beings have to take care of the natural world. First, in Book V, speaking of land distribution, he writes: "Each man who receives a portion of land should regard it as the common possession of the entire state. The land is his ancestral home and he must cherish it even more than children cherish their mother; furthermore, Earth is a goddess, and mistress of mortal men" (*L.* 740a; see also *L.* 923a-b).[41] Then again, near the conclusion, the Athenian indicates that "the earth and every household hearth are already sacred to all the gods" (*L.* 955e).[42] Furthermore, Carone notes the example in the *Phaedrus* of Plato's exaltation of the natural beauty surrounding Socrates and Phaedrus as an example of Plato and his Socrates *not* loathing the natural environment.[43] She also refers to the *Critias* where Plato has Critias mention deforestation and soil erosion (*Criti.* 111b-c).[44] These examples verify that Plato's metaphysical dualism does not require ignoring or hating the natural world.

These passages about the natural world and natural beauty are part of a *very highly developed* set of conceptions of nature, beauty, and *kosmos* that we find in Plato. But reading Plato as an austere dualist obscures what a resource Plato's dialogues are for those working on issues pertaining to the natural environment.[45] If early commentators had paid proper attention to Plato revering nature, then Plato's influence on Western civilization might have kept us from the current global environmental crisis and the massive reduction in biodiversity.

Second, we should consider those who have been particularly associated with the body and nature. When austere dualist thinkers have encouraged human beings to renounce nature and to treat the physical with disdain, they license the disregard, disrespect, and devastation of whoever is associated with the body. I am in agreement with those who contend that women as well as non-Western, nonwhite people are oppressed insofar as they are subsumed into nature.[46] Furthermore, I imagine much more could be said by way of making connections between the condemnation of nature and various other forms of oppression too, if it were not beyond the scope of this book to study such connections in detail. For instance, other commentators have argued that the poor and working class are also associated with animals and the body in a classist hierarchy.[47] Here I cannot give a thorough account of these forms of oppression, but consider, for instance, the racist convention of associating people of color, especially African American women, with wild animals.[48] As Bordo writes, "[T]he racist ideology and imagery that construct non-European 'races' as 'primitive,' 'savage,' sexually animalistic, and indeed more *bodily* than the white 'races' extends to black women as well as to black men."[49] This exemplifies how the abhorrence of the physical world and nature can also translate into racist disdain and disregard. Consequently, women who live at the intersection of racism and sexism are doubly oppressed by this association between women and nature.

Misreading Plato as a philosopher who ignores or demeans the physical results in failing to see Plato as a resource for those working on a wide variety of women's issues. Let's consider several dimensions. Women have borne the brunt of the austere dualist interpretation's influence[50] in part because the austere account of asceticism became pervasive throughout Western culture as the epitome of purity and goodness.[51] The prevalence of this interpretation in effect established a standard for sexual morality. Yet, living up to the austere standard of chastity has historically been imposed upon women rather than men.[52] Even when the expectation of chastity is imposed more universally, many feminists have observed the "impossible monsters" that arise from sexual repression and the particular toll they have taken on women in various forms of violence.⁵³ Maybe we would not live in a culture of rape, violence, and female disempowerment if austere dualism had not appeared to condone the degradation of anything associated with the physical. Now that we can push aside that misguided view, scholars and others working on contemporary problems surrounding sexual morality would benefit from utilizing Plato as a resource.

Another example of Plato's contemporary relevance pertains to the feminine association with reproduction. Thinkers looking to emphasize a positive connotation between women and nature should turn to Plato as a very special resource. Historically human beings have experienced women as the caretakers of their infant bodies. Despite the fact that men are also embodied and also have a biological role in the process of creating new life (and, like women, can learn to raise children), men have been traditionally linked to culture and rationality, while women have been traditionally linked to nature (as well as emotion).⁵⁴ These connections have shaped society's attitude toward and treatment of women. According to Karen J. Warren, nature is construed as feminized, and women are seen as naturalized, with women called "cows, foxes, chicks, serpents, bitches, beavers, old bats, pussycats, cats, bird-brains, hare-brains."⁵⁵

However, Plato goes to great lengths to indicate how foolish it is to reduce women to their biological function (R. 454d-e). Nonetheless, he associates nature with women when he has Socrates refer to the Earth as our "nurturer" or wet nurse (*trophon*) (*Ti.* 40b) and "mother" (*mêtêr*) (*R.* 414e, *Mx.* 237e-238a). He also links the body with Earth when he has Socrates refer to the bodily as "earthy" (*geôdes*) (*Phd.* 81c)⁵⁶ and to the soul becoming covered in "wild, earthy, and stony profusion" because of its association with the body (*R.* 612a). And in the *Timaeus*'s reincarnation scheme Plato has Timaeus align women with other animals (*Ti.* 42b-d, 90e-92c).⁵⁷ Tong captures the problem at hand well when she writes, "If man is the lord of nature, if he has been given dominion over it, then he has control not only over nature but also over nature's human analog, woman. Whatever man may do to nature, he may also do to women."⁵⁸ We have already determined that Plato does *not* reduce women merely to their capacity to give birth and nurse and his dialogues do *not* in fact sanction contempt for nature. Yet, the problem with the association of women with nature arises in the reception of Plato's thought. Reading him as disdaining the body has assisted in the subsequent aspersing of whatever is commonly associated with the physical, particularly women.

In addition to connecting the feminine with nature, Plato also aligns philosophy with the feminine. Plato makes a robust connection between philosophy and the feminine when he includes in the dialogues notions that philosophers are all pregnant (*Smp.* 206c), that Socrates helps philosophers deliver their ideas much like his mother who was a midwife (*Tht.* 149a–151d), and that Socrates learned everything he knew from a woman—a priestess named Diotima (*Smp.* 208c, 201d). Plato even uses the term *kuma* (wave) in laying out the *Republic*'s paradoxes, which comes from "*kuô*" meaning to swell which is used in the context of pregnant women's swelling bellies.[59] The commentators who think Plato ignores the physical or that he dishonors nature and women are missing some powerful moments of Plato paying tribute to the body, especially women's bodies.

Furthermore, Plato also connects the feminine with the political, as we shall see in chapter 4's examination of the *Republic*'s First City where Plato has Socrates emphasize physical survival and an admiration for the cooperative community effort to achieve it in a peaceful, sustainable fashion. The tendency of those who interpret Plato as an austere dualist is to ignore the *Republic*'s commanding warnings about poverty as well as the description of the poverty-free First City. Consequently, the influence of the austere dualist interpretation has had an impact on our notion of what constitutes the political. Establishing a focus on these neglected aspects of Plato's work gives us a lot to think about in terms of the contemporary applications of Plato's political philosophy. Scholars working on wealth inequality, food justice, diplomacy, peace and nonviolence, and the like would be aided by studying the aspects of Plato I will emphasize in chapter 4. But listening to an austere dualist interpreter, one would never recognize Plato's relevance for our contemporary problems. Although it is not my primary task in this project to examine the details of Plato's views in their applicability to contemporary issues, my project makes it unmistakable that Plato's conceptions would be a tremendous resource for people working on these sorts of issues.

1.4 Strange Claims and the Analogy Strategy

Plato's influence on Western culture, especially religious thought, makes it difficult for us to appreciate how strange some of his ideas have seemed to his audiences. In Annas's words, Plato was a "revolutionary" with "radical ideas."[60] While many Platonic notions may seem relatively familiar now, Plato recognizes the innovative nature of his worldview, which includes having his Socrates claim both that the soul is one's most valuable possession and that the soul's healthy state is preferable to its diseased state. Plato is aware that one might respond to this type of worldview by declaring it outlandish to suggest something nonphysical could possibly be more real and more valuable than the physical body. As I will show here, Plato then uses analogies with the physical to help interlocutors and readers alike make sense of unfamiliar claims and help them aspire to virtue.

Throughout the corpus, those whom Socrates considers "body-lovers" (*Phd.* 68b-c) are said to be plagued by impediments to living justly, such as the fear of death and the desire for pleasure, because they prioritize the physical body, advocate hedonism, and lack concern for the health of the soul. Body-lovers do not fathom that their lifestyle causes disharmony. For example, when body-lovers consider the potential negative consequences of their actions, they envision consequences that are physical in nature, such as being imprisoned or put to death. Think, for instance, in the *Crito* of Crito initially thinking of harm only in terms of physical harm, while Socrates tries to get him to imagine the serious harm is to the soul.

This body-loving worldview is what makes it difficult for interlocutors such as Callicles and Thrasymachus to accept the claim that living unjustly is inherently unchoice-worthy. For such a person justice is "a mug's game,"[61] the silly business of serving the weaker; it is nothing serious that would require substantial reflection and practice. Often, Plato has Socrates deal with interlocutors who have a difficult time thinking about justice and injustice as anything more than "crowd-pleasing vulgarities" (*Grg.* 482e).[62] For example, Callicles is candid about his belief that being a "just" person is not an admirable character trait. He thinks that "justice" as it is conventionally construed is not real (*Grg.* 483b-484b). And in the *Republic*, Socrates also faces challenging questions put forth by Glaucon and Adeimantus concerning why one should be moral and why one should care about anything other than the rewards and punishments offered up by society. Despite claiming to convey popular opinion rather than his own (*R.* 358c-d), Glaucon represents the position that no one is willingly just, that people are just only for fear of punishment (*R.* 359c-360d). Adeimantus reinforces Glaucon's position, claiming that one need not be just so long as one learns how to use persuasion to convince others that one is just (*R.* 365b-d). When Glaucon and Adeimantus solicit from Socrates an account of what justice or injustice "does of its own power by its presence in the soul of the person who possesses it, even if it remains hidden from gods and humans," Plato has Adeimantus say that no one "has adequately argued that injustice is the worst thing a soul can have in it and that justice is the greatest good" (*R.* 366e). Having already failed to convince Thrasymachus in

Book I of the *Republic* that justice is better than injustice, Socrates worries that, on its own, his view of justice is not compelling.

Even though Glaucon and Adeimantus insist they are already sympathetic to Socrates's contention that being just is better for an individual than being unjust, they excel at playing the devil's advocate such that they both appear not to accept completely the truth of Socrates's position (*R.* 365b–367e). As Socrates says, "For you must indeed be affected by the divine if you're not convinced that injustice is better than justice and yet can speak on its behalf as you have done. And I believe that you really are unconvinced by your own words. I infer this from the way you live, for if I had only your words to go on, I wouldn't trust you" (*R.* 368a-b). Thus, Socrates needs a way to help his interlocutors experience justice as something real, not merely a crowd-pleasing idea, something that demands reflection on one's own character, and to see that moderation is indispensable for justice.

Given, then, that Plato recognizes the controversial nature of his worldview, it should not surprise us that he devises an overarching strategy to put the interlocutors and readers of his dialogues in a position to grant the importance of living the just life. What could help Socrates demonstrate that the way one lives has consequences on both one's soul as well as one's political community regardless of who else knows about it? Plato focuses on health and disease in order to construct educational analogies about both individual justice and social justice. He frequently employs what cognitive scientists call analogical reasoning to make his strange, obscure views more conceivable.[63] An analogy is the systematic relationship between two analogs, a "target" analog and a "source" analog. The target analog represents the new situation that one is trying to figure out, and the source analog represents an old experience that is being adapted and applied to the target analog.[64] Analogical reasoning relies on the ease with which one can adapt and apply one's knowledge of the source analog to the target analog.[65] It is common to find Plato using source analogs that rely on knowledge of the embodied world of everyday life in order to pave the way for him to later introduce very abstract target analogs. Think, for example, of the *Phaedo* where Plato has Socrates use an analogy to prepare the interlocutors to be introduced to the abstract notion of recollecting Forms. He talks about how a beloved's lyre or cloak can bring the beloved to mind (*Phd.* 73d) because he can presume widespread familiarity with this erotic phenomenon, and it therefore makes a well-designed source analog.

Another example of Plato's use of analogical reasoning unfolds in the *Republic*. When the conversation hits some confusion about what justice

Interpreting Asceticism in Plato   15

is in Book 2, Plato has Socrates employ an analogy concerning physical sight and rational inquiry, which is a body-soul analogy, in order to set up Plato's introduction of the city-soul analogy, which is his other central analogy that claims similarity between physical and nonphysical entities. Socrates says:

> The investigation we're undertaking is not an easy one but requires keen eyesight. Therefore, since we aren't clever people, we should adopt the method of investigation that we'd use if, lacking keen eyesight, we were told to read small letters from a distance and then noticed that the same letters existed elsewhere in a larger size and on a larger surface. We'd consider it a godsend, I think, to be allowed to read the larger ones first and then to examine the smaller ones, to see whether they really are the same. (R. 368c-d)

As soon as Glaucon and Adeimantus challenge Socrates, Socrates immediately advances his case with them by utilizing analogical reasoning to set up further usage of analogical reasoning in hopes of making his claims more persuasive about what justice is and what its benefits are. In so doing, he is putting Glaucon and Adeimantus in a position to apply their understanding of the source analogs, eyesight and the city, to the target analogs, rational inquiry and the soul, respectively.

The main shared trait driving the city-soul analogy is that both souls and cities can be just or unjust (R. 368e). On this basis, Plato has Socrates assert isomorphism, namely, that the city and the soul have the same structure. Blössner critiques Plato for considering the analogy hypothetical at 368d-369a but assuming it as established in Book 4.[66] And he observes that Plato "is dramatically extending the boundaries of the analogy" when he concludes not just that cities and souls are both entities that can be just or unjust but that they both also have the same number of component parts and that justice for both consists in the proper comportment of the components.[67] These fallacious extensions lead directly to claiming at 441c-d that if the virtues associated with the city are wisdom (R. 428b-429a), courage (R. 429a-430c), moderation (R. 430e-432b), and justice (R. 432b-434d), then the virtues of the soul must also be wisdom (R. 442c), courage (R. 442b-c), moderation (R. 442c-d), and justice (R. 441d-442a, 442d). As Ferrari observes, Plato makes this choice and has his reasons for doing so, which he does not reveal.[68] So we must consider why he extends the analogy in the direction of proportional structure.

The other examples are legion of Plato operating through metaphors and analogies that try to teach us something about the nonphysical by relying upon our understanding and values in the physical realm. Cooper points out that Socrates focuses on "how to conceive and appreciate the value of the various highly rated traditional virtues (justice, courage, temperance, etc.), in comparison with other things apparently also of value (such as bodily health, physical strength, wealth, bodily or other pleasures, and so on)."[69] Plato's messages about justice and the care of soul are driven by a particular kind of reasoning that analogizes the physical and the nonphysical, specifically the body and the soul.

On one hand, Plato relies on the physical body as a source analog in hopes of Socrates seeming clearer and more credible when expounding his claims about souls, which is his main target analog. To make his strange claims about the soul and its proper care realistic and true to life, Socrates appeals to that with which his interlocutors are well acquainted, the human body, its skills, its needs, its health and disease, and so on. For instance, at *Gorgias* 521a Plato has Socrates suggest that the political craft is the quest to make citizens "as good as possible, *like a doctor*" (emphasis added). This is a promising strategy because interlocutors and readers are literally at home with the physical and the crafts that attend to the physical, and consequently it is typically easy to adapt and apply knowledge of health and disease. Plato has Socrates explicitly compare justice to health because he knows that human beings usually value physical health as inherently good.[70] No one should be confused as to why someone prefers physical health over sickness. Given this function, medicine is a powerful analogy. Knowing how intuitive the concepts of physical health and disease are to his audience, Plato uses the continuum between health and disease to describe the condition of souls, even though they are not physical. In this way, Plato is using familiarity with the physical as a pedagogical tool and renovating vocabulary that typically pertains to the physical.

In particular, Plato employs health and disease to explain the consequences of just and unjust ways because health plays out in internal rather than external consequences.[71] It does not matter if other people (or the divine) ever discover one's just or unjust character because justice and injustice have an immediate effect on one's soul, just as it does not matter whether one's neighbor or doctor ever discovers one's healthy or unhealthy lifestyle, for health and disease are authentic states occurring in one's body even if they remain concealed from other people.

On the other hand, however, Plato is ultimately making the case that virtue and the care of the soul are of greater value than such valuable things as bodily health and physical strength.⁷² Here Plato assumes that his readers may be ignorant or even resistant to claims about the soul, but that drawing an analogy to the physical will make the claims about the soul more intelligible and less outlandish. Plato is a normative dualist, and thus he values the soul over the body, but he still uses the body to educate others about the value of health in the soul. In so doing, Plato is transforming the vernacular of physical health to apply to something nonphysical.

Plato often has Socrates analogize the body (the source analog) to the soul (the target analog) in order to persuade interlocutors and readers of the following: (1) the health of the soul is inherently good just as the health of the body is inherently good; (2) living unjustly results in a diseased soul; and (3) one should pursue the health of the soul by living justly. In crafting this particular analogy, Socrates intends to make more plausible his message that when one does not take proper care of the soul, say, by living immoderately, there are real consequences regardless of who knows it. He aims to demonstrate to his interlocutors that the negative consequences of living unjustly are not even limited to the ill health of one's own soul. Not properly caring for the soul also affects one's *polis* and the other souls in the *polis*. In fact, Plato does not only have Socrates say that what health is to the body justice is to the soul (*Grg.* 464b-c, *R.* 444c), but in the *Republic* he also signals that justice is to the city what health is to the body (*R.* 372e-373a).

There are a variety of additional ways that Plato uses physical vocabulary to illustrate new concepts about philosophy and philosophers.⁷³ He frequently makes use of all sorts of imagery in service to various philosophical lessons. In his account of the nonphysical soul and the nonphysical Forms, Plato often employs either erotic vocabulary⁷⁴ or the language of food and nourishment.⁷⁵ For instance, let's look at *Republic* 490a-b, where Socrates claims that the philosopher is driven by erotic love of the Forms and has intercourse with the Forms, while the Forms provide nourishment for the person who is truly a philosopher by nature. He says:

> Then, won't it be reasonable for us to plead in [the philosopher's] defense that it is the nature of the real lover of learning to struggle toward what is, not to remain with any of the many things that are believed to be, that, as he moves on, he neither loses nor lessens his erotic love until he grasps the being of each nature itself with the part of his soul that is fitted to grasp it, because of its kinship with it, and that, once getting

near what really is and having intercourse with it (*kai migeis*) and having begotten understanding and truth, he knows, truly lives, is nourished (*kai trephoito*), and—at that point, but not before—is relieved from the pains of giving birth? (*R.* 490a-b)

When Plato utilizes such analogies, does he mean to import something significant from the source analog to illuminate something about the target analog (Forms and the soul), or is he turning the original connotation of the source analog's vernacular entirely on its head?

Plato intends to refashion the meaning of the physical vocabulary he employs in nonphysical contexts, such as souls being nourished or philosophers having intercourse with the Forms. He had to adapt existing vernacular in order to create a lexicon for concepts for which the Greek language had no words.[76] The metaphorical usage relies upon the literal meanings but modifies the terms' original connotations, such as feeding a physical body with physical food or physical bodies having sexual intercourse, into something new and nonphysical, such as "feeding" a soul with contact with nonphysical Forms or a soul "having intercourse with" Forms. Furthermore, despite his project to transform certain physical vocabulary, Plato still also regularly uses food vocabulary with its original, literal physical connotation. So, Plato can continue to use erotic vocabulary with its original sexual meaning alongside strategic use of transformed erotic vocabulary.[77] The central question here is how much weight Plato gives to the literal meanings of this physical vernacular after he transforms the original connotation by pointing beyond it.

Some scholars reject out of hand the possibility that Plato chooses this language while conserving the original connotations.[78] However, I argue that, while it is obvious that there is a sematic shift happening, Plato must import something significant from the original connotation in order for the original vocabulary to function as a source analog that sheds light on the target analog. I urge that we bear in mind the rich dynamic involved in Plato making use of the original meanings as source analogs. As Classen explains, even though these metaphors are initially intended to serve as illustrative comparisons, they also provide important suggestions into the relationships under examination.[79] Even if we remember how Plato makes use of concepts such as physical nourishment or erotic attraction as source analogs, that is not mutually exclusive of his also playing with those original connotations as they are refashioned for the target analogs.[80]

1.5 Pedagogical Irony

This project will demonstrate, for the first time in the scholarly literature, that Plato does value the body and the role it plays in the philosophical life. He values the body because rational inquiry includes particular physical and erotic experiences that facilitate the understanding of true reality (eternal, nonphysical Forms), and, as I just explained, because the physical regularly functions so well as a source analog to facilitate learning about the abstract and invisible. Certain positive roles for embodied experience are a persistent feature of Plato's thought, not just referenced in a stray passage here or there. Plato does say some disparaging things about the body, but I argue that these vilifying remarks operate in a provocative, ironic way for the sake of a pedagogical aim.[81] Although I will underscore the evidence for his normative dualism, I contend that Plato intends to speak to two different categories of readership.[82] His audience is heterogeneous, and being aware of this, he imbues his texts with multiple layers of meaning. In this regard, his message is not unlike the enigmatic oracular prophesies people received at Delphi. His dialogues offer much that is directed toward those who are not yet philosophers or caretakers of the soul, and simultaneously they are geared toward those who have already made the transition to prioritizing the care of the soul and loving wisdom. On one level he addresses those who are already more philosophically inclined in order to encourage them to discern a positive role for the physical within the philosophical life; on another level he speaks to those who are less philosophically inclined in order to warn them off overindulging the physical through an excessive appetite.

Plato warns us about the danger of being a slave to the body, what he calls a "body-lover" (*philosômatos*) (*Phd.* 68b-c). Body-lovers are characterized by the fear of death as well as by slavishness with respect to such things as wealth and the pleasures of food, wine, sex, and sleep. Body-lovers use sense perception of "visibles" without also engaging in philosophical reasoning about what Plato calls "intelligibles" (*R.* 509d). The aim of a body-lover is pleasure alone, even if it comes at the expense of one's psychic or physical health. Plato's Socrates's main pursuit in the dialogues is encouraging his interlocutors to put soul before flesh so that they may flourish as human beings. For instance, in the *Apology*, he says, "For I go around doing nothing but persuading both young and old among you not to care for your body or your wealth *in preference to or as strongly as* for the best possible state of your soul" (30a-b; emphasis added).[83] While Plato's

Socrates refrains from utilizing disingenuous devices, such as apologizing, crying, or parading his family in front of the jury, to save his own life in the *Apology*, he is quite willing to use rhetorical tools in order to prompt his interlocutors to accept that, even though the body plays some positive roles in inquiry, the body's value pales in comparison to that of the soul. So, sometimes Plato has Socrates make use of unsympathetic claims about the body in order to jar the body-loving members of his audience away from their conventional attitude of being solely or chiefly concerned with the state of one's body.

My contention is that, according to Plato, one flourishes as an individual human being when one learns how to care for the soul *without* disregarding the body's needs and desires, rather than by learning how to deny the body's needs and desires. The dialogues make clear that the antidote to body-love is loving wisdom rather than loving only pleasure, wealth, and/or power. However, one must learn how to be properly disposed toward the body before one can love wisdom and flourish as a human being. Ultimately, Plato hopes that the interlocutors and readers will learn to esteem the soul sufficiently to be able to coordinate its needs with those of the body so that body and soul can live in harmony with each other. This enables one to include moderate physical pleasures in one's contemplative life without becoming a slave to the body. However, if Plato were explicitly to convey that there is room for enjoying physical pleasure within a contemplative life, body-lovers would likely latch on to the familiar concern for pleasing the body and ignore (or reject) the idea that one should prioritize the care of the soul. Thus, for pedagogical reasons his messages about the importance of the body must be embedded within his call for all human beings to abandon body-love.

This pedagogical strategy invites interlocutors and readers to initiate a transformation that involves making two transitions. First, one needs to make a transition to loving the soul instead of the body. In the second transition, one moves away from the extreme of caring *only* for the soul to caring for both the soul and the body in a way that prioritizes the soul without renouncing the body. These transitions do not necessarily happen in discrete instants; instead, making these transitions is an ongoing process that moves at different speeds for different individuals, depending on their individual predispositions. For example, someone who has made the transition to loving the soul instead of the body may still be vulnerable to a relapse into body-love. So, what might seem like mixed messages about the body's value are actually Plato's attempt to write different prescriptions for two different audiences. The body-lovers need the dialogues' more austere-sounding aspects, while those who have transcended body-love in favor of soul-love are properly ready for Plato's appeals to moderation.

Plato plants in the dialogues numerous indications that the body is indispensable in the inquirer's quest for knowledge, and as such, condemning the body is counterproductive for a Platonic inquirer. For example, by using dialogue as his literary genre, Plato presents dialogue as the main mode of philosophical investigation.[84] In the mutual exchange of dialogue, the interlocutors are speaking and listening, and these activities require the bodily faculties of speech and hearing. As Saxonhouse writes, "The production of words has an effect on and is dependent on the body. To engage in *dialegein* is not to be free of the body."[85] Thus, without the body Socrates and the interlocutors could not exchange ideas in this particular way. Secondly, Plato frequently uses analogies that rely upon one's existing grasp of physical things (such as the health of the human body, functions of body parts, physical crafts such as medicine, physical training, agriculture, shoemaking, etc.) in order to facilitate consideration of his ideas about the nonphysical (such as how one ought to care for the human soul). Thirdly, Plato acknowledges with his theory of recollection that sense perception has a role in rational inquiry. In all instances, the ascent to knowledge begins with sensory perception, and in special cases, what instigates the ascent process is sense perception linked to erotic desire, such as the perception of a beloved's physical beauty (*Smp.* 210a-b, 211c).

However, the austere dualist interpretation contends that Plato's philosophers leave everything worldly behind in pursuit of philosophy. This view obfuscates our conception of the ascetic lifestyle epitomized by Socrates. Philosophers like Socrates need not reject this world in order to honor the Forms they love. I will demonstrate that Plato's attitude toward embodiment acknowledges that philosophers still eat physical food to nourish their physical bodies while they have the Forms as food for thought; that under the right conditions philosophers may have sexual intercourse with the right beloved alongside having intellectual intercourse with the Forms; that they can be in love with the Good and still want to engage as leaders in the community in order to make cities and souls as orderly and good as possible. Yes, Plato's philosophers can be thinkers, lovers, and governors.

1.6 Plan for the Chapters

Despite various indications that Plato believes the body is central to the practice of philosophical inquiry, the Western tradition became preoccupied with a literal interpretation of the Plato's call for a "separate soul" (*Phd.* 64c). Focusing on the *Phaedo* in chapter 2, I describe the paradoxical nature of calling for embodied philosophers to separate the soul from the body. The central aim of that chapter is to resolve this paradox by reconsidering what exactly it means for philosophy to be "training for death" (*Phd.* 64a). I will undercut the literal interpretation of the separate soul, arguing instead that living with a separate soul consists of abandoning body-love and its concomitant focus on physical "sensibles" in favor of the care of the soul and its focus on philosophical thought about "intelligible" Forms. In calling for the philosopher to separate soul from the body, Plato distinguishes himself as a Pythagorean ally, but he reflects not the rigid Pythagorean asceticism but rather a carefully qualified normative dualism, which prioritizes the care of the soul without neglecting the subordinate management of the physical.

Overlooking Plato's pedagogical project and misunderstanding his dualism have led many to consider activities such as eating, sleeping, and having sexual intercourse at odds with rational inquiry. However, each of these physical endeavors in its own way is part of what can enable the human being to live philosophically, to pursue knowledge of the Forms. In fact, as we shall see in chapter 3, Plato highlights the crucial role of erotic ascent in learning the Forms. Nevertheless, Alcibiades's account of Socrates's abstinence with him has misled some readers into assuming that there is no room for erotic experiences within the philosophical life. We must reassess Platonic love; after all, the colloquial meaning of the adjective *platonic* presumes the ascetic dualist interpretation.

In chapter 3, I develop an account of the *Symposium* and *Phaedrus* that makes clear that philosophers like Socrates can be seduced but only by someone of similar character who shares the passion for dialectic and there are advantages that come from such experiences. Erotic encounters lie mysteriously between the physical and the nonphysical, and as such *erôs* is a gateway between physical sensibles and intelligible Forms. *Erôs* brings us toward an individual body and then has us reach for something beyond it. Plato recognizes the sort of erotic desire that reaches for the Form of Beauty (rather than for yet another body) as a fitting element of the human condition.

Chapter 4 raises two main questions of the political sort. First, what is Plato's vision of the relationship among health, justice, and peace as well as between individuals and the community? Second, does Plato's normative dualism require philosophers to withdraw from the social-political arena? I will examine the connection between Plato's attitude toward embodiment and his theory of justice—both individual justice and social justice—in the *Gorgias* and the *Republic*. The first part of chapter 4 focuses on the recognition in these dialogues of a conception of the philosophical life centered on moderation rather than austere asceticism. I will show how the austere dualist interpretation conflicts with the moral psychology offered in the *Republic*, especially Books IV, VIII, and IX. If a human being were to embrace the austere dualist approach to self-discipline, then the soul's rational aspect will rule over the spirit and appetite in the fashion of a tyrant. If the individual soul aims to cultivate the virtue of justice, then the aspiration to austere asceticism is unquestionably injudicious. Given Plato's contention that a human being flourishes when the psychic aspects live harmoniously together, each doing their own work well, the ideal of austere asceticism represents a profound lack of self-knowledge.

The second part of chapter 4 takes up the issue of whether a philosopher, fully engaged in the pursuit of wisdom, will or should "go down again to the prisoners in the cave and share their labors and honors" (*R.* 519d). Much like the examples I mentioned earlier, Plotinus's own commitments may have shaped the vision of Platonism that comes to us through Neoplatonic interpretation. In particular, as concerns political engagement, Plotinus assumes that a good philosopher puts civic virtue aside.[86] Socrates mentions that his *daimon* urged him to stay out of politics (*Ap.* 31d, *R.* 496c), and Plato himself chose the private life of doing and teaching philosophy over the public life of political service that his family presumably would have anticipated for him. Despite these appearances, I argue that Plato's philosophers are deeply engaged in civic life. Throughout the dialogues, Plato reveals his own curiosities about embodied human beings and the universe they inhabit; of course, we also see this in the daily activities of his Socrates, the street philosopher. So, chapter 4 will challenge the interpretation that political dialogues such as the *Republic* and the *Gorgias* contain a version of Platonism that derides philosophers wasting their time, energy, and talents on anything to do with the physical universe, including the messy business of governing embodied human beings. For Plato, real philosophers do not disdain human affairs just because they love the Forms.

The last part of chapter 4 investigates Plato's discussion of poverty and the simple First City in the *Republic*, both of which have been largely neglected on account, I believe, of the influence of the austere dualist interpretation. Chapter 4 will demonstrate that to decipher Plato's attitude toward the body and asceticism we must examine his warnings about poverty and the brief sketch of the First City where good health and peace are the order of the day. Finally, chapter 4 meditates briefly on Plato's philosophy of peace. Plato plants the seeds for the "know justice, know peace" or "no justice, no peace" notion (*R.* 372a-d). In Plato's dynamic concept of peace, harmony is initiated within each individual and extends through the web of their interrelations. Peace will be possible on both the individual and community levels when human beings reject both hedonism and strict austerity in order to honor the moderate care of human beings.

I will conclude with a summary fifth chapter in which I will sketch out how the *Philebus*, *Timaeus*, and *Laws* could be read in light of my interpretation. I shall point to evidence that these late dialogues have three themes in common with the great middle dialogues I will analyze. First, there is positive attention given to the physical, and the value of the body is made explicit. Second, these dialogues generally champion moderation rather than austere denial. And finally, various political motifs are grounded in consideration of embodiment, particularly Plato's commitment to the pursuit of peace, the importance of civic unity, and the elimination of poverty. Examination of these themes will give support to the claim that Plato's view of the physical in the late dialogues is consistent with my reading of the *Phaedo*, *Symposium*, *Phaedrus*, *Gorgias*, and *Republic*.

In the course of reflecting on one exemplar—Plato's Socrates—and three conceptions—philosophy as training for death; philosophy as erotic ascent; and philosophy as psychic health—we shall see that, for Plato, philosophy is the practice (*askesis*) dedicated to the mastery of embodied inquiry. Making sense of a wide variety of puzzles throughout the corpus by interpreting Plato as a normative dualist, I will conclude that loving wisdom requires not only acceptance of our embodied condition but also appreciation of the important positive roles the physical plays in philosophy. In arguing for this unconventional reading, I hope to gift to my reader the challenge of seeing embodiment and asceticism in Plato with fresh eyes.

Chapter 2

Moderation and Training for Death in the *Phaedo*

2.1 Introduction

Plato's Socrates associates philosophy with training for death (*meletê thanatou*) in the *Phaedo* (64a). To explain this claim, he says that philosophers separate the soul from the body (*Phd.* 64c) and "live in a state as close to death as possible" (*Phd.* 67d). This seeming paradox leaves the reader to wonder what positive role, if any, Plato envisions the body playing in the philosophical life, which is defined by devotion to abstract inquiry. Scholars who interpret Plato as an austere dualist turn to the *Phaedo* for their strongest evidence that Plato believes that the philosophical lifestyle requires the discipline to deny the body completely in order for the soul to be "most by itself . . . having no contact or association with [the body] in its search for reality" (*Phd.* 65d).[1] The conventional understanding of the *Phaedo* is that engaging in bodily activities makes one too at home in the physical world, not yearning for disembodied communion with the Forms.[2] I will argue for a more nuanced reading of this dialogue.

The *Phaedo* depicts Socrates's last words as: "Crito, we owe a cock to Asclepius; make this offering to him and do not forget" (*Phd.* 118a). Many scholars[3] follow Nietzsche in assuming that this insistence on a sacrifice to the god of health means life is an illness that is cured by death.[4] This famous interpretation of the remark dovetails with the austere dualist interpretation of Plato, especially in the *Phaedo*. According to commentators such as Olympiodorus, Damascius, and Nietzsche, Plato says no to life and denounces the physical world of impermanence.[5] Such readers might point to *Phaedo* 95d2 for support. In this passage, Socrates is representing Cebes's concerns when he says, "That [the soul] existed for a very long time before, that it knew much and acted much, makes it no more immortal because of that; indeed, its very entering into a human body was the beginning of its destruction, like a disease; it would live that life in distress and would in the end be destroyed in what we call death." However, in this passage Socrates appears to be representing Cebes's concern rather than his own view. Perhaps in attributing this concern to Cebes, a young Pythagorean, Plato's Socrates is emphasizing the Pythagorean tendency to see embodiment as a disease.

Austere dualist interpreters read Plato's dialogues as hostile to embodied life, indicating that there is no proper enjoyment of embodied pleasures, but I contend that this caricature of Plato is not supported by the text of the *Phaedo*. Plato has been construed this way as a result of confusion surrounding his contention that the separation of the soul from the body will solve the two problems that embodiment poses for an inquirer, the problems of distraction and deception. In this chapter, I will argue that, despite the call for a separate soul, Plato is not the austere dualist he has been made out to be, even in the *Phaedo*, and he does not ultimately recommend that philosophers absolutely deny the body.

Unlike most commentators, Roochnik, Woolf, Russell, Peterson, Saxonhouse, Williams, Weiss, Burger, Spitzer, and Tenkku agree that what I call austere dualist asceticism is not espoused in the *Phaedo*.[6] Plato's conception of philosophy as training for death should not be interpreted as a withdrawal from the physical world of everyday life. As Roochnik aptly remarks, the lesson of the *Phaedo* is "far from teaching its readers to feel 'revulsion at imperfection' and a deep distaste for the 'passingness' of human life, far from urging them to become theoretical optimists who are hungry only for a glimpse of the Eternal Forms."[7] Instead, for Plato, philosophy entails normative dualism, which is the view that the soul is worthy of being taken more seriously than the physical. Nevertheless, it is crucial to note that Plato believes the role of the body is *secondary* to the role of reason, rather than having no place at all in the philosopher's life. As I indicated in chapter 1, the notion that the soul and its abstract reasoning is superior to the body troubles feminist philosophers, who fully desegregate rationality and physicality. However, as my reading will demonstrate, Plato sees the body as instrumentally valuable for doing philosophy. Feminists would disagree that the body is only valuable because it is able to make a positive contribution to the process of rational inquiry. Still, with my normative dualist interpretation, we will see that Plato's view of the body is not as objectionable to feminists as austere dualist interpreters led us to believe.

In the course of arguing against an austere dualist interpretation of Plato's *Phaedo*, I will closely examine several passages, often thought to be illustrative of Plato's austere dualism, that in fact undermine the austere dualist interpretation. In section 2.2, I will show that, while Plato is cognizant of two central problems that embodiment poses for an inquirer, he presents a prospect for resolution in the shape of normative dualism, which is the prioritization of the soul over the body and form over matter without the repudiation of the physical. I will argue that maintaining this sort of perspective is what it means to live with a separate soul. In this section I will also demonstrate that there are three grave problems with the austere dualists' literal interpretation of the call for a separate soul. These concerns, which will be addressed in turn, are that (1) this interpretation neglects to account for the role of sense perception in the theory of recollection; (2) it ignores the fact that literal separation of the soul from the body is plainly unachievable during life and thus conflicts with the suicide prohibition; and (3) according to this reading, Socrates cannot be considered an exemplar of the philosophical life, which is at odds with Plato's unmistakable celebration of Socrates as the ideal philosopher.[8] After explaining these aspects of why the literal reading is untenable, I will marshal evidence for my reading of the call for a separate soul as an invitation to transform one's thinking, an invitation to become a philosopher.[9] This inducement goes out to both the body-lovers and the soul-loving Pythagoreans, who have more work to do if they are to practice philosophy in what Plato's Socrates would have called the right way.

I dedicate 2.3 toward showing that in the *Phaedo* Plato holds moderation in high regard and advocates for its inclusion in the philosopher's lifestyle, which, once again, is at odds with an austere dualist interpretation. In 2.4, I question some of the assumptions commonly made in how we think about "practicing philosophy the right way" (*pephilosophêkotes orthôs*) (*Phd.* 69d), which turns out to have more to do with being a good Bacchant (a worshipper of Dionysus, the god of wine and fertility) and less to do with withdrawal from this world. Finally, in 2.5 I will defend Plato against the criticism that his conception of human virtue requires human beings to transcend human nature. According to Plato, one fulfills one's highest potential as a human being by engaging in the pursuit of wisdom and goodness. This philosophical quest can only be successful if the soul is prioritized over the body while valuing the body enough both to make use of its contribution to the process of learning and to respect it with the proper care.

2.2 Resolving Two Problems with Embodied Inquiry

In the *Phaedo*, we see that Socrates is concerned with two problems that stem from being embodied—distraction and deception. First, there is the problem of an inquirer being distracted by the many needs and wants of the human body. For example, the rumble of hunger will distract one from work just as the need for sleep will put an end to work for the day. Second, bodily senses can deceive one inquiring after truth. He says, "[W]henever [the soul] attempts to examine anything with the body, it is clearly deceived by it" (*Phd.* 65b). As a result, the soul gets "confused and dizzy" by being dragged toward the ever-changing physical world (*Phd.* 79c). For example, hallucination, *trompe l'oeil* paintings, holograms, a pencil looking bent when in a glass of water, and the like all demonstrate that the senses do not necessarily provide reliable information for the would-be knower. This leads Taylor to conclude that "the man who is really 'in love with knowledge' must confess that his heart's desire is either only to be won after death, when the soul has achieved her independence of her troublesome partner, or not at all."[10] I disagree with Taylor's conception of the role the human body plays in Plato's view of philosophy. Plato recognizes the problems that embodiment poses, but he also envisions a resolution to these two challenges in the form of separating the soul from the body. The question is, What does Plato mean by this?

My view challenges the conventional, austere dualist interpretation of the separate soul, which is typified by Grube's translation of the *Phaedo*. Plato calls for the philosopher to separate the soul from the body as follows: "[T]he soul of the philosopher most dishonors (*atimazei*) the body, flees from it and seeks to be by itself" (*Phd.* 65d).[11] Grube's translation renders *atimazei* as "disdains," which echoes his translation of 64e, where he translates Socrates as saying that "the true philosopher despises" things such as the pleasures of food, drink, sex, and other bodily enjoyments.[12] However, the verb at 64e is also *atimazein*, which would be better translated as "esteeming lightly" or "not honoring." Grube's translation enforces the presumption of austere dualism at the expense of illuminating what it really means to separate the soul, practicing for death.

In this section, I will examine what exactly it means to live with a soul separated from the body.[13] Austere dualist interpreters take the call for a separate soul literally.[14] If one assumes that death-training and soul-separating is a simple matter of abandoning concern for the physical, and even despising the body, it might appear that if philosophers were to renounce the body, then they would no longer be susceptible to either the distraction or deception problem. I will now demonstrate three central problems with this literal interpretation of the separate soul before moving on to detail my own view of what it means to live with a soul separated from the body.

Following his description of the philosopher as a soul-separator, Socrates asks, "Is what is most true in [the Forms] contemplated through the body, or is this the position: whoever of us prepares himself best and most accurately to grasp that thing itself which he is investigating will come closest to the knowledge of it?" (*Phd.* 65e). Socrates and Simmias conclude that the latter is the case. How should this mode of contemplation be interpreted? Those who interpret the separate soul literally find this mode of contemplation encapsulated when Socrates says that the Forms "can only be grasped by the reasoning of thought" (*Phd.* 79a; translation modified). The austere soul-separator would strive not to develop any beliefs based upon sensory experiences because, in terms of immediate representation, sensory perception fails to disclose the existence of Forms.[15]

The presence of the theory of recollection in the *Phaedo*, however, flies in the face of the austere dualist interpretation of the separate soul. The austere dualist interpretation obliges philosophers to steer clear of the "unceasing influx of sensory information."[16] In this regard, the literal view of the separate soul fails to account for the physical senses' role in the investigation of the Forms. In the words of Prior:

> This rather elaborate theory of recollection softens somewhat the harsh critique of sensory experience given earlier, at 65a–66e, and evades the conclusion that knowledge of the Forms is possible only after death. Plato had previously condemned the senses utterly, stating that they were a hindrance to the acquisition of knowledge and that the philosopher was better off without them; but here he gives them the role of catalysts for recollection and states that our knowledge of the Forms is derived from nothing else but the senses (75a). It now appears that, although the senses are not adequate for knowledge, they are necessary for it, at least while the soul is embodied.[17]

Understanding true reality cannot be done *by* the body, but, for Plato, it is also true that it cannot be done *without* the body, given that sense perception, which works through the body, sets in motion the process of recollection, as Socrates indicates at 73c–75b. As Frede confirms, "In fact Plato goes out of his way to make clear that sense-perception is necessary for this type of recollection."[18]

Plato uses the theory of recollection to highlight the important role of sense perception in rational inquiry. I agree with Woolf, who notes, "It is very hard to apply the ascetic reading to Socrates' remarks on sense perception without a degree of absurdity. . . . Socrates is surely not suggesting that the philosopher walk around with his eyes shut and his ears plugged."[19] Indeed, Plato believes that sense perception is useful to philosophers. This works in two ways. First of all, sense perception does tell us something. For instance, Cebes's and Simmias's eyes tell them that Socrates is sitting before them in his prison cell. That is important in itself. Yet, sense perception can also stimulate another kind of thinking, philosophical reasoning, when senses exhaust their explanatory power. For example, Socrates explains that we derive knowledge of the Equal Itself from sense perception of particular equal things (*Phd.* 74b-c).[20] A moment later he goes as far as to propose that in fact knowledge of the Equal Itself could not be achieved in any way except one derived from sense perception. Plato has Socrates declare, "Then surely we also agree that this conception of ours derives from seeing or touching or some other sense perception, and cannot come into our mind in any other way" (*Phd.* 75a). Even though the process of recollecting the Forms does not rest with sensory perception, it must make good use of it, being propelled forward on a philosophical journey. So, it would be counterproductive for a Platonic inquirer to abhor or ignore the physical at the same time as undertaking to comprehend the Forms.[21] Because the austere dualist reading just bemoans the negative implications of the body, it fails to see the positive role that sensory experiences (and consequently the body) play in coming to understand the Forms. Separating the soul from the body for the sake of trying to grasp the Forms should not be interpreted as the literal abandonment of sense perception, because sense perception is indispensable to the process of recollecting the Forms, as we see at *Phd.* 75a5–8.

Sensory experiences also serve to remind us of things we have forgotten during our lives. For example, Simmias tells Cebes that he cannot remember the theory of recollection at the moment, even though Socrates mentions it frequently (*Phd.* 73a), and Simmias is reminded of the theory through his own faculty of hearing and Cebes's and Socrates's faculties of speech. Of course, in order for sensory experience to inspire philosophical reasoning the inquirer must have the correct attitude toward sense perception. Certainly, the philosopher must use reason to judge cautiously the information gleaned from sensory experience, but it is neither possible nor advantageous for the Platonic learner to eschew sensory experiences entirely. In Woolf's words, "Philosophy does not come along and, in some absurd or perhaps sinister fashion, *deprive* us of the evidence of our senses. What it does is reform our *attitude* towards that evidence. . . . The task of philosophy is to prevent us from being taken in by the body and to recognize the radically subordinate place of the bodily in the nature of things."[22] Plato's epistemology draws attention with his theory of recollection to the necessary role sensory experience plays in philosophy. Philosophers enjoy rational inquiry concerning unchanging truth, but this process begins with the body's sense perception of the physical world. Thus, in Plato's epistemology we see the positive role Plato has Socrates assign to the body in the philosophical life.

The reformation of one's attitude toward sensory data and the body is a substantial aspect of Plato's normative dualist point of view. However, it absolutely does not require the withdrawal from daily life constituted by living a life devoid of bodily experiences.[23] There is a difference between the separation of the soul from the body that occurs at death and what it means to separate the soul from the body during life. It is a paradox to suggest that the soul can be literally separated from the body *while* living in a body. Taken literally, the separate soul is human death. Socrates underscores this when he asks Simmias, "Is [death] anything else than the separation of the soul from the body? Do we believe that death is this, namely, that the body comes to be separated by itself apart from the soul, and the soul comes to be separated by itself apart from the body? Is death anything else than that?" (*Phd.* 64c).[24] It is impossible to separate the soul from the body literally while alive, and thus pursuing this literal separation of the soul from the body is not a strategy that will successfully inoculate the embodied inquirer against either the deception problem or the distraction problem.

Having established that the literal separation of the soul from the body is unachievable without dying, we must ask if the call for a separate soul is a recommendation of suicide for those wanting to be wise and good. It would be natural to consider this as Plato has Socrates describe philosophers as training for *death* (*Phd.* 64a). However, in the *Phaedo*, Socrates emphasizes that the philosopher refrains from expediting the reunion with the Forms by committing suicide because it is impious (61c–63c). Even for a Platonist, ethical and religious considerations trump the joy of disembodied communion with the Forms. So, Socrates's call for philosophers to separate the soul from the body cannot be a demand that philosophers literally end their lives. Consequently, the literal interpretation of the separate soul associated with austere dualism is incompatible with the suicide prohibition.[25]

What then can the call for philosophers to live with separate souls mean if not literal death? To avoid these issues (the contradiction of death during life and the suicide prohibition), the austere dualist interpretation tries to take the idea of a separate soul one degree less literally, contending that the separate soul is a separation of one's body from the material world.[26] However, we must see that separating one's body from the material world is not the same as separating one's soul from one's body.[27] So an austere way of life does not constitute a separate soul properly training for death. No matter how abstemious one might become about shelter, sleep, food, and drink, those bodily needs would never disappear entirely.[28] Ultimately, only actual death, not the absolute denial of the body's needs and desires, ends the soul's involvement with the body. Certainly, that fact alone does not make the satisfaction of bodily needs something to be glorified. The philosopher living with a separate soul does not abide bodily needs simply because they are inevitable but rather because the body turns out to play several important roles in the life of one inquiring after truth and goodness. The intellect cannot do its work without the body. For instance, the body's need for sleep appears to disrupt philosophical inquiry, but cognitive scientists have more recently understood that we should not construe sleep as time away from intellectual work. They confirmed that sleep is a crucial step in the learning process, given that it is only during deep sleep that the brain transfers memories from short-term storage to long-term memory. While Plato did not have access to this information, we can glean from his emphasis on memory's role in rational activity that he could see any activity that facilitates memory as consistent with the philosopher's overall goals.

Nevertheless, in the course of reflecting on the distraction and deception problems, Socrates does express some austere-sounding views. The core of his apparent dispute with the body is summed up when he says, "Indeed the soul reasons best when none of these senses troubles it, neither hearing nor sight, nor pain nor pleasure, but when it is most by itself, taking leave of the body and as far as possible having no contact or association with it in its search for reality" (65c). This claim epitomizes Socrates's commitment to rational inquiry and foreshadows his quest for a separate soul. One of the most unflattering indictments against the body arises soon after this remark. Socrates says:

[A]s long as we have a body and our soul is kneaded together with (*sumpephurmenê*) such an evil we shall never adequately attain what we desire, which we affirm to be the truth. The body keeps us busy in a thousand ways because of its need or nurture.... Only the body and its desires cause war ... for all wars are due to the desire for wealth, and it is the body and the care of it, to which we are enslaved, which compel us to acquire wealth, and all this makes us too busy to practice philosophy. (*Phd.* 66b-d; translation modified)

Austere dualist interpreters conclude from this passage that the body is not only irrelevant to philosophy but disruptive of it too because bodily necessities lead to conflict and war.[29] Plato does have Socrates indicate that "body-love" is opposed to the love of wisdom. Socrates says, "Any man whom you see resenting death was not a lover of wisdom but a lover of the body, and also a lover of wealth or of honors, or both" (*Phd.* 68b-c). Austere dualist readings tend to equate Plato's emphasis of the danger involved in body-love with the conclusion that the embodied life is inherently diseased and abominable.

Peterson points out the central flaw in this view. She explains that when Socrates cautions against being a death-fearing body-lover (*philosômatos*) (*Phd.* 68b-c),

the statement does not show explicit connection between embodied life and disease. To say that the body-lover's condition has nothing healthy about it speaks only about somebody's life, not everybody's. It connects only a *certain kind* of embodied life and disease.... Socrates may think that anybody who loves riches and prestige is diseased; but we have no evidence that everybody, and especially Socrates himself, is thus diseased. Socrates neither resents death, nor loves riches or prestige.[30]

Plato depicts Socrates as an exemplar of the lifestyle most conducive to inquiring after the Forms, and it is quite clear that his body has not kept him too busy to practice philosophy. At 61a, Socrates straightforwardly describes himself as someone who has been practicing the art of philosophy. In so doing, he has reached the point of not taking death as something to be feared. Socrates is not a body-lover, but he does not disdain the body either.

Socrates's own life, which includes regular involvement with his body, exemplifies that satisfying certain needs and desires does not necessarily inhibit one from leading a contemplative life. Peterson gives a splendid accounting of Socrates's manifold ways of consorting with the body not at all out of the necessity demanded by 64e's account of the philosopher: (1) Socrates gathers with at least fourteen other bodies throughout his final conversation (*Phd.* 59b-c); (2) he spent his last night with his wife (*Phd.* 59e–60a), whether they discussed their concern for bodily matters in going over "*post-mortem* household management" or having the sort of sexual experience that created their young sons; (3) he gained insight about closely connected opposites from his physical experience of the pains of being shackled and the pleasures of being released (*Phd.* 60a); (4) his body leads him to thoughts of the Equal itself from his sense perceptions of the lengths of sticks and stones (*Phd.* 74–76); (5) he attended closely to sound in writing poetry (*Phd.* 60d–61a); (6) his wife observes that his whole life, including his final thirty days, has been spent in conversation (60a). I concur with Peterson, who concludes, "If he strongly wanted his soul to be alone by itself undistracted by the body the better to think of items like justice itself, this is all odd behavior."[31]

There is, in fact, a severe dissonance between Socrates's way of life and the austere dualists' version of the philosophical life. Given Plato's unquestionable portrayal of Socrates as the philosophical exemplar par excellence, this dissonance casts a pall over the austere dualist version of the philosophical life. Only when we equate asceticism with austere self-denial can Plato's Socrates be said to diverge from the philosophical paradigm. But if we bear in mind the original sense of asceticism as practice, discipline, or training, then there is nothing discordant about asceticism and Socrates's way of doing philosophy. Socrates is embodied and connects himself regularly with other flesh-and-blood human beings, and his engagement with this world has not at all hindered his ability to contemplate. This ought to give readers serious pause before adopting a literal interpretation of the separate soul. Plato's readers must figure out what else exactly is entailed by *living* with a separate soul.

We have now detected several serious difficulties with the literal interpretation of the separate soul. In summary: This view fails to account for the role of sense perception in the theory of recollection. It ignores the fact that literal separation of the soul from the body is plainly unachievable and conflicts with the suicide prohibition. And, perhaps most crucial of all, according to this interpretation, Socrates has not been practicing philosophy the right way, which flies in the face of Plato's incontrovertible depiction of Socrates as the exemplar of philosophy par excellence. We can now conclude that the call for philosophers to separate the soul from the body must not be interpreted literally.[32]

When Plato has Socrates call for philosophers to live with a soul that has been separated from the body, what he has in mind is for philosophers to undergo a transformation in their way of thinking. Plato emphasizes the changes Socrates's thinking has undergone in order to exemplify the transformation involved in becoming a philosopher. The foremost transition involved in thinking as a philosopher is to abandon the sort of thought that focuses *only* on the body, its sensory data, and its needs and desires.[33]

Crito and Socrates are illustrative of life before and after making this first transition, respectively. The central point of *Phaedo* 82d–83b is to elucidate the difference between the soul that philosophy "gets hold of" and the one it does not. Plato uses Crito to typify the sort of thinker whose attention is directly toward the physical but not far beyond it. He writes, "We shall be eager to follow your advice, said Crito, but how shall we bury you?" (*Phd.* 115c). To this Socrates responds, "In any way you like . . . if you can catch me and I do not escape you. . . . I do not convince Crito that I am this Socrates talking to you here and ordering all I say, but he thinks that I am that corpse which he will soon see, and so he asks how he should bury me" (translation modified). Here Plato depicts Crito's concern for Socrates's burial as driven entirely by thinking of Socrates as merely his body. His mistake is seeing Socrates as his body. Crito has not undergone the transformation toward abstract thought, and Socrates is aware of that. Crito's way of thinking revolves entirely around the body; he is not adept at consideration of the soul.[34]

Instead, Crito is the sort of person Socrates talks about whose soul is "forced to examine other things through [the body] as through a cage and not by itself" and "wallows in every kind of ignorance" (*Phd.* 82e). One might think that this passage is evidence of austere dualism in Plato because of its conception of the body as a prison.[35] However, the fuller context of the passage reminds us that it is *only* the souls of nonphilosophers, such as Crito, whose bodies are like prisons. To use Plato's notion of "the one" and "the many," these prisoners are stuck on "the many." Their liberation comes with the transition to seeing "the one" in relation to "the many."

Plato has Socrates explain that "philosophy gets hold of their soul when it is in that state, then gently encourages it and tries to free it by showing them that investigation through the eyes is full of deceit, as is that through the ears and the other senses" (*Phd.* 83a). Instead of relying on the body as the soul's only source of information, the soul relies on the body for safekeeping. Linforth reminds us that the most probable derivation of *sôma* comes from the Orphic tradition; he writes, "it comes from *sôizein*, 'to keep safe,' because the soul is 'kept safe' in the body as in a prison until it has paid certain penalties."[36] Properly under the influence of philosophy, it is no longer necessary to construe the body as a cage or even a tomb.[37] Socrates has been active in the process by which philosophy "gently encourages" the souls of his interlocutors to transform the way they think. But despite Socrates's coaching, Crito's body continues to be a prison for his soul because he has not abandoned his trust in empirical thinking.

In his response to Crito's question about the burial, Socrates is advising his friends to consider the possibility that he is really his soul, which may be imperishable. In doing so, Socrates attempts to demonstrate the value of thinking beyond what can be observed with sense perception. He exemplifies what it means to live with a soul separated from the body. In making the transition away from focus on the physical, the philosopher is conscious that investigating the world *solely* through the body is "full of deceit" (*Phd.* 83a). So, the philosopher's soul is persuaded "to withdraw from the senses in so far as it is not compelled to use them" (*Phd.* 83a). However, this thinker is not withdrawing from using the body in everyday life, but is, rather, moving away from sheer reliance upon the senses. Once one has made the transition toward contemplating the nonphysical Forms, one is in a position to recognize that the soul is an even more valuable tool than the body for inquiring into reality. However, the final aspect of the transformation into philosopher comes with the acknowledgment that in caring for the soul one cannot denounce the physical because it is indeed the starting point for all inquiry. Although Socrates goes on at 83a to use language that might make it sound as if the soul does all its philosophical work "by itself" without the aid of the body's senses, even in pursuit of nonphysical reality, philosophers are compelled to use the senses as a starting point for inquiry. Ultimately, Socrates's concern is not literally for the separation of the soul from the body, but for philosophical reasoning to be distinguished from total dependence on the senses.

In the *Phaedo*, Plato has Socrates give his interlocutors some insight into how his way of thinking came to be philosophical. He describes his own prior fascination with natural philosophy, which takes up "the causes of everything, why it comes to be, why it perishes and why it exists" (*Phd.* 96a-b). Plato portrays Socrates as having spent time wondering about questions such as: What brings the body to life? What causes the body to grow? What causes one to act? Socrates notes that he did not have much talent for thinking about the world this way (*Phd.* 96c). Let's turn now to some of the examples Socrates uses to demonstrate how he has separated the soul from the body by transforming his way of thinking. At 96c-e, Socrates raises the question of what causes the body to grow. Describing his own transformation, he says:

> This investigation made me quite blind even to those things which I and others thought that I clearly knew before, so that I unlearned what I thought I knew before, about many other things and specifically about how men grew. I thought before that it was *obvious to anybody* that men grew through eating and drinking, for food adds flesh to flesh and bones to bones, and in the same way appropriate parts were added to all other parts of the body, so that the man grew from an earlier small bulk to a large bulk later, and so a small man became big. (*Phd.* 96c-d; emphasis added)

This seemed obvious to Socrates precisely because at the time to which he is referring, his thinking relied primarily upon his sensory experience, which confirms that eating coincides with growth. He continues to explain the process of how his thinking changed, alluding to an intermediate step in how he answered the question of what causes the body to grow. He notes that he came to think that the cause of a body's growth is one becoming taller by standing next to someone or something shorter (*Phd.* 96d-e). About this Socrates says, "I thought my opinion was satisfactory, that when a large man stood by a small one he was taller by a head, and so a horse was taller than a horse. Even clearer than this, I thought that ten was more than eight because two had been added, and that a two-cubit length is larger than a cubit because it surpasses it by half its length" (*Phd.* 96d-e). However, Socrates abandons even this view as he moves away from thought that is focused upon the physical toward a kind of thinking that goes beyond mere empiricism. Ultimately, Socrates realizes "that I am far, by Zeus, from believing that I know the cause of any of those things" (*Phd.* 96e). Socrates's *aporia* develops the instant that he sees the deficiency of his empirical thinking. The *aporia* is resolved once Socrates eventually realizes that "it is through Bigness that big things are big and the bigger are bigger, and that smaller things are made small by Smallness" (*Phd.* 100e). His thinking has transformed into abstract philosophical inquiry.

Before this *aporia* was resolved, Socrates turned to Anaxagoras, who claims that "it is Mind that directs and is the cause of everything" (*Phd.* 97c). Addressing Anaxagoras's empirical thinking about what causes one to act, he says that he was hopeful of a good explanation when he read Anaxagoras's account of Mind, but that

> this wonderful hope was dashed as I went on reading and saw that the man made no use of Mind, nor gave it any responsibility for the management of things, but mentioned as causes air and ether and water and many other strange things. That seemed to me much like saying that Socrates' actions are all due to his mind, and then in trying to tell the causes of everything I do, to say that the reason that I am sitting here is because my body consists of bones and sinews, because the bones are hard and are separated by joints, that the sinews are such as to contract and relax, that they surround the bones along with flesh and skin which hold them together, then as the bones are hanging in their sockets, the relaxation and contraction of the sinews enable me to bend my limbs, and that is the cause of my sitting here with my limbs bent. (*Phd.* 98b-d)

Anaxagoras's explanation is correct insofar as it characterizes the physical phenomena involved in action. Socrates accepts physical phenomena as "that without which the cause could never be a cause" (i.e., the bones, sinews, etc.) (*Phd.* 99b; translation modified), but he is disappointed because Anaxagoras has failed to look beyond his perception of physical phenomena for the real cause of action. The question of what causes one to act will not be answered as fully as possible by someone who has not made the transition away from thinking only about the physical. Instead, Socrates prefers an explanation that looks beyond the physical. He conceives of having "chosen the best course" (*Phd.* 99a) as a cause of one's action, playing, in fact, even more of a causal role than the physical phenomena. This is, of course, a very philosophical way of thinking about behavior. Thus, in Socrates's disappointment with Anaxagoras's account of action, we see Plato's emphasis on the importance of transforming how one thinks.

Plato has Socrates describe a similar development in how he thinks about the question of what causes two. He indicates that this question can be answered in two different ways. One way involves answering in terms of mathematical operations. This sort of thinking holds that the cause of two is either the addition of one and one or division (*Phd.* 101b-c). This approach to thinking this question through is similar to thinking that what causes the body to grow is eating and drinking, which add "flesh to flesh and bones to bones" (*Phd.* 96c-d). Just as Socrates eventually abandons this way of thinking about what causes the body to grow, so too does Socrates in time give up the account focused on a conception of mathematical operations that is rooted in corporeal thinking, such as taking one apple, physically moving it close to another apple, and declaring that you have two apples. Plato has Socrates say, "I will not even allow myself to say that where one is added to one either the one to which it was added or the one that is added becomes two, or that the one added and the one to which it was added become two because of the addition of the one to the other" (*Phd.* 96e–97a). What he came to find misguided in this approach to the question of what causes two is that it is focused entirely on the physical. For example, with respect to addition, this focus on the physical involves thinking that two separate entities "come near to one another" or that "the coming together and being placed closer to one another" is the cause of two (*Phd.* 97a), and with respect to division this physical sort of account maintains that two is caused "because one is taken and separated from the other" (*Phd.* 97b). Socrates's approach to inquiry has undergone a transformation, pushing him beyond merely physical phenomena. This development leads him to say that "in these cases you do not know of any other cause of becoming two except by sharing in Twoness, and that the things that are to be two must share in this, as that which is to be one must share in Oneness" (*Phd.* 101c). In reaching this account of what causes two, Socrates is thinking philosophically, and here too we see the prominence of transformation in the *Phaedo*.

Socrates is careful to note that in undergoing this transformation in how he thinks about these sorts of questions he had to "unlearn what [he] thought [he] knew before" (*Phd.* 96c). It may be expected that human beings, even Socrates, start out their thinking focused entirely on sensory data about physical phenomena. And there is a certain psychological discomfort involved in taking the risk to include in one's inquiries considerations that are nonphysical and cannot be taken in via the senses. But wondering about the nonphysical Forms is of the utmost value, for Plato. Accordingly, Plato envisions that the philosopher will develop a hierarchical orientation toward the nonphysical and the physical, which I refer to as normative dualism, that considers the soul more important than the body. In doing so, the philosopher prioritizes investigation of the nonphysical Forms over empirical thought concerning the physical world, which is to separate the soul from the body. However, as Plato demonstrates, the search for knowledge could not be commenced without our bodily senses; so, a philosopher should acknowledge that the body plays a positive role in the philosophical life. Even after their transformation philosophers continue to employ thinking about physical phenomena acquired through sensory data, but they rely upon the soul to organize the different streams of input. The philosopher keeps empirical thinking in perspective as a starting point for philosophical inquiry. In light of that, the philosopher who embarks upon trying to understand the Forms recognizes how counterproductive it would be to abhor or even just to ignore the physical.

Plato's authorial choices in the *Phaedo* show him to be the kind of thinker who pursues philosophical thought with empirical consideration still in mind. For example, his Socrates might contend that life comes from death (*Phd.* 71a), but Plato knows that only when Xanthippe and the other women are removed from the scene can such a claim get off the ground. As Saxonhouse writes, "All this is claimed, as if there were no process of procreation that depended on sexual commingling, no interaction of the sexes to produce the child who sits with his mother in his father's prison cell. . . . Plato himself made sure that we recognize this by putting Xanthippe there for us to notice before there is this discourse in isolation from the mutuality of the family and of the city. He chose to include it; he need not have done so."[38] However, by dismissing Xanthippe from the scene, Plato does make it easier for the reader to ignore the empirical aspects of procreation. Saxonhouse adds that, even though Socrates expresses his dissatisfaction with Anaxagoras's focus on the body, Plato himself is not at all interested in ignoring the body. She observes how often "Plato makes mention of the facial expressions that accompany the speeches (a smile here, the look of one's eyes there, e.g., 64a, 101b, 102d, 115c)."[39] I would add that Plato also mentions Socrates's physical movements, such as lying down, sitting up, and rubbing his legs at 60a-c, and stroking Phaedo's head and hair at 89b. Think too of Socrates's mention of Thrasymachus's sweat and blushing (350d) and Glaucon's laughter in the *Republic* (398c, 451b). Indeed, Plato prioritizes the soul over the body without ignoring the body at all. Socrates may not direct much of his attention to his body in the *Phaedo*, but Plato reliably makes sure to direct the audience to the body.[40]

Plato's authorial choices in the *Phaedo* indicate his divergence from the austere claims about the body being made in the conversation that Socrates is having with a group of young, Pythagorean men. In light of this, Saxonhouse offers an intriguing explanation of why Plato might have chosen to write himself into the *Phaedo*, which is very rare for him, only to indicate that he was too sick to be present at Socrates's final day of philosophizing (*Phd.* 59b). To say the least, it is doubtful that illness could keep Plato away from an occasion that must have been of the utmost magnitude to the man who would spend the rest of his life eulogizing

Socrates. Saxonhouse wonders if this authorial decision indicates that Plato "would not be satisfied by the stark dichotomies between body and soul that are meant to quiet the objections of the Pythagorean, non-Athenian youth with whom Socrates speaks in the *Phd*."[41] Similarly, Davis cleverly observes that "to stay home because you are sick suggests that ultimately some value is being placed on staying alive, contrary to what Socrates seems to suggest in the *Phaedo*."[42] This sort of dramatic moment is useful for putting into context the ascetic-sounding remarks Plato has the interlocutors make at times. I propose that Plato is interested in addressing his work to two different kinds of audiences, one of whom is represented by these Pythagoreans.

If I am correct that Plato is a normative dualist rather than an austere dualist, then one might wonder why Plato incorporates austere-sounding remarks into the *Phaedo*. Why might he choose not to put additional emphasis on his position that philosophers should concentrate on getting good at *embodied* inquiry? Why does he not propose straightforwardly that people ought to become *more* interested in their souls and only secondarily interested in the physical? Plato's disparaging remarks about the body operate in a provocative, ironic way for the sake of a pedagogical aim. To begin with, we should never expect Plato to be straightforward in communicating his positions, because that sort of undemanding transparency would clash with his dialectical approach to pedagogy. It is certain that Plato intends to leave his audience with work to do for themselves. Alongside a host of other issues, we must think through for ourselves the merits of different conceptions of the soul.

Plato discerns two fundamental attitudes concerning the body and the soul. The many care only for the body, altogether neglecting the care of the soul, while there are a few who have already attempted to transcend body-love in favor of caring for the soul. In the *Phaedo*, young Pythagoreans are representative of this minority.[43] For Plato, both the many and the few have to undergo further transformation in how they think of the soul. Plato's use of austere-sounding remarks is directed at both audiences simultaneously. In this regard, the *Phaedo* is delicately poised between advocating for an austere asceticism and a normative asceticism.

Plato has Socrates initiate his educational project with the many by using his austere-sounding remarks at times in order to upset body-lovers because being in a state of psychological disequilibrium jars one into taking notice. If Plato were explicitly to communicate *anything* positive about the body, such as that it plays a positive role in philosophical inquiry, the many might latch on to the familiar call for safeguarding the body and reject or ignore the idea that one should prioritize the care of the soul. He hopes the austere-sounding claims about the desirability of a separate soul will shift attention away from the conventional attitude of being solely or chiefly concerned with the concrete state of one's body. Before one can master embodied inquiry, one must acknowledge the "terrible danger" that one is in when one does not care for the soul (*Phd.* 107c). We should think first of the political and interpersonal tyranny that can result from Socrates's interlocutors being plagued body-love. Being privy to this dialogue puts body-lovers in a position to take notice of Plato's warning about the danger of body-love. One who takes this danger seriously is prompted to make a transition away from honoring the body above all else to prizing the soul most of all.

It is instantly recognizable that Plato intends to draw attention to the dialogue's Pythagorean overtones. For example, making Echecrates Phaedo's interlocutor in the frame conversation announces the Pythagorean connection from the start of the dialogue, given that Echecrates is in Aristoxenus's list of the last Pythagoreans.[44] In Phlius, where Aristoxenus tells us many Pythagoreans lived, these two discuss Socrates's last day.[45] Furthermore, Socrates's main interlocutors in this dialogue, Simmias and Cebes, are known associates of the Pythagorean Philolaus,[46] and this status reveals their familiarity with Pythagorean notions such as the transmigration of soul.[47] These Pythagoreans are symbolic of having made the choice to focus on the care of the soul instead of the body. The transformation that body-lovers must initiate is already underway with a few, represented here by Pythagoreans.

Yet, Plato depicts the Pythagorean interlocutors as needing Socrates's guidance, and if they are to understand his conception of the philosophical care of soul, then he must first find a way to get their attention. So, when Socrates makes austere-sounding pronouncements in the *Phaedo*, Simmias and Cebes are easily focused and more than ready to agree. As Roochnik writes, "Far from trying to conceal this high level of agreement between Socrates and his interlocutors, Plato makes it explicit. In fact, at one point Socrates says this: 'let us speak with one another, and give up trying to talk to others' (64c1). The resulting conversation, which takes place in the isolation of Socrates' jail cell, is permeated with a feeling of cultic solidarity: it is a gathering of believers."[48] However, if Plato's Socrates is interested in facilitating the second part of the transformation in how one thinks about the soul, then these men are precisely the ones with whom Socrates needs to be in dialogue.

Plato suspects that the great majority of people are deeply entrenched in believing that the soul is insignificant and inconsequential. Cebes describes the dominance of this notion when he says to Socrates, "Men find it very hard to believe what you said about the soul. They think that after it has left the body it no longer exists anywhere, but that it is destroyed and dissolved on the day the man dies, as soon as it leaves the body; and that, on leaving it, it is dispersed like breath or smoke, has flown away and gone and is no longer anything anywhere" (*Phd.* 70a). Here, Plato reveals his awareness that the many will not accept the claim that the intangible soul is immortal and in fact more real than the body. What's more, by putting this commentary in the mouth of Cebes, Plato is flagging for his audience the difficulty that even aspiring Pythagoreans (such as Simmias and Cebes, as well as Echecrates[49]) have transcending body-love. Simmias, for one, still has a view of the soul that prioritizes the body (*Phd.* 86d).

Again, this group is portrayed as being in need of Socrates's guidance concerning how to do philosophy properly. Only having already acknowledged the primacy of the soul is one ready to grapple with the question of how one can separate the soul from the body *while* remaining incarnate. This is the paradox of the separate soul. For Plato, these young Pythagorean interlocutors must acknowledge that, even though the value of the body pales in comparison with that of the soul, the body need not be disdained, given that it makes positive contributions to philosophical inquiry. They must figure out how to transition away from prizing *only* the soul to honoring the soul *more than* the body *without* denouncing the body. Making this transformation is to resolve the separate soul paradox.

However, as Pythagoreans, they are not likely to see philosophy this way. Instead, like austere dualist interpreters, they are likely to believe that the philosophical life is austere, thinking, as Bluck does, that "much of the energy which in other men is expended upon emotion or appetite may in [the philosopher] be diverted to the acquisition of knowledge."[50] In the *Phaedo*, Plato does not give Socrates any interlocutors who are likely to be opponents of this view. However, in addition to the dialogue that Plato coordinates between Socrates and these Pythagoreans, Plato also arranges a conversation between the reader and the dialogue.[51] Consequently, the *Phaedo* has two simultaneous agendas. The austere-sounding comments are designed to jolt the body-loving reader into consideration of the value of the soul, while passages such as the Bacchant analogy (*Phd.* 69c-d) are intended to give the soul-loving Pythagorean interlocutors pause before they exclude moderate pleasure and the body in general from the philosopher's life. Let's turn now to the aspects of the *Phaedo* that should disturb the Pythagorean interlocutors' commitment to the austere lifestyle.

2.3 Moderation and the Separate Soul

An austere dualist denies the body, attempting to practice the sort of severe self-discipline that leaves no room for indulging in even moderate pleasures. Hence, if Plato were an austere dualist, then advocacy of moderation would be strange. Yet, a reader of the *Phaedo* can safely conclude that Plato holds moderation in high regard and advocates for its inclusion in the philosopher's lifestyle. This point is suggested by numerous aspects of the *Phaedo* where Socrates gestures toward moderation both implicitly as well as explicitly. The centrality of moderation in the philosopher's life stems from moderation being the outcome of a certain attitude or disposition. Let's begin by examining the *Phaedo*'s implicit discussion of moderation.

Within the context of his harsh remarks about the activities of the body, Socrates leaves ambiguous the question of *just how much* bodily indulgence is acceptable for a philosopher. Socrates claims that "we shall be closest to knowledge if we refrain as much as possible from association with the body and do not join with it more than we must" (*Phd.* 67a). At stake here is whether or not a philosopher should enjoy the pleasures involved in tending to necessary bodily concerns. What Socrates and Simmias have agreed to at this point in the *Phaedo* is that the philosopher will be the least concerned with (*espoudakenai*) pleasures such as food and drink. Following this, they agree that the true philosopher holds all matters of service to the body in fairly low esteem (*atimazein*), participating in them when necessary (*Phd.* 64e). Later he makes a similar remark, that the philosopher keeps away from pleasures and desires and pains *as far as possible* (*Phd.* 83b; emphasis added). Plato puts into Socrates's mouth verbs concerning not taking bodily matters seriously, concerning holding bodily matters in lower esteem than matters of the soul. But these verbs do not go as far as to indicate that a philosopher abhors the body or considers bodily matters of no importance whatsoever. Instead, with his call for a separate soul, Plato offers a conception of the philosophical life that is primarily about attitude.[52]

Bluck describes Socrates as possessing an "indifference to worldly pleasure."[53] This is not false, but without contextualization this assertion is potentially misleading. At neither 64d-e nor 83b does Socrates comment on the fact that he is a philosopher who experiences the pleasures of sex, food, wine, long walks, and so on. But Plato reminds us that Socrates has not one but two small sons in addition to the older one (*Phd.* 60a, 116b), making clear that even at seventy Socrates wasn't keeping too far away from the natural but unnecessary pleasures of sexual experience. In the

Symposium, Alcibiades tells us that Socrates "was the one man who could really enjoy a feast; and though he didn't much want to drink, when he had to, he could drink the best of us under the table" (220a).[54] As we shall see in chapter 3, this echoes Socrates's attitude toward physical beauty in the *Symposium* where we learn from Alcibiades that Socrates is "crazy about beautiful boys," even though "it couldn't matter less to him whether a boy is beautiful" (216d-e). And gastronomic pleasure must have been fairly dear to Socrates given that he requests free meals as his reward for doing the gadfly's duty for Athens (*Apology* 36d-e). So, Socrates may be indifferent to worldly pleasures, but he is no stranger to them.

While Socrates does participate in pleasurable human activities, he is not unduly serious about worldly pleasure. It is not the object of his enthusiasm; the care of the soul is. Notwithstanding Socrates's ambiguity about how much pleasure is acceptable in the life of a philosopher, he is calling attention to the expectation of at least some pleasures (presumably the classes of necessary pleasures, such as eating, and natural but unnecessary pleasures, like sex) being involved in the philosophical lifestyle. Socrates's position, thus, implicitly suggests that philosophers should train themselves to be moderate, rather than aspiring to the austere version of asceticism, because under the control of *phronêsis* moderation will be exercised correctly (*Phd.* 69b-c). Dorter agrees:

> The usual view of [64d-e] as an advocation of asceticism has been a source of perplexity because of the non-ascetic behavior attributed to Socrates in other dialogues, but in fact there is nothing here that goes against Socrates' usual views. First, he is not arguing against pleasure in general here but only the false or "so-called" pleasures (*tas hêdonas kaloumenas*). . . . He does not advocate the unnecessary and non-natural pleasures of adorning oneself with especially elegant clothing, but there is nothing unusually ascetic for him in that view. In the case of food, drink, and sex, however, he urges not abstinence but only that we refrain from taking them seriously (*espoudaikenai*). . . . One allows oneself to appreciate the charms a certain experience has to offer without forgetting their triviality in comparison with important matters.[55]

Dorter captures well the particular attitude Plato's Socrates has toward physical pleasure. Pleasure can be enjoyably included in a philosophical life, even though it is not the sort of thing that one should be disproportionately serious about.⁵⁶ And if one needs time and energy for the sort of thinking that makes a human life worth living, then one must never be immoderate in directing one's attention toward trifling pleasures. Philosophers train themselves to be moderate concerning trivial delights; and moderation is under the control of *phronêsis*, and so will be exercised correctly (*Phd.* 69b3–4 and 69c1–2).⁵⁷

Unless Plato goes out of his way to demonstrate that his understanding of moderation differs from the typical meaning, then it remains difficult to establish an austere dualist interpretation of Socrates's persistent references to moderation in the *Phaedo*. If Plato does not make a strong and consistent case for an austere construal of *sôphrosunê*, then the reader will fall back upon the understanding of moderation that was as traditional then as it is now. Currently, Aristotle's doctrine of the mean pervades the West's understanding of moderation, and there is absolutely no reason to assume that moderation meant something drastically different before Aristotle. Plato himself tells us how commonplace it was to hear the Delphic maxim "*mêden agan*" (nothing in excess) mentioned around town (*Protagoras* 343b), and Hesiod, too, provides a pre-Platonic literary version of the Delphic maxim.⁵⁸ Let's turn now to the passages in which moderation is explicitly mentioned. In these we shall see that, since Plato does not make a substantial case for any other meaning, moderation in the sense of *mêden agan* is recommended for the philosophical life. Maintaining this sense of moderation as a philosophical ideal, Plato consistently conceives of the philosophical lifestyle as one that does not necessarily require abstinence from physically pleasurable experience.

At 68c-d, Plato's Socrates explicitly mentions *sôphrosunê*, referring to the popular conception of the term and describing it as "not to get swept off one's feet by one's passions, but to treat them with disdain (*oligôrôs echein*) and orderliness." Grube's translation makes for a perplexing explanation of moderation because being orderly about one's passions is not the same thing as disdaining them. Grube's rendering of the phrase "*oligôrôs echein*" as "treating with disdain" would be better translated as "treating carelessly" or "treating neglectfully." To conceive of *sôphrosunê* as treating the passions carelessly or neglectfully is consistent with the idea at 64d of refraining from taking trivial pleasures seriously (*espoudaikenai*). However, with a presumption of austere asceticism, Grube's translation excessively amplifies the negativity in the tone of this passage. For example, he misleadingly translates a remaining part of this sentence at 68d, rendering it as follows: "[I]s this not suited only to those who most of all despise the body (*malista tou sômatos oligôrousin*) and live the life of philosophy?"

"*Malista tou sômatos oligôrousin*" should be translated as "making the body of small account" or "esteeming the body little."[59] This too would correspond to 64d's sketch of refraining from taking trivial pleasures seriously (*espoudaikenai*). Being orderly about passions and treating them neglectfully goes hand in hand, then, with treating the body as of little account. This way of behaving corresponds to the normative dualist's general attitude toward pleasure, which leaves room for enjoying pleasure in moderation while never being seriously concerned with pleasure. However, this kind of ordering of one's concerns stands in sharp contrast with disdaining pleasure per se, which is the mark of the austere dualist position. Thus, in order to sensibly interpret this use of "*sôphrosunê*" we must abandon these erroneous aspects of Grube's translation. Once liberated from the influence of Grube's ascetic dualist interpretation, we are able to recognize Plato's normative dualism.

The second of the five explicit allusions to moderation occurs within a rather strange passage about reincarnation.[60] This reference comes as part of a schema in which Socrates and Cebes agree to the following: that the soul is more like the divine, while the body is more like the mortal (*Phd.* 80a-b); that a pure soul will "spend the rest of time with the gods" (*Phd.* 81a);[61] and that inferior persons will be "bound to such characters as they have practiced in their life" (*Phd.* 81e). He offers us examples of how he thinks reincarnation operates. He says that those who based on their habits were gluttonous, violent, and drunk will join donkeys (*Phd.* 81e-82a), that those who esteemed injustice, tyranny, and plunder will join wolves and hawks, and that those who "practiced popular and social virtue, which they call moderation (*sôphrosunên*) and justice and which was developed by habit and practice, without philosophy or understanding" join "a social and gentle group, either of bees or wasps or ants, or then again the same kind of human group, and so be moderate (*metrious*) men" (*Phd.* 82b). This indicates that the moderate life, even when it is not formed by philosophy and *nous*, is recommended above the Calliclean life of gluttony, injustice, tyranny, and plunder and the Alcibiadean life of violence and drunkenness. Yet, given that those who lead lives of demotic moderation are reincarnated rather than being freed from embodiment, this appears prima facie to be a critique of moderation.[62]

Does Plato reject the conventional understanding of moderation (*mêden agan*)? If so, there would be no reason to ever praise moderation, which Socrates does indeed do in the other four passages that refer to moderation. Ultimately, nor does 82c-d present any alternative, austere sense of moderation. Socrates's criticism here is directed only at moderation that is developed aphilosophically out of habit and common sense. In passing judgment on the moderation of nonphilosophers, Socrates reveals his preference for the kind of moderation that is forged by understanding rather than out of habit. And so he transitions to some important comments about his conception of philosophers. First, sounding more austere than most anywhere else in the corpus, Socrates says:

> [T]hose who practice philosophy the right way keep away from all bodily passions, master them and do not surrender themselves to them [*hoi orthôs philosophoi apechontai tôn kata to sôma epithumiôn hapasôn kai karterousi kai ou paradidoasin autais heautous*]; it is not at all for fear of wasting their substance and of poverty, which the majority and the money-lovers fear, nor for fear of dishonor and ill-repute, like the ambitious and lovers of honors, that they keep away from them. (*Phd*. 82c)

And right after that, we learn two things from Socrates's comments about philosophers and their moderation at 82d. First, they "care for their own soul and do not live for the service of the body" (*alla mê sômati plattontes zôsi*) (*Phd*. 82d). I interpret this as indicative of the philosopher's indifferent attitude toward something such as physical pleasure rather than being about the philosopher's rejection of any experience of or participation in something such as physical pleasure.[63] One might even suggest that austerely rejecting the experience of physical pleasure altogether very much involves keeping bodily passions in the forefront of one's mind.[64] Second, philosophers do not travel the same road as the aphilosophically moderate people (*Phd*. 82d). What does Plato mean here by saying that philosophers keep away from the bodily passions? What two "roads" are diverging from each other at 82d? To make sense of this, let's compare some translation possibilities.

In my view, the stronger translations of 82d come from Rowe and Gallop, who are similarly oriented toward rendering the passage like this: that those who care for their own souls and do not live for the service of the body *say farewell to* or *disregard* (*chairein eipontes*) those people who are moderate by habit but not through philosophical understanding.[65] On this reading, the object of "*chairein eipontes*" is the people who are aphilosophically moderate rather than the bodily passions referred to at 82c. However, this is not what comes through in Grube's translation.[66] He translates 82d as follows: that those who care for their own souls and do not live for the service of the body "dismiss all these things." First, *who* or *what* is the object of *chairein eipontes*? For Grube, it is the bodily passions being dismissed. The grammar here does not rule out taking the object to be the bodily passions, but the lines immediately after this do not encourage it either, because they refer to the aphilosophical people not the bodily passions. So I think the stronger translation takes the aphilosophical people as the object rather than the bodily passions. However, it is interesting that Plato makes both objects of *chairein eipontes* and the concomitant interpretations possible, encouraging the reader to choose. Second, and of even greater significance, is the question of how *chairein eipontes* should be translated. Grube chooses "dismiss," which would not be inaccurate if we take "*chairein eipontes*" metaphorically, thereby arriving at the notion of dismissing someone or something from one's thoughts.[67] Yet, using a verb that underscores a mental disposition rather than anything concerning experience of something would better capture the spirit of Plato's use of *chairein*. For instance, when Socrates uses *chairein auton* at 63e, Grube renders it with "take no notice," and at 64c he translates *chairein epontes ekeinois* as "nevermind them." Taken together, these occurrences indicate that Plato's philosophers dismiss bodily pleasures as an *attitudinal* project moreso than an austere stance to not ever *experience* them. Consequently, what it means for philosophers to keep away from bodily passions is not necessarily to reject the experience of them. Instead, as we shall see throughout this book, to not *live for* serving the body is to think of the body as of little importance in comparison with the soul, and to *keep away from* bodily passions is to eschew the perspective that is unduly concerned with physical pleasures as if they were more significant than contemplative pleasures.

The third and fourth references to moderation also leave the reader free to use its customary meaning, namely, nothing in excess. At 83e, Socrates says that genuine lovers of learning are moderate (*kosmioi*), which he means to contrast with those he has just mentioned who are riveted to the body (*Phd.* 83d). In mentioning those who are riveted to the body by pleasures and pains, I take Socrates to have in mind body-lovers for whom *only* the body has sway, that is, those who not only experience bodily pleasures and pains but also take them very seriously. In contrast, Gallop reads this passage as an absolute condemnation of pleasures and pains.[68] If this passage were intent on admonishing pleasure and pain in general, then it would be strange to mention moderation as the philosopher's virtue unless accompanied by making a case for an alternative, austere meaning. If we look at 83b8 and 83c6, however, it is clear that Plato is intent on criticizing excessive (*sphodra*) pleasure, rather than pleasure in general. Meanwhile, when Socrates concludes his story about the afterlife he says that "the soul that has led a pure and moderate (*metriôs*) life finds fellow

50   Plato and the Body

travelers and gods to guide it, and each of them dwells in a place suited to it" (*Phd.* 108c). These two passages make generally positive remarks about being moderate, and the context of each does nothing to contest the Delphic connotation. Thus, these four sections of the *Phaedo*, which we have examined thus far, do not provide any reason to abandon the Delphic connotation of moderation in favor of an austere sensibility.

At 114e–115a, Plato has Socrates raise the topic of moderation for the fifth time. He says:

> A man should be of good cheer about his own soul, if during life he has ignored the pleasures of the body and its ornamentation as *alien to him* [*hôs allotrious te ontas*] and doing him more harm than good, but has *seriously concerned* [*manthanein espoudase*] himself with the pleasures of learning, and adorned his soul not with alien but with its own ornaments, namely, moderation, righteousness, courage, freedom and truth, and in that state awaits his journey to the underworld. (*Phd.* 114e–115a; emphases added)

One might think that this passage goes the farthest toward realigning *sôphrosunê* with an austere version of asceticism. If this were the case, then this passage would stand alone, as the remainder of the references to moderation do not endeavor to diverge from the traditional Delphic understanding. On the other hand, it seems more likely that Socrates is not criticizing pleasures absolutely; rather, he qualifies his remarks by observing that this person has recognized that the pleasures of the body are not all important. This echoes the tone of Dorter's reading of the *Phaedo's* first mention of moderation and my reading of the second. This tone calls not for abstinence but for the philosopher to acknowledge that the pleasures of the body pale in comparison to matters that deserve to be taken seriously (*espoudaikenai*). This interpretation is further supported by the fact that Socrates includes moderation among the soul's proper ornaments and does so without contesting the traditional Delphic understanding at any point in the dialogue.

2.4 How Bacchants Train for Death

A damaging blow is also dealt to the austere dualist interpretation when Plato points out an analogous relationship between Bacchants and philosophers. Although I said earlier that physical desire is not a substantial topic in the *Phaedo*, it is hinted at by a peculiar reference to Dionysus. In the *Phaedo*, one of Plato's central projects is to illuminate the difference between the many who neglect the soul and the few who properly nurture it through the practice of philosophy. He has Socrates declare that philosophy is practiced in the right way when one wants most of all to free the soul from the body (*Phd.* 67d). He says, "[T]he philosopher more than other men frees the soul from association with the body as much as possible," not caring at all for the pleasures of the body (*Phd.* 65a). However, we have now seen that there are two competing interpretations of claims such as this. Austere dualist interpreters read these passages literally, while normative dualist interpreters do not. Sensing the interlocutor's need for some further orientation, Socrates constructs an analogy. Although this analogy is very significant, it has been virtually overlooked in the scholarly literature.[69] Plato writes:

> It is likely that those who established the mystic rites for us were not inferior persons but were speaking in riddles long ago when they said that whoever arrives in the underworld uninitiated and unsanctified will wallow in the mire, whereas he who arrives there purified and initiated will dwell with the gods. There are indeed, as those concerned with the mysteries say, *many who carry the thyrsus but the Bacchants are few. These latter* are, in my opinion, no other than those who have practiced philosophy in the right way [*houtoi d' eisin kata tên emên doxan ouk alloi e hoi pephilosophêkotes orthôs*]. (*Phd.* 69c-d; emphasis added)[70]

The choice to construct this analogy around the worship of Dionysus should be shocking to commentators who read Plato as an austere dualist. This analogy is intended to set apart those who do things improperly from those who do things properly, in addition to pointing out the rarity of outstanding practitioners.[71] It is strange that Plato chooses proper and improper Bacchants as the example filling out this analogy. Bacchants are well known for their interest in the pleasures of the body; they religiously drink and enjoy sexual pleasure. We do not expect Plato to use an analogy for understanding this that asks us to see philosophers as similar to worshippers of Dionysus, whom the Greeks associated with debauchery. As Morrow writes, Dionysus is "scarcely the god one would choose as patron of an Academy of taste and morals."[72] If Plato is going to create the analogy around proper and improper worshippers of a god, we might expect him to make the analogy revolve around Apollo, whom the Greeks associated with order and rationality. And certainly Plato could have chosen to use the proper and improper practitioners of some craft completely unrelated to any of the gods, such as medicine or sculpting.

The decision to emphasize the Bacchants is not at all arbitrary. Plato's authorial selection of the Bacchant analogy coheres with one of the boldest claims in the entire corpus. The term *houtoi* (in the last line of the passage) grammatically refers back to the true Bacchants. As a result, the last line of the quoted passage claims that these worshippers of Dionysus are good philosophers. Even the general connection between good philosophers (i.e., the purified, soul-separators) and worshippers of Dionysus should give us pause. To link the practice of philosophy with the Dionysian lifestyle contradicts the austere dualist interpretation. Still, we must wonder, if practicing philosophy the right way entails separating the soul from the body, then in what way can Bacchants be considered soul-separators? In what way are Bacchants training for death?

While Plato makes conscious literary choices to place the dialogue against a Pythagorean backdrop, the *Phaedo* is shot through with both Bacchant and Pythagorean elements. In addition to the Bacchant analogy and the claim that the Bacchants are practicing philosophy the right way, there is Plato's heroization of Socrates when he alludes to Socrates playing the role of Heracles, while Phaedo plays the role of Iolaus (*Phd.* 89c). There is also another reference at 109b to Heracles, who was the exemplar of the hero for both the Pythagoreans and the Bacchants.[73] It may strike the reader as odd that the dialogue puts Dionysian elements in communication with Pythagorean elements. However, Kingsley argues that it is a mistake to treat Pythagoreanism as fundamentally incompatible with the worship of Dionysus. He writes, "Apollo may have been important for Pythagoreans, but at a purely theoretical and general level we need to bear in mind that the Apollonian and Dionysiac elements of Greek life were intimately intertwined."[74]

At 85b5, Socrates says that he is consecrated to Apollo (*hieros*). In Euripides's *Bacchae*, Apollo's avatar, Teiresias, gives a lengthy defense of the worship of Dionysus (170–369, especially 266–328). Thus, if the worship of Dionysus is properly understood and practiced, then it is not in conflict with the ordered life that is associated with Apollo. In fact, this sort of worship actually allows one to practice the moderate way of life. Character and nature allow one to comprehend and achieve the mean. In this regard, Dionysian worship assists one in keeping a balanced soul.

Contrarily, failure to align one's life properly with Dionysus puts one at risk of being destroyed by the god, as, for example, King Pentheus is in the *Bacchae*. Many an extreme hedonist and austere ascetic have met their end through the kind of psychological disintegration that Pentheus's dismemberment symbolizes. Furthermore, Apollo and Dionysus are opposites (*ta enantia*) in the specialized sense of being opposed psychological forces, held together in soul by a tension of force. If the balance between them is not struck, then one can never attain the eudaimonic manner we so admire in Socrates.

The Apollonian and Dionysian elements come together for the Bacchants and Pythagoreans in their interest in death, rebirth, and immortality. The central myth about Bacchants that needs debunking is that the worship of Dionysus was simply about hedonism and debauchery. The pleasures associated with true Bacchants (in contrast to mere thrysus carriers) were quite distinct from the debauchery of an Alcibiades and the hedonism of a Callicles. The dilettante enjoys the drinking and sex associated with worshipping Dionysus simply because those activities yield immediate pleasure; the pursuit of immediate pleasure is a body-lover's way of approaching being a Bacchant. But the genuine Bacchant has moved beyond this way of thinking about wine and sex. True Bacchants' interest in wine and fertility differs from that of those who merely carry the thyrsus, insofar as true Bacchants approach their rituals with a focus on piety.

The genuine Bacchant drinks and enjoys erotic pleasure for the sake of a higher religious purpose, namely, to be reborn. One of the central phrases associated with the Bacchants is "I am a kid who has rushed for the milk" (*eriphos es gal' epeton*), which Kingsley has argued is a reference "to the process of immortalization."[75] Someone newly born rushes for the mother's milk; Bacchant initiates were thought of as newly reborn. Meanwhile, the young goat was a traditional representative of Dionysus. And "lastly, it may apply to the capacity of a Bacchic initiate to imitate or identify with Dionysus while remaining, in certain fundamental respects, distinct from him."[76] In the latter regard, the Bacchic phrase is strikingly parallel to the Platonic process of becoming like god (*homoiôsis theôi*). (I will return to the subject of becoming like a god in 2.5.) In the course of enjoying physical pleasures for the higher purpose of imitating Dionysus, the true Bacchant has trained for death. The exclusive reliance on thinking about physical pleasure prevents the dilettante Bacchant from training for death.

For the philosopher with the proper attitude about the hierarchy of soul to body, the transition from a life of only empirical thought to a life that includes philosophical thinking as well is crucial. The dialogues attempt to push our thinking beyond our inclination to depend solely on sensory experience. For example, when asked about the ritual activities the dilettante Bacchant relies for information entirely on his/her actual experiences in this physical realm with those activities (i.e., what s/he has directly experienced for her/himself as well as what s/he has heard from others). Meanwhile, philosophical thought looks for answers beyond mere physical phenomena, because thinking that depends entirely on sensory experience will always be deficient. Yet, philosophers do not entirely abandon the information collected through sense perception. They know that drinking and sex yield physical pleasure but put that empirical information into the perspective gained by successfully transitioning to philosophical thought. This transition from empirical thinking to philosophical thought enables one to consider the immortality of the soul and to see that the health of the immortal soul is of the utmost importance, *without* vilifying the body.

Plato aspires to prompt a transition to philosophical thought so that a new, more sophisticated perspective on sensory experience in particular and the physical in general will emerge. It is *erôs* that moves us from the physical to the nonphysical, and in the case of the body, the transition to philosophical thinking makes one care principally about virtue, as that is the healthy state of the soul, which one will be in possession of forever. As a result, one develops a new perspective that being embodied is merely one facet of being human; the body is important (especially insofar as it assists the soul in loving wisdom), but ultimately it is a less important aspect of being human. Thus, successful transformation to being a lover of wisdom causes the lifestyle that revolves solely around the pleasures of the body to dissolve and a new, intellectual, moderate lifestyle to surface.

2.5 Becoming Like God in a Life Raft

Echoing the *Phaedo*'s call for the philosopher to be liberated as much as possible from the body, Plato indicates in the *Theaetetus* that human beings should eagerly attempt to become as much like god as possible. He has Socrates say, "That is why a man should make all haste to escape from earth to heaven; and escape means becoming as like god [*homoiôsis theôi*] as possible; and a man becomes like god when he becomes just and pure, with understanding [*homoiôsis de dikaion kai hosion meta phronêseôs genesthai*]" (176a-b).[77] According to Annas, Plato's ideal of becoming like god "runs against the current of ancient ethical thought, which takes virtue to be an ideal fulfillment of human nature and its potential, not an attempt to transcend it and to become another kind of being altogether in a quest for perfection that can be attained only in a withdrawal from everyday life."[78] Austere dualist interpreters tend to read Plato this way.[79] Yet, I take issue with the assumption that, for Plato, the ideal of becoming as godlike as possible is different from the concept of virtue as fulfilling human nature and its potential. When Plato calls for us to become as much like the divine as possible, there is confusion about what he is idealizing.

Both in the *Theaetetus* passage and elsewhere, Plato holds up as ideal the fulfillment of human nature and its potential. In the *Theaetetus* passage, he has Socrates single out becoming just (*dikaion*) and pure (*hosion*) with the aid of practical wisdom (*meta phronêseôs*) as what it means to become as much like god as possible. If being "pure" (*hosion*) means disdaining the physical in the manner of austere dualism, then Annas would be right to see it as withdrawal from everyday life. However, before we assume that "*hosion*" should be associated with an austere version of *askesis*, it should be mentioned that *hosion* can also be translated as pious, religious, or divinely ordained. Furthermore, Plato's use of the phrase *meta phronêseôs* underscores that practical wisdom, or prudence, aids in becoming pure and just. It seems unlikely that practical wisdom would be of assistance in withdrawing from everyday life. Conversely, *phronêsis* would be of great use to a philosopher trying to figure out how to be wise and good while embodied.

Socratic piety[80] demands that we avoid being so hubristic as to attempt to position oneself on par with god, which is what one does if one attempts to excise one's incarnation while living in a God-given body. Human beings may strive after the greatest possible imitation of the divine, but being divine is off limits for us. We can become *like* god; we cannot *be* god. Plato does not envision human beings transcending the human condition altogether because the soul cannot actually become god even after death. What sort of existence does a disembodied, godlike soul have? This is a question that Plato asks but does not clearly answer. Socrates tells Simmias that when our souls existed apart from the body before birth "they had intelligence" (*Phd.* 76c). Each human soul is said to encounter the Forms prenatally, while disembodied. Plato reminds us that the philosopher is eager for disembodied communion with reality (*Phd.* 68a).[81] Yet, because this intelligence is inferior to divine cognition but superior to embodied human cognition, the status of a disembodied soul appears to be intermediate between the human and the divine.

Returning to this state does appear to be the preference of a Platonic inquirer. But why should this entail seeing human existence "as an aberration or as a punishment"?[82] Why should it necessitate disinterest in and even disdain for the physical? Even though philosophers long for disembodied communion with the Forms, disembodied existence is impossible for human beings. Human beings do come to life in the flesh for whatever mysterious reason, and, as a result, it would be unwise to hate the body and the sensible realm, especially given the positive role the body plays in philosophizing about the world we inhabit. Human flourishing is accomplished when one masters embodied inquiry rather than when one attempts to transcend being human. To fulfill human potential and try to imitate the divine, Plato emphasizes that human beings should attempt to become as wise and good as possible.[83]

One might wonder why, if philosophers concentrate on getting good at *embodied* inquiry, would Plato ever call that training for *death*. At *Phaedo* 68a, Plato has Socrates compare the philosophers' longing for reunion with the Forms at death to the desire of grieving men to be with their loved ones who are not present here and now. The two examples of longing for death at 68a have in common love and the desire for being together with their beloved. The central difference between the two examples is that for the grieving men the loss is a recent one, while for the philosophers their beloveds have not changed from being here to not being here. The philosophers' relationship with the Forms has been long distance, so to speak, since birth.

Socrates invites us to think nautically, comparing life to rough seas (*Phd*. 85d). Let's play with this theme a bit. If we compare the situation of a soul becoming embodied to being lost at sea, and the body to a life raft, then we can suppose that, until the soul reaches the long-sought-after shore of disembodied communion with the Forms, it should be glad to have had the body as a life raft.[84] It would be lacking in practical wisdom to disdain the life raft just because one prefers the safety of the shore. Perhaps one can appreciate the body, even though one would be glad to do without the body someday, just as, even though one is glad to have had a life raft, one is happy to reach the shore.[85]

The piety that commits philosophers to the suicide prohibition assumes there is a divine reason for our existence in the physical world. Therefore, it would be a bit puzzling for philosophers to resent the body, because it disrespects the very entity that they attempt to respect by refraining from suicide.[86] The philosopher who piously observes the suicide prohibition focuses instead on living properly, and the dedication to piety is less of a struggle because rational inquiry makes embodied existence worth living. Of course, in Socrates's own nautical musing, philosophical beliefs serve as the "firmer vessel" compared to the initial life raft (*Phd.* 85d). Here he invites the philosopher to jump from mere embodiment, our initial raft, to the philosophically oriented life, the better boat. As the affinity argument suggests, if trained, even the embodied soul will naturally incline toward that which is real and pure (*Phd.* 79c-d). In the words of Gordon, "Philosophy, therefore, provides the means for limited beings to stay afloat amidst the sometimes tumultuous seas of human embodied life."[87] Plato has given us grounds for believing that, in our embodied condition, the ideal toward which we ought to strive is a life of reasoning with pleasure. Living with a soul oriented toward the Forms is not to transcend human nature; it is to realize the highest potential of human nature by becoming a philosopher.

Therefore, we can understand Plato's goal of becoming as much like the divine as possible as a way of living that does not necessitate total withdrawal from life. Vainly avoiding a full human life is not the proper way to train for death. Denying the body's needs and desires is a way of hiding from human nature that is hardly philosophical or courageous. A philosopher training for death is engaged in an *askesis*[88] that is much more complex than the simplistic austere version of asceticism. The normative dualist point of view maintains that the body is a tool through which the soul explores the world.[89] And, as we have seen, the body performs a positive function in the process of rational inquiry. If one makes the transformation to philosophical thought, then one can see the body for what it really is. This is the sense in which philosophy encourages the soul to be released from its excessive attachment to bodily desires. The philosopher will not attempt to repress the body but will instead coordinate its needs with those of the soul. It is the life of reflective moderation that enables the inquirer to deal with the challenges that embodiment poses for a thinker. That is, we should care for our souls, exercising reason and enjoying the moderate pleasures that are actually conducive to inquiry. We must use reason itself to identify these pleasures, avoiding an excessively hedonistic lifestyle, the life of body-lovers. But so too must the inquirer use reason to avoid the errant path of the austere lifestyle that tries to deny the physical.

If Plato were the austere dualist that the Neoplatonists and so many others make him out to be, then he would be encouraging a vain lifestyle at odds with what is ultimately endorsed in the figure of Socrates. Plato's Socrates stands as the exemplar of becoming as much like god as possible. He has cultivated justice and piety with the aid of practical wisdom, but neither piety nor practical wisdom makes him repudiate the human body or the physical aspects of everyday life. Rather, in pursuit of justice and piety Socrates has prioritized the soul over the body. We shall see in chapter 3 that philosophers aspiring to wisdom and goodness need not withdraw from the sexual aspects of life, and in chapter 4 that philosophers honor their love of the Good most highly when they resist the temptation to withdraw from political leadership. In fact, the remaining chapters will both demonstrate that when philosophers practice erotic love and engage in political leadership in the right way they are advancing their aspirations to be as much like the divine as possible. We will see Socrates exemplify this.

Chapter 3

Beauty, Education, and Erotic Ascent in the *Symposium* and *Phaedrus*

3.1 Introduction

While the orientation of the *Phaedo* puts more emphasis on the embodied inquirer's problems with deception, the *Phaedrus* and *Symposium* highlight the human being's struggle with distraction, particularly the troublesome disruptions erotic attraction can initiate for one who is struggling to be wise and good. We have already seen in chapter 2 that the philosopher solves the deception problem by living with a separate soul and that soul-separating is not a matter of abandoning concern for the physical. Plato's philosophers are not in a position to disregard the corporeal entirely because the process of calling to mind the reality of eternal being begins with sensory perception of the physical world. Instead, philosophers deal with the deception problem by making a transition from empirical thinking to philosophical thought. The embodied inquirer's susceptibility to being deceived by the physical senses is lessened by developing the capacity to use empirical data but not depend entirely on it.

In contrast to the human body's indispensable desire for food, drink, sleep, and shelter, it might seem that the inquirer could repress and ignore erotic desire in order to avoid being distracted from philosophical inquiry. Many scholars have read Plato as though he believes that *erôs* ought to be conquered, leaving desexualized "platonic love" in its wake.[1] However, in the erotic dialogues, Plato designates philosophy as a form of erotic pursuit. In fact, these dialogues demonstrate that philosophers should not even try to eliminate erotic desire because it is on account of this erotic nature that philosophers long for and begin to access Plato's Forms. Both the *Phaedrus* and *Symposium* emphasize the role of *erôs* in a thinker's life, making suggestions about what *erôs* should and should not be for the philosopher. Plato's Socrates advises that *erôs* should be undertaken only with a proper beloved. It should not be something shameful or unhealthy; it should not be allowed to distract the lover of wisdom from rational inquiry. In the final analysis, erotic desire should be an impetus to learning rather than a distraction from it.

Plato prioritizes erotic desire that is channeled into philosophical understanding and, in turn, the cultivation of human virtues, and he presents his Socrates as the exemplar par excellence of practicing philosophical inquiry as a form of erotic pursuit. So, I begin this chapter, asking in 3.2 why, despite his attraction to them, Plato's Socrates refrains from having sexual experiences with Phaedrus (3.2.1) and Alcibiades (3.2.2). Also, I'll examine why he married and procreated, if the philosophical lifestyle supposedly requires sexual abstinence (3.2.3). After investigating Socrates's erotic life, I will show in 3.3 how erotic desire can facilitate knowledge of the Forms. To recognize this, we must delineate two versions of *erôs*—a healthy, divine *erôs* and an unhealthy, vulgar *erôs* (in 3.3.1) and clear up some confusion about Plato's the Forms (in 3.3.2) that stem from the ascent language used in the erotic dialogues (and elsewhere) with the help of Plato's comparisons of physical and psychic beauty (in 3.3.3).

My analysis will demonstrate that the embodied inquirer who learns how to manage erotic attraction properly will experience two distinct but mutually consistent advantages. The first and most important advantage that the erotic dialogues emphasize is the educational function of erotic desire that I discuss in 3.3, which orients the soul's journey toward knowledge of the Forms. To use Gordon's words, "Eros is the engine of what we call philosophy."[2] Second, Plato hints that erotic consummation may be an enjoyable reward earned through the hard work of philosophical endeavor and commitment to pursue and enjoy good pleasures only, that is, those that are beneficial. I will study the evidence for interpreting Plato this way in 3.4.

My discussion will establish that Plato leaves room for sexual experience in the philosophical life because erotic consummation can occur under the guidance of reason. This is suggested by the drama of Aristophanes's hiccups and the "sneeze treatment" that cures him in the *Symposium* (which I take up in 3.4.1) as well as by Plato's discussions of divine horses being rewarded for hard work and patience with nectar and ambrosia (which I consider in 3.4.2) and philosophers loving boys with the help of philosophy (which I analyze in 3.4.3). Plato does not go as far as to necessitate sexual consummation for the philosopher, but I will show that he does accept it as potentially compatible with the life dedicated to philosophy. The course of this discussion will confirm that it is a mistake to assume that Plato's view of *erôs* endorses an austere dualist version of asceticism. As we uncover Plato's belief that *erôs* helps embodied inquirers understand both self and reality, we will see further evidence for his normative dualism.

3.2 The Erotic Philosopher

When Plato has his characters admit the difficulty involved in knowing oneself, he draws our attention to the importance of self-knowledge for living well and understanding reality. Early in the *Phaedrus*, Plato has Socrates indicate that he is still unable to know himself; he says that he studies himself, asking, "Am I a beast more complicated and savage than Typhon, or am I a tamer, simpler animal with a share in a divine and gentle nature?" (230a).[3] Why is self-knowledge so elusive? Together, the *Phaedrus* and *Symposium* suggest that the struggle to understand oneself stems in large part from our nature as erotic beings. Plato depicts Socrates as not only a model inquirer but also as an erotic philosopher, that is, one who experiences erotic desire as uniquely adjoined to the pursuit of knowledge.[4] Our first indication of the worrisome effect *erôs* has on Socrates comes from a comparison of two moments in the *Symposium*. Plato's Socrates tends to disavow knowing anything worthwhile, contending instead to possess "human wisdom," which he describes as knowing that he knows nothing (*Ap.* 21b-d). Yet, Socrates breaks from this claim when Plato has him say, "[T]he only thing I say I understand is the art of love [*ta erotica*]" (*Smp.* 177e). However, later in the *Symposium* he recants, saying, "I realized how ridiculous I'd been . . . to say that I was a master of the art of love, when I know nothing whatever of this business" (198d). What does this tension reveal about Socrates? What sort of thing is *erôs* that Socrates could be so confused about his own understanding of it?

It is not a coincidence that Socrates is both an erotic person and a model inquirer. These dialogues establish that being a lover of wisdom is about making an erotic ascent. Plato's Socrates exemplifies how to circumnavigate well the distractions that erotic desire causes, but he also draws to our attention that erotic desire is not a coincidental feature of the pursuit of understanding the Forms. The embodied philosopher is distracted from rational inquiry by erotic desire, but erotic desire simultaneously performs the function of getting the philosopher close to the beauty of a beloved, which is crucial to the process of being reminded of the Form of Beauty. Once we are near something beautiful, our instinct to love beauty takes over from there.[5] One might be inclined to disagree, thinking that our instinct to love beauty inevitably makes erotic desire a source of distraction from philosophical inquiry. However, Plato takes seriously the idea that loving the beauty of one's beloved puts us on to something special. He is well aware that erotic desire can take a lover away from philosophical inquiry and self-cultivation, but he goes to lengths to show the positive roles erotic desire can play in the life of an inquirer.

The *Symposium* in particular portrays Socrates as a philosopher with *erôs* on his mind. He has "just bathed and put on his fancy sandals—both very unusual events"[6] and when asked "why he was looking so good," he replies, "I took great pains with my appearance: I'm going to the house of a good-looking man; I had to look my best" (*Smp.* 174a). This smartening makes public Socrates's intention to spend the night flirting with Agathon, the host of this symposium. Having readied himself for a night of flirtation, Socrates winds up being the last one awake when the sun rises over Agathon's party. He spends the last few hours of the night talking with Aristophanes and Agathon, long after Alcibiades fell asleep or left and Eryximachus and Phaedrus "made their excuses and left" (*Smp.* 223c). A body-lover such as Alcibiades might consider Socrates's effort to look good a waste so long as he goes home by himself. Why must Socrates leave the party alone?

The *Phaedrus* and *Symposium* depict our erotic philosopher as abstinent with two handsome men, Phaedrus and Alcibiades. Austere dualist interpreters would have us believe that Plato and his Socrates endorse the position that sexual experiences are incompatible with the philosopher's life of rational inquiry.[7] For example, Nussbaum says of the *Symposium*, "You think, says Plato, that you can have this love and goodness too, this knowledge of and by flesh and good-knowledge too. Well, says Plato, you can't."[8] Ascetic dualist interpreters have assumed that Socrates' rejection of Alcibiades's sexual advances is evidence of Socrates's austere asceticism, and they have assumed in turn that Plato's admiration of Socrates implies that he too endorses austere asceticism.[9] However, nowhere in the *Symposium* or the *Phaedrus* is it said that sexual experiences should be banned from the philosopher's life.[10] Nails confirms, "It is not as if Socrates is an ascetic, some celibate moralist; we know that he was not."[11] Instead, these dialogues recommend that the philosopher should not consummate a relationship with someone lacking a beautiful soul. What Socrates's abstinence in these situations actually confirms is that Phaedrus and Alcibiades are not fitting beloveds for Socrates; they are not properly equipped for seducing Socrates.

3.2.1 Socrates's Abstinence with Phaedrus

The attentive reader of the *Phaedrus* picks up on the variety of clues intended to signal some special chemistry between Socrates and Phaedrus. First of all, Plato has Socrates indicate close personal knowledge of Phaedrus (*Phdr.* 228a), and Socrates mentions loving Phaedrus dearly (*Phdr.* 228d). Second, Plato makes the authorial decision to have the *Phaedrus* be the only dialogue in which Socrates is completely alone with just one interlocutor secluded from urban society. Moreover, Plato makes their environment out to be a seductive setting in a variety of ways. This includes having Phaedrus recall the myth of Boreas carrying Oreithyia off, which "serves as an image of the natural seduction scene taking place" between Socrates and Phaedrus.[12] Plato's intention to depict Socrates as an erotic philosopher is also signaled by Phaedrus telling Socrates that Lysias's speech is just the sort he will find interesting because it is about love (*Phdr.* 227c). After learning that the speech addresses why a beloved should offer his sexual favors to someone who does not love him rather than to someone who does, Socrates jokes that he wishes Lysias "would write that you should give your favors to a poor rather than to a rich man, to an older rather than to a younger one—that is, to someone like me and most other people: then his speeches would be really sophisticated, and they'd contribute to the public good besides!" (*Phdr.* 227c-d). While it should not surprise us that an erotic philosopher is interested in the sexual favors of beautiful boys, the ascetic assumptions about Socrates make it easy to forget that perhaps there is truth in jest here.

Phaedrus leads Socrates on a pastoral walk beyond Athenian city limits so that he can rehearse for Socrates a speech by Lysias that he has just heard. The city limits had a reputation for being a place for prostitution.[13] Although de Vries notices that Socrates discerns "the natural beauties of the spot with a connoisseur's eye and uses a connoisseur's language to describe them,"[14] Socrates describes himself as inexperienced with the countryside outside of Athens—a "stranger outside the city" (230d).

In spite of the traditional expectation that younger men be passive in their interactions with older men, Phaedrus is proactive in using his role as guide to lead Socrates into quite seductive territory. He proposes that they "walk right in the stream" until they reach the slope perfectly suited for lying down on the grass (*Phdr.* 229a-b). This slope comes complete with mood lighting, music, and fragrance in the form of shade, singing cicadas, and the sweet smell of tree blossoms (*Phdr.* 230b-c). Seduction imagery continues to abound when Socrates describes the process by which he gets Phaedrus to recite Lysias's speech in terms of the dynamic between lovers playing hard to get. Socrates refers to himself as "a man who is sick with passion for hearing speeches" and "a partner for [Phaedrus'] frenzied dance" (*Phdr.* 228b-c). Meanwhile, Socrates says that Phaedrus "played coy and pretended that he did not want to. In the end, of course, he was going to recite it even if he had to force an unwilling audience to listen" (*Phdr.* 228c). Furthermore, Phaedrus replicates this erotic tone later when he wants Socrates to make the speech that he promised would be better than Lysias's. He even orders Socrates to "Stop playing hard to get!" (*Phdr.* 236c-d) Socrates then returns flirtation with flirtation, saying both that he wants the Muses to help him impress Phaedrus and that he doesn't want to get distracted and lose his train of thought as a result of looking at Phaedrus (*Phdr.* 237a-b). The fact that this setting does not inspire Socrates to be seduced by Phaedrus leaves readers to wonder whether this is meant to signify that Socrates is an austere sort of ascetic who sees erotic consummation as shameful.

When Phaedrus finishes reciting Lysias's speech, Socrates says, "I'm in ecstasy. And it's all your doing, Phaedrus: I was looking at you while you were reading and it seemed to me that the speech made you radiant with delight; and since I believe you understand these matters better than I do, I followed your lead, and following you I shared your Bacchic frenzy" (*Phdr.* 234d). Given Socrates's earlier statement about desiring beautiful lovers (*Phdr.* 227c-d), we are left to wonder whether or not Socrates is being sarcastic here, making a joke about how reading speeches aloud compares with the other activities that could occupy them in such a romantic environment. Yet, it is more likely that Socrates is lampooning Phaedrus's fanaticism about speeches.[15] In both the *Phaedrus* and *Symposium*, Phaedrus is depicted not as a lover of wisdom but as a lover of speeches. Moreover, he does not even want to analyze the speeches about which he is so passionate. He just wants to hear speeches and memorize his favorites so that he can recite them for others. It is Phaedrus's preference for rhetoric and memorization over dialectic and understanding that precludes his seduction of Socrates.[16]

In the *Symposium*, Phaedrus's enthusiasm for speeches influences his lover Eryximachus to suggest that the men spend the evening making speeches in honor of *Erôs*. It also leads Phaedrus to make the first of these speeches, and, finally, his passion for speeches causes him to interrupt Socrates's effort to arrive at knowledge through dialectical discussion. With Socrates beginning to ask Agathon questions, Plato writes:

At that point Phaedrus interrupted: "Agathon, my friend, if you answer Socrates, he'll no longer care whether we get anywhere with what we're doing here, so long as he has a partner for discussion. Especially if he's handsome. Now, like you, I enjoy listening to Socrates in discussion, but it is my duty to see to the praising of Love and to exact a speech from every one of this group. When each of you has made his offering to the god, then you can have your discussion." (*Smp.* 194d-e)

Phaedrus sees Socrates's desire to have a discussion with Agathon as a fruitless departure from speechmaking. He does not share Socrates's interest in dialectic. This is demonstrated again at the end of Socrates's palinode, where Phaedrus does not have even one question about the palinode.[17] Phaedrus's lack of interest in dialectic makes clear why at the conclusion of the palinode Socrates reiterates his hope that Phaedrus will be converted to philosophy (*Phdr.* 257b).

We learn from Socrates's own words that knowing how to do dialectic is central to attracting his attention. Socrates says, "I am myself a lover of these divisions and collections, so that I may be able to think and to speak; and if I believe that someone else is capable of discerning a single thing that is also by nature capable of encompassing many, I follow 'straight behind, in his tracks, as if he were a god.' God knows whether this is the right name for those who can do this correctly or not, but so far I have always called them 'dialecticians'" (*Phdr.* 266b). It should be noted that this passage indicates that Socrates loves the collections and divisions themselves, but we can also gather from this passage that Socrates will not be seriously interested in one who lacks the ability to make these collections and divisions. So, it would behoove Socrates's suitors to learn how to be erotic—to collect and divide, to do dialectic, to do philosophy. It is clear from both the *Phaedrus* and *Symposium* that Phaedrus is a long way off from knowing how to engage in philosophical inquiry. Phaedrus cannot do the one thing that would make Socrates follow him around as if he were a god. After all, Phaedrus is portrayed as even less philosophically inclined than Alcibiades.[18]

3.2.2 Socrates's Abstinence with Alcibiades

Because Socrates twice declares that he loves Alcibiades (*Grg.* 481d and *Smp.* 213d), we should wonder why Socrates repeatedly refuses Alcibiades's attempts to seduce Socrates. In interpreting this aspect of Alcibiades's speech in the *Symposium*, there has been a presumption that sexual activity is incompatible with philosophical contemplation either because the philosopher just is not interested in sexuality, or worse, because of the inherent baseness of sexuality.[19] Perhaps that view crept into the interpretation of Plato because of Plotinus's influence. Porphyry explains that when Plotinus heard the rhetorician Diophanes read in Plato's *Symposium* that Alcibiades "asserted that a pupil for the sake of advancing in the study of virtue should submit himself to carnal intercourse with his master if the master desired it" he could barely resist the urge to get up and leave the reading and that when it was over he instructed Porphyry to write a refutation.[20] It is difficult to say with certainty whether Plotinus takes sexual intercourse to be incongruous with the ethical-philosophical life or if his reaction simply reflects his opposition to a form of *paiderastia* that falls outside of the accepted custom. In my view, the choice to remain abstinent with Alcibiades represents Socrates's recognition that it would be improper to consummate a sexual relationship when presented with a sexually eager,[21] physically appealing, but morally and philosophically stunted individual.[22] Although Alcibiades turns out to be by far one of the most interesting interlocutors in the Platonic dialogues, his life is plagued by his moral shortcomings. Considering Alcibiades's inadequacy, Socrates's refusal to consummate their relationship sexually is evidence neither that Socrates prefers abstinence nor that Plato intends an austere ascetic lesson.[23]

Erotic desire has long been considered trouble as a result of its ability to blind lovers, and so we might fear that Socrates's loving feelings for Alcibiades would blind him to Alcibiades's weaknesses. Yet, somehow Socrates sees his beloved Alcibiades as he really is. If Alcibiades had transcended his body-love and mastered the care of the soul, then Socrates could have guided him in the moderate sort of erotic experience that still prioritizes the pursuit of philosophical knowledge. However, Socrates sees all too clearly that Alcibiades has not yet succeeded at making the transition from body-love to the care of the soul. Owing to this, Alcibiades is not at all ready to make the transition to prioritizing the soul over the body in a way that allows for satisfying desire under the guidance of reason. Even though Socrates thinks that Alcibiades has psychic promise, at least three aspects of his soul strike Socrates as ugly.

First of all, Alcibiades is uncouth. He arrives at Agathon's party uninvited, drunk, and acting wildly (*Smp.* 212c–213a). Given that Alcibiades's historical namesake was implicated in two scandals in the same year (the alleged profanations of the Eleusinian mysteries and the mutilation of the Hermae, which was perhaps the Western world's most astonishing act of drunken vandalism), we can assume that this is not meant to be considered out of character.²⁴ Furthermore, despite being with a noisy crowd of men, Alcibiades is "half-carried" into Agathon's house by a shrieking flute-girl (*Smp.* 212c-d). The mention of the flute-girl evokes Socrates's disparaging remarks about "the second-rate parties of the agora crowd," at which men "are unable to entertain themselves over their wine by using their own voices to generate conversation" and "pay premium prices for flute-girls" (*Prt.* 347c).²⁵ In comparison with such a group, Socrates says, "When well-educated gentlemen drink together, you will not see girls playing the flute or the lyre or dancing, but a group that knows how to get together without these childish frivolities, conversing civilly no matter how heavily they are drinking. Ours is such a group, if indeed it consists of men such as most of us claim to be" (*Prt.* 347d-348a). Being not only entertained but physically supported by a flute-girl thus signals the difficulty Alcibiades has being urbane, being a man such as most of them claim to be.

Jealousy is Alcibiades's second psychic problem. We learn of his jealousy from his reaction to finding Socrates on the same couch as Agathon (*Smp.* 213c-d). Furthermore, Socrates perceives in Alcibiades's jealousy a proclivity for jealous rage. Socrates accuses Alcibiades of yelling and threatening, claiming that he thinks Alcibiades barely refrains from slapping him around (*Smp.* 213d). In fact, Socrates claims that he finds "the fierceness of [Alcibiades's] passion" terrifying, and he asks Agathon to "please try to keep him under control" (*Smp.* 213d). Is Socrates really so afraid of Alcibiades's temper? Or are Socrates's worries here just a flirtatious show that he puts on both to forge an allegiance with Agathon against Alcibiades (who, like Socrates, is angling to be alone on a couch with Agathon, the handsome guest of honor) and in turn to flirt with Alcibiades by making him jealous of Agathon?²⁶ While this particular scene is replete with signals of flirtation within a love-triangle, it appears likely nonetheless that Socrates is sincerely worried about Alcibiades's psychic shortcomings with respect to his temper. As Nussbaum writes, "The atmosphere of mock-threat and mock-violence surrounding Alcibiades' speech goes deeper than a game, since we know it to be the speech of a man who will soon commit real acts of violence."²⁷

Third, Alcibiades is shameless and extremely arrogant. Presumably these qualities are exactly what landed the historical Alcibiades in trouble time and again. We first glimpse Plato's Alcibiades's arrogance in the *Alcibiades*,²⁸ but the picture is completed in the *Symposium*. He is incredibly self-assured about his good looks (*Smp.* 217a, 219c; cf. *Alc.* 104a), his family background and wealth (*Alc.* 104a-c), and his popularity with suitors (*Alc.* 103a-104d). Furthermore, Alcibiades exhibits the ambitions for political power that are symptomatic of believing oneself to be superior to all other people. His arrogance is evident each time he expresses his considerable surprise that Socrates could make him feel as though *his* life "is no better than the most miserable slave's" (*Smp.* 215e). Unfortunately Alcibiades's overconfidence hampers his recognition of his own need for further education.

Nevertheless, Socrates is not the only one to recognize the psychic potential Alcibiades is wasting; Alcibiades sees it too. Alcibiades describes Socrates's conversations with him as having an "extraordinary effect" on him (*Smp.* 215d-e). This effect and his account of how he handles it are worthy of being quoted at length. He says:

> Let anyone—man, woman, or child—listen to you or even to a poor account of what you say—and we are all transported, completely possessed. . . . The moment he starts to speak, I am beside myself: my heart starts leaping in my chest, the tears come streaming down my face, even the frenzied Corybantes seem sane compared to me—and, let me tell you, I am not alone. I have heard Pericles and many other great orators, and I have admired their speeches. But nothing like this ever happened to me: they never upset me so deeply that my very own soul started protesting my life—my life!—was no better than the most miserable slave's. And yet that is exactly how this Marsyas here at my side makes me feel all the time: he makes it seem that my life isn't worth living! You can't say that it isn't true, Socrates. I know very well that you could make me feel that way this very moment if I gave you half a chance. He always traps me, you see, and he makes me admit that my political career is a waste of time, while all that matters is just what I most neglect: my personal shortcomings, which cry out for the closest attention. So I refuse to listen to him; I stop my ears and tear myself away from him, for, like the Sirens, he could make me stay by his side till I die. (*Smp.* 215d–216b)

Even though Alcibiades is not immune to Socrates's captivating manner, he chooses not to give himself over to Socrates's values. Here Alcibiades pinpoints why Socrates's teaching ability is limited; Socrates can guide only those who give him "half a chance."

Alcibiades chooses not to give Socrates that opportunity, knowing what consequences will follow from that decision, saying, "I know perfectly well that I can't prove he's wrong when he tells me what I should do; yet, the moment I leave his side, I go back to my old ways: I cave in to my desire to please the crowd. My whole life has become one constant effort to escape from him and keep away" (*Smp.* 216b). Not only does Alcibiades keep away from Socrates, eventually he steers clear of philosophy too. Alcibiades repeatedly leaves Socrates too soon;[29] as a result, Alcibiades is left alone with his psychic shortcomings. As Gordon writes, "Dying at the hands of assassins in his forties when most men are in their prime, disgraced by two cities that he betrayed, Alcibiades' life exemplifies the continuing misguidance of powerful eros. Alcibiades' was a life in pursuit of glory, power, and repute, ending ultimately in infamy."[30] He remains a body-lover who fails to make the transition to the care of the soul. This puts Alcibiades on the path to his end.

Despite the fact that Alcibiades will not commit to the care of the self that Socrates encourages, he is perceptive enough to understand Socrates in a way that few do.[31] The commentary about Socrates that Plato puts into his mouth is largely discerning and insightful.[32] Plato has Alcibiades say about Socrates, "None of you really understands him. . . . I'm going to show you what he really is" (*Smp.* 216d). More than any other interlocutor Alcibiades sees Socrates as he really is. Erotic desire has not blinded Alcibiades to Socrates any more than it blinded Socrates to the reality of Alcibiades. One might even go so far as to imagine that their erotic desire for each other is what enables them to see each other so truthfully.[33] Alcibiades hints at how he is able to understand Socrates so well when he says, "I don't know if any of you have seen him when he's really serious. But I once caught him when he was open like Silenus' statues (*agalmata*)" (*Smp.* 216e). This is a deeply strange declaration. By way of a partial explanation Alcibiades says, "Isn't he just like a statue of Silenus? You know the kind of statue I mean; you'll find them in any shop in town. It's a Silenus sitting, his flute or his pipes in his hands, and it's hollow. It's split right down the middle, and inside it's full of tiny statues of the gods" (*Smp.* 215b).[34] Nussbaum takes the frequent mention of statues in the *Symposium* as intentional foreshadowing of the mutilation of the Hermae to which Alcibiades would be linked a year following the dramatic setting of January in 416.[35] Meanwhile, duBois interprets these tiny gods inside Socrates as Alcibiades's vision of Socrates as pregnant—pregnant with Diotima and her teachings.[36] But let's examine other possibilities as well.

Another possible meaning of seeing Socrates "open like Silenus' statues"[37] could be that Alcibiades has heard something privately from Socrates to which no one else is privy. However, this interpretation would entail Socrates being dishonest when he says, "If anyone says he has learned anything from me, or that he heard anything privately that the others did not hear, be assured that he is not telling the truth" (*Ap.* 33b). If seeing Socrates "when he was open" does not refer to private conversation, an alternative interpretation of Alcibiades's statement is that it refers to some private physical intimacy.[38] Alcibiades himself rules out this possibility. He tells us of Socrates's abstinence in the face of his repeated and assorted attempts to seduce Socrates (*Smp.* 217a–219e). A reader might question whether Plato's Socrates, who is in love with Alcibiades, could in actuality resist Alcibiades's efforts to seduce him.[39] In confessing the details of how he proactively attempted to seduce Socrates, Alcibiades risks being ridiculed for upending the traditional dynamic between lover and beloved that strictly demands passivity from the younger *erômenos* and proactivity from only the older *erastês*.[40] Alcibiades even alludes to the fact that the entire story of his effort to seduce Socrates cannot be told publicly (*Smp.* 218b), and the reader is left to infer that the story Alcibiades tells is intended to represent the truth. What, then, does it mean for Alcibiades to have seen Socrates "open like Silenus' statues"?

Perhaps we can better answer this question by thinking less literally. Alcibiades is somehow discerning enough to figure out that Socrates's "whole life is one big game—a game of irony" (*Smp.* 216e). Alcibiades's use of the Silenus simile suggests that in his effort to know Socrates he finds that there is always more to understand.[41] Using the Silenus simile reveals Alcibiades's awareness that, for one who is willing to dig deeper, there is always more to Socrates than meets the eye. To see Socrates open like Silenus's statues is to understand that the one thing we know for certain about Socrates is that we do not know anything about Socrates for certain. Yet, Alcibiades intentionally turns away from Socrates, away from inquiring alongside him, and thus away from the full erotic experience for which Socrates might have hoped.

After hearing Alcibiades say, "Nothing is more important to me than becoming the best man I can be, and no one can help me more than you to reach that aim" (*Smp.* 218d), Socrates replies:

> If I really have in me the power to make you a better man, then you can see in me a beauty that is really beyond description and makes your own remarkable good looks pale in comparison. But, then, is this a fair exchange that you propose? You seem to me to want more than your proper share: you offer me the merest appearance of beauty, and in return you want the thing itself, "gold in exchange for bronze." (*Smp.* 218e–219a)

Rather than contending that sexual experiences are wrong always and everywhere for men of their kind, Socrates appeals to a principle of fair exchange. If Plato or his Socrates were to consider sexual experiences inherently shameful, wouldn't Plato have Socrates or Alcibiades communicate that? Yet, Plato chooses not to have Alcibiades attribute any such belief to Socrates, nor does he put into the mouth of Socrates any revisions of Alcibiades's account. Instead, we are left to gather from Socrates's abstinence that it would be a mistake for him to have a sexual experience with Alcibiades not because sexual experiences are inherently debauched, but rather because Alcibiades has failed to cultivate his psychic potential. As a result, he is not a suitable beloved for Socrates. And Socrates goes away thinking that Alcibiades has disappointed him by not choosing to do the sorts of things that would enable them enjoy both the pleasures of philosophy and sex together.[42]

Von Blanckenhagen complains, "Had Socrates slept with Alcibiades not 'like a father or older brother' but as a true *erastês*, he might well have channeled the manifold gifts of this most gifted of all Athenians in a classical, a 'Periclean,' direction and would have made him the best statesman Athens ever had."[43] In my view, this would be impossible. Alcibiades has impeded his own seduction of Socrates by repeatedly rejecting the opportunity to engage in philosophical inquiry with Socrates.[44] If only Alcibiades would choose the philosophical life over the life of popular politics, he could inquire alongside Socrates and learn how to collect and divide, how to have dialectic discussions, how to do philosophy, in other words, how to make Socrates "follow 'straight behind, in his tracks, as if he were a god'" (*Phdr.* 266b). How different things would be if it were actually true that nothing is more important to Alcibiades than becoming the best man he could be (*Smp.* 218d). However, Alcibiades allows his avoidance of feeling shame to get in the way of making the transition toward the care of the soul, and this makes all the difference in his relationship with Socrates. So, Socrates must look beyond Alcibiades for a fair exchange of psychic beauty.

3.2.3 A Philosopher Married with Children

Despite the ways in which Alcibiades is disappointing, Socrates still professes to have two loves: philosophy and Alcibiades (*Grg.* 481d). His wife, Xanthippe, is absent from this list. Yet, we know that Plato's Socrates does have intercourse with Xanthippe because they have children (*Cri.* 45d, *Phd.* 60a). Since austere dualist interpreters read Plato and his Socrates as committed to the view that sexual desire and consummation are shameful, they need an account of why Socrates has sex with Xanthippe. That interpretation presumes that Socrates consummates his relationship with Xanthippe for the sake of procreation in a merely conventional fashion. In the *Symposium*, Diotima claims that it is a natural human tendency to desire to give birth to children because "it is what mortals have in place of immortality" (206e–207a). Is Socrates like most human beings with respect to being interested in prolonging his earthly presence by leaving behind children to keep alive his legacy and his family line, or what today we would call his genetic material?[45] I do not think so.

In particular, the *Apology* and *Crito* establish Socrates's ambivalence toward physical survival; his concern is for the state of his soul. In the *Apology*, Socrates acknowledges that his philosophical mission has put his life in danger and says, nevertheless, "You are wrong . . . if you think that a man who is any good at all should take into account the risk of life or death; he should look to this only in his actions, whether what he does is right or wrong, whether he is acting like a good or a bad man" (28b-c). Socrates also discloses that he knows the jurors at his trial expect him to make an obsequious defense in order to avoid being put to death (*Ap.* 38d-e). Yet, Socrates refuses to be untruthful in his defense, going to great lengths to explain that it matters only *how* one lives not *how long* one lives. He says, "I would much rather die after this kind of defense than live after making the other kind" (*Ap.* 38e). Socrates's commitment to his ethics over his existence is also featured in the *Crito* when he refuses to escape from prison as the government and his friends expect him to (47e-48b). He will not preserve his body at the expense of his soul by committing any of these ignoble acts (that is, abandoning his philosophical mission, making false claims in his defense, and escaping from prison). If Socrates will not take part in any of these acts for the sake of avoiding death, it follows that he would not advocate any shameful behavior, regardless of whether that behavior is conventional or would consequently prolong his physical existence in some way. If Socrates considers sexual consummation a shameful self-indulgence, he would not do it even for the sake of prolonging life by immortalizing himself through having children. Given Socrates's record of living life in accord with his values, the fact that his life does include sexual experiences indicates that he must not find them inherently shameful.[46]

Having discounted the austere dualist assumptions about the implications of Socrates's abstinence with Alcibiades and his procreation with Xanthippe, we must now ask why Socrates does with Xanthippe what he refuses to do with his beloved Alcibiades. It is impossible to answer this question with any certainty. Unfortunately, we know very little about either the historical Xanthippe or Plato's Xanthippe. The picture of the historical Xanthippe is formed mostly out of apocryphal stories, and Plato's Xanthippe is a relatively undeveloped but pleasant character. Someone mistakenly believing that physical beauty alone is relevant to the seduction of Socrates might wonder if Xanthippe possesses a beauty that surpasses Alcibiades's. However, in terms of Socrates's physical connection to Xanthippe, we simply never hear anything, which is noteworthy given that Socrates does not shy away from noting his physical attraction to others, such as Charmides, Alcibiades, Phaedrus, and Agathon. Does Socrates have a more substantial intellectual connection to Xanthippe than he does to Alcibiades? When Socrates sends Xanthippe away from the conversation over his deathbed, it appears that he considers her a dispensable interlocutor, leading us to believe that he does not have a great intellectual connection to her (*Phd.* 60a-b).

One might argue that Socrates has lower intellectual expectations of Xanthippe than he does of Alcibiades because Xanthippe is a woman and Socrates is living in a misogynistic culture. If so, she can meet these second-rate standards and be taken as a lover by Socrates. However, Plato gives us reason to believe that his Socrates is much less misogynistic than the prevailing culture. After all, Plato's Socrates believes that guardian-women should receive the same education as guardian-men (*R.* 451e), and his most important teacher is "most wise Diotima," "a woman who was wise about many things" (*Smp.* 208c, 201d). Furthermore, if the consensus that Plato invents Diotima is correct,[47] then Plato's choice of a woman as Socrates's most important teacher indicates that he too is substantially less misogynistic than the prevailing culture. It is clear that Socrates experiences a deep intellectual connection with Diotima. In comparison, it appears that Xanthippe, like Alcibiades, cannot offer Socrates a gold-for-gold sort of exchange.

It is, however, interesting to note that in the *Phaedo* it appears Xanthippe spent the night with Socrates on eve of his execution.[48] While some might be inclined to see Xanthippe as nothing more than the mother of Socrates's children, perhaps Socrates and Xanthippe did share something more substantial. Still, we are left without a full understanding of why he has sexual experiences with Xanthippe while he remains abstinent with Alcibiades. Either Socrates only limits himself to gold-for-gold partners in the context of the pederasty or he does not generally confine himself to gold-for-gold partners. But in conversation with Alcibiades, he does imply that a bronze-for-gold exchange is not what he seeks (*Smp.* 218e–219a). However, such a position cannot stand without accounting for Xanthippe's role.

Concerning both the historical Socrates as well as Plato's Socrates, there is so much that we simply cannot know. Why Socrates chooses to marry and have children with Xanthippe will remain a mystery as will the question of whether Plato's Socrates ever experiences sexual pleasure with those who *do* know how to collect and divide, how to have dialectical discussions, how to do philosophy. We wonder if Socrates might have followed "straight behind" dialecticians such as Diotima, Plato, or Theaetetus. Whether he did or not, Socrates is neither a practitioner nor a proponent of abstinence. Rather, in the figure of Socrates Plato gives his readers a role model with a godlike wisdom for steering clear of bad relationships. The fact that he is an erotic philosopher who did not abstain from sexual experiences in all cases demonstrates that, for Plato's Socrates, sexual experiences are not inherently incompatible with the philosophical lifestyle. Even though Plato never married or had children that we know of, the fact that he admiringly characterizes a sexually active older man as the exemplar of the philosophical lifestyle indicates that Plato is not a proponent of abstinence either.

3.3 *Erôs* the Educational

We have now seen from Plato's Socrates's own example that someone who lives in accord with philosophical values need not reject sexual experiences in every instance. His wisdom is illustrated by his good sense not to have sexual experiences with unsuitable beloveds. If *erôs* can facilitate knowledge, one might worry that Socrates is missing out on something important because of his bad luck in not finding suitable beloveds. Luckily, even when Socrates must choose abstinence, erotic desire is nevertheless accessible to him. In both the *Symposium*'s ascent passage and the *Phaedrus*'s palinode, Plato portrays the inquirer's epistemological starting point as the perception of physical beauty and his/her epistemological motivation as erotic desire. In this section, I will discuss the role that erotic desire plays in facilitating knowledge of the Forms. And in 3.4 ("Nectar and Ambrosia for Plato's Philosophers"), I will discuss the conditions wherein a philosopher could choose to satisfy erotic desires in order to experience the enjoyable reward that provides temporary satisfaction and thereby prevents erotic desire from disrupting philosophical work.

3.3.1 Two Versions of *Erôs*

The speeches of Pausanius and Eryximachus in the *Symposium* have much to teach us about *erôs*' manner of facilitating wisdom, even though these speeches tend to be overshadowed by those of Socrates, Alcibiades, and Aristophanes.[49] Both Pausanias's and Eryximachus's speeches announce a dichotomy of love. For Pausanius, the split is between common or vulgar love, which is attached more to body than soul, and heavenly love, which takes "pleasure in what is by nature stronger and more intelligent" (*Smp.* 181b-d). He says, "These vulgar lovers are the people who have given love such a bad reputation that some have gone so far as to claim that taking *any* man as a lover is in itself disgraceful" (*Smp.* 182a).[50] Meanwhile, for Eryximachus, the division is between diseased love, which cannot enjoy pleasures without slipping into debauchery, and healthy love, which is able to enjoy fine pleasures without unhealthy aftereffects such as decadence and addiction (*Smp.* 186b-d). Plato intends for us to consider this speech seriously, and its main conclusion is that *erôs* can be manifest in two different versions, only one of which is objectionable.[51]

Having seen the two different versions of *erôs*, we can appreciate Pausanias's claim that criticisms of erotic desire should be directed at common and diseased love rather than its positive counterpart, heavenly and healthy love. He says that *erôs* has an undeservedly bad reputation because of the rarity of lovers of the right sort and the incidence of lovers of the vulgar sort. Vulgar lovers are attached "to the least intelligent partners, since all they care about is completing the sexual act" (*Smp.* 181b). Those who care only for the pleasures of sex are, by definition, body-lovers who have yet to make the transition to soul-love, whereas heavenly lovers value intelligence in particular because they understand its usefulness in thinking about all facets of reality, including the abstract and nonphysical. This reinforces the notion that Socrates prefers philosophically inclined beloveds because his erotic desire is not directed toward pleasure as such but rather at philosophical inquiry as a form of erotic pursuit.

If we keep in mind that Plato writes the whole dialogue and is not just speaking through Socrates's character,[52] then we are in a position to see that Pausanias's and Eryximachus's speeches demonstrate Plato's esteem for heavenly and healthy love. Sheffield notes that, even though Socrates explicitly claims that the previous speeches do not aim for truth (*Smp.* 198d-e), the inclusion in Socrates's speech of some views from the earlier speeches, including the position in Pausanias's and Eryximachus's speeches that *erôs* for the soul is more valuable than *erôs* for the body, "suggests that these are indeed 'nuggets of truth.'"[53] If *erôs* were indistinguishable from *epithumia*, then *erôs* would be rightly criticized as the simplistic attachment to the body, which disrupts the attainment of knowledge.[54] However, establishing that there is a heavenly, healthy kind of love precludes the identification of *erôs* with *epithumia*. Heavenly, healthy *erôs*, in contrast with epithumetic or vulgar love, facilitates wisdom rather than diverting it.

76   Plato and the Body

In Roochnik's words, "Without Eros there would be no philosophy."⁵⁵ To understand the Form of the Beautiful, that is, what it means to be beautiful, is the educational goal of the healthy version of love. This version of love makes knowledge possible by getting inquirers near the beautiful people and things that initiate the process of calling to mind, recollecting, the Form of the Beautiful. Let us turn now to an examination of why Plato would take so seriously the idea that pursuing an understanding of the Forms is an erotic endeavor.

3.3.2 Desire, Recollection, and Confusion about the Forms

In the *Symposium*, Socrates claims that a desiring entity "desires something of which it is in need; otherwise, if it were not in need, it would not desire it" (200b). According to this definition, the lover is involved in a naturally progressive movement, going from something that one now possesses (as a result of having previously desired it) toward another thing that one desires because one does not yet possess it. As various dialogues make clear, Plato recognizes that all human beings are subject to desire. So, regardless of whether one is a healthy lover or a vulgar lover, if Socrates is right about desire, then all lovers will be subject to progressive movement. This progressive movement takes body-lovers in the lateral direction of an endless bed-hopping parade.⁵⁶ In contrast, healthy lovers, who have made the transition away from body-love toward the care of the soul, are not interested in that sort of progressive erotic movement. Instead, the heavenly, healthy lover agrees with Agathon that love resides in character (*Smp.* 195e), with Aristophanes that love is not just about sex but something more (*Smp.* 192c-d), and with Eryximachus that the fullest sexual desire is attached just as much to a proper soul as to a body perceived as beautiful (*Smp.* 183e–184a). However, Socrates learned from Diotima that the healthiest lover is interested in moving closer to knowledge. Here we see the main reason why Plato casts philosophical inquiry as a form of erotic pursuit. According to Socrates's definition of *erôs* in the *Symposium*, philosophers are engaged in erotic ascent because they desire something they lack. Philosophers aim to acquire any missing understanding of the Forms, and through philosophical inquiry, they pursue the objects of their desire.

Plato has Socrates give an account of Diotima's lesson about how to harness properly the progressive motion so that it will move one closer to knowledge. Socrates summarizes Diotima's account of this ascent as follows:

> That is what it is to go aright, or be led by another, into the mystery of Love: one goes always upwards for the sake of this

> Beauty, starting out from beautiful things and using them like
> rising stairs: from one body to two and from two to all beau-
> tiful bodies, then from beautiful bodies to beautiful customs,
> and from customs to learning beautiful things, and from these
> lessons he arrives in the end at the lesson, which is learning
> of this very Beauty, so that in the end he comes to know just
> what it is to be beautiful. (*Smp.* 211c-d)

For the healthy lover, the progressive erotic movement is actually an ascent toward the Forms. This passage echoes what we have already seen of the Platonic inquirer's commitment to pursuing the best possible understanding of the Forms. The *Phaedrus*'s palinode also offers readers an explicit account of how an inquirer might accomplish this level of understanding. There, Plato has Socrates suggest that the soul is like a winged chariot equipped with a charioteer and two horses. As others have noticed, the horses invoke sexuality in the ancient tradition of using horse metaphors for sex, and the wings also strike a sexual chord.[57] Meanwhile, Plato meditates extensively on psychic wings, which he has Socrates say are nourished by "beauty, wisdom, goodness, and everything of that sort" and are poisoned by "foulness and ugliness" (*Phdr.* 246e). When nourished, these wings lift the soul up to "the plain where truth stands" (*Phdr.* 248c). That *erôs* facilitates the lover's understanding of the Forms is indicated by Socrates saying, "Human nature can find no better workmate for acquiring [the Form of Beauty] than Love (*Erôs*)" (*Smp.* 212a-b). The phenomenon of erotic desire is, after all, physical only in part; *erôs* is also an aspect of the soul.[58]

Erotic desire can have an educational function, what Frede calls "education through enchantment."[59] But it must be kept in mind that not every human being who feels erotic desire will find that *erôs* facilitates knowledge. At *Phaedrus* 250a, Plato has Socrates say, "But not every soul is easily reminded of the reality there by what it finds here." And the ascent passage makes clear that, while some people direct *erôs* toward the contemplation of Beauty itself, first as instantiated in the physical and then as exhibited in the nonphysical, most people direct *erôs* only toward either one particular beautiful body or toward all beautiful bodies. For the many who never make the ascent to understanding Beauty itself, *erôs* is not facilitating a philosophical pursuit. So, erotic desire does not perform an educational function for everyone. Conversely, philosophers, who direct *erôs* beyond the corporeal, are taking a course not easily followed to its end, even though erotic desire assists in the process. Diotima is not confident in even Socrates's prospects to follow her account (*Smp.* 210a, e). Nevertheless, the philosopher who directs *erôs* toward understanding the

Form of Beauty and the other Forms has found a way for *erôs* to serve a crucial educational function. The palinode reiterates the centrality of the educational function of *erôs*, putting even more emphasis on the details of how the educational function of *erôs* operates.

The palinode designates erotic desire as both a blessing and a curse for the philosopher. It is a curse insofar as it distracts the inquirer from focusing on one's contemplative work. However, the very source of this disruption is also the source of insight into what the inquirer wants to contemplate. Plato characterizes this irony in his portrayal of the relationship between the charioteer and the dark horse. The charioteer and the dark horse appear at odds with each other, but it turns out that the charioteer's agenda is actually facilitated by the dark horse. In the palinode, the soul's aspects negotiate with each other with their own concerns in mind. The charioteer is interested solely in true Beauty, while the dark horse is interested in the pleasures of sex. The white horse, focused on honor but mainly interested in being compliant with the charioteer, is happy to go along with the charioteer's agenda. Yet, the charioteer needs the dark horse just as much as the white horse. The charioteer pines for the Forms, but on his own will not recollect this true Form as easily as when he is made by the dark horse to be near the sight of a beautiful beloved.

The erotic desire for beautiful beloveds serves the philosopher well because this desire prompts the philosopher to be near physical beauty present in the beloved, which initiates the process of recollecting the Form of Beauty. As Gordon justly remarks, "The cause of the charioteer's being reminded of the true nature of beauty is the dark horse's strong pull and his intemperate approach to the beloved! The charioteer, left only to his own devices, would not have gotten a glimpse of beauty."[60] It is strange, then, to consider the dark horse a "bad" horse when the dark horse contributes the erotic desire for a person whose beauty participates in the Form of Beauty. This attraction to beauty that has a share in the Form of Beauty is crucial for helping embodied philosophers to grow the wings they need to "depart" (*Phdr*. 249a) and return to the realm of the Forms.

Interestingly, Plato's use of directional language in the palinode has led to a great deal of confusion about the Forms. He gives readers cause for asking where Forms are as well as for believing that the Forms are somewhere above us when he has Socrates propose that the souls that "go to feast at the banquet [of Forms] . . . have a steep climb to the high tier at the rim of heaven" (*Phdr*. 247a-b). Socrates also refers to this plain of truth as "the top" and "what is outside heaven" (*Phdr*. 247b-c). This location-oriented language may incline a reader to suspect that the Forms are literally in a "place beyond heaven" (*Phdr.* 247c). The artist Raphael might very well have pointed to this directional tone if he were to explain why he depicts Plato with a finger pointing upward in "The School of Athens." This type of ascent language is echoed at various points in the corpus, most prominently in the ascent passages of the *Symposium* (211c) and *Phaedrus* (*Phdr.* 246a–248d) and the prisoner's upward passage out of the *Republic*'s cave (517a-c).[61]

Nevertheless, Plato has also given readers subtle cues that encourage a different, non-location-oriented understanding of the Forms. A reader who has transitioned away from mere empirical thinking toward philosophical thought will understand that the Forms are not physical and therefore do not exist anywhere physically. However, the things in our physical world are said to participate in Forms. For instance, an individual dog participates in what it means to be a dog, that is, an individual dog participates in the Form of Dog. In this way, the Forms are enmeshed in the physical world we actually inhabit. They are here, but in a unique fashion that brings one to see that the physical is real but its reality is inferior to what has eternal, nonphysical being. This unconventional worldview expresses the dualized Platonic value system. We are in a better position to understand what reality and knowledge are for Plato if we focus not on the directional language that he uses when discussing reality but rather the description of reality as "the plain where truth stands," a "pasture (*nomê*)" that has "grass (*leimônos*) that is the right food for the best part of the soul" (*Phdr.* 248c). Here we see Plato once again turn to physical vernacular to make his abstract point.

An inquirer interested in knowledge will then want to understand the duality of being, that is, *both* the reality of true being (e.g., what it means to be good, what it means to be beautiful, what it means to be a dog) and the physical manifestations of goodness, beauty, dogs, and so on. Philosophers will be curious about the world of things that have a share in the Forms. Platonism does not entail resenting physical entities. Rather, a philosopher who values eternal, unchanging being should still understand the value of being curious about the world. To be "like an oyster in its shell" (*Phdr.* 250c) and not properly utilize "reminders of these things [the Forms]" (*Phdr.* 249c) is to miss opportunities for wondering, for making the transition to philosophical thinking. Instead, the philosopher observes and contemplates the physical world and its events, beginning the process of gleaning what can be learned about the Forms of which each particular thing or occurrence has a share.

So it is that to recollect is simply to call to mind something that always lies beneath the surface, something easily ignored by those who are not intent on inquiring into all the facets of reality. What Platonism asks us to call to mind is the robust reality that could be described in much the same way that Alcibiades describes Socrates in the *Symposium* (215b). Real being is also like a Silenus, a figurine inside of which there is always more for the one who will dig deeper, going beyond the surface. Any inquirer who understands the Form of Beauty itself will see the importance of the one physical body whose beauty first begins to call the Form to mind. If the perception of beauty accelerates the calling to mind of the Form of Beauty, then a Platonic inquirer should want to perceive beauty as fully as possible, including through erotic desire for a beloved's beauty, which participates in beauty itself. Consequently, the philosopher who has had erotic experiences of a beautiful person for the sake of being reminded of the Form of Beauty is better off than an inquirer who has not taken pleasure in beauty. As Carson writes:

> As Sokrates tells it, your story begins the moment Eros enters you. That incursion is the biggest risk of your life. How you handle it is an index of the quality, wisdom and decorum of the things inside you. As you handle it you come into contact with what is inside you, in a sudden and startling way. You perceive what you are, what you lack, what you could be. What is this mode of perception, so different from ordinary perception that it is well described as madness? How is it that when you fall in love you feel as if suddenly you are seeing the world as it really is? A mood of knowledge floats out over your life. You seem to know what is real and what is not. Something is lifting you toward an understanding so complete and clear it makes you jubilant. This mood is no delusion, in Sokrates' belief. It is a glance down into time, at realities you once knew, as staggeringly beautiful as the glance of your beloved. (249e–50c)[62]

3.3.3 The Combination of Physical and Psychic Beauty

Alcibiades points out how puzzling it is that Socrates is "crazy about beautiful boys" even though "it couldn't matter less to him whether a boy is beautiful" (*Smp.* 216d-e). If something is more important to Socrates than one's physical appearance, then why does he follow beautiful boys "around in a perpetual daze" (*Smp.* 216d)? There are numerous occasions where Plato notes Socrates's interest in the beauty of bodies: *Ly.* 204b, 207a; *Chrm.* 153d, 154b-c, 155d, 158c; *Crt.* 44a. Socrates explains this when he says that someone pregnant with ideas "is much more drawn to bodies that are beautiful than to those that are ugly; and if he *also* has the luck to find a soul that is beautiful and noble and well-formed, he is even more drawn to this combination (*panu dê aspazetai to sunamphoteron*); such a man makes him instantly teem with ideas and arguments about virtue" (*Smp.* 209b-c). We see this exemplified in the *Charmides*. With everyone in the palaestra gazing upon Charmides "as if he were a statue," Chaerephon says, "If he were willing to strip you would hardly notice his face, his body is so perfect" (*Chrm.* 153c-d).[63] In response, Socrates says, "You are describing a man without equal—if he should happen to have one small thing in addition . . . a well-formed soul" (*Chrm.* 153d). Plato encourages us to think of the beautiful soul as the moral nature that has such presence as to be distinguished as beautiful.[64] Clearly, psychic beauty is more important to Socrates than physical beauty. This is again suggestive of Plato's normative dualism. Only one who holds the soul in the highest regard recognizes that its beauty is more precious than that of the body. But all the while the philosopher realizes that the beauty of the body is worthy of being appreciated, although not taken seriously. For Plato, only the inquiry after true reality and the pursuit of goodness are to be taken seriously. Thus, if one's beloved is philosophically inclined, one can put up with a beloved who lacks the more trivial manifestation of beauty.

However, being around someone who possesses both physical and psychic beauty is more conducive for prompting the philosopher to "[conceive and give] birth to what he has been carrying inside him for ages" than being around someone with physical beauty alone (*Smp.* 209c). This notion of labor inducement explains why Socrates has such a constant and unabashed appreciation for beautiful boys (e.g., *Ly.* 204b, 207a; *Chrm.* 153d, 154b-d, 155d, 158c, *Smp.* 216d, 223a). He follows them because he is eager for "giving birth in beauty," which, according to Diotima, is the real purpose of love, whether in body or in soul (*Smp.* 206b-c). Those who are pregnant in body desire to give birth to children through sexual intercourse (*Smp.* 208e), while those who are pregnant in soul desire to give birth to ideas through dialectic (*Smp.* 209a-c). Socrates's erotic experiences have yielded both children and ideas, which would not surprise Diotima, given that she believes that all human beings are pregnant both in body and in soul (*Smp.* 206c).

Despite going to lengths to champion the combination of a beautiful body and soul over an exclusively beautiful body, these passages in the *Symposium* oddly neglect to compare the beautiful body-soul combination with an exclusively beautiful soul. There are a variety of possible reasons for Plato to leave the reader in the dark about this. First of all, passages such as *Symposium* 209b and *Republic* 402d demonstrate that the combination of psychic and physical beauty will be victorious over whichever particular beauty with which it is compared. Second, it may also be the case that human beings cannot isolate psychic beauty from corporeality. In other words, perhaps having a beautiful soul contributes to the perception of one's physique as beautiful. For example, in the *Theaetetus*, Theodorus tells Socrates that Theaetetus is not beautiful (*Tht.* 143e), though truly remarkable in other ways, and later, after Socrates has been extraordinarily impressed by the beauty of Theaetetus's soul, he disputes Theodorus, indicating that Theaetetus *is* beautiful because "handsome is as handsome says" (*Tht.* 185e). In an example at the other end of the spectrum, Socrates is set aflame by Charmides's renowned beauty, but that occurs *after* Socrates is told that Charmides is a philosopher and has a beautiful and good soul (*Chrm.* 154e). In that scene, Socrates ultimately "never questions [the] suggestion that physical bearing and carriage, the general way one 'handles oneself,' in every situation, expresses an inward temperance (or the opposite)."[65] Finally, Plato may not bother with the neglected comparison because his concern is to undermine the tendency to assess someone only with respect to physical appearance. Body-lovers are concerned only for the beauty of the body, and Plato hopes passages that compare the physical-psychic beauty combination with a merely beautiful body will put his readers in a position to become accustomed to assessing psychic beauty (or lack thereof) as well.

Although the *Symposium* neglects to compare the combination of physical and psychic beauty with psychic beauty alone, the *Republic* does address that comparison. Socrates and Glaucon agree that "the most beautiful sight for anyone who has eyes to see" is "if someone's soul has a fine and beautiful character and his body matches it in beauty and is thus in harmony with it, so that both share in the same pattern" (*R.* 402c-d). While they agree that the beautiful body-soul combination is most desirable, Glaucon contends (and Socrates agrees) that someone with an appetite for goodness will nevertheless "put up with it" if someone's beauty defect is physical rather than psychic (*R.* 402d-e). Given the reports of Socrates's physical appearance, it is conceivable that Alcibiades considers his attraction to Socrates a case of "putting up with" physical defect because of extraordinary psychic beauty. One might complain that if only Socrates were more physically beautiful, then Alcibiades would have been more easily induced to give birth to good ideas. However, Plato's Alcibiades accepts responsibility himself for neglecting his own potential. As we have already seen, Plato has Alcibiades explain that it was Socrates who tried to prompt him to live a more virtuous life, while Alcibiades himself neglects the care of the soul (*Smp.* 215d–216b). In this case, what hinders Alcibiades's philosophical progress is his own lack of psychic beauty, not Socrates's lack of physical beauty.

The Greek appreciation of the combination of *kalos k'agathos* raises a vital question. If a philosopher is lucky enough to find a beloved with both psychic and physical beauty, should the philosopher still appreciate the physical beauty of the beloved during the ascent toward the Form of Beauty itself? As one ascends toward the Form of Beauty does one discard one's previous esteem for the objects lower on the ladder?[66] Vlastos, Moravcsik, and others argue for the "exclusive" interpretation of the ascent passage in which, as one ascends to the Form of Beauty, one loses all esteem for the objects lower on the ladder.[67] On the other hand, Kosman, Price, Irwin, and others espouse the "inclusive" interpretation in which one's advance toward the Form of Beauty reconfigures one's attitude toward the objects lower on the ladder without any loss of esteem.[68] The exclusive reading is linked to the austere dualist interpretation of Plato, whereas the inclusive reading is consistent with interpreting Plato as a normative dualist.

The exclusive reading appears to be supported by one aspect of the ascent passage: 210b5–6. Nehamas and Woodruff translate the text there as, "When he grasps this, he must become a lover of all beautiful bodies, and he must think that this wild gaping after just one body is a small thing and despise it [*henos de to sphodra touto chalasai kataphronêsanta kai smikron hêgêsamenon*]."[69] What exactly is despised here, the beautiful body that the ascendant first appreciated or the ascendant's initial attitude of "wild gaping after" that body? Thinking that the ascendant no longer values at all what is lower on the ladder is the hallmark of the exclusive reading.[70] This translation is not inaccurate, but the verb being rendered as "despise" (*kataphronêsanta*) can also be accurately translated as "to look down upon." In view of that, the exact meaning here is ambiguous. This ambiguity leaves room for either the exclusive or inclusive reading. Is there reason to choose one of these translations of *kataphronêsanta* over the other?

At 210b6–7, Plato writes, "After this he must think that the beauty of people's souls is more valuable [*timiôteron hêgêsasthai*] than the beauty of their bodies." Here there is no indication of any contempt for what was lower on the ladder. Rather, there is clear indication that the beauty of souls is simply "more valuable," which in turn signifies that the lower rungs on the ladder are considered less valuable. There is greater resonance between this passage and 210b5–6, which immediately precedes it, if "*kataphronêsanta*" is rendered as "look down upon" rather than as "despise," because finding something "less valuable" corresponds to "looking down upon" something. Finding something less valuable is not at all the same thing as despising it.[71] Taking the word choice at 210b6-7 into consideration, we can conclude that choosing "despise" over the other possible translation ("look down upon") creates dissonance in the ascent passage, whereas translating *kataphronêsanta* as "look down upon" maintains the passage's consonance.

At 210c5-6, Plato indicates that after appreciating the beauty of activities and laws the ascendant will regard the beauty of bodies as "small" (*hina to peri to soma kalon smikron ti hêgêsêtai einai*). In Nehamas and Woodruff's translation, *smikron* is "a thing of no importance." Thinking of something as "small" goes hand in hand with "looking down upon" something but not with "despising" something or thinking of something as "of no importance" whatsoever.[72] Robin Waterfield's translation also leaves physical beauty as "unimportant."[73] Normative dualism looks at all the things in the physical world as *inadequate* or subordinate,[74] but that is rather different from being unimportant. While "negligible" or "unimportant" are fair translations, translating *smikron* as "small" still leaves room for the *smikron* entity to have lesser value rather than being entirely valueless.

My own view, then, is not only that the inclusive reading is better supported by the Greek but also that the inclusive reading is consistent with the Platonic metaphysical principle that Forms are causes of things and that things participate in or have a share in Forms. Given this principle, the ascendant "looks down upon" or "regards as small" the lower rungs of Diotima's ladder because they are not Beauty itself. Yet, the philosopher should continue to appreciate the way in which the Form of Beauty *is* manifest to a certain degree in an individual body, even once one has ascended closer to grasping Beauty itself.[75] To the degree that something participates in the Form of Beauty there is reason to appreciate it, even though it is not Beauty itself.[76] As Irwin comments, "The correct account allows us to love the lower objects to the right extent, and for the right reasons, in so far as they are really beautiful; but we have no reason to stop loving them altogether."[77] Appreciation for the lower manifestations of Beauty need not be eliminated from a life like Socrates's.[78]

Since the embodied philosopher cannot be engaged with the Forms themselves literally all of the time (even Socrates breaks from his trances!), the philosopher must still live amid the physical. If we consider another example beside the Form of Beauty, we can imagine that a philosopher who has grasped the Form of Justice would still be curious about earthly manifestations of justice as well as of injustice. How could the philosopher not appreciate the lower manifestations of justice (or beauty or goodness, etc.) wherever they are found? Indeed, post-ascent encounters with physical particulars will be bittersweet: bitter because the ascendant now knows the things as mere images of Forms and sweet because as images they occasion remembrance of the philosopher's true beloved, the Forms.

Having knowledge in the Platonic sense will cause the ascendant to understand why these images were adored in the first place as well as what limitations there are to such adoration, and the ascendant's erotic attraction will be moderated accordingly by this understanding. Inherent in normative dualism is the conviction that there is, in fact, a hierarchy among Forms and their physical images. The ascendant can be trusted to maintain the proper hierarchical perspective on the objects lower on the ladder, such as the body of the human beloved.[79] The normative dualist point of view entails knowing that when Diotima talks of "loving boys correctly" (*Smp.* 211b), she means that their beauty should never be mistaken for Beauty itself, and that the act of taking pleasure in their beauty shouldn't be limited to, or oriented primarily toward, the appreciation of corporeal beauty. As a result, the philosopher can reconcile a supreme love for the Form of Beauty with an everyday desire for beloved human beings. This is Platonic love.

Nussbaum disagrees. Looking at Socrates as a model ascendant, Nussbaum contends that Socrates "is reliably virtuous—courageous, just, temperate—all without lapses of weakness or fatigue. And this seems intimately connected with his imperviousness to the happenings in the world."[80] While I agree with Nussbaum that Socrates epitomizes the benefits of having made the ascent,[81] I think she is mistaking his logical and focused life for imperviousness to what she calls "mortal rubbish."[82] Indeed, things that matter a great deal to ordinary people are of little concern to Socrates. Nussbaum repeats numerous well-known examples of Socrates's strangeness, such as his steadfastness in the face of Alcibiades's seduction, his remarkable tolerance with respect to drinking, his lack of concern for clothing, and his endurance of cold and hardship. While I agree that Socrates is an exemplar of "what a human life starts to look like as one makes the ascent,"[83] I disagree with Nussbaum's conclusion that what accounts for these exceptional aspects of Socrates's biography is his withdrawal from the physical world.[84]

Even though contemplation is paramount in Socrates's life, he is not withdrawn from the physical world. In fact, erotic desire is still attached to particular bodies for him, too. As Carone writes, "Socrates refuses to sleep with Alcibiades, but not because getting higher on the ladder has killed every sort of sexual attraction in him. Indeed, he is far from minimizing his feelings toward him: on the contrary, he describes his love (*erôs*) for Alcibiades to Agathon as 'no trivial matter' (*ou phaulon pragma*, 213c)."[85] Socrates's pursuit of knowledge overrides his concern for matters such as clothing, but he still kitted himself out for Agathon's party, as we saw earlier. And his commitment to using erotic desire to help him ascend to understanding the Forms precludes succumbing to the sexual temptation of unworthy beloveds such as Alcibiades or Phaedrus, but erotic desire still exists even in old age for him at least with Xanthippe (or Myrto),[86] as is demonstrated by having young children.

3.4 Nectar and Ambrosia for Plato's Philosophers

Earlier, I asserted that, even though the charioteer and dark horse appear to be at odds with each other, the charioteer needs the dark horse to best accomplish its aim of understanding the Forms. Now we will see that the dark horse's agenda is also facilitated by its fellow team members, the charioteer and the white horse. With their help, the dark horse can best accomplish its aim of enjoying the pleasures of sex. One might wonder why we should care if the dark horse's plan is ever accomplished at all. A philosopher may wish that erotic desire did not transpire, given the risk of being interrupted from its contemplative pursuits. However, if philosophers are to possess self-knowledge, then they must accept having a tripartite nature. Both the *Phaedrus* and the *Republic* indicate a tripartite soul in which each aspect has important business to accomplish (more on this in chapter 4). In the *Republic*, Plato has Socrates go as far as to define justice for an individual as having a soul in which each aspect does its own important work (433a–435b). Thus, one who wants to live justly cannot anticipate success without appropriately nourishing all our psychic aspects. Despite this principle of psychic harmony, austere dualist interpreters read Plato as calling for us to *not* provide nourishment for all the psychic aspects.

Imagining that Plato insists upon the starvation of the appetite fails to distinguish between Socrates's two speeches in the *Phaedrus*. As Ferrari has aptly pointed out, Socrates's first speech, which he offers while covering his face (*Phdr.* 237a), condones puritanism. In contrast to Lysias's speech, which advocates hedonism, in Socrates's first speech we hear "the voice of puritanism: by which I mean an automatic hostility toward pleasure as such, and an inability to integrate pleasure in an honest fashion with the pursuit of the good. In the popular and encyclopedic conception of the history of Western philosophy, this is of course often thought of as Plato's own voice."[87] Ferrari rightly calls attention to Plato's efforts to dissociate Socrates from the first speech he makes. In advance of giving the first speech, Socrates distances himself from it by indicating that he is simply relaying a speech that represents ideas about love that he heard "somewhere" (*Phdr.* 235c-d). Then, during the interlude between Socrates's first and second speeches (*Phdr.* 241d-243e), Socrates plainly recants this puritanical speech, calling for a palinode of his own. Reading the palinode as the middle ground between the hedonism of Lysias's speech and the austerity of Socrates's first speech, Ferrari succeeds in pointing out the mistake of interpreting Plato austerely.[88] Furthermore, he describes well the danger of a Platonic learner attempting to adopt an austerely ascetic lifestyle. He writes, "Not really understanding *why* he should keep his appetite for pleasure in check, he simply represses it; with the result we might expect. The repressed appetite, as Plato imagines it, is disavowed in public but burns bright within the secret recesses of his soul; and he will sate it in private lovenests."[89]

For the very same reason that *erôs* is powerful enough to enable one to see the world differently, it can also be intolerably distracting to leave that desire frustrated. In the soul's quest for knowledge, erotic desires will undoubtedly arise. Austere dualists would have us believe that Plato despises incarnation, given the inevitable distraction caused by sexual desire. Despite the troublesome disruptions *erôs* can initiate, I have already shown that *erôs* performs an educational function indispensable for the philosopher. Now the embodied inquirer must decide what to do about erotic desire when it arises. The philosopher trying to decide whether or not to satisfy an erotic desire can look for guidance in Plato's dialogues. I will demonstrate that, for Plato, the life ruled by reason can include the fulfillment of erotic desires, so long as it occurs under the guidance of reason and with the proper beloved. These are the conditions under which a philosopher can be seduced. The austere dualist interpretation is adamant that these conditions could never be met, but denying the possibility of an ideal beloved with whom to philosophize is much like denying the possibility of the ideal city ever coming to exist (Cf. *R.* 472d-e).

When philosophers take lovers under these conditions, they satisfy their sexual appetite in order to renew their focus on the project of understanding the Forms. Aristophanes describes this sort of thing as follows in his speech: "[W]hen male embraced male, they would at least have the satisfaction of intercourse, after which they could stop embracing, return to their jobs, and look after their other needs in life" (*Smp.*

191c-d). In this way, sexual experience delivers one from the distraction caused by erotic desire at least temporarily, making full concentration on philosophical inquiry possible. Plato invites us to imagine the possibility of a pair of philosophers inquiring together and then culminating their erotic experience of the Forms and each other in a sexual experience that satisfies their sexual desire. Philosophers who accept that reward would experience relief, albeit temporary, from the pangs of desire. Freed temporarily from the distraction of their desire for each other, the philosophers return to focusing on their shared desire to understand the Forms.

Experiencing relief from the pangs of desire functions as a prevention against the distraction that takes the philosopher away from the journey toward knowledge. This is suggested in particular by three passages: *Symposium* 185c-e (in conjunction with 189a), *Phaedrus* 247e and 256a (in conjunction with 248a), and *Phaedrus* 249a (in conjunction with 252e). In these passages, Socrates intimates a pattern of inquiring by day and then, once one brings to a close one's contemplative work, nourishing our other psychic aspects. Considered together, these passages advocate for the fulfillment of the right sort of erotic desire (the heavenly, healthy sort that values psychic beauty more than physical beauty) because this appropriate route to contenting the soul's appetitive aspect returns one from erotic distraction to erotic inquiry.

I will now turn to exploring these passages, but first I want to make clear that Plato is certainly not licensing the appetitive aspect of the soul to usurp the control that is supposed to be maintained by the soul's rational aspect, if one is to live justly. Nussbaum suggests that the "small interval of calm" that would follow sexual satisfaction is not useful to the philosopher and that being "in the grip of these recurring needs" will in fact take the inquirer away from philosophical work.[90] However, I will show that these passages reveal instead that the appetitive aspect is more likely to attempt to usurp rationality's control over the human being when its desires are *always* left unsatisfied. In turn, rationality's control is more likely to be preserved if the other aspects of the soul are satisfied when that can be done under the guidance of reason. Once one understands this, then s/he is well on the way to making the final transition to loving *both* the soul and the body in just that order of priority.

3.4.1 Hiccups and the Sneeze Treatment

Given the order of speeches that Agathon's guests have decided on, Aristophanes is scheduled to speak after Pausanias and before Eryximachus.

However, he is sidetracked by a case of hiccups, and Eryximachus takes his turn instead. This hiccups attack could be symbolic of a bodily distraction sidetracking one from rational inquiry. Aristophanes has been diverted from an intellectual discussion, just as he would be if he were preoccupied with unfulfilled sexual desire. Unable to take his turn, Aristophanes pursues the potential cures suggested by Eryximachus, who is a physician. Eryximachus says, "While I am giving my speech, you should hold your breath for as long as you possibly can. This may well eliminate your hiccups. If it fails, the best remedy is a thorough gargle. And if even this has no effect, then tickle your nose with a feather. A sneeze or two will cure even the most persistent case" (*Smp.* 185d-e). A Platonic reader who fails to consider the importance of the dramatic events in the dialogues would miss the possible significance of this hiccups episode. Wondering why Plato would bother to include this scene, we can leave it aside as just a comic moment[91] or we can construe it as a philosophically suggestive joke, seeing the palpable correspondence between the three potential cures for the hiccups and the three possible ways of responding to sexual desire.[92] Holding one's own breath is as denying and futile as sexual abstinence, and sneezing, which is symbolic of explosive but temporary loss of control, coincides with the explosive but temporary loss of control that accompanies orgasm. Gargling does not appear to have an obvious specific analog. While I won't speculate about what sexual act would correspond to gargling, it is clear that it would be something that is working up to but falls short of the loss of control involved in orgasm. If we think of the distraction by hiccups as analogous to distraction by sexual desire, it becomes of the utmost interest that only the "Sneeze Treatment" gets Aristophanes back to the discourse at hand.

Curiously, Aristophanes adds, "Makes me wonder whether the 'orderly sort of Love' in the body calls for the sounds and itchings[93] that constitute a sneeze, because the hiccups stopped immediately when I applied the Sneeze Treatment" (*Smp.* 189a). This off-the-cuff remark may suggest that even the right sort of erotic desire (that is, the heavenly/healthy love eulogized by Pausanias and Eryximachus) can be a distraction from inquiry, but unlike its vulgar/diseased counterpart, it does not necessarily need to go unfulfilled. The noble lover, who is defined by greater concern for the soul than for the body, is actually served by sexual experience because the satisfaction of erotic desire returns the noble lover to inquiry rather than creating further distraction. Lending weight to this interpretation of the drama of the sneeze, Plato has Aristophanes say of sexual intercourse that "when male embraced male, they would at least have the satisfaction of intercourse, after which they could stop embracing, return to their jobs, and look after their other needs in life" (*Smp.* 191c-d). Plato's philosophical lover satisfies erotic desire wherever not doing so would cause an unnecessary distraction from inquiry. For philosophers, the relief of desire enables one to return to the pursuit of wisdom, just as Aristophanes sneezes for the sake of getting back to the discussion.

One might argue that putting the observation that the right sort of love calls for the noises and ticklings that constitute a sneeze in the mouth of Aristophanes, a comedian, signals that Plato intends to poke fun at this view. As I indicated before, this may indeed be a joke, but it could very well be a philosophically suggestive joke. Looking at the drama holistically, we should not presume that Plato wants us to take seriously only what comes from the mouth of Socrates. In this case, Plato would indeed advocate Aristophanes's insinuation because the heavenly/healthy lovers understand that the soul matters more than the body and thus can be trusted to engage in sexual activity under the guidance of reason rather than pursuing sexual pleasure as an end in itself. What these lovers share is not limited to sexual gratification. These lovers keep their sexual experiences in the proper normative dualist perspective, as an activity that delights the body in service to the soul's philosophical education. Just as the sneeze returns Aristophanes to the conversation, so too can orgasm return an inquirer bursting with desire to intellectual work. In this respect, sexual experiences can facilitate wisdom by satisfying the distracting desire and allowing the philosopher to get back to work.

3.4.2 Nectar and Ambrosia for the Divine Horses

The idea that philosophical work and the satisfaction of appetites are not mutually exclusive is also expressed in Socrates's palinode. Claiming that "to describe what the soul actually is would require a very long account," Socrates chooses instead to say that the soul is like "the natural union of a team of winged horses and their charioteer" (*Phdr.* 246a). Socrates then offers an account of a day in the life of a divine charioteer. The charioteer spends the day "feasting at the banquet" where the "mind is nourished by intelligence and pure knowledge" (*Phdr.* 247b, d). Once the charioteer has "feasted on" the Forms, the soul "goes home" and "on its arrival, the charioteer stables the horses by the manger, throws in ambrosia, and gives them nectar to drink besides" (*Phdr.* 247e). This passage announces that once the work of nourishing the rational aspect of the soul is completed, it is appropriate for the divine soul then to nourish the other psychic aspects. As Nussbaum says, "Even divine beings have horses; even these horses need their food (247e)."[94]

Given that in this passage the charioteer and horses are symbolic of the divine soul, one might wonder whether the same lifestyle is best for a *human* soul. For the weaker human intellect, does the day of nourishing the soul's rational aspect ever reach an end? And is it best for our other psychic aspects to be nourished too? Socrates does make clear that the life of a human soul is not nearly as "well under control" as that of its divine counterpart (*Phdr.* 247b); "chariot-driving in our case is inevitably a painfully difficult business" (*Phdr.* 246b). So, the human team is deficient when measured against the divine team. The human and divine teams experience feasting on the Forms quite differently. The myth encourages us to believe that the attempt to nourish the rational aspect of a human soul is less easily accomplished. As a result, austere dualists take Plato to resent the human soul's exile in embodiment because it entails that there is no end to the human charioteer's work, that is, no end to the effort to grasp the Forms. Accordingly, they interpret Plato as suggesting that there is never a call for rest and nourishing the human soul's horses; they portray him as failing to acknowledge the place of the horses' needs in the life of the whole chariot team.

Having considered the possibility that the dissimilarity between the divine and the human precludes using the account of a day in the life of the divine chariot as model for living our own lives, let us ask why it is that Plato gives the gives the divine charioteer horses at all. Plato includes horses in his depiction of the human soul in order to depict the human soul as complex, having three aspects of different "stock" and "bloodlines" (*Phdr.* 246b). Our horses are not only different from our charioteer but they are also different from each other. In contrast, Plato indicates that the divine soul is not essentially complex, explaining that "the gods have horses and charioteers that are themselves all good and come from good stock besides, while everyone else has a mixture" (*Phdr.* 246a-b). If the divine soul's horses are from the exact same stock as the divine charioteer, then they would be redundant, and Plato need not have included them. Furthermore, if we believe that our rationality alone is what gives us a kinship with the divine, then it is really strange for Plato to assign horses to the divine soul.

It could be suggested that the divine charioteer needs horses for transportation, needing to move around heaven "looking after everything and putting all things in order," as well as to go to feast on the Forms "at the rim of heaven" (*Phdr.* 246e–247b). However, one might ask why the gods of this myth could not be self-moving. I contend instead that Plato chooses to depict the divine chariot team with horses in order to establish a paradigm for the human soul. At 248a, Plato has Socrates complete his account of the life of the divine charioteer and refer immediately to a human soul that makes itself as much like the god it follows as possible. If we are to live similarly to the god our soul has followed, then we too will occupy ourselves with trying to grasp the Forms, and we will also need to draw the contemplative work to a close for the day, resting, as Socrates does in the final line of the *Symposium*, and nourishing and rewarding our horses. Just as the divine charioteer gives the horses a reward of nectar and ambrosia at the end of the day's work (*Phdr.* 248a), so too does the human black horse feel entitled to a reward (*Phdr.* 256a).[95] Let's now examine the prospects for the erotic experiences this horse desires.

3.4.3 Loving Boys with the Help of Philosophy

The austere dualist interpretation represents Plato as vilifying the dark horse, which causes the soul to "barely make it" to the sight of the Forms because of its bad training (*Phdr.* 247b). The danger of "barely making it," according to the *Phaedrus*, is that today's trip to the Forms refuels the soul's wings for the next trip. The soul's wings must be nourished in order to arrive in the position for beholding the Forms, and yet the vision of the Forms is what nourishes the soul's wings. Barely making it jeopardizes one's fuel supply and ultimately this causes one's psychic wings to wither (*Phdr.* 248c-d). Socrates claims that the shedding of wings causes the soul to come into a body (*Phdr.* 246c, 248c-d). He explains the consequence of this:

> No soul returns to the place from which it came for ten thousand years, since its wings will not grow before then, except for the soul of a man who practices philosophy without guile [*philosophêsantos adolôs*] *or who loves boys in the midst of philosophy* [*paiderastêsantos meta philosophias*].[96] If, after the third cycle of one thousand years, the last-mentioned souls have chosen such a life three times in a row, they grow their wings back, and they depart in the three-thousandth year. (*Phdr.* 248e–249a; emphasis added; translation modified)

Because of desire, which causes the fall into the physical world, we return to the realm of the Forms at best after three thousand years and at worst after ten thousand. Why are philosophers on the fast track back to grazing in "the pasture that has the grass that is the right food for the best part of the soul" (*Phdr.* 248c)? Socrates claims that philosophers are fast-tracked because those souls that have "seen the most" of the Forms are incarnated as philosophers or people "prone to erotic love" (*Phdr.* 248d). Philosophers alone have winged souls (*Phdr.* 249c). Thus, philosophers become embodied after having seen the Forms but not well enough to prevent their exile from that pasture, leaving them with unfinished philosophical work and a penchant for *erôs*.

Socrates's view of what can be done with that propensity for erotic love has been largely overlooked in the literature. Plato has Socrates make explicit that, so long as it is done in conjunction with philosophy, erotic love facilitates the soul's return from exile in embodiment just as efficiently as "practicing philosophy without guile" (*Phdr.* 249a). In other words, Plato's philosophers can suitably use erotic love *either* for the sake of primarily loving wisdom, which Socrates calls practicing philosophy without guile (*philosophêsantos adolôs*), *or* for loving wisdom alongside taking as a beloved of similar character.[97] This is a bold pronouncement, given that the philosopher's endgame is reunion with the Forms; it speaks well of the choice to "love a boy with the help of philosophy" that it leads to the same positive outcome as choosing to "practice philosophy without guile." Yet, prominent commentators have largely ignored Socrates's assertion that so long as philosophy aids one's love for a beloved (*paiderastêsantos meta philosophias*) one is situated on the same speedy path to reunion with the Forms as when one practices philosophy alone (*philosophêsantos adolôs*).[98]

It has been easier to overlook this point because *paiderastêsantos meta philosophias* has been translated in ways that deemphasize Socrates's claim or explain it away as something else. For example, Nehamas and Woodruff translate this phrase as "loving boys philosophically," and Jowett translates it as being "a lover, who is not devoid of philosophy."[99] Nehamas and Woodruff's rendering of *meta philosophias* as "philosophically" is rather vague, and their translation of *paiderastêsantos* as "loving" is fair but too conservative because it tames the erotic tone of the Greek verb, which means to be a *paiderastês*. If Plato wanted to be clear that this does not include the sexual relationship, he could have, but he does not. Meanwhile, Jowett's choice of an English verb (being "a lover") approximates the erotic tone of *paiderastêsantos*, but his rendering of *meta philosophias* as "not devoid of philosophy" is imprecise. These translations have reinforced the assumption that the reincarnative fast track consists solely of philosophy and sexual abstinence.

Readers would more readily detect the nature of Plato's claim here if they read the more accurate translations offered by Rowe, Hackforth, Burger, and Ferrari. Rowe translates the phrase as "has united his love for his boy with philosophy."[100] Hackforth renders it as "has conjoined his passion for a loved one with that seeking" (namely, seeking after wisdom).[101] Burger reads it as "one whose love for boys is conjoined with philosophy."[102] And Ferrari and Waterfield[103] both translate the phrase as combining "his love for a boy with the practice of philosophy."[104] Even these translations do not preclude austere dualist interpreters from reading *paiderastêsantos* as a verb that is being reinvented without its original sexual connotation. The Greek here does not exclude the hypothesis that Plato intends to strip the erotic terminology of its sexual meaning, but it does not encourage it either.

Perhaps Plato intends for there to be two ways of interpreting his erotic vocabulary, the straightforward sexual reading as well as a nonsexual meaning that turns the original connotation on its head.[105] Plato's usage here must metaphorically rely upon the literal meaning but transforms the term's original connotation into something nonphysical. As I discussed in chapter 1, Plato does this often throughout the corpus, especially with the language of nourishment (*R.* 401c, 498b; *Prt.* 313c-d, 320a; *Sph.* 223e; *Phdr.* 246e, 248b-c, 251b-c). And he certainly intends to shift the original meaning to something other than the literal meaning, but the semantic shift in meaning only works because it also maintains an aspect of the original connotation. Just as we know that Plato often still uses food vocabulary with its original physical connotation, even though he transforms that vocabulary and regularly uses it nonliterally, so too must we see that Plato can continue to use erotic vocabulary with its original sexual meaning alongside occasional use of transformed erotic vocabulary.

One might find this ambiguity in Plato's vocabulary dissatisfying, but for Plato it is pedagogically useful. He can simultaneously direct a more austere message to his body-loving readers, while presenting a non-austerely ascetic message to his readers who have transcended body-love in favor of soul-love. The body-lover needs to be given the message that it is hubristic to behave as Lysias's hedonistic non-lover does; the body-lover needs to hear that desire should not command the whole soul, dragging one around without reasoning (*Phdr.* 238a). However, the reader who has prioritized the care of the soul over body-love has no need to persist in believing the "dangerous falsehoods" (*Phdr.* 243a) that assert sexual love is shameful in every circumstance.

Ferrari and I agree that the second speedy path to reunion with the Forms proposed by Socrates at 249a should be read with the original sexual association. Put differently, we concur that *Phaedrus* 249a allows philosophers to consummate sexual desire for each other in conjunction with pursuing knowledge together. While Rowe, Hackforth, and Waterfield offer helpful translations, their commentaries do not assist us in figuring out whether

Plato is using *paiderastêsantos* with the straightforward sexual connotation or reinventing the term's original sexual connotation in a nonsexual way.[106] What Hackforth does note in a footnote to his commentary is that the person who practices philosophy without guile and the person who conjoins philosophy with his passion for a loved one are the same person.[107] If he intends that the same person could take either the path of just doing philosophy or the path of loving boys with the aid of philosophy, then I would agree with Hackforth. However, given his lack of commentary on this important line, it isn't at all clear that this is what he means.[108]

In my view, the conclusion of the palinode, where the cycles of reincarnation are mentioned again, has been misinterpreted, leaving austere dualist interpreters to ignore passages that stand in tension with the austere conclusion that has been drawn from *Phaedrus* 256a–257a. Their view of this passage holds first that the life being recommended for philosophers in love is to do only philosophy together, and second that this life is different from and superior to the life that includes sexual consummation of erotic desire.[109] On the contrary, a close reading of this passage does not convey that austere ascetic message. At *Phaedrus* 250e–251a, Plato has Socrates explain that the nonphilosopher, who is most removed from the experience of the Forms, "surrenders to pleasure and sets out in the manner of a four-footed beast, eager to make babies; and wallowing in vice, he goes after unnatural pleasures too, without a trace of fear or shame."[110] Austere dualist interpreters see in this comment a condemnation of all sexual consummation, concluding that the philosopher does not do this. But of course we know that Socrates has fathered children while being a model philosopher, and this should give us pause before we conclude that 250e–251 is a criticism of all sexual consummation. Instead, this passage criticizes those for whom sexuality is nothing but lust. In this we see Plato's Socrates's aversion to the hedonistic sort of person who never wonders whether a particular desire is the sort that should be satisfied. This recent initiate does not even consider the possibility that erotic desire can be directed toward something other than the human body. This failure to examine one's own assumptions confirms the position that this person is not a philosopher. This nonphilosopher does not see what Diotima sees, namely, that erotic desire for physical beauty can be the beginning of something other than just a seduction.

This discussion of the recent initiate, the nonphilosopher, is all given by way of contrast with the philosopher, who referred to as a "recent initiate," "one who has seen much in heaven" (*Phdr.* 251a). When this philosopher sees a beautiful beloved, s/he feels reverence for that beauty which is a reminder of true beauty. At *Phaedrus* 251b–252b, Plato provides an image of what happens when beauty provides nourishment for the soul's wings. The irony of Plato's description of what ensues from the philosopher's reverence is that it is the sexiest passage in all of Greek and Roman literature.[111] Following this spicy passage, Socrates quickly reiterates the sort of lover he is discussing, namely, the one who was attendant on Zeus (*Phdr.* 252c), who turns out to be the philosopher. In particular, Socrates emphasizes that those who follow[112] Zeus "make sure [the beloved] has a talent for philosophy and the guidance of others" (*Phdr.* 252e).[113] Having the ability to do philosophy is the chief criterion for being a suitable beloved for the philosopher. Together, this pair works to make each other and themselves as noble of the soul, as Zeus-like, as possible (*Phdr.* 252e–253c). After focusing on the priority of doing philosophy together and making each other and themselves as good as possible, Socrates announces that "if he follows that desire in the manner I described, this friend who has been driven mad by love will *secure a consummation*[114] for the one who he has befriended that is as beautiful and blissful as I said—*if*, of course, he captures [*hairethêi*] him" (*Phdr.* 253c; emphases added). Plato then has Socrates remark that he will proceed to describe "how the captive [*hairetheis*] is caught" (*Phdr.* 253c).

Socrates sketches for us the negotiations that occur among the psychic aspects that lead up to the consummation he mentions at *Phaedrus* 253c. As I noted earlier, each aspect of the soul has its own agenda. The dark horse wants to have sex with the beautiful beloved, while the honor-loving white horse contributes the sense of shame that "prevents itself from jumping on the boy" (*Phdr.* 254a). Together, the white horse and the charioteer delay the dark horse's ambition, resisting because they are "angry in their belief that they are being made to do things that are dreadfully wrong" but "at last, however, when they see no end to their trouble, they are led forward, reluctantly agreeing to do as they have been told" (*Phdr.* 254b). Two questions arise: What exactly is "dreadfully wrong" about what the dark horse desires? And what kind of agreement is made here? In order to discern Plato's answers, we must pay close attention to what happens as the negotiations continue. In describing "how the captive is caught," Plato has Socrates underscore how undisciplined the dark horse is. This wild horse still needs training, but its passion has put the charioteer close enough to the beloved's beauty to serve the educational function I have already explored. Before, I suggested briefly that the charioteer's awe in the presence of this beauty winds up being useful for the dark horse's plan. Let's now investigate how that comes to pass.

At *Phaedrus* 254b-c, the charioteer and good horse renege on their earlier agreement, begging the dark horse to "wait till later" (*Phdr.* 254d).[115] Even though the charioteer and good horse pretend to forget "when the promised time arrives" (*Phdr.* 254d), the black horse aims again to propose the pleasures of sex to the beloved. However, once again the charioteer is struck with fear at the sight of the beloved's beauty and violently reins in the black horse. Being fiercely reiged in on every occasion of being near the beloved eventually conditions the undisciplined horse to be fearful in the presence of this beauty (*Phdr.* 254e). The once-insolent dark horse is now "humble enough to follow the charioteer's warnings . . . with the result that now at last the lover's soul follows its boy in reverence and fear" (*Phdr.* 254e; translation modified). Nussbaum takes this respect and love to be the source of the demand that the lovers reject intercourse.[116] While I disagree with Nussbaum that intercourse must continue to be rejected after the pair loves and respects each other, I agree that the palinode calls for rejecting intercourse before reverence and fear are properly developed. Reverence and fear give the philosopher the chance to spend time with the philosophical beloved. The pair become friends, and slowly they get to know each other. Consequently the beloved grows wings in the presence of the goodness of the lover, and the beloved falls in love with the lover in return (*Phdr.* 255d). Burger calls this "the evolution of mutual friendship into mutual desire."[117]

Being in love like this is hard for the beloved to understand (*Phdr.* 255d). As Halperin indicates, "Plato's departure from conventional norms of thought and speech is striking. Socrates claims that the beloved youth comes to participate in his lover's passionate desire for him."[118] Neither the lover nor the beloved speaks of this as love, just friendship. Nevertheless, the beloved desires the lover too: "He wants to see, touch, kiss, and lie down with him; and of course, as you might expect, he acts on these desires soon after they occur [*poiei to meta touto tachu tauta*]" (*Phdr.* 255e).[119] With their mutual love and desire established, the beloved acts on these desires.

Despite the fact that Sinaiko takes the consummation to be nonsexual, he writes, "The special emphasis of this section is on the consummation of the love affair, which is achieved only when the painfully won self-disciplined love of the lover is reciprocated by his beloved and their relationship becomes mutual."[120] The mutuality Plato has Socrates describe here is in sharp contrast with the cultural norms established concerning *paiderastia*.[121] Let us not forget that this long description is of how the philosophical lover "captures" the philosophical beloved. The verb initially used to describe this process is *capture* (*hairethêi*), but by the time the entire process of coming to know and love each other is disclosed the verb used is *to lie down with* (*sugkatakeisthai*). In fact, LSJ takes this passage as a typical instance of *sugkatakeisthai* indicating sexual intercourse.

Austere dualist readers would find this sexual vocabulary peculiar, given that they want to interpret the dark horse's humbled state as a desexualized state. Conversely, Vlastos asks:

> Now would it be reasonable to think that Plato expects this liaison to start with such raw, all-but-overpowering, lust, and then become totally desexualized as it matures? If so, why does he tell us (255e) that the body, when he comes to return the lover's passion, "wants to see, touch, kiss, and share his couch," a desire which "ere long, as one might guess, leads to the act," so that we now find the pair "sleeping together"?[122]

Vlastos agrees with me, then, that erotic desire continues in the dark horse, even though it has become humbled.[123] My point is that being in the humbled state actually facilitates getting what the dark horse wanted all along. Plato depicts being reverent with the beloved as a necessary condition for the beloved reciprocating the lover's erotic desire.

Despite my agreement with Vlastos that erotic desire continues after the humbling of the black horse, I disagree with Vlastos's overall view of the nature of the philosophers' relationship. He believes the mention of consummation at 253c is not a sexual consummation.[124] Taking 256a-b as evidence that the consummation cannot be sexual, he writes, "Plato discovers a new form of pederastic love, fully sensual in its resonance, but denying itself consummation, transmuting physical excitement into imaginative and intellectual energy."[125] On this transformation of vocabulary, Griswold and Nussbaum agree with Vlastos.[126] Quite the opposite, I will show that *Phaedrus* 256a-c does not deny sexual intercourse in the philosophical life. For those who prioritize philosophy, the Forms are the ultimate objects of desire, while erotic desire for a beloved is secondary. Precisely because philosophers' desire for a beloved is secondary to their desire for the Form of Beauty of which a beloved's beauty is a mere reminder, philosophers are said to be using "reminders of these things [the Forms] correctly" (*Phdr.* 249c). Platonic love can involve sexual consummation.

The time has finally come for the lover's dark horse to get what he's been waiting for, what he was promised. Socrates says, "When they are in bed, the lover's undisciplined horse has a word to say to the charioteer—that after all its sufferings it is entitled to a little fun" (*Phdr.* 256a). I have already demonstrated that this "bad" horse isn't so bad after all, but it is fair to consider the dark horse undisciplined; throughout the day, before any work had been done, the dark horse was already calling for its own nectar and ambrosia. As Ferrari writes, "[T]he horses require their own special food."[127] However, the dark horse makes his strongest case to his chariot-mates when he argues that after all his suffering he has now *earned* what he's wanted all along.

This paints a different picture of the dark horse than the initial description at 253e. There, Plato has Socrates describe the dark horse as unresponsive to reason, being "deaf as a post." Here, the dark horse has become a negotiator. The phrasing of his request at 256a strikes us as articulate precisely because it corresponds to the pattern indicated at 247e, where the divine charioteer offers nectar and ambrosia to the horses after a long day of working to carry the divine charioteer around heaven and to its rim. Meanwhile, Ferrari has noticed that the charioteer's methods also become reversed. He writes, "Although the charioteer seems to stand for the control of reason and the bad horse for brutish, uninhibited lust, in the allegorical struggle between the two it is the bad horse who adopts persuasive language and the methods of reason, while the charioteer maintains control by sheer strength and wordless violence."[128]

With the dark horse now believing his work has entitled him to his nectar and ambrosia, Plato has Socrates indicate two possibilities. They can either adopt the best way of life, or a second-rate way of life. This passage, popularly taken to advocate abstinence, emphasizes that the best way of life is characterized by doing philosophy and having a well-ordered soul (*Phdr.* 256a), whereas the inferior life is marked by putting "ambition in place of philosophy" (*Phdr.* 256a-c). This contrast tells us that when the dark horse is not trained to be reverent, then the lovers just jump into bed, forgoing important activities such as doing philosophy together, shaping each other's character, and falling in love; but when the dark horse's ambitions are "enslaved" (*Phdr.* 256b) the lovers have time to do philosophy while developing what Plato calls "backlove" (*Phdr.* 255e). So, we see the contrast between Socrates's first speech, in which the lover tries to keep the beloved away from philosophy because it would make the beloved a better person (*Phdr.* 239a-b), and the second speech, in which the lover aims to improve (and be improved by) the beloved by pursuing philosophy together (*Phdr.* 249a, 252e–253c, 256a-b).[129]

The conclusion of the palinode reiterates the idea of reincarnation cycles that we first find at *Phaedrus* 248e–249a, and I find that passage important for deciphering what is left implicit about the first-rate life at

256a-b. If 256a-b indicates that the reincarnation fast track consists exclusively of abstinence and doing philosophy, then it would stand in tension with 249a, where Plato has Socrates point out that there is not one but two paths to that three-thousand-year shortcut. However, if the first-rate life at 256a-b can include either "practicing philosophy without guile" (*philosophêsantos adolôs*) or "combining his love for a boy with the practice of philosophy" (*paiderastêsantos meta philosophias*), these two passages are not inconsistent. I see no reason to believe that the first-rate philosophical life at 256a-b is incompatible with the first-rate philosophical life at 249a. Plato's main concern in both passages is that the lovers do what it takes to prioritize philosophy and maintain a well-ordered soul.[130]

What relegates a soul to the ten-thousand-year plan is putting ambition in the place of philosophy, which inherently involves disorder in the soul. It is these disordered, unphilosophical souls for whom Plato does not advocate consummation of erotic desire. Yet, it should be noted that Plato is not very harsh on these unphilosophical lovers, describing even their second-rate life as "bright and happy" (*Phdr.* 256e). But, while "ordinary people" would take the sexual experiences of these nonphilosophers to be "the happiest choice of all" (*Phdr.* 256c), philosophers know that by failing to order their souls properly and do philosophy together these second-rate lovers have doomed themselves to waiting ten thousand years for their reunion with the Forms. Thus, Plato has Socrates bring the palinode to a close with a protreptic to philosophy directed toward both readers and Phaedrus, who is not a philosopher but a lover of speeches, as we have already seen. Satisfying one's sexual desire for another lover of wisdom after pursuing knowledge together is what the philosopher feeds to the black horse. What would be a more motivating protreptic to philosophy than discovering that doing philosophy with another dialectician entitles philosophers to sexual consummation with a beloved partner in dialectic?

3.5 The Unlucky Erotic Philosopher

We might wonder which of the two fast-track paths recommended at *Phaedrus* 249a Plato's Socrates is on. Does he attempts to return expeditiously to the Forms by practicing philosophy straightforwardly or by combining his love for a boy with the practice of philosophy? Our erotic philosopher may practice philosophy "guilelessly" sometimes, either in private (*Smp.* 175a-c and 220c-d) or with the interlocutors to whom he is not attracted, but combining the practice of philosophy with loving boys would clearly be his preference. Plato has Socrates commence the palinode with a comment about a man "in love with a boy of similar character" (*Phdr.* 243c), and the erotic philosopher we observe in the *Symposium* and *Phaedrus* is approved to be on the prowl for a boy of similar character, a philosopher who would be his partner in dialectic, the care of the soul, as well as in *erôs*.[131] Plato's Socrates knows there is no shame in this; in fact, at the beginning of the palinode, he highlights for us "the shame he feels before a decent and generous man who, having experienced genuine love, knows how untrue his first speech was."[132]

Yet, Socrates's abstinence with handsome, young boys reminds us of his difficulty in finding a beloved who is both willing and able to philosophize with him. Considering this difficulty, one might wonder why any companion, philosophically inclined or not, couldn't serve as a philosopher's beloved. Couldn't a philosopher such as Socrates satisfy his erotic desire with any willing partner and then return to philosophical inquiry with a philosophically inclined interlocutor? At *Phaedrus* 252c–253c, Plato has Socrates emphatically declare that philosophers need to make sure their beloveds are philosophically inclined. We might then wonder why Plato takes seriously the idea that philosophical aptitude is the chief criterion for being a philosopher's suitable beloved. In my view, he aims to show something about the philosophical life, particularly that for true lovers of wisdom the erotic experience is not oriented toward the desire for pleasure as such. If Socrates were to take as his lover someone who is either not a philosopher or not of similar character, he would fall into the class of lovers he describes at the end of the palinode who are not able to approve of their own erotic experiences "with their whole minds" (*Phdr.* 256c). In this way, Plato indicates that when one takes a beloved who is *not* endeavoring to understand the Forms, then one finds erotic experiences that are oriented merely toward lust. This sort of erotic experience fails to facilitate understanding of the Forms. Therefore, Plato believes it is only when philosophers find a suitably philosophical beloved that they may have erotic experiences that are oriented toward the pursuit of knowledge.

In his erotic dialogues, Plato depicts loving boys with the aid of philosophy as unavailable to Socrates because his prospective beloveds are not suitable. They are not dialecticians. They cannot trade gold for gold. In the words of Ferrari:

> Because it is to some extent a matter of luck whether the philosophic lover encounters a truly appropriate beloved, there is a genuine possibility that he will have to practice philosophy

without the special benefits of philosophic love—just as there is a far stronger possibility (which we saw from the *Republic*) that he will have to practice philosophy without the benefit of doing so in the ideal society.[133]

Socrates's bad luck in both of these regards helps to account for why the conversations he has with just about every interlocutor end in failure on a certain level.

Miller has noticed Plato's frequent choice to have Socrates's testing end in failure,[134] and this point reinforces my contention that Plato's remarks vilifying the body operate in a provocative, ironic way for the sake of a pedagogical aim. Miller writes, "Obviously, Plato's real interest lies not with his *dramatis persona* but with the audience that the *persona* mimes. The failure of an interlocutor to meet the philosopher's test within the drama is, in its basic function, Plato's test and provocation of his hearer. . . . Plato challenges the hearer *to recover* [what is lost in the interlocutor's failure] *for himself*."[135] Similarly, I argue that Plato's most austere-sounding comments are directed at his hearers who have not yet succeeded in making the transition to prioritizing the care of the soul over the care of the body; and for those in his audience who have managed to prioritize the care of the soul over the care of the body, Plato leaves numerous indications that the care of the soul does not require the total denial of the needs and desires of the body. Plato's ultimate recommendation for the philosopher is to care for both the soul and the body in a way that prioritizes the soul without renouncing the body.[136]

Having seen that neither the *Symposium* nor the *Phaedrus* indicates that the philosophical life must be abstinent, we are once again faced with wondering why Plato is not more explicit in conveying the message that it is acceptable to satisfy erotic desire for one's philosophically inclined beloved after doing philosophy together. I contend that he anticipates the likelihood of body-lovers latching onto an overt message about the fulfillment of appetitive desires. Body-lovers, who have yet to make the transition to caring for the soul, would see such a straightforward message as permission to fulfill any sexual desire because body-lovers fail to acknowledge the necessity of doing so under the guidance of reason. Only those who have already been successful making the transition away from body-love toward the care of the soul are ready to satisfy sexual desire with the help of philosophy.

Socrates is ready to acknowledge that lovers are mad (*Phdr.* 244a), but he contends that "this sort of madness is given us by the gods to ensure our greatest good fortune" (*Phdr.* 245b-c). We have now seen the shapes this good fortune takes. *Erôs* educates philosophers. It facilitates the philosophical pursuit of understanding the Forms. And when philosophers draw that work to a close, they have earned the nourishing reward that for a time relieves the distraction caused by erotic desire. If a proper beloved is available, then these philosophers may choose to include sexual consummation in their lives. Depicting Socrates's trouble with finding himself in that lucky position, Plato highlights in his erotic dialogues how difficult it is for philosophers to find philosophical beloveds. Whether he ever had an erotic experience with a soul-loving philosopher with whom he also did philosophy is beyond our ability to know. After all, let's not forget the cultural expectation that *erastês* and *erômenos* maintain the discretion required to keep what goes on between them private. Yet, the association maintained by both the historical Socrates and Plato's fictive Socrates with rare philosophical souls such as Plato and Theaetetus makes clear that Socrates would not have to look too far to find "a boy of similar character" with whom he could love wisdom and grow wings, *if*,[137] of course, he could capture him.

Chapter 4

Health, Justice, and Peace in the *Republic* and *Gorgias*

4.1 Introduction

My project has focused on refining our interpretation of Plato with respect to his attitude toward the physical world in general and human bodies in particular. Chapters 2 and 3 have demonstrated the serious challenges facing the austere dualist interpretation, and I have shown the inaccuracies involved in assuming that Plato's focus on contemplation necessitates despising the human body and the physical world. Plato is candid about the fact that being wise and good is difficult when sensory deception and erotic distractions can jeopardize the philosopher's goals. But I have already shown that if one learns how to manage, not repress and deny, the body's needs and desires, then being wise and good is not unattainable for human beings. Whereas chapters 2 and 3, respectively, uncovered that neither training for death nor the erotic ascent to knowledge should be construed as austere ascetic projects, this chapter will investigate Plato's attitude toward the human body and its needs and desires in the context of social and political life. I will argue against the interpretation that claims Plato has no concern for human bodies in particular or the physical world in general. In fact, we shall see that Plato puts the goal of physical survival at the heart of what he construes as political.

I will examine Plato's analogical treatment of health and justice in both the *Republic* and *Gorgias*. Plato has Socrates describe justice as the health of both political associations and individual souls. I will show that the pursuit of austere asceticism jeopardizes the health of individuals' bodies and souls and their communities. Moderation, rather than the repressive immoderation of austere asceticism, is essential to both individual justice and civic justice. One of the main tasks here is to make sense of the associations Plato has Socrates suggest among health, justice, and peace. The other is to discern the relationship between the individual human being and the community of others. In the *Republic*, Plato offers that moderation fosters health, health fosters justice, and justice fosters peace.[1] The key to understanding how health and justice relate to peace is discerning Plato's theory of the interconnectedness of individual souls and the political community. In a variety of ways we see that for Plato justice is relational; justice brings good relations, "friendship and a sense of common purpose," whereas injustice "causes civil war, hatred, and fighting" (*R.* 351d).[2]

In 4.2, this chapter will take up the moral psychology that comes out of the *Gorgias* and *Republic* in order to focus on the treatment of appetitive desire for physical pleasure. Like the dialogues we have already considered, both of these political dialogues endorse moderation rather than austere asceticism as conducive to harmony within the soul. These dialogues put readers in a position to recognize that attaining this sort of personal peace is an important part of living well as an embodied inquirer.

Section 4.2.1 takes up the moral psychology offered in the *Gorgias*. I will inspect three passages in particular that in one way or another all make use of the craft of medicine and/or its principles: 464b–465d, where Socrates discusses the crafts that care for both the body and the soul; 493a–494a, where Socrates uses the water-bearers myth and the jar image to endorse moderation rather than austere asceticism, which is in line with medicine's concepts of filling and emptying; and 505a-c, where Socrates continues to work with the analogy between medicine and the love of wisdom in order to claim that just as doctors do not give the same prescriptions to healthy patients and sick patients, so too would soul-doctoring philosophers not give the same recommendations to those with healthy souls as they would to those with unhealthy souls. This theme dovetails with the notion of pedagogical irony that I introduced in chapter 1.

In 4.2.2, I will explore the *Republic*'s account of this inner harmony. There, Plato has Socrates indicate that individual justice consists in a soul that orders the psychic aspects in proportion to their natures. Inquirers with properly ordered souls are able to nourish the body in a way that does not put either psychic or physical health in jeopardy. Consequently, as I will show, the rational aspect should not rule by acting despotically toward the appetite, as the austere dualist interpretation of *askesis* would hold. My normative dualist reading shows that a just person cares for the soul without disregarding the body's needs and desires, which requires anticipating and confronting obstacles in the way of cultivating the virtue of justice.

Section 4.3 examines the possibility of the philosopher as a political leader. Here, I will contest the claim that a real philosopher disdains human affairs and prefers to stay out of the political fray in favor of paying attention to the invisible realm of nonphysical Forms. One of the central issues in the *Republic* concerns whether or not those who care about justice should have to be compelled to offer their talents to their cities and fellow citizens. We should be puzzled by the strange aversion to civic engagement depicted in the allegory of the cave. How we conceive of the physical, including the human body and its value, has a lot to do with whether or not we value the social-political arena and the pursuit of social justice. For instance, if one construes human excellence as requiring one to transcend everything worldly, then one will attempt to live an austere asceticism. One who aspires to be this sort of philosopher does not want to pay attention to the physical world at all. This is the alleged lover of wisdom who rejects out of hand the prospect of political leadership.

Austere dualists make sense of this by assuming that anything but the life of exclusive contemplation is of no importance to a philosopher. I will debunk the austere dualist notion that, for Plato, philosophers are only authentic if their lifestyle consists exclusively of contemplation of the Forms. In 4.3.1, I will investigate Plato's Socrates's repeated claims that good leaders have rare, peculiar natures capable of combining different and even opposing traits, such as reluctance toward and commitment to political leadership. In 4.3.2, I will show how various misunderstandings about philosophers contribute to the confusion about whether they want to rule. In 4.3.3, I will question the circumstances under which even decent rulers who love the Good may take refuge from politics. And finally, in 4.3.4, I will show that for one who truly loves the Good, the desire to try to order cities and souls after that model will be greater than one's desire to avoid the disorderly, petty political arena. This effort to engage the world for the sake of making cities and souls imitate orderly Goodness is compatible with the philosopher's love of the Form of the Good. Here too we are reassessing Platonic love, and we shall find that philosophers' love for the Forms draws them into the community.

In 4.4, I will argue that Plato is not guilty of dismissing the physical in the context of his political philosophy. In particular, 4.4.1 will show that Plato's Socrates is deeply concerned about poverty and its destabilizing effects on individuals' bodies and souls and, in turn, on society as a whole.

The variety of concerns about which he warns us is so extensive that it is astonishing how little scholarly attention this theme has garnered in the literature. Further, in 4.4.2, I will take up Socrates's brief discussion of the healthy city in *Republic* Book 2 in order to demonstrate the connection Plato's Socrates envisions between the quest for physical health/survival and the pursuit of political harmony. The First City has attracted more scholarly attention than Plato's view of poverty, but most scholars do not take the account of this city at all seriously. I will show that Plato's inclusion of the First City is very significant for understanding his attitude toward the body in the political arena. Plato's brief sketch of the First City calls our attention to the serious idea that when people are provided for in a way that makes healthy survival possible, then they are in a position to make valuable contributions to the world around them and, importantly, not to disrupt the conditions for harmonious relations with others. Finally, in 4.5 I will discuss Plato's belief that if there is no justice there will be no peace and that if we do know justice we will know peace.

4.2 Justice as Individual Harmony

Plato takes a wide variety of approaches to elucidate his notion of the just individual, all of which involve the concept of internal harmony. In chapter 3, we saw that Plato's tripartite moral psychology figured into the *Phaedrus*'s attention to sexuality and love. Now let's see how Plato has Socrates develop the concept of justice as harmony in the context first of the *Gorgias* and then of the *Republic*. In both of these political dialogues, health and the practice of medicine are crucial to Plato's way of conceiving of individual justice. In the *Gorgias*, justice is construed as the health of the soul, specifically the corrective treatment of the diseased soul, and in the *Republic*, justice is pronounced the health of the soul and the city. This notion of justice as health underscores the desirability of a harmonious relationship among unequal parts.

4.2.1 Care of the Soul in the *Gorgias*

Socrates utilizes analogical reasoning in the *Gorgias* in order to assert the existence of expertise in the field of psychic care.[3] He does this so frequently that Callicles grouses, "By the gods! You simply don't let up on your continual talk of shoemakers and cleaners, cooks and doctors, as if our discussion were about them!" (*Grg.* 491a). However, for Socrates, their discussion does concern such craftsmen; as I noted in chapter 1, Plato has Socrates use analogical reasoning regularly to make his seemingly strange claims more persuasive. Let's consider three passages from the *Gorgias* in particular: 464b–465d, where Socrates accounts for the four crafts involved in caring for the body and soul; 493a–494a, where he relays the myth of the water-bearers with its significant jar metaphor; and 505a-c, where Socrates writes different prescriptions for life for souls with different needs.

In the *Gorgias*, Socrates notes that just as there are two crafts that combine to make the body healthy, so too are there two crafts that work together to make the soul healthy. While he rests with calling the expertise about physical health the care of the body, Socrates gives the field of psychic care a technical term: *politics* (*Grg.* 464b). Here, Plato has Socrates indicate the broad nature of politics. We tend to use the word *politics* to refer narrowly to public governance, but in the *Gorgias*, Socrates steers us away from this narrow understanding of politics toward a sense of politics that also includes individual self-governance. This assumption that virtue is connected with the political life is typical of ancient Greek conceptions of politics.

Gorgias 464b–465d surveys all that is necessary for healthy self-governance, as well as how authentic self-governance (the care of the body and the soul) can be imitated by "knacks." Socrates says that the care of the body is, on one hand, gymnastics and, on the other, medicine (*Grg.* 464b). These crafts are imitated by the knacks of cosmetics and pastry baking, respectively (*Grg.* 465c). The cosmetic knack is the shortcut to appearing healthy just as confections merely imitate medicine's power to make someone feel better. Resting on the couches of the *Republic*'s luxurious city (*R.* 372d) is the antipode of the exercise that Socrates refers to as gymnastics in the *Gorgias*, and eating the pastries Glaucon demands in the *Republic* (373a) is exactly what Socrates cautions us against in this passage in the *Gorgias*. Later in the *Gorgias*, Socrates calls the city that has been made physically worse by the imitative body-care knacks "swollen and festering" (*Grg.* 519a), which echoes the language he uses in *Republic* II to describe Glaucon's unjust city (372e), as we shall see in section 4.4.2.

Analogously, Socrates claims that politics consists, on one hand, of legislation and of justice, on the other. Just as one engages in physical training (what Plato calls gymnastics) in order to prevent physical disease, one must engage in psychic training (what Plato calls legislation) in order to prevent psychic disease.[4] And just as one submits to medical treatment in order to correct physical disease, one must submit to psychic medicine (what Plato here calls justice) in order to correct psychic disease. Furthermore, just as the healthy appearance caused by practicing gymnastics can be mimicked by cosmetics, so too can a healthy psychic appearance be given off by one who has mastered sophistry. This is exactly what Adeimantus had in mind in the *Republic* when he worried that one need not actually possess a well-ordered soul (that is, a just soul) so long as one learns how to use persuasion to convince others that one is just (*Rep.* 365b-d). Finally, just as pastry baking can mimic the way that medicine makes someone sick feel better, so too does oratory mimic the way that justice actually corrects psychic illness. Whereas the crafts for self-care operate "with a view to what's best" (*Grg.* 464c), the knacks use "flattery" and "guessing" to give off the impression of being worthwhile, despite focusing on what's pleasant instead of what's best (*Grg.* 464c-d).

Body-lovers concentrate at best on fitness and nutrition (and medicine too, whenever necessary),[5] but at worst a body-lover uses cosmetics to appear healthy and eats pastries to feel better physically. The one who comes to see the necessity of devoting oneself to the care of the soul makes a transition toward politics, as Socrates broadly construes politics. At that point, one must either exercise one's own psychic legislation or submit oneself to a psychic trainer. However, if one requires the guidance of a psychic trainer, ideally the psychic trainer would teach one how to legislate one's own psychic aspects. The ideal psychic trainer is someone who is always informed by what is best rather than by what is pleasurable. Socrates defines a true politician exactly in these terms (*Grg.* 521d) as he reminds us how rare such psychic trainers are.

And whenever a soul has fallen into need of psychic medicine due to either bad legislation or bad circumstances, soul-lovers must take their psychic medicine if they are to care for the soul properly. They may either see to justice on their own, such as by making an apology, or through the legal system, such as by turning oneself in for punishment. The *Gorgias* demonstrates that one can avoid the need for corrective justice by engaging in what we can either call legislation or self-control. This healthy life entails learning how to rule oneself and be moderate in satisfying one's appetites. The interlocutors in the *Gorgias*, especially Callicles, find the notion of "ruling oneself" extremely foreign. They are accustomed to the notion of ruling over others (*Grg.* 452d, 491c-d). In response to Socrates's declaration that self-rule matters as much and more than ruling over others, Callicles finds this incomprehensible and asks Socrates, "What do you mean by one who rules himself?" (*Grg.* 491d). He must ask because he has no idea what Socrates has in mind.

Many people for whom political activity is important focus on the quest to rule over others (cf. *Grg.* 452d) rather than attending to the self-rule. What Socrates is doing is "assimilating self-government [*heautou archein*] to self-mastery [*enkratê auton heautou*] with regard to pleasures,"[6] a view Irwin suspects is original to Plato.[7] Similarly, in the *Republic*, Adeimantus suggests to Socrates that true understanding of justice is the mechanism by which one develops self-rule, that is, being one's *"own best guardian, afraid that by doing injustice he'd be living with the worst thing possible"* (*R.* 366d–367a; emphasis added). Here, Adeimantus instructs the interlocutors about ruling over oneself, a concept so foreign to Callicles that, as we have seen, he has no idea what Socrates is talking about when Socrates initially raises it in the *Gorgias* at 491d-e.

As we saw in chapter 2, body-lovers can transform themselves into people who prioritize the care of the soul. Here in the *Gorgias*, Plato emphasizes that the care of the soul is ideally accompanied by the care of the body. If the psychic crafts are put into practice, the soul will be in good shape, just as when one implements the physical crafts, the body will be in good shape. He has Socrates grasp the value of physical health and the importance of living under the guidance of all four of the self-care crafts. Practiced together, this is Plato's science of living well, which ensures psychic harmony.[8] The scheme of self-care for both soul and body that Plato offers in the *Gorgias* further reinforces the commitment to holistic medicine to which I alluded in chapter 1.

Let's now turn to the passage that sets out to show the benefits of moderation and self-rule. At *Gorgias* 493d–494a, Plato has Socrates argue that, while one might imagine that the hedonistic life is pleasurable, it is actually a life of pain and frustration. For Callicles, moderation is not choice-worthy, because it involves governing oneself in a way that limits one's chances for pleasure. For Socrates, immoderation is not choice-worthy, because it prevents one from truly enjoying a pleasure at hand in the present. We shall see Socrates concentrate on the pleasure and freedom involved in moderate self-control as opposed to the pain and constraint he associates with hedonism. The underlying theme here is the desirability of being self-sufficient.

In the *Gorgias*, Callicles balks at the idea that not all desires for pleasures ought to be satisfied (491e–492a). He claims to believe that pleasure and goodness are identical (*Grg.* 492c), and Socrates charges himself both with refuting Callicles's position that the good life is hedonistic as well as with helping him to understand something important about the soul. Socrates's refutation of Callicles involves three main claims: first, that pleasure is not the same as the good; second, that some pleasures are better than others; and finally, that beneficial pleasures are those that produce something good such as physical health and the bad pleasures are the ones that cause harm like physical disease.[9]

Upon hearing Callicles's position, Socrates remembers having heard someone compare the appetitive aspect of the soul to a jar (*Grg.* 493a). Socrates fumbles around with his recollection of the wise man from whom he heard this account,[10] but tells it in hopes of convincing Callicles "to choose the orderly life, the life that is adequate to and satisfied with its circumstances at any given time" (*Grg.* 493c). Socrates compares the hedonistic soul to a leaky jar (*Grg.* 493b) and contrasts the leaky jar with a jar kept full by a tight lid. He says:

> Consider whether what you're saying about each life, the life of the self-controlled man and that of the undisciplined one, is like this: Suppose there are two men, each of whom has many jars. The jars belonging to one of them are sound and full, one with wine, another with honey, a third with milk and many others with lots of other things. And suppose that the sources of each of these things are scarce and difficult to come by, procurable only with much toil and trouble. Now the one man, having filled up his jars, doesn't pour anything more into them and gives them no further thought. He can relax over them. As for the other one, he too has resources that can be procured, though with difficulty, but his containers are leaky and rotten. He's forced to keep filling them, day and night, or else he suffers extreme pain. Now since each life is the way I describe it, are you saying that the life of the undisciplined man is happier than that of the orderly man? When I say this, do I at all persuade you to concede that the orderly life is better than the undisciplined one, or do I not? (*Grg.* 493d–494a)

The leaky jar metaphor is meant to illuminate the difference between how a hedonist and a normative dualist thinks of a satisfied soul.[11] Even though Socrates calls this account "on the whole a bit strange" (*Grg.* 493c), Plato has Socrates introduce the jar metaphor precisely because he is aware of how effective it is to analogize the soul with physical things, given how well the physical functions for all human beings as a source analog, especially a hedonist such as Callicles.

Linforth suggests that the fundamental analogy is between the jar and the appetitive aspect of the soul. He writes, "The uninitiated (*amuêtoi*) are the unintelligent (*anoêtoi*). The jar which the unititiated must ever try to fill is the part of the soul in which the desires are located, and the sieve in which they try to carry water is the soul itself."[12] Part of what happens here is wordplay that takes advantage of the similar sounds in *pithos* (jar), *epithumêtikon* (appetite), and words pertaining to persuasion such as *peithein* and *pithanos* in order to emphasize that the appetitive aspect of the soul is persuadable—either to temptation or to self-discipline.

And Callicles needs this recommendation, given the hedonist's response he offers in his response to Socrates's use of the jar metaphor. He says, "The man who has filled himself up has no pleasure any more, and when he's been filled up and experiences neither joy nor pain, that's living like a stone, as I was saying just now. Rather, living pleasantly consists in this: having as much as possible flow in" (*Grg.* 494a-b). Callicles does not recognize the pain and difficulty of maintaining the hedonistic lifestyle before Socrates's use of the leaky jar image. As Irwin writes, "Socrates uses the image of the leaky jar . . . to suggest that Callicles' advice to cultivate desire is less attractive than it might have seemed. For the desires which are cultivated will be insatiable; the more they are satisfied, the more demanding they will become, requiring further satisfaction creating further desire."[13] With the mention of a jar leaky like a sieve, Plato's Socrates imports notions of filling and emptying that Plato is borrowing directly from medicine.[14] Socrates uses the image to reject the hedonist way of life and to recommend for the way of living symbolized by a full jar with a tight lid.

What exactly does the full jar with a tight lid symbolize? If moderation is represented as the full jar with a tight lid, does this image correlate with the austere interpretation of ascetic self-discipline or the normative dualist interpretation? The contents Plato chooses for the jars possessed by the self-controlled person are the first indication that this metaphor is not intended to recommend the austere version of asceticism. Plato chooses wine, milk, and honey as the contents of the jars, and these choices are rather symbolic, not at all arbitrary. Wine, milk, and honey are traditionally associated with Dionysus, and consequently they would be unfitting symbols of austere asceticism, as we saw in chapter 2. Furthermore, if Socrates were trying to encourage the soul-lover to deny the body altogether, then it strikes me as rather ineffective to represent the austere ascetic lifestyle as a *full* jar with a tight lid. An *empty* jar would be a much more suitable representation of the austere denial of appetites. The point of the jar metaphor passage is, rather, to instruct us to be moderate about the satisfaction of our desires so as to be self-sufficient and enjoy life.[15] The image of a *full* jar tells us that pleasures have "flowed in" to use Callicles's expression. From there, the question is whether to call that satisfaction, as is Socrates's position, or to see that as a death-mimicking act of settling, as is Callicles's view.[16]

Let's turn now to look at Socrates's discussion of who shall be allowed to let the pleasures flow in the soul and how the filling of jars works, so to speak.

At 505a-b, Socrates observes that, while one might consider the hedonistic lifestyle one entirely free from constraint, it is marked by the constraints imposed by medical doctors and psychic trainers like Socrates. Meanwhile, the doctor of either the soul or the body can permit the intake of pleasures for one who is healthy (*Grg.* 504e–505a). He points out that a doctor does not give the same prescription for health to all patients. Plato writes, "[D]octors generally allow a person to fill up his appetites, to eat when he's hungry, for example, or drink when he's thirsty *as much as he wants to when he's in good health,* but when he's sick they practically never allow him to fill himself with what he has an appetite for" (*Grg.* 505a; emphasis added). Compare this to Eryximachus's admonition against heavy drinking for a party that imbibed excessively the night before (*Smp.* 176e). The context there makes clear that this doctor would not similarly restrict a party that had not overconsumed so recently. Thus, in Eryximachus we have a good example of a doctor who writes different prescriptions for those who are well and those in need of recovery.

The doctor need not ever restrict the sort of patient who has an understanding of how much and what to eat and drink, whereas the doctor must rein in a patient who has not mastered self-rule. Once Callicles agrees to this, Socrates adds, "And isn't it just the same way with the soul . . . ? As long as it's corrupt, in that it's foolish, undisciplined, unjust and impious, it should be kept away from its appetites and not be permitted to do anything other than what will make it better" (*Grg.* 505b).[17] Callicles agrees, and soon thereafter realizes that his agreement refutes his initial claim that it is better for the soul to be undisciplined rather than disciplined. Although Callicles does not remain a cooperative interlocutor, it is clear that the body-soul analogy has done its work. It made Socrates's claim (that it is better for the soul to be disciplined in satisfying its appetites) more intuitive for Callicles. In fact, the use of analogical reasoning made Socrates's call for moderation so intuitive that it led Callicles to refute himself (*Grg.* 505b-c).

The fact that a different prescription is given to the healthy patient and a much more restrictive prescription to the diseased patient is of great analogical significance for one trying to interpret Plato's messages about how a philosopher ought to treat the body.[18] The tension in Plato about whether the life of someone who wants to be wise and good can properly include the enjoyment of moderate pleasure is not due to Plato's being conflicted or indecisive about how he thinks an embodied inquirer should treat the body. If different prescriptions are written for the healthy and the sick, then one should expect Plato's Socrates—the model of soul doctor—to offer different prescriptions for psychic health to his patients as well. And indeed the reader finds in Plato's dialogues not one but two sets of messages about how to treat the body as well as the soul's appetitive desires.

For his body-loving patients, Socrates writes a prescription that calls for caring for the soul rather than prioritizing the body. It is to this patient that the most austere-sounding remarks are directed as the antipode of hedonistic body-love and inattention to the care of the soul. Just as a sick patient is given a restrictive prescription, so too is the patient riddled with psychic illness in need of an austere prescription, what Socrates describes as not being "permitted to do anything other than what will make it better" (*Grg.* 505b). However, someone who has already made the transition away from body-love toward soul-love is not suffering from psychic illness in need of correction. As a result, Socrates writes a different, more permissive, prescription for this patient. Just as a doctor allows a healthy man "to fill up his appetites . . . *as much as he wants to*," so too is the psychically healthy patient allowed to satisfy his/her appetites as much as s/he wants to. There is no danger in allowing psychically healthy people to satisfy their appetites because healthy people have healthy desires. Thus, there is no need to prescribe austerity in such cases. Healthy patients know how to be moderate because they see beyond the mere appearances of what they want, knowing instead which pleasures and how much pleasure to include in a healthy life. Precisely because their erotic motivation is not primarily directed at appetitive pleasures, the prescription for them is permission to enjoy both intellectual and physical pleasures rather than instruction to avoid such experiences.

This picture is consistent with the conclusions Plato has Socrates draw in the *Republic*. There, people have healthy desires as a result of having worked to put the soul's appetitive and spirited aspects under the guidance of the soul's rational aspect. Their health results from continued success with satisfying the right sorts of desires, namely, the ones that are approved of by the soul's rational aspect and satisfy the appetite enough to facilitate harmonious unanimity within the soul. Let's turn there now.

4.4.2 Care of the Soul in the *Republic*

The *Republic* draws a parallel between the health of the soul and the health of the city and construes both in terms of the harmonious interplay of different and unequal parts. Socrates reminds the interlocutors that they got to talking about cities in order to see what justice looks like there so that they could see it more easily in the case of the individual. Although he warns them off from taking the analogy to be more precise than is possible (R. 435c), he contends that "we are surely compelled to agree that each of us has within himself the same parts and characteristics of the city" (R. 435d-e). They "hypothesize" that this is correct and move forward with the discussion (R. 437a).

In order to convince Glaucon and Adeimantus that justice and injustice have immediate psychic consequences, as Adeimantus suspects and hopes, Socrates uses health as a source analog to assist them in understanding their target analog. He says:

> Just and unjust actions are no different for the soul than health and unhealthy things are for the body. . . . Healthy things produce health, unhealthy ones disease. . . . Just actions produce justice in the soul and unjust ones injustice. . . . To produce health is to establish the components of the body in a natural relation of control and being controlled, one by another, while to produce disease is to establish a relation of ruling and being ruled contrary to nature. (R. 444c)

Here, Plato uses the health analogy to make more concrete the grasp we have of the negative outcomes that result from being unjust and the positive rewards of being just. In Book 4, Plato has Socrates puts forward a tripartite conception of the soul in addition to the principles that the soul is healthy when it is just and that it is just when each of the soul's aspects does its own work (R. 441e-442d, 443c-e). The picture of the just person in Book 4 is complete once Plato has Socrates explain that the harmony within the soul is psychic health. Plato has Socrates say, "Virtue seems, then, to be a kind of health, fine condition, and well-being of the soul, while vice is disease, shameful condition, and weakness" (R. 444d-e).

Importantly, this theory of justice relies upon the notion of function. Plato's Socrates contends that justice is "the having and doing of one's own" (R. 433e-434a), and Plato has Socrates indicate that the aspects of the soul have different natures and accordingly have different functions. In Book 4, he focuses on the business each aspect of the soul ought to be minding and the hierarchical order that is best for the soul overall. The business of the soul's spirited aspect is to be courageous whenever one perceives that one has been wronged (R. 440c-d), while the business of the soul's appetitive aspect is to desire what is moderate (R. 442a-b), leaving the rational aspect free to wonder and try to be wise (R. 442c-d). The soul's aspects are not the same but they are interdependent, and Book 4 makes clear that each aspect of the soul has important work to do. Thus, the virtue of justice is health cultivated in three interdependent respects, with each aspect of the soul doing its important work. What is good for a human being is the life constituted by each aspect of the soul doing what is natural for it to do and doing so in proper amounts.

In terms of the ideal psychic order, the interlocutors agree with Socrates that reason is fit to rule over the spirit and appetite on account of its superior nature. The rational part of the soul is fit to lead the other aspects "since it is really wise and exercises foresight on behalf of the whole soul" (R. 441e). It is for spirit and appetite to obey reason's guidance. But the spirit is reason's natural ally (R. 441e) and is supposed to help reason govern the appetite (R. 442a). Plato writes, "They'll watch over it to see that it isn't filled with the so-called pleasures of the body and that it doesn't become so big and strong that it no longer does its own work but attempts to enslave and rule over the classes it isn't fit to rule, thereby overturning everyone's whole life" (R. 442a-b).

The fundamental question here concerns what the rule of reason over the rest of the soul involves. What type of leader is the rational aspect of the soul supposed to be? The austere dualist interpretation contends that the rational aspect of the soul should not merely lead but ought to dominate the soul's nonrational aspects in a tyrannical manner,[19] squashing the functions of the rest of the soul, especially the appetite. The austere dualist reading holds that it would be more ideal if one could never feel desires because the appetite's desires for food, drink, sex, and so on tie the soul more closely to the body and the physical world. Even though the moral psychology of the *Republic* makes clear that each aspect of the soul must be given the opportunity to do its important work well (R. 433a–435b; 441d-e), austere dualist interpreters have presumed that the proper order of the soul is one wherein reason quells appetitive desires for physical pleasure,[20] and what's more, they fail to recognize or reconcile the inconsistency between calling for reason to dominate the subjugated aspects of the soul as well as to harmonize all the parts of the soul.[21]

If one aims for inner harmony, then ruling over the other parts of the soul should not involve suppressing the other functions within the whole soul.[22] Schultz agrees that the harmony model of justice in the *Republic* requires giving "a voice" to even the appetitive part of the soul because it "provides necessary notes on the scale of internal justice."[23] Schultz,

Annas, Rice, and Russell see an ambiguity in the *Republic* between two pictures: one that emphasizes harmony and one that emphasizes force.[24] However, proponents of this view believe Plato is more keen on a model that emphasizes harmony. Annas claims that the harmony view is "what Plato most of the time wants, for he would hardly liken moderation to harmony if he thought that the behavior it required was enforced and accompanied by resentment."[25]

In Book 4, Plato has Socrates instruct us to expect all aspects of the soul, even the appetite, to be active when their work is what's best for the overall human being. No part of the virtuous soul will be squashed through domination. As Annas writes, "As well as describing the just person as unified and harmonious, Plato makes a comparison with health (444c–445b); he wants us to think of justice as a state where the person is completely fulfilled . . . because no aspect of him or her is being repressed or denied its proper expression."[26] So, according to the logic of the *Republic*'s theory of justice, reason ruling in an authoritarian way would hinder the soul's effort to survive and flourish, given that the soul functions best when each psychic aspect plays its own natural role and does so virtuously. Reason should rule over the other parts of the soul, but not as a tyrant.

Plato's theory of justice very much relies upon the idea of cooperation, friendliness, and harmony among the parts of a soul or a city. Putting oneself in order is all about bringing harmony to the interrelations among one's psychic aspects (*R.* 443c–444a). This is the fundamental principle driving the *Republic*'s account of individual justice. When the largest and most disruptive aspect of the soul (*R.* 442a), the appetite, does its work well, the soul achieves moderation, which Socrates describes as bringing the soul into harmonious "unanimity" wherein "the naturally worse and the naturally better" "all sing the same song together" (*R.* 431e–432a). Here we see Plato link his theory of justice to a vision of peace—both personal and political—through good leadership focused on cooperative harmony instead of domination.

For instance, Plato has Socrates say that one "who is healthy and moderate" "best grasps the truth" when one "neither starves nor feasts his appetites" (*R.* 571d–572a). Socrates reiterates this twice in Book 9 when he concludes, "Therefore, when the entire soul follows the philosophic part, and there is no civil war in it, each part of it does its own work exclusively and is just, and in particular it enjoys its own pleasures, the best and truest pleasures possible for it" (*R.* 586e–587a). In line with what we found in the *Gorgias*, here too Plato's thinking about pleasure and pain relies upon the medical doctrine concerning filling and emptying. At both *Republic*

363d and 586b, we find the same "leaky" vessel motif[27] that Plato initiates at *Gorgias* 493a–494a being used to portray the suffering experienced by hedonistic souls. The Book 9 passage warrants quotation. Plato writes:

> Those who have no experience of reason or virtue, but are always occupied with feasts and the like, are brought down and then back up to the middle, as it seems, and wander in this way throughout their lives, never reaching beyond this to what is truly higher up, never looking up at it or brought up to it, and so they aren't filled with that which really is and never taste any stable or pure pleasure. Instead, they always look down at the ground like cattle, and, with their heads bent over the dinner table, they feed, fatten, and fornicate. To outdo others in these things, they kick and butt them with iron horns and hooves, killing each other, because their desires are insatiable. For the part that they're trying to fill is like a vessel full of holes, and neither it nor the things they are trying to fill it with are among the things that are. (*R.* 586a-b)

In this passage, Plato is in the midst of a comparison of hedonism and moderation, and he counts on the medical view of replenishment and emptying to help make the case against hedonism.

Additionally, Plato's Socrates alludes to the importance of the just person's "accustoming [the aspects of the soul] to each other and making them friendly" (*R.* 589a) and claims that the just person "should take care of the many-headed beast as a farmer does his animals, feeding and domesticating the gentle heads and preventing the savage ones from growing" (*R.* 589b).[28] Even the inquirer who is ruled by the rational aspect of the soul must satisfy the appetitive aspect's "gentle" desires. Plato demonstrates Socrates's acceptance of natural pleasures, which actually reinforce psychic harmony according to the *Republic*'s logic.

In contrast, reason's tyrannical mode of leadership would starve even what Socrates thinks of as our more domesticated desires. This domination would make justice unfeasible because it precludes harmonious unanimity.[29] If it austerely represses the appetite, the appetite certainly will not be friendly with reason. Leading like a tyrant would even estrange reason's natural ally, the spirit. Plato has Socrates indicate that the spirited aspect is not allied with the appetitive aspect, but given the spirit's recoil from what is unjust, our spirited aspect should be expected to rile up when the appetite is denied even moderate satisfaction, either from a tyrannical rational aspect or the deprivation caused by poverty (to which we shall return in 4.4.1).

A just life requires confronting, not ignoring, the question of how to include pleasure in the rational life. It requires attention to the appetite's agenda. Talent for managing one's appetite properly does not, however, follow from the austere ascetic rejection of all things physical. As Patterson wisely remarks:

> In Book IX . . . Socrates gives full and emphatic recognition to the important fact . . . that all three parts or aspects . . . have desires and pleasures peculiar, even natural, to them. Further, proper enjoyment of learning by the reasoning part, of victory and good repute by the spirited part, of food, drink, and so on by the appetitive part, reinforce the psychic harmony called justice in Book IV, since each part not only has and sticks to its own job, but positively enjoys doing so. Further still, these natural and proper pleasures, including those of the lowliest sector now contribute significantly—as benefits accruing to the just person simply through the presence of justice in his soul, whether or not its presence is known to gods or men—to the victory of the just life over the unjust.[30]

Thus, we see from Book 9 that the just person figures out both how to avoid overindulging in pleasures (letting appetite be the soul's dictator) and being too austere about the denial of pleasures (letting reason be the soul's dictator). Both are avoided by learning to be moderate, which can happen only under the guidance of—but not tyranny of—reason.

In these ways, Plato consistently has Socrates give the impression that in the soul of a just person we should not expect any aspect of the soul to be quashed. Plato could have had Socrates say that reason ought to dominate and crush emotion and appetite, but in fact he does not. Careful readers will conclude that Plato's theory of justice holds that *domination* by any part of the soul undermines the cultivation of justice as a virtue and is, consequently, deemed unjust.

The just person focused on rationality and the care of the soul should not try to withdraw from this world by denying the appetite austerely. Embodied inquirers live well when they learn how to order the psychic aspects in proportion to their natures. Importantly, Plato's Socrates clarifies:

> And when [the just person] does anything, whether acquiring wealth, taking care of his body, engaging in politics, or in

private contracts—in all of these, he believes that the action is just and fine that preserves this inner harmony and helps achieve it, and calls it so, and regards as wisdom the knowledge that oversees such actions. And he believes that the action that destroys this harmony is unjust, and calls it so, and regards the belief that oversees it as ignorance. (*R.* 443e–444a)

The just person can still seek wealth as long as one still manages to keep perspective on the worth all things considered of wealth. *Republic* 476c-d, 479e, and 485b all speak to the ways in which philosophers can keep the status of things in perspective because of their genuine understanding of the Forms. The just person can and does take care of the body without being overly attached to physical pleasure.[31] And as we shall examine in the next section, the just person can participate in the political arena without being overly attached to honor and reputation. The just person can undertake these activities all while maintaining the proper prioritization of rationality over spirit and appetite and the soul over the body. While the unjust person struggles to discern the appropriate amount of activity for the irrational aspects of the soul, which usually leads to the appetite being too active, the just person only wants to do what facilitates inner peace. Inquirers with properly ordered souls are able to engage the physical world in a way that does not put psychic health in jeopardy. In other words, just people integrate pleasure in an honest fashion with their pursuit of the good. They prioritize the care of the soul while enjoying life in the body.

In addition to the possibility of out-of-control appetites (an oft-considered danger) and tyrannically dominating rational aspects (a danger neglected by the austere dualist interpretation), there are other possible threats to the harmonious state of the soul that concern the spirited aspect. While Plato is clear that the spirit is more readily obedient to the rule of reason than the appetite (*R.* 441e), the spirit may nevertheless become overactive too, causing the whole soul to become disjointed. Plato's honor-lovers exemplify this state of the soul. We can easily add people with "anger management issues" as well. Furthermore, what Plato has Socrates lay out gives us every reason to recognize that experiencing injustice, especially with frequency and/or intensity, will be a serious threat to the harmony within the individual soul because it will inflame the spirit. His account of the spirited part of the soul highlights the impact that experiencing injustice has on the spirit. Whether one experiences injustice directly or as a bystander, he thinks it will have an arousing effect on the spirited aspect of the soul. If that reaction were intense enough, the effect would not be limited to the spirit; it would destabilize the whole soul.

Anger felt on the occasions where injustice is detected is natural, but if that anger were felt more than the proper amount, this excess would infringe upon the other aspects of the soul. For instance, one can be too angry to study, to eat, to refrain from homicide, and so on. As a result, excess anger ought to be avoided. Yet, given the injustices that occur in the world, even one with righteous anger is vulnerable to having a disharmonious soul, if anger dominates the soul. Reeve highlights Plato's example of the "small children . . . full of spirit right from birth" (R. 441a); he writes, "An infant cries to be fed. If it is not fed soon enough, its cries turn to cries of rage. It is crying, not only because it is hungry, but out of awareness that its desire for food is being frustrated."[32] This distinction between the pain of hunger and the painful anger of feeling denied would be just as apt in the case of those without the resources for nourishment, the poor and the extremely poor. Julia Annas once observed, "Plato does not face the question of whether one could be happy if one had psychic harmony but had to cope with external problems, like being terribly poor."[33] However, Plato does explicitly indicate that both poverty and affluence disrupt psychic harmony (R. 591e),[34] and, as we shall see in 4.4.1 and 4.4.2., Plato's broader commentary on poverty also commits him to that position.

4.3 The Peculiar Nature of Leaders in Plato's *Republic*

Having considered Plato's highly developed view of self-care for both body and soul, we must now ask whether the people who thus live well will act as leaders. One of the central themes in the *Republic* is how rarely one finds a leader among their fellow citizens. Plato has Socrates contend that good leaders are seldom found because their nature is so peculiar and rare. In particular, Plato's Socrates maintains that the rare nature of a good leader combines qualities that "*mostly grow in separation and are rarely found in the same person*" (R. 503b; emphasis added). Plato's leaders are the ones who can pull off counterintuitive feats, being living paradoxes, so to speak. So, in looking for leaders one pursues unusual people.

4.3.1 Rare Combinations

Plato initiates his emphasis on the seemingly impossible nature of those who should lead the community when he has Socrates first discuss who will "guard" the city. He says, "Where are we to find a character that is both gentle and high-spirited at the same time? After all, a gentle nature is the opposite of a spirited one. . . . If someone lacks either gentleness or spirit, he can't be a good guardian. Yet it seems impossible to combine them. It follows that a good guardian cannot exist" (*R.* 375c-d).[35] Despite what appears to be the case, Socrates asserts the rare type of guardian who indeed does combine these two traits, and he begins to formulate the program that trains these rare peculiar people to cultivate properly the balance between these opposing qualities. The discussion of guardians who have a nature that is at once both gentle and fierce—two opposing qualities—is the first instance in the *Republic* of the peculiar case of opposing qualities being found in one and the same rare person.[36]

There is a second instance, at 503b-c, where we learn that philosophers are quick-witted but instead of being mercurial they are stable.[37] These passages indicate that good leaders can combine two qualities that are typically impossible to find in the same person.

However, at 485d-e it appears that Plato has Socrates say philosophers are thought not to engage in both the pleasures of body and of soul. Readers have been getting to know Plato's leaders up to this point in the *Republic*, and we have been led to expect these rare individuals to be able to combine within their character the ability to possess differing and even opposing traits. So, it ought to surprise us when that is not at all the picture at *Republic* 485d-e. There, Socrates acts as if the philosopher were not the rare one who can combine differing and even opposing traits. Plato writes:

> Now, we surely know that, when someone's desires incline strongly for one thing, they are thereby weakened for others, just like a stream that has been partly diverted into another channel. . . .
>
> Then, when someone's desires flow towards learning and everything of that sort, he'd be concerned, I suppose, with the pleasures of the soul itself by itself, and he'd abandon those pleasures that come through the body—if indeed he is a true philosopher and not merely a counterfeit one. . . .
>
> Then surely such a person is moderate and not at all a money-lover. It's appropriate for others to take seriously the things for which money and large expenditures are needed, but not for him. (*R.* 485d-e)

I will focus on a critical interpretation of the conception of philosophers that comes out of this passage at 485d-e, asking why Plato should think it would be impossible for philosophers to enjoy physical pleasures as part of the lifestyle that truly revels in intellectual pleasures. The standard interpretation of this passage is in tension with the example of Socrates's life. So either Socrates is a counterfeit philosopher or the austere interpretation of the hydraulic passage is incorrect. The former is a possibility Plato would not have us take seriously. So, we must question the standard interpretation of this passage, which scholars have used to define the philosophical lifestyle.

One possibility that I take quite seriously is that this odd position at 485d-e functions purposefully as a pedagogical moment in order to test Socrates's interlocutors, specifically Glaucon and Adeimantus. If this is a moment they (along with careful readers) should protest, saying something like, "Socrates, why would you say that, as it contradicts not only your own status and behavior but also the theme you have laid out concerning the philosopher's peculiar nature, which can paradoxically combine qualities that are not typically found in the same person?" But Glaucon and Adeimantus do not say any such thing, and many readers are in that position as well. As with several other tests that Glaucon and Adeimantus both fail and even fail to recognize,[38] this could be another instance of them "yessing" Socrates when they ought to challenge what he is claiming as inconsistent with other claims he has made about philosophers. They would succeed at Plato's pedagogical test if they understood the philosophical life well enough to know why philosophers are capable somehow of pulling off the counterintuitive feat of being passionately interested in intellectual pleasure while still participating in the act of enjoying physical pleasures, such as those of sating thirst, eating a delicious meal, being warmed by the fire in the hearth or erotic love in the bed, and so on.

Conversely, if Plato did not intend for the passage to be not a test for Adeimantus and Glaucon, what does Plato intend for it to mean? We must ask what the hydraulic model conveys about philosophy and the nature of philosophers and their way of life. Melissa Lane describes the drive portrayed in this passage as a "form of love . . . so powerful as to exert . . . a hydraulic effect: psychic energy flows into this love, depriving other desires of the energy to oppose or distract one from the desire to learn."[39] According to Lane, the hydraulic model indicates that real philosophers are so wholly occupied with their pursuit of the Forms that they have no energy for anything else, such as desire for physical pleasures. The logic of the hydraulic model asserts the following:

> Philosophers are lovers (*erôsin*) of learning (485b1), whose psychic energy flows so strongly into a loving pursuit of truth (485d3) that it saps the flow into bodily desires. This does not originate in a reasoned judgement [*sic*] that bodily desires

and experiences are unimportant, or in a deliberate policy of asceticism, by which they are forcibly suppressed. It originates rather in a hydraulic redirection of psycho-physiological energy effected by the sheer power of the love of learning in the soul of the natural philosopher.[40]

According to Lane, it takes the philosopher no reasoned judgment whatsoever to love nothing but the pursuit of truth. By this logic, it is not merely "bodily desires and experiences" for which the philosopher has no energy; anything that is not perceived as conducive to the pursuit of truth would not hold the philosopher's attention.[41] This sort of interpretation of 485d-e is characteristic of austere dualism.

On one hand, depending on how broadly we interpret what is conducive to the pursuit of truth, I would agree with Lane. If Lane were to include certain embodied activities as part of the pursuit of truth, such as the right kind of *erôs* or political engagement, then I would agree with her point about what the philosopher takes seriously and what the philosopher may manage, such as the body's needs, without considering important. But Lane does not interpret the pursuit of truth as broadly as I do. So, I take issue with her view that the authentic philosopher would never have any energy for engaging in this-worldly matters, such as political leadership or the right kind of erotic experiences.

In contrast to the austere view that Lane offers, I argue that the philosopher's attitude toward physical pleasure in the hydraulic model passage is one of *indifference* toward physical pleasure relative to intellectual pleasures rather than being an outright rejection of such pleasures. Plato's philosophers rank their love for the Forms ahead of the pleasures of the body in terms of importance, but they are not necessarily disinclined to experience and even enjoy embodied pleasures.[42] But they do not love pleasure. Still, philosophers need not operate at a distance from worldly pleasure even though it does not matter compared to the Forms.[43]

For instance, imagine the good feeling experienced by leaders working to improve their communities, whether it helps food get to the mouths that need it or to better educate the citizens. Even the work to improve education is a process that very much utilizes the body. Education may develop the life of the mind, but it involves all sorts of physical processes; even though the body has physical needs such as for food and sleep that can appear disruptive, teachers and students use voices that one way or another come through the body to communicate and as such the body enables human inquiry. How nice it would be for philosophers to appreciate the body on account of this.

126   Plato and the Body

Authentic philosophers can simultaneously be on a quest for understanding truth *and* engage in activities that may bring pleasures that come through the body. In particular, the normative dualist interpretation of Plato shows that the philosopher may enjoy physical pleasure, as we see Socrates do frequently, but the philosopher's soul is moderate and is not controlled by the appetite for such pleasure. While Plato's philosophers travel within the physical universe, it is easy to know what really matters and what is more trivial by comparison. However, while prioritizing their love of the Forms, Plato's philosophers will enjoy this-worldly pleasures.

How could Plato believe the philosopher does not experience physical pleasures, when Socrates clearly did? For Plato, Socrates is the model philosopher and certainly not a counterfeit. Socrates exemplifies a soul ordered properly enough to experience physical pleasures without attaching any inherent importance to them.[44] Socrates epitomizes the philosopher's unusual nature, which is uniquely capable of combining traits that usually grow only in separation.

The theme Plato imbues through the *Republic*—that philosophers can pull off rare feats of combining opposing qualities when the masses cannot—helps draw the oddity of the hydraulic passage to our attention. That passage offers up a distinction between real philosophers and other people, but what the interlocutors agree to misses the whole point. The *Republic* has been teaching us to be on the lookout for the rare natures that can somehow combine even opposing qualities (and Plato follows that up at *Timaeus* 18a).

We need look no farther than Socrates to see the paradox in action. Alcibiades emphasizes Socrates's extraordinary nature in his speech in the *Symposium*; he calls it Socrates's "bizarreness" (*Smp.* 215a) when he attributes both knowledge (217a) and a disavowal of knowledge (216d) to him. This bizarre human being is Plato's exemplar of the philosophical life. Part of what it means to examine Plato's conception of philosophy is to acknowledge his admiration for Socrates as the exemplar par excellence of the unusual philosophical nature. Plato's Socrates prioritizes the rational life over that of physical pleasure, while still participating in the enjoyment of physical pleasures. It should not be considered impossible for Plato's philosophers to desire physical pleasures as part of the lifestyle that so enjoys intellectual pleasures.

4.3.2 Misunderstandings and Mistaken Identities

Interpreting the hydraulic model passage also raises the question of whether or not the philosopher's love of learning is compatible with civic leadership. Can a genuine philosopher, who sincerely loves learning and whose desires totally flow in that direction, engage in political activity? Plato seems to think so when he has Socrates boldly claim that happiness can only be found where philosophers rule as kings and queens (*R.* 473c-e, 487e, 499a-b, 500e, 521a-b).[45] At 474b, after Glaucon warns him that saying such a thing would prompt many to do terrible, violent things to him on the spot, Socrates says, "If we're to escape from the people you mention, I think we need to define for them who the philosophers are that we dare to say must rule. And once that's clear, we should be able to defend ourselves by showing that the people we mean are *fitted by nature both to engage in philosophy and to rule in a city,* while the rest are naturally fitted to leave philosophy alone and follow their leader" (emphasis added). Plato's insistence that the philosophical life should involve concern for human affairs is on display. Here, we have a definition of the philosopher that includes *both* philosophizing and political leadership as integral to Plato's Socrates's conception of philosophy itself. When Plato later introduces the hydraulic model Adeimantus and Glaucon fail to make any connection between this definition of the philosopher and what is implied by the hydraulic model, failing what strikes me as another crucial test Plato has Socrates give them.

Socrates recognizes that he must define the philosopher, as he is aware that when he says philosophers should rule, his listeners probably imagine different people than he does (*R.* 499e–500a). In fact, Socrates reiterates many times that the biggest obstacle to people agreeing with him that philosophers are the ones best suited to rule is the problem of mistaken identity (*R.* 474b-c, 485a, 495c, 498d–499a, 499d–500b).[46] For Plato's Socrates, sophists and others who may be mixed up with philosophers are not philosophers.[47] Yet, philosophers are confused with those who persist with "the sophistications and eristic quibbles that, both in public trials and in private gatherings, aim at nothing except reputation and disputation" (*R.* 499a). Philosophers are mistaken for "those outsiders who don't belong and who've burst in like a band of revellers, always abusing one another, indulging their love of quarrels, and arguing about human beings in a way that is wholly inappropriate to philosophy" (*R.* 500b). The sophists and other quarreling quibblers have given philosophers the bad reputation that drives the violent response Glaucon anticipates for Socrates's claim that philosophers ought to rule.[48]

However, Socrates is certain that clearing up the philosophers' identity will immediately bring his doubters to agreement.[49] Consequently, in Book 5, Plato has Socrates define a philosopher as "someone who readily and willingly tries all kinds of learning, who turns gladly to learning and is insatiable for it" (*R.* 475c), "those who love the sight of truth" (*R.* 475e), "those who in each case embrace [*aspazomenous*] the thing itself" (*R.* 480a). Furthermore, he notes that those who meet these criteria will be few (*R.* 476b). The few who have knowledge of and love for the Forms are the ones Socrates envisions having the right nature for governing (*R.* 476d–480a).

After Plato has made political leadership integral to the conception of philosophy itself (*R.* 474b) and has emphasized the philosopher's rare nature, which is capable of being different and even opposing things, we should be taken aback when in Book 7 we learn of philosophers who "are unwilling to occupy themselves with human affairs" (*R.* 517c) and "refuse to go down again to the prisoners in the cave" (*R.* 519d), and that this is the outcome of their love of the Form of the Good (*R.* 517b-c). The conventional view of Platonism maintains that due to their passionate devotion to knowledge philosophers disdain human affairs and stay out of the political fray.[50] For austere dualist interpreters, the philosopher bogged down in civic leadership is a counterfeit or a has-been. According to this reading, real philosophers abandon the physical realm. The austere dualist interpretation would have us believe that if any of a person's desires flow toward something besides learning, then one's quest for learning is undermined. They define commitment to learning in terms of the outright rejection of the physical world,[51] which, in turn, requires shirking one's duty to the community.

"According to the contemplative ideal," McKeen writes, "philosophers should prefer a life far away from politics where they can practice philosophical contemplation without needless interruption and without any of the messy business of governing."[52] The interpretation McKeen aptly describes ignores the very title of the *Republic*, which could just as easily be translated "Public Business."[53] I would add that, when Plato sets up the conversation in the *Timaeus* as what occupied Socrates the very next day after the *Republic*'s discussion of human matters such as our personal and political character, he further directs us to recognize the philosopher's curiosity about the physical universe and the human beings in it.[54] Additionally, Mahoney observes that in many of Plato's judgment myths (*Grg.* 523a–527a, *Phd.* 107c–115d, *R.* 614b–621d, *Tim.* 41a–42d, *L.* 904a-c) "one's activities in the physical world profoundly affect how one fares on the next step in the journey; dying does not allow one to escape the ill effects of shirking one's this-worldly responsibilities."[55] Only on the austere dualist reading is shirking one's duties to one's community recommended as part of the best life a human being can choose. This interpretation deeply misunderstands the philosopher's love of the Forms and the commitments that spring from this love.

The few who by nature are passionately devoted to the philosophical life have a love for justice so deep that it creates an inclination for political matters, matters that affect them and their communities. The complication is that simultaneously authentic philosophers are aware that the political arena is messy and maddening for one who loves order and the Good. So, the natural philosopher is willing to rule in order to help repair the world through leadership but is also loath to be concerned with petty human affairs. Alongside their passion for improving cities and souls, these philosophers have their aversion to the disorder and corruption that typify the political arena. How does the philosophers' desire to lead fit together with their aversion to ruling? This may seem like a paradox. Yet, as we have already seen, throughout the *Republic* Plato emphasizes that philosophers are the rare, quirky sort of people capable of this peculiar combination of opposing qualities. In fact, for Plato's Socrates this combination of willingness and aversion is precisely what distinguishes the philosopher from the crowd of all too willing would-be rulers who do not love the Form of the Good and would, consequently, make bad rulers.

From the start of the *Republic*, Plato has Socrates establish an emphasis on the status of political leadership, raising concerns about eagerness to rule. Socrates warns about the voluntary rulers of the wrong sort and dreams of the right type of reluctance to rule (*R.* 347b-d). In Book 1, a good ruler is one who exhibits an important reluctance. In a conventional setting, where many construe political rule as an opportunity to use power to seek one's own advantage, it is philosophers who think they have better things to do with their own time and energy than to get involved in petty politics. They exhibit the same unattached attitude toward conventional politics that philosophers exhibit toward bodily passions in the *Phaedo*, *Symposium*, and *Phaedrus*, as we saw in chapters 2 and 3. Their preference for a contemplative life rather than the life of acquiring wealth and power over others accounts for their reluctance to take part in conventional politics.

These reluctant but willing rulers stand in sharp contrast with the candidates who are nothing but eager for the chance to use their power in service to their own personal agenda, say, to help their friends and harm their enemies. Once we are certain that leaders are not ruling in order to pursue their own petty agendas we can rest assured of their intention to rule with a focus on their individual mission to care for the city and the souls of its citizens. The citizen who prefers to do something other than rule is a great candidate for public trust (*R.* 520e–521b), and at *Republic* 521a-b Plato has Socrates say that only those who live a good and rational life look down on political offices. So, the principal tension here is that the ideal candidates for leadership seem to be the very people who are not eager to be involved in politics because there is a better life available to them, and that better life seems to be the life of exclusive contemplation. Let's investigate.

4.3.3 Loving the Good and Taking Refuge from Politics?

When philosophers are involved in the political matters of their communities, as Plato says they should be, despite their healthy aversion, are they making a personal sacrifice of their own happiness?[56] Many commentators think so, contending that Plato's philosophers wish they could be exclusively concerned with their own knowledge of the Forms but recognize that political duty requires a considerable personal sacrifice on the part of philosophers.[57] This position relies upon two main premises: (1) that exclusively contemplating the Forms is what philosophers prefer to do, if they are free to choose their activities in accord with their own nature, interests, and goals,[58] and (2) that involvement in political matters is an interruption from contemplation of the Forms.[59] Making such assumptions, these interpreters conclude that philosophers pursuing self-interest would not have time for or interest in looking down at human affairs, echoing the picture in the allegory of the cave. On the whole, I disagree with this point of view.[60] I will primarily argue against the second premise, which is wholly false owing to equivocations concerning the meaning of phrases such as "human affairs" and "political matters." Meanwhile, I will contend that the first premise is not quite accurate, even though it is a popular caricature of Plato's view.

What is misleading about the first premise, in my view, is that contemplating the Forms is what the philosopher *exclusively* prefers and expects.[61] Additionally, the first premise assumes that loving the Forms would require exclusive contemplation. The premise is built from the portrayal of the philosopher in the allegory of the cave. By indicating that the freed prisoner should not simply stay outside the cave but rather must go back into the cave to try to perform for others what someone did for him by coming back inside to drag him outside, the allegory of the cave reiterates the call for philosophers to take their turn when their leadership is needed (*R.* 519b–521b, 540b). There, Plato has Socrates describe a type of philosophers who become unwilling to do anything but direct their focus exclusively at the Form of the Good once they have seen it (*R.* 517c, 519d), who have a better life than ruling (*R.* 520e) just "living the greater part of their time with one another in the pure realm" (*R.* 520d), who would not fight with each other in order to rule (*R.* 521a), who despise political rule (*R.* 521b), who would have to be compelled to rule (*R.* 519e, 520a, 520e, 521b, 539e, 540b). Scholars have been eager to see the allegory of the cave's philosophers as good, decent men who care about justice and submit to rule, despite having to be compelled.[62] It ought to surprise us that those who allegedly care most about justice have to be compelled to offer their talents to their cities and fellow citizens.

These passages characterize contemplation of the Forms as particularly rewarding for the philosopher. Does that mean philosophers have something more important to do than being concerned with the happenings of the world inhabited by embodied human beings?[63] Not according to Irwin, who writes, "[S]upreme value does not imply all-inclusive value; [the philosopher] will also have reason to value other activities expressing his view of the best activities for all his life, and they will include more than philosophical thought."[64] Glaucon and Adeimantus would prove themselves to be more philosophically adept if at this point in the allegory of the cave they made an observation like Irwin's, noticing how different this philosopher in the allegory is from the philosopher Socrates introduced in Book 5. But they do not.

The main indications that philosophers are averse to ruling occur after Socrates turns his attention away from what Roslyn Weiss calls the "natural philosophers" of Books 5 and 6.[65] Weiss's thesis contends that in the *Republic* Plato presents us with not just one rendering of the philosopher. Weiss shows that the "natural philosopher," who is the subject of Books 5 and 6, is willing and able to lead, while the "philosopher by design," who is taken up in Book 7 and its allegory of the cave, is unwilling to lead despite having been trained to be able. I agree with Weiss that only the philosophers Plato discusses in Book 7's cave allegory mistake the transitory political matters of their cities as a waste of their understanding and love of unchanging Forms. Weiss's identification of Plato's distinction between these two philosophical paradigms successfully solves the puzzle that has long occupied commentators concerning why the philosophers in the cave allegory must be compelled to rule. The natural philosopher exhibits no reluctance whatsoever toward political leadership under the right conditions.[66]

Natural philosophers will be eager to rule if and when their leadership is needed to serve their communities. Weiss writes:

> The philosophers of Book 7, then, who do not wish to rule, and have to be persuaded or compelled to do so, have little in

common with the philosophers of Book 6, who do not wish to rule under reasonable conditions. . . . Book 6's philosophers do not share Book 7's aversion to the human realm: on the contrary, their souls always "reach out . . . for everything divine and *human.*" . . . Whereas Book 6's philosophers are thus generously willing to rule—without compensation—for the sake of improving the souls of others but are prevented from doing so by the corruption of their cities' regimes, Book 7's are selfishly averse to ruling even when their city has groomed them for just this task and eagerly awaits their guidance. (486a)[67]

Weiss's project of distinguishing two different philosophical paradigms in the *Republic* undercuts the assumption that all philosophers prefer the exclusively contemplative life. Thus, the first of our two questionable premises derives from what Socrates says of Book 7's "philosophers by design" who are precisely the ones *trained to prefer* the intelligible realm.

In the *Republic*, mysteriously, Plato has Socrates leave unvoiced the amount of time and energy he has invested in political activity. In fact, he goes out of his way to imply that he is one of the natural philosophers who does not engage in politics, who does his own work, taking refuge from the political storm around him (*R.* 496c-e). Additionally, in his trial defense Plato's Socrates uses himself as an example of one who has to keep away from politics. For instance, at *Apology* 31c-32a he explains that his divine sign turned him away from public affairs and that had he attempted political involvement he would "have died long ago." Then again at *Apology* 36b-c he indicates that he was "too honest to survive" if he occupied himself with "wealth, household affairs, the position of general or public orator or other offices, the political clubs and factions that exist in the city." Here, we see that Socrates felt compelled to disavow conventional political leadership; he did not attempt to rule over Athens. Is he really one of the "decent but useless" natural philosophers who are scared off from political leadership?

Despite believing that Weiss's distinction between natural philosophers and philosophers by design is accurate, I am inclined to disagree with her about how to classify Socrates using the framework of four philosophical types she examines. According to Weiss, *all* natural philosophers back away from political leadership; they never get the chance to be useful as leaders because "they've seen the madness of the majority and realized, in a word, that hardly anyone acts sanely in public affairs" (*R.* 496c). Weiss's interpretation of Book 6 concludes that the natural philosopher *inevitably* becomes unwilling to lead under bad circumstances. She focuses on 496a-e, where friends of justice take shelter from the storm in order to "lead a quiet life and do their own work" (*R.* 496d), and 501a, where leaders who want to make cities and souls imitate the Good as much as possible seem willing to do this work only if they can work with a clean slate.[68] Thus, Weiss finds it impossible to classify Socrates with these natural philosophers of Book 6 because his piety makes him actively fight for justice and try to improve human souls. Socrates never disengages, despite operating in the same maddening political arena as those who take "refuge under a little wall from a storm" (*R.* 496d). Weiss and I agree that, even though Socrates's daemonic sign keeps him out of conventional politics, he does not lead an apolitical life. In the *Apology,* Plato has Socrates state: "I have deliberately not led a quiet life" (36b). Socrates's life was not private at all. He did not simply enjoy grazing freely in the pastures of philosophy and doing nothing else (*R.* 498b-c). He was a deliberate leader, intentionally civically engaged. As a result, Weiss suggests Socrates is a fifth type of philosopher who exists implicitly in the *Republic.*

The minor disagreement I have with Weiss is in wondering whether Book 6 definitively rules out the possibility of a bifurcation of the natural philosophers who never get corrupted, who always want to promote goodness—with one subset who sits out of civic leadership because of living in exile among those who will not fight for justice (like the philosophers at 496b-d) and another subset who also lives exiled among those who will not assist in the fight for justice but who cannot resist the desire to try to improve cities and souls even if that will jeopardize one's survival (like Socrates).[69] Unlike Weiss, I consider Plato's Socrates a natural philosopher who is simply less scared off from the active life than the other natural philosophers who lack allies with whom to fight for justice. It is worth asserting this divergence from Weiss because the model of Socrates is so crucial to Plato. Using my suggested bifurcation of the natural philosopher category enables us to learn more about natural philosophers from Socrates's example.

Despite Plato's portrayal of the natural philosophers of Books 5–6 as disciplined students of *and* eager practitioners of the Good, one might imagine that political leadership undermines the philosopher's focus on contemplation of the Forms. Cooper imagines a philosopher, who has engaged in "the constant practice of philosophical argument and examination,"[70] assuming or resuming the political life. Cooper's conception of the philosophical way of life precludes the possibility of the philosopher-ruler. Of the philosopher who gets into politics, Cooper writes, "Their philosophically arrived at and supported commitments would be evident in many ways in their life, and it would not be unreasonable to call it a philosophical life. Nonetheless, the life would henceforward be that of an ordinary citizen, showing the effects of philosophy, but not itself a life *of* philosophy, of constant engagement in philosophical argument and analysis."[71] Cooper offers the example of the Roman statesman Cato, whom Seneca considers a wise man but not a philosopher because his life was not that of constant philosophical engagement.[72] Cooper himself notes that Cato supposedly even read philosophical books during campaigns.[73] How much more constantly would Cato need to engage in thinking about philosophy to count as a philosopher than if he immediately gets to it when back in his tent even in the middle of a military campaign? I'm not interested in pursuing a case for classifying Cato as a philosopher; rather, I'm intent upon showing that Cooper's definition of the philosophical way of life is hyperbolic.

While I agree with Cooper that, given Socrates's commitment to an ongoing examination of ideas, he exemplifies the philosophical way of life, I nevertheless disagree with Cooper's expectation of *constant* philosophical contemplation.[74] This exaggeration is born from ignoring the philosophers' embodiment as well as their regular occupation with the messy matters of trying to improve the souls around them as well as their cities. Even those who engage philosophical ideas enough to be considered philosophers by Cooper or Seneca do not engage in philosophical thinking constantly. Consider the example of Socrates, who is a philosopher interested in worldly matters. He pulls himself from his philosophical trances to engage the human world more often than not.

He demonstrates this variously, as I noted in chapter 1: Socrates eats and really enjoys a good feast (*Smp.* 220a); and, as we have already seen, he even requests meals as his reward for civic engagement (*Ap.* 36e–37a); he drinks, quite a bit (*Smp.* 220a); he sleeps (*Crt.* 44a; *Prt.* 310b-c; *Smp.* 223d); he enjoys the physical beauty of various people he knows (*Smp.* 212c, 216d, 218e; *Prt.* 309a-b, 316a; *Chrm.* 153d–154d, 155d); more importantly, Socrates is interested in the well-being of all human beings, his interlocutors, his friends and their loved ones; he has "given birth in beauty" to multiple children, creating and caring for his family (*Ap.* 34d; *Crt.* 60a); he has done military service (*Smp.* 219e; *Chrm.* 153b-d); he has served as a member of the Council and has responded when summoned by the Thirty (*Ap.* 32b-c); he has traveled to Piraeus for a religious festival (*R.* 327a);[75] and so on. Given Cooper's expectation of *constant* philosophical engagement, it's a wonder that Socrates's assorted activities do not disqualify him from being a philosopher in Cooper's view.

Cooper talks of those who neglect the good of the soul "by ranking some other value or values ahead of the soul's good condition: whatever the other values are that they go off, leaving philosophical argument aside, to pursue."[76] Cooper repeatedly uses the word *unrelenting* to describe the philosopher's effort to possess wisdom. He explains that "this they do day by day and as much of the day as they can manage."[77] How much of the day ought to be dedicated to philosophical endeavors is a matter of controversy. As we saw from Porphyry's comments in chapter 1, Plotinus looks at this issue much like Cooper appears to, demanding constant engagement in abstract contemplation. But Socrates is not Plotinus. For a philosopher such as Socrates, his whole life is teleologically oriented toward the love of wisdom and the care of the soul, even when he engages the world around him. His personal happiness absolutely stems from his rational lifestyle, but he illustrates that a rational life need not be *exclusively* contemplative. He not only includes erotic experiences of pleasure as part of his rational existence, as I showed in chapter 3, but also the political endeavors of a gadfly.

To think of the philosophical way of life as that of *constant* engagement in dialectic is an exaggeration. Consider in particular Socrates conversing with interlocutors for the sake of improving their souls. We can call this teaching, even though Socrates does not, especially if we keep in mind the sort of "teaching" Socrates does, instead of having in mind the more conventional sort of teaching that involves the simple transfer of ideas or information from a knower to a non-knower. Socrates routinely suggests that the mutual exchange of dialogue is beneficial for all involved in terms of facilitating the pursuit of knowledge.[78] Yet, usually Socrates is discussing a matter about which his interlocutor is clearly more novice than he.[79] If Socrates has previously thought something through, either on his own[80] or in dialogue with others, and he takes time to refute another person's ignorance concerning the matter that he has already understood, then his effort to assist another in making progress could be construed as an interruption from furthering his own understanding. In this regard, Socrates's philosophical coaching, his main form of civic engagement, could be seen as disrupting his own pursuit of any new knowledge.

However, there is no doubting that Plato sees his Socrates's life as one oriented toward philosophical contemplation at *every* turn—when he teaches a novice, when he readies himself for the next day's work by sleeping (which is not every night, as we know from the *Symposium*), and so on. We can get past thinking of the moments Socrates spends teaching as moments when he isn't philosophically engaged if we recall that, typically, sharing knowledge increases one's own knowledge.[81] We can say that Plato's own life is telling in this way as well. His deep attraction to the Forms is clear, but rather than exclusively contemplating them on his own or with others, he writes dialogues in hopes of shaping souls and cities.[82] For both Plato and Socrates, philosophy happens when human beings exchange dialogue rather than by any sort of withdrawn communion with the Forms. But it has been easy for many to misunderstand this because Plato puts such heavy emphasis on rejecting "sham values" and withdrawing from circles where they are upheld.[83] However, trying to rise above pernicious norms so commonplace that they are conventional is not at all equivalent to withdrawal from the physical world.

Whether we have in mind Socrates's or Plato's engagement with the world, either way none of it "fastened" them to the physical world in a way that impaired their ability to pursue truth. Throughout the corpus, Socrates's experiences in the human world are not at all depicted as "leaden weights," pulling his focus away from true things. Yet, at *Republic* 519a-b Plato has him suggest to Glaucon that these undesirable outcomes will occur unless one is "freed from the bonds of kinship with becoming." There is a tension between the model of Socrates (and the account of philosophers in Books 5 and 6) and the account here in Book 7. One way to think about what Plato has Socrates say in Book 7 is a strategy we have seen already in previous chapters, where we compare the attitude of someone like Socrates with that of a nonphilosopher. The nonphilosopher takes things such as "feasting, greed, and other such pleasures" as important, and because of this mistake they weigh the nonphilosopher down like "leaden weights." Think, for instance, of Glaucon's reaction to Socrates's vision of the healthy city for a clue as to Glaucon's nonphilosophical commitments to luxurious feasting, lounging on couches, and other pleasures (*R.* 372c-e). Because a philosopher such as Socrates has the proper perspective on such pleasures he can experience the physical world without compromising his sense of what is truly important.

In particular, Plato's Socrates exemplifies the leader's peculiar, apparently contradictory nature. He does engage passionately in political leadership, while eschewing conventional politics. In the *Gorgias*, he candidly admits his political inclination when he declares: "I believe I'm one of a few Athenians—so as not to say I'm the only one, but the only one among our contemporaries—to take up the true political craft and practice the true politics" (521d). However, in the *Apology*, Socrates offers a more ambiguous report on his own civic leadership. At two key points in his defense he offers a picture that dovetails with the account in the *Gorgias*:

I was attached to this city by the god—though it seems a ridiculous thing to say—as upon a great and noble horse which was somewhat sluggish because of its size and needed to be stirred up by a kind of gadfly. It is to fulfill some such function that I believe the god has placed me in the city. I never cease to rouse each and every one of you, to persuade and reproach you all day long and everywhere I find myself in your company. (*Ap.* 30e-31a)

I went to each of you privately and conferred upon him what I say is the greatest benefit, by trying to persuade him not to care for any of his belongings before caring that he himself should be as good and wise as possible, not to care for the city's possessions more than for the city itself, and to care for other things in the same way. (*Ap.* 36c-d)

As we see in these two parts of his defense, because of his daily endeavors to be a dialectical gadfly to anyone and everyone in his city Socrates could never be guilty of Cicero's charge that "hampered by their pursuit of learning they [the philosophers of the *Republic*] leave to their fate those whom they ought to defend" (1.9.28).[84] Socrates need not be ordered to be a leader in his community; he cannot stop himself. In this way, Plato uses Socrates as a counterpoint to the picture of the philosopher in the allegory of the cave, who must be compelled to be a leader. But even Socrates finds it more attractive to serve as gadfly-leader than to be a conventional ruler.[85]

In so many ways, Plato emphasizes our interdependence, hinting that justice has so much to do with the ways human beings need each other. Socrates makes clear that philosophers trying to lead require allies in their mission to repair the world by fashioning it as closely as possible after the Forms of Goodness, Justice, Beauty, and the like. Socrates worries that without such partners a philosopher fighting to instantiate Goodness might not even survive to labor another day. Of course, this foreshadows the trial and death of Socrates, which makes this sort of concern so tangible. And because would-be philosophers grow up already "kept down by exile" (*R.* 496a) from the sort of community that would be led by philosopher-rulers, they have "no ally with whom they might go to the aid of justice and survive" (*R.* 496c). Even if a philosopher can manage to be just, even when enveloped by an unjust society, s/he will be alone in the struggle to foster justice. So, with respect to public affairs the philosopher has at least two problems: (1) managing the temptations involved in being surrounded by injustice and (2) being alone in the struggle to foster justice.

It is no wonder, then, that Plato has Socrates muse that the best natural philosophers can hope for while being kept down by exile is to live quiet lives, being satisfied if somehow they can live "free from injustice and impious acts and depart from it with good hope, blameless and content" (R. 496d-e). Does Plato's Socrates sincerely believe that the natural philosophers who turn away from leadership truly love the Good? Is it possible for a philosopher to love the Good and nevertheless take refuge from ruling? Brown thinks so. He writes, "Plato recognizes, that the circumstances matter to what is just and unjust, and so it is reasonable to think that under some circumstances, the philosopher would prefer not to rule while under other circumstances, they would prefer to rule."[86] Meanwhile, Mahoney questions the permanence of any disengagement; he interprets Plato as suggesting a pattern of disengagement followed by reengagement.[87] I am inclined to agree that perhaps those who temporarily take refuge return to their journey eventually after taking shelter from the storm (R. 496d), after a rest and time for reflection.

Observe the sharp contrast in tone between the quietism at *Republic* 496 and Callicles's claim in the *Gorgias* when he indicates that the philosopher "becomes unmanly and avoids the centers of his city and the marketplaces . . . and, instead, lives the rest of his life in hiding, whispering in a corner with three or four boys, never uttering anything well-bred, important, or apt" (485d-e).[88] Callicles's pejorative characterization of the quiet philosophical life will not be attractive to Adeimantus and Glaucon, but the type of quietism Socrates mentions at 496d-e appeals to them a great deal. Ferrari argues:

> What [Glaucon and Adeimantus] want to hear now from Socrates is a proof that the quietist is a just man too, indeed, the most just of men. They are not so interested in the proof that justice beats injustice; they are already confident that it does (347e). What they want is a new account of justice that fits with the path of withdrawal and self-containment that they have chosen. (358b, 367b, e)[89]

Hence, Socrates takes on the challenge of leading Glaucon and Adeimantus away from the view that "quietism is the best recourse in their imperfect world."[90] This is difficult because a quiet life of doing philosophical work (R. 496d) is a very tempting refuge in an unjust circumstance. The conclusion of the *Republic* reinforces this lure when Odysseus is depicted as "looking for the life of a private individual who did his own work" (620c). But Odysseus is of course not a philosopher, and neither are Glaucon and Adeimantus. Perhaps the life of quiet refuge merely baits them as Socrates prepares to introduce a few pages later his notion that anyone who really loves the Good looks in both directions, so to speak, using the Good as the model and the world's souls and cities as the canvas (*R*. 501b). More on this important passage shortly.

4.3.4 Loving the Good and Leading Communities

According to the logic that Lane proposes in interpreting the hydraulic model at *Republic* 485d-e, Socrates should not have any psychic energy left for any political endeavors, given that as a philosopher his love of learning flows so strongly into the pursuit of truth. According to the austere dualist interpretation of the hydraulic model, Socrates ought to be just like the philosophers in the allegory of the cave who have no interest in, let alone passion for, civic engagement at all. Yet, Plato's Socrates is an exemplar of a leader who need not be compelled; instead, he exhibits the kind of piety that drives one to be a leader even when forces, such as the threat to one's survival, constrain one in favor of not leading.[91]

For Socrates, being a good man who cares about justice necessitates being what Vlastos calls "a street philosopher" and Goldstein calls "a philosophical urban guerrilla."[92] In fact, Russell contends that "no philosopher has ever been portrayed as more fully a part of his world and the lives of the neighbors he finds in it."[93] And Vlastos explains that Socrates took "to the streets, forcing himself on people who have neither taste nor talent for philosophy, trying to talk them into submitting to a therapy they do not think they need."[94] This did not make Socrates popular, but it did make him a leader. And to hear Alcibiades tell it, Socrates "transported, completely possessed" everyone—"man, woman, or child"—whether they were inclined to take public speakers seriously or not (*Smp*. 215d). As Klosko writes, "In keeping with the traditional Greek view that a chief responsibility of the *polis* is to see to the moral betterment of its citizens, Socrates' goal must be judged 'political.' "[95]

The Socrates of the *Apology* is very pessimistic about the prospects of someone like him being able to engage in a sustained public effort to defend and pursue justice, to improve his city (31c-32a). Bobonich remarks, "If the likelihood of educational success in Athens and other extant cities is sufficiently low and the costs of trying sufficiently high, Socrates might reasonably recommend withdrawal from public activity."[96] Think, for example, of how Plato has Socrates tell Protagoras that he will withdraw from their conversation and depart unless Protagoras ceases giving long speeches (*Prt.* 335a–336b).

However, in reality nothing could keep Socrates out of the agora, out of the Piraeus, out of people's business at Callias's or Agathon's or the courthouse steps or the outskirts of town, and so on, even when pressured to not make such trouble, even when not terribly optimistic about the characters he was trying to mold. Miller reminds us that "nothing external has either 'compelled' or enticed him to this extraordinary generosity."[97] For Miller, it is being moved by the Good that results in Socrates's extraordinary generosity. Miller continues:

> In his repeated descents "into the cave," Socrates [is] "imitating and fashioning himself after the model of" the Good, he gives himself to others . . . it is only fitting that Socrates chooses to "take the Good as a model" and, as a consequence, gives himself over to the task of ruling, that is, of "bringing order to the city and other individuals and himself." He is only, as it were, "being what he is," expressing in his deeds what he has come to know as his own substance.[98]

The model of Socrates must give us pause before we presume that the rational ideal is incompatible with a desire to pay attention to such worldly considerations as erotic love or the political concerns of human communities.

Yet, multiple passages in the corpus seem to relay the message that philosophers stand apart from this world. Consider, for instance, *Republic* 604b-c where Plato has Socrates say that "human affairs aren't worth taking very seriously" (*ti tôn anthrôpinôn axion on megalês spoudês*), or *Laws* 803b where the Athenian says, "Not that human affairs are worth taking very seriously—but take them seriously is just what we are forced to do, alas" (*esti dê toinun ta tôn anthrôpôn pragmata megalês men spoudês ouk axia, anagkaion ge mên spoudazein: touto de ouk eutuches*). Meanwhile, at *Phaedrus* 249c-d, Plato has Socrates mention philosophers "standing outside of human concerns" (*existamenos de tôn anthrôpinôn spoudasmatôn*). At first glance this may seem to reflect an "otherworldly" view of philosophy. However, Socrates refers to the philosopher's focus on what is truly real in comparison with what merely passes for real in the earthly realm of things. And the very wings Plato's Socrates claims are essential to trying to grasp the Forms in the *Phaedrus* are fueled by this-worldly beauty. The

Forms as more real than, say, petty human concerns, but many human concerns still matter; they just are not worth taking as seriously because of their ever-changing, temporary nature. (See also 2.3.)

Let's now explore how philosophers could classify their political engagement as congruent with the philosophical commitment to lead a contemplative life. In other words, if the natural philosophers do not experience an *exclusively* contemplative life because they are involved in political leadership when their turn comes, how is that they are still focused on their beloved Forms, even when they are engaging in civic leadership? The two critical passages shedding light on the issue of the philosopher's attitude toward this world of human beings and earthly institutions are *Republic* 500c–501c and 540a-b. After Plato has Socrates say, "No one whose thoughts are truly directed towards the things that are . . . has the leisure to look down at human affairs" (*R.* 500b), he begins to finesse what he means by this claim. At first glance, this appears to suggest that the philosopher is exclusively dedicated to the study of the Forms, never taking on civic leadership. But in fact we shall see that Socrates advocates for a conception of the philosopher's work that is emphatically *not* otherworldly. At every turn, the *Republic* reminds us that philosophers ought to be concerned with the community's problems and put right what they can.

The passage makes use of a craft analogy, comparing philosophers to painters, the cities and souls they can improve to canvases, and the Forms to the models (*R.* 500e–501a).[99] Plato writes:

> Then the philosopher, by consorting with what is ordered and divine and despite all the slanders around that say otherwise, himself becomes as divine and ordered as a human being can. . . . And if he should come to be *compelled* to put what he sees there into people's characters . . . instead of shaping only his own . . . [would] look often in each direction, towards the natures of justice, beauty, moderation, and the like, on the one hand, and towards those they're trying to put into human beings, on the other. (*R.* 500c–501b; emphasis added)

Here, Socrates has confidence that a philosopher who truly understands the Form of Justice will also try to repair the world by transforming it as much as possible into something that participates in the Form of Justice.[100] At the conclusion of Book 7, Plato has Socrates reiterate the idea, using the same language of the Form of the Good being the philosopher-ruler's model (*R.* 540a-b). There, Plato writes, "And once they've seen the good itself, they must each in turn put the city, its citizens, and themselves in order, using it as their model" (*R.* 540a-b).

Plato has Socrates make clear that philosophers can and should use the Good as their model for ordering the city and the souls of others and themselves. In Weiss's words, "The philosophers do not simply impose their vision of the just, noble, and moderate on human souls, but rather, in an iterative procedure, they 'look away frequently (*pukna*) in both directions' (501b) and 'rub one thing out and draw in another again (*palin*)' (501c)."[101] Commentators are familiar with the aspect of Plato's thought that looks *from* things *toward* Forms, but this passage calls significant attention to the need to look in the other direction as well, *from* Forms *toward* things (*R.* 501b). The philosopher-leader honors the Good by steering the community toward a greater share of it. Put another way, Plato's philosopher-leaders have a sense that their community could be better than it is; they recognize the potential in themselves, in their fellow citizens, and in their civic institutions to imitate Forms such as the Good, Beauty, and Justice, in particular.

The philosopher's love for the Forms flows toward ordering the physical universe as much as possible after the Form of the Good. As Irwin puts it, "Plato assumes that the philosopher's knowledge of the Forms will create the desire to express his knowledge in his actions. . . . Plato assumes that whatever someone comes to value in the ascent he will also want to propagate . . . he wants to create as well as possess."[102] Philosophers can love the Form of the Good *and* use it as the model they imitate as they lead their communities. In Socrates's daily routine, we see the way in which the thoughtful pursuit of the Forms is relevant to the philosophical-political work of shaping characters and communities into their most virtuous versions. Philosophers' self-interest and overall chosen goals to love, pursue, and imitate Justice, Goodness, Beauty, etc. are not surrendered but furthered when they bring their rational nature to the work of serving as leaders in their communities.

An important question that emerges is whether or not this broadly construed notion of leadership should be referred to as political rule. We saw above that Miller takes Socrates to be engaged in the task of ruling. One might object to this on the grounds that ruling is a more narrow concept than merely bringing order to a disorderly world. One might suggest that there is an important difference between being a leader, which I have demonstrated Socrates was, and being a ruler, the sort of position from which both Plato and his Socrates took refuge. However, I am inclined to agree with Miller's broader construal of the task of ruling. In the *Gorgias*, Plato has Socrates reject the narrow notion of politics as holding public office when he defines politics as the care of the soul, which he says consists of legislation and justice (464b).[103] Following that lead, we can construe the political craft broadly enough that it does not require being a conventional ruler. Leaders can be rulers *or* gadflies, because leadership is not about a position or title but about a way of being.

I would also include an additional reason for the philosopher to see shaping cities and souls as compatible with philosophical goals. A philosopher pursues knowledge of the Form of Justice through philosophical contemplation, but it is typical that this learning process begins with thinking through what is gathered from sense perception of things that participate—to whatever extent—in the Form of Justice. Philosophers find access to the Forms, at least in part, through paying attention to whatever has a share in those Forms, as we have already seen in chapters 2 and 3. So wherever rulers can make their communities more exemplary of the Forms, especially Justice, Goodness, and Beauty, they will try to, and when they do, they will be further enabling thinkers in the community to begin the process of recollecting the Forms from their sensory experiences of those earthly things that participate in the Forms of Justice, Goodness, and Beauty.

Neither finding nor creating images of the Forms in physical things and earthly institutions will provide the philosopher with the same happiness as the beatific vision of the Forms. Yet, Plato's notion that things *participate* in the Forms is central to his understanding of how visible things are associated with invisible Forms (see *Phd.* 73c–75b). As we have already established, sense perception of the things that have a share in the Forms is a significant aspect of theoretical contemplation insofar as sense perception begins the process of recollecting the Forms. So, one who loves the Forms will want others to come to greater knowledge of the Forms through perceptions of a world with the greatest possible share in the Forms.[104] I argue that this is one of the ways a philosopher can "return to the cave" because the more philosophers enable their communities to embody the Good, the more readily future philosophers may begin the process of recollecting the Form of the Good.

Genuine philosophers love wisdom and the Forms, and yet they want to shape cities and souls in the image of the Form of the Good. My normative dualist interpretation allows real philosophers to engage the embodied world in any manner that honors the Good. Here, the Form of the Good is their primary beloved. Nonetheless, when the philosopher-leader wants cities and souls to be improved as much as possible, having the greatest possible share of the Form of the Good, this is an act of love for this-worldly cities and souls.[105] The work philosophers do with this second set of beloveds is imitative. By this I mean that the philosophical leader wants to help cities and the souls in them to be remade in the image of the Good as far as possible. Of course, imitation and images have a second-rate status in Plato's metaphysics of authenticity.[106] However, the nature of the critique of imitation in Book 10 applies to those who are *not* using the Form of the Good as their model and thus would not be applicable to the philosopher who is trying to make this world and the souls in it imitate the Form of the Good as much as possible.[107]

The philosopher-leader's imitation ranks higher for Plato than the imitations performed by craftsmen such as painters and carpenters who imitate mere appearances rather than Forms. At 500d, the philosopher is compared favorably with other craftsmen due to imitating the Form of the Good while shaping souls and cities. A more direct comparison occurs where Socrates alludes to the craftsman who "tries in each case to imitate the thing itself in nature" (*R.* 597e–598a). This imitator is judged more favorably than the painters and sculptors who imitate appearance instead of Forms.

Even though the task will not be easy, natural philosophers are fervent about molding themselves, the city, and their fellow citizens after the Forms. It is the pettiness, which so often typifies political life, that the philosopher loathes. Nonetheless we must be cautious to equate looking down on pettiness neither with abhorrence of the physical world nor with disengagement from civic leadership.[108] The philosopher is the one who serves the community by actually knowing how to do what is best, while would-be leaders dream of how nice it would be if good outcomes could only happen somehow. On this reading, Plato's philosopher "is a good maniac,"[109] willing and eager to do this work wherever conditions are such that the work needs to be done. A "good maniac" would most enjoy living in pure, disembodied kinship with the Good, but given that that is not available to the embodied philosopher, the next best thing would be to operate in a world that already participates in the Forms to the greatest extent possible. If philosophers were fortunate enough to inherit such a world, then it would be optimal enough not to need to be put into better order by philosopher-rulers.[110] Yet, even under such circumstances philosophers would still be needed as leaders in order to sustain this participation in the Good. And, of course, when the world's cities and souls are in need of a greater share of Goodness, then philosophers must both contemplate the Forms and use them as models for shaping souls, institutions, and cities in need of repair.

Commitment to political leadership is, therefore, an essential aspect of a real philosopher's commitment to the Forms. For philosophers, especially those situated in adverse conditions, the desire to attend exclusively to the Forms is unfitting.[111] The leader who understands the Form of the Good will want to see the world participate in that Goodness as much as possible. A life focused on one's own virtue and knowledge is an achievement, involving love of the Forms, and the life focused on both the care of one's own soul as well as the souls of others too—the life of political leadership—is certainly focused differently, albeit no less focused on the Form of the Good. The political life is different insofar as it involves not just self-care but also an obligation to look after others.[112] However, for Plato, the love of human beings is still secondary to loving the Forms, especially the Form of the Good.[113] When philosophers take up the mantle of political leadership we should not presume that this interrupts the philosophical life. Socrates hints that ruling a city is part of the very same love at play in loving wisdom, immediately after defining the philosopher as one who loves truth and learning, when he claims that one loves all of what one loves (*R*. 474c). Philosopher-rulers are not disrupting their study of and love for the Forms; they are working on their mastery of the Forms from a different direction, in a very impactful way. Thus, it would be a mistake to assume that one whose energy flows toward learning could not be focused on the Forms while simultaneously welcoming participation in the effort to improve cities and souls.[114]

My view coincides with the position that Irwin, Kraut, and some others take,[115] that real philosophers will understand how their political leadership is actually in line with their philosophical interests and goals.[116] Good leadership must constantly be mindful of the Form of the Good. These natural philosophers see leadership as part of their project to love and embrace the Forms, relishing the chance to fashion their community as much as possible after the beatific vision of the Forms. In this regard, *R*. 500c–501c and *R*. 540a-b echo Diotima's claim in the *Symposium* that "by far the greatest and most beautiful part of wisdom deals with the proper ordering of cities and households, and that is called moderation and justice" (*Smp*. 209a-b). In an intriguing way, Plato has Diotima indicate that the best of wisdom involves the art of politics. Philosophers love wisdom, and therefore of course they will actually love the part of wisdom that deals with the proper ordering of cities and souls.

I agree with Kraut when he argues that Plato's conception of philosophy is one single-mindedly focused on "the project of imitating the Forms" rather than "more narrowly" just contemplating them.[117] Kraut contends that ruling instead of living the purely theoretical life does not involve rejecting the ideal of imitating Forms, whereas to refuse to lead is to reject the Forms as models.[118] And he explains that "the best sort of human life is one which is dedicated to the project of imitating the Forms and in which one never does anything to reject them as a model."[119] Authentic philosophers can have enthusiasm for civic engagement because they understand that if one loves the Forms, then one will feel compelled to express that love by, as Diotima says in the *Symposium*, giving birth in beauty (*Smp.* 206a–208b).[120]

In the context of political leadership, one expresses this love with the compulsion to model cities and souls after the Forms as much as possible. To be clear, the compulsion that moves the "natural philosophers" of Book 6 is quite different in nature from the compulsion referred to later in the *Republic* in connection with the "philosophers by design." The natural philosophers' compulsion is a *desire from within* about which they are enthusiastic and from which they would never and could never relent.[121] In contrast, the compulsion of the philosophers by design is imposed externally through law, and ruling is a position about which they are not at all happy and which they would keenly relinquish.

Concerning compulsion, there is also a key distinction in terms of the upbringing of the two types of philosophers. The very category of "designed" philosopher exists because in Book 7 Plato has Socrates make clear that one way to produce a kind of philosopher is to have the city educate a certain type of person "better and more completely" than the others (*R.* 520b). Philosophers by design owe a debt for their upbringing, and what the city planned all along was for that debt to be paid by these people taking on the work of educating others so that down the road "the city will be governed, not like the majority of cities nowadays, by people who fight over shadows and struggle against one another in order to rule—as if that were a great good—but by people who are awake rather than dreaming" (*R.* 520c-d). Justice requires the designed philosophers to be leaders, but the same is not exactly true of natural philosophers, those who have "grown spontaneously, against the will of the constitution." Book 7 contends that natural philosophers would be "justified in not sharing in their city's labors" (*R.* 520a-b) because they have not received an education provided by the city. Should one think that natural philosophers are compelled to be leaders because they owe the city for the elite education they received from the city they would be wrong. What drives natural philosophers like Socrates to shape cities and souls for the better is something altogether different: love for and attention to the Form of the Good compels the natural philosopher to take the lead in helping this world and its people and institutions better imitate the Form of the Good. It is this *erôs* that provides the philosopher's political energy and initiative.[122]

4.4 Justice as Political Harmony

The main appeal of the quiet individual life is that it appears to protect oneself from the additional vulnerabilities involved in putting oneself out there in the political arena. Concentrating on the individual soul, Socrates tells us that "nothing terrible will happen to you if you really are an admirable and good man, one who practices excellence" (*Grg.* 527d). This suggests that the soul is one's real self and that our precious true selves are fortunately in no danger from the injustice of others. This point of view puts all the responsibility for the state of one's soul on oneself. That seems fortunate, given that one's own virtue and therefore happiness are thus within one's own control. The consolation offered by this position is encapsulated by Plato's Socrates's claim that "a good man cannot be harmed either in life or in death" (*Ap.* 41d).

For all the solace that derives from this belief, there is much that can be perilous in believing that the soul alone is one's true self. This view may tempt us to think that what happens to bodies does not really matter. For instance, Plato asserts that it matters how one lives rather than how long one lives (*Grg.* 512e; cf. *Ap.* 38e and *Cri.* 48b). If we were to adopt this perspective completely, we would not necessarily worry about victims of starvation or physical attack, such as those who are assassinated, because they are not perpetrators of injustice. In addition, where people operate with a paradigm that considers physical bodies insignificant, injustice against bodies may not even strike us as all that unjust, as unfortunately happens at times, for instance in cases of rape. The danger posed by thinking of the soul as the real self is that it downplays the vulnerability of our bodies, highlighting that victims' souls have nothing to fear. Plato reminds us not to fear death, but he is nonetheless concerned about bodies and interested in fostering health and peace.

While this project has certainly demonstrated that the body has secondary status to the soul in Plato's thought, that status is not to be confused with utter disregard for human bodies. For instance, in the *Phaedo*, Socrates does not think it matters how his friends bury his body (115c–116a) but that is not the same as loathing the body or thinking of the body as so trivial that it does not warrant respectful, customary treatment. Plato goes out of his way to indicate his sense of the appropriate way to respect a corpse. First, he has Socrates explicitly say that they should bury his body "in any way you like and think most customary" (*Phd.* 116a). And Socrates is portrayed as believing that cleansing the body is customary, and he chooses to experience the bath "and save the women the trouble of washing the corpse" (*Phd.* 115a). This is an additional instance of Plato regarding something as secondary in status but still worthy of thoughtful treatment.

If it doesn't really matter how long one gets to live, should we not take it as an injustice when someone is murdered or starves to death? Austere dualists might interpret Plato as maintaining that so long as one is not the doer of injustice, then one need not devote one's attention to world's events. While Plato's Socrates argues that being the perpetrator of injustice is far worse than being the victim of injustice (*Grg.* 466c–469c), I disagree with those who think that Plato and his Socrates are indifferent to the world's events.[123] I shall demonstrate that real-world matters of injustice are of great concern to Plato, even if how long one gets to live is less important to Plato than how virtuously one lives. He has Socrates worry deeply about issues of violence, war, poverty, disease, and so on.

4.4.1 Plato's Emphasis on the Dangers of Poverty

Let's look for a moment at a contemporary situation. In the twenty-first century there is a tremendous difference between the average life expectancy of, for example, a Japanese or Swiss person (more than eighty years) and that of a resident of, say, Lesotho or Sierra Leone (less than fifty years). If it doesn't really matter how long one gets to live, then we would not be disturbed by the factors that give citizens of sub-Saharan Africa nearly half the life expectancy of citizens of developed nations such as Switzerland. Even within the United States there are noteworthy differences in life expectancy across the population. For example, African Americans have a shorter life expectancy than any other racial group in the U.S. except Native Americans. There are many relevant factors here, including political life in one's neighborhood. For instance, within the city of Baltimore, the life expectancy of the residents of the Federal Hill/Inner Harbor area is on average just about twenty years longer than the life expectancy of the residents of West Baltimore (location of the 2015 uprising). Such a divergence among citizens' experience of life suggests the city may not be cohesive, that is, not as healthy and stable for some as for others. This discrepancy is just one among many signals that, as Lötter writes, "[p]hilosophers today still have to confront the dramatic consequences of the vastly unequal distributions of poverty and wealth on both local and global scale."[124] As I will show, Plato was the first philosopher to recognize this.

However, one disturbing aspect of the austere dualist interpretation of Plato is its presumption that bodies and what happens to them (and, by extension, social-political communities that are linked to the body's needs) are irrelevant to a philosopher's sphere of interest.[125] However, I reject the interpretation that claims Plato has no regard for human bodies in particular or the physical world in general. Such an interpretation cannot be correct because it is incompatible with Plato's significant emphasis on poverty and its divisive effect upon communities. Most commentators have neglected to appreciate the centrality in the *Republic* of Plato's warning about the calamity of poverty.[126] In contrast, I will show that Plato is deeply concerned about poverty and its destabilizing effects on individuals as well as on society as a whole.

Before Plato, Thales had already demonstrated that philosophers are able to make money but that they are not interested in financial pursuits, and after Plato, the Cynics and Stoics esteem the choice to live a simple life, eschewing wealth. Plato is at the center of this landscape.[127] Nonetheless, despite this detachment from wealth and admiration of chosen poverty and despite the aristocratic tenor Plato plants in the *Republic* through interlocutors such as Glaucon and Adeimantus,[128] Plato's Socrates certainly understands the material requirements of embodied life.

Not once but twice in the *Republic*. Plato has Socrates explicitly assert that poverty rips communities apart. At *Republic* 422e–423a, Socrates claims that a city containing poverty may appear to be one city while it is in fact "two cities at war with one another, that of the poor and that of the rich. . . . If you approach them as one city, you'll be making a big mistake." More than one hundred Stephanus pages later, Plato has Socrates reiterate his contention that a city containing a disparity of wealth and poverty will lack unity and stability when he says that the oligarchic city is "not one city but two" (*R.* 551d). Between these instances, Plato has Socrates indicate the importance of community cohesion when he uses the finger argument to define civic unity as the pleasures or pains of anyone in the city being felt by the city as a whole (*R.* 462). While he does not expressly mention poverty there at 462a-b, he again declares that there isn't "any greater evil we can mention for a city than that which tears it apart and makes it many instead of one," and no greater good "than that which binds it together and makes it one." He has Socrates use the finger analogy to lead Glaucon to the conclusion that the best governed city will be so cohesive that "whenever anything good or bad happens to a single one of its citizens" it "will say that the affect part is its own and will share in the pleasure and pain as a whole" (*R*. 462d-e). He commits to this again when Socrates reminds Glaucon that for a city the "height of good government" includes having a common way of life for all, whether in war or peace (*R*. 543a). I agree with Waterfield's contention that "Plato simply takes the value of the unity of the state as self-evident."[129] Plato depicts the harmonious ordering of a soul's aspects and of a city's classes as being of paramount importance. Having defined civic unity as the pleasures or pains of anyone in the city being felt by the city as a whole, Plato's Socrates has committed himself to the claim that in a truly cohesive community poverty would never be tolerated, because the pains of the poor would be felt by all, motivating the community to establish the conditions that stamp out poverty as thoroughly and swiftly as possible.

What disrupts harmonious unity within souls and cities? On one hand, scholarly attention has made embodiment out to be practically the entire cause for Plato of "war, civil discord and battles" (*Phd*. 66c), and on the other hand, the secondary literature has infrequently addressed the role of embodiment in the pursuit of justice and peace at all. For instance, it is striking that many scholars have been so underwhelmed by the accomplishments at hand in Socrates's healthy city, the *Republic*'s First City.[130] To consider a community working collaboratively to meet all of its citizens' needs as a small thing intimates how irrelevant the demands of embodied existence appear to such a mind.[131] Andrew sees Plato as someone who makes that sort of mistake, as someone whose wealth caused him to disregard the material realities of embodiment.[132] I disagree. Let us turn now to the rest of my evidence that Plato does not leave the physical body outside the sphere of a philosopher's concern, first considering Socrates as an exemplar of the ideal philosophical nature, who is himself not at all inattentive to the physical, and then looking more broadly at the claims throughout the *Republic* concerning the political problems posed by poverty.

In the *Apology*, Plato has Socrates explain the burden that his chosen poverty placed on his family (31b). Then, after being found guilty Socrates proposes a "penalty" for himself that feeds "a poor benefactor who needs leisure to exhort you" (*Ap*. 36d). He continues:

> Nothing is more suitable, gentlemen, than for such a man to be fed in the Prytaneum much more suitable for him than for any one of you who has won a victory at Olympia with a pair or team of horses. The Olympian victor makes you think

yourself happy; I make you be happy. Besides, *he does not need food, but I do.* So if I must make a just assessment of what I deserve, I assess it as this: free meals in the Prytaneum. (*Ap.* 36d; emphasis added)[133]

Here, Plato uses the son of working-class parents (a stonemason and a midwife) to remind us that philosophers cannot make their important contributions to society without something to eat and leisure time to philosophize.[134] Normally, an aristocrat would prize these meals at the Prytaneum for their glory rather than for the financial reward,[135] but for Plato's Socrates both are relevant, given his poverty. Plato also has Socrates indicate his poverty at *Republic* 338b, saying "I have no money." Saxonhouse notes that in the *Symposium*, Poverty (Eros's mother) has characteristics that remind us of Socrates himself—shoelessness, taking breaks on porches, sleeping on bare ground, always living in need.[136] And Ferrari observes penniless Socrates's prayer at the end of the *Phaedrus* (279b-c) for external possessions "in friendly harmony with what is within" and for "gold . . . as much as a moderate man could bear."[137]

Andrew suggests that in proposing a punishment of free maintenance by the state in the *Apology*, "Socrates may have been demanding something akin to state support for philosophers, an early form of tenured professorship or an alternative to dependence on the wealthy."[138] The idea here is that Socrates earns this support through his work as a philosopher, conversing with and questioning anyone who is interested. This might seem a strange thing for Andrew to suggest, given Socrates's repudiation of having been anyone's teacher and of taking fees in exchange for the questioning and discussion he conducts in the agora (*Ap.* 33a-b). He disavows the teaching profession, but Socrates's important work would not be possible if he lacked any and all means of support, especially given that he offers himself not only to the wealthy but also to the poor (*Ap.* 33b).

Instead of being a wage laborer, Socrates receives gifts from wealthier friends;[139] Plato alludes to his own and others' eagerness to support Socrates financially (*Ap.* 38b).[140] Without his own independent wealth or his wealthy friends' gifts, Socrates would not be in a position to make his philosophical contribution to his community. His opportunity to work on philosophy would either be limited or made altogether impossible if Socrates had to attend to the constant routine of providing for himself and his dependents the basics needed for survival. Consider, for instance, how Plato's Socrates sees the need to spare the guardians "the perplexities and sufferings involved in . . . making the money necessary to feed the household" (*R.* 465b-c) by depriving them of private property and making sure the producer class provides them with what they need (R. 416c–417a).

Plato's experience as an aristocrat probably would not have helped him to understand the consequences of not having one's basic needs for food, water, and shelter met. So, perhaps it was the influence of the historical Socrates, one of the "have-nots,"[141] that helped Plato develop his perspective on the realities of embodied existence.[142] In any event, Plato is intent on demonstrating his sensitivity to the way people need each other; in the *Republic* particularly, he exhibits deep concern about poverty and a multidimensional understanding of its impact on individuals and the community. It is very significant that Plato recognizes poverty as an enemy of individual health and civic unity.

He takes up all the following variety of concerns about poverty. He has Cephalus indicate that poverty can put one in a circumstance to feel forced to cheat or deceive others "against our will" (R. 331b); he has Socrates follow that up, saying that wherever there are beggars there will be thieves (R. 552d). Socrates also claims that while people honor the vicious for their wealth and power (R. 364a), "they dishonor and disregard the weak and the poor, even though they agree that they are better than the others" (R. 364a-b).[143] Later he adds that poverty leads to flattery of the rich (R. 465b). It also humbles one and can led to a propensity for being appetitive toward money, valuing money above all else (R. 553b-c); that valuing money above all else leads to inattention to education (R. 554b); that valuing money above all else leads to the neglect of virtue (R. 550e, 555c). He expresses concern for the vulnerability of those in the care of foster families (R. 554c). In addition to criticizing predatory lending (R. 555c), Plato notes that poverty leads one to get into debt and then have to pay it off (R. 464c). He observes that lacking property can lead to disenfranchisement (R. 553a). Poverty causes one to lack the proper tools or resources to do one's work well (R. 421d) and to lack the time to notice and plot against an emerging tyranny (R. 566e–567a). He emphasizes that poverty leads to complex emotions, such as resentment and hatred, toward those who have profited from the losses of the poor (R. 555d-e); poverty can even cause the desire for revolution (R. 422a, 555e). He even goes as far as to observe that the money makers "with their eyes on the ground, pretend not to see" the poor (R. 555e) who "sit idle in the city" (R. 555d). Finally, as we saw earlier, Socrates says that poverty disrupts psychic harmony (R. 591e).

In all these ways, Plato has a firm grasp of the array of consequences of living in poverty, especially about the exploitation of the poor by the rich,

Health, Justice, and Peace in the *Republic* and *Gorgias* 153

and he is profoundly concerned about poverty, especially given poverty's destabilizing effect on individuals and their cities. The most primal threat to the harmonious ordering of souls and cities is the community's inability to meet individuals' basic needs for a healthy life. If an individual suffers from serious poverty, the picture Plato paints suggests that the consequences of this poverty threaten to disrupt both psychic and civic harmony. It should now appear simplistic to make embodiment itself out to be the cause of all discord. Discord erupts not in every case of embodiment but where the human being's needs go unmet, as in the case of being impoverished.

Simultaneously, Plato aims to raise our concern about the pervasive lack of reflection on the impact one's lifestyle has on oneself as well as on the global network of political associations. In place of such reflection, human beings tend either to suppose that justice is not actually important or to operate on the assumption that of course most people are decent and therefore just. These tendencies are depicted in the attitudes of many of Socrates's interlocutors. For example, when Thrasymachus asserts something like "nice guys finish last" he is supposing that justice is not at all important in "the real world." And Glaucon would presumably see himself as a basically decent person, even though it is his unthinking petition for delicacies and luxuries that leads to the city's "fever." Incorporating his desired luxuries, such as meat, into the city's lifestyle first leads to illness (*R*. 373c-d) and ultimately causes war (*R*. 373e). One evades serious inquiry into what justice really is whenever one assumes that justice doesn't really matter, that justice is attainable without difficulty, or that one is a "good person" even though one lacks an account of justice. These aspects of the *Republic* give us reason to believe that peace can only occur where citizens learn the value of reflecting on the consequences of their lifestyle.[144] Plato construes philosophy as psychic medicine, because loving wisdom includes this sort of reflection. Peace continues to elude us today precisely because this sort of reflection about the consequences of one's lifestyle on not only oneself, but also the rest of the world's citizens, is so rare. But Plato gives a brief outline of the kind of city where the conditions for peace are met and are even sustainable for the future, Socrates's First City. Let's turn our attention toward the First City.

4.4.2 Socrates's First City

Many scholars entirely ignore the First City of Plato's *Republic*[145]—for instance, Plumwood, who on account of ignoring the First City thinks that Plato believes war is a part of an ideal society,[146] and Keuls, who contends that Plato "seems never to have contemplated a world without constant armed conflicts."¹⁴⁷ The scholars who do not overlook Socrates's account of the First City tend to consider it either a passage that does not contribute anything to our understanding of what Plato is up to in the *Republic*¹⁴⁸ or a naive, unrealistic fantasy.¹⁴⁹ Of course, the latter criticism could also be made of the *Kallipolis*.¹⁵⁰ In Rachel Barney's view, the First City, the one Socrates calls the healthy, true city, is "a strictly *impossible* city."¹⁵¹ Barney insists that Plato intends for it to be a city where there is no role for the soul's rational and spirited capacities, only for the exercise of the soul's appetitive aspect.¹⁵² I challenge Barney's claims that there is no political activity¹⁵³ or constitution, no exercise of the rational or spirited aspects of the soul, and that the city is austere.¹⁵⁴

I join a small group of scholars in taking the First City of the *Republic* seriously.¹⁵⁵ As we shall see, Plato does not depict life there as austere. Furthermore, there are also clues and implications about the role of rational reflection and spirited concern in such a community. Specifically, I will show that in order to live as moderately as they do the citizens *must* exercise the whole soul (rather than just the appetitive aspect of the soul). We will do well to take this "tantalizing" passage seriously, given that it offers "a vision of a community in which harmony within the individual psyche, among inhabitants, and with other communities is the norm."¹⁵⁶

In Socrates's conversation with Glaucon and Adeimantus about the theoretical formation of a city, Plato has Socrates ask what justice and injustice are and how they come to exist in a city, and in response Adeimantus admits that he has "no idea" (R. 371e-372a). However, at 372a, Plato has Adeimantus casually wonder whether justice "was somewhere in some need that these people have of one another." This is a demonstration of Adeimantus's humility and insight even though his character is generally dwarfed by his brother. In response, Socrates proceeds to describe a city where the citizens are healthy and peace prevails, all in hopes of making justice clear for his interlocutors.¹⁵⁷

Plato has Socrates conjure up an image of a city where health and unity are of the utmost importance. In fact, the account points out that citizens come together to form a community in order to meet more easily the needs of each individual, reminding us of the central importance of satisfying the body's basic needs in the social-political arena (R. 369b-c). As Annas notes, Plato "sees it as simply obvious that each individual is not self-sufficient (369b)."¹⁵⁸ Instead of competing with each other, the citizens use a cooperative approach (R. 369b-c) because they were not all born alike (R. 370a-b), and the principle of specialized labor is introduced so that their needs can more easily be satisfied (R. 370a-c).¹⁵⁹ Furthermore, as McKeen writes, "All transactions among inhabitants are made on the assumption of mutual advantage (369c)."[160] This in particular enables Socrates's city to enjoy tremendous unity. Concerning the way of life in this city, Socrates says:

> First, then, let's see what sort of life our citizens will lead when they've been provided for in the way that we have been describing. They'll produce bread [*siton*], wine, clothes, and shoes, won't they? They'll build houses, work naked and barefoot in the summer, and wear adequate clothing and shoes in the winter. For food, they'll knead and cook the flour and meal they've made from wheat and barley. They'll put their honest cakes and loaves on reeds or clean leaves, and, reclining on beds strewn with yew and myrtle, they'll feast with their children, drink their wine, and, crowned with wreaths, hymn the gods. They'll enjoy sex with one another but bear no more children than their resources allow, lest they fall into either poverty or war [*hêdeôs sunontes allêlois, ouch huper tên ousian poioumenoi tous paidas, eulaboumenoi penian ê polemon*]. (R. 372a-c)

Socrates's comments about the healthy city immediately lead to grumbling from Glaucon about the lack of "relishes" (*opson*), and so Socrates adds a bit more detail to his account, introducing additional foods that are consumed, such as salt, olives, cheese, figs, chickpeas, beans, and acorns, and noting that these citizens drink moderately (R. 372c-d).[161] The brief but important sketch of the healthy city concludes with Socrates saying, "And so they'll live in peace and good health, and when they die at a ripe old age, they'll bequeath a similar life to their children" (R. 372d).

Socrates's account ends there because of Glaucon's interruption, but at its heart is the view that peace will be manifest wherever human beings are provided for in a just and moderate fashion through cooperation rather than competition. Glaucon bristles that this "communal life of rustic contentment"[162] sounds good enough only for sows (R. 372d).[163] McCoy has shown that Glaucon is hostile to the First City because "it is a city that lacks the masculinity of politics, war, and the honors that accompany war" and it places "feminine practices at the heart of civic practice."[164] Glaucon is used to a different political framework, and he deems luxury to be the only desirable lifestyle.

To this, Socrates replies, "All right, I understand. It's not merely the origin of a city that we're considering, it seems, but the origin of a *luxurious* city. And that may not be a bad idea, for by examining it, we might very well see how justice and injustice grow up in cities. Yet the true city [alêthinê polis], in my opinion, is the one we've described, the healthy one [hugiês tis], as it were" (R. 372e).[165] So, Socrates gives up his discussion of the First City and moves on to talk about the sort of city that interests Glaucon, the feverishly appetitive city of luxury (truphôsa polis).[166] Plato depicts the interlocutors as being rather nonchalant about moving on to discuss a very different sort of city, and this has made it easier for commentators to underestimate what Plato writes about the kind of city Socrates thinks is healthy and true.

The healthy city becomes feverish once commodities that are unnecessary for a healthy life, such as perfumes, pastries, prostitutes, and other such luxuries, are incorporated (R. 373a). For example, he explains to Glaucon that if the citizens are going to eat meat, then they will need more doctors for the individual citizens as well as an army for the city to seize more land for pasture from their neighbors. And if their neighbors "too have surrendered themselves to the endless acquisition of money and have overstepped *the limit of their necessities*," then war will be inevitable.[167] Socrates then says, "We won't say yet whether the effects of war are good or bad but only that we've now found the origins of war. It comes from those same desires that are most of all responsible for the bad things that happen to cities and the individuals in them" (R. 373c-e). It may be difficult for Glaucon to understand why the inclusion of luxuries such as couches and meat cause such problems for the city, but he nevertheless agrees with Socrates's prognosis (R. 373e). Plato does not envision that the end of warring will come as a result of denying the body. Rather, he envisions that the end of warring will come once citizens of the world learn how to measure what they really need, seeing beyond mere appearances of what they want.

Peace will prevail when individuals foster justice by cultivating the health of the soul, the body, and the political state. Correlatively, peace will be impossible where not enough attention is paid to meeting the needs of the bodies and souls in the community, where individuals are distracted by their *pleonexia* ("having and wanting more than one is entitled to")[168] becoming competitive rather than cooperative. Where Glaucon's interruption and his city are driven by a pessimistic sense of *pleonexia*, Socrates's account of the First City is markedly optimistic and just. Cooper emphasizes the contrast between their competing notions of justice. According to Cooper, "mutual aid, not mutual restraint, is the key to Socrates' notion of justice."[169] Meanwhile, Glaucon asserts that "justice is a matter of each person leaving the others alone—not harming them, not interfering with them, not preventing them from doing what they want."[170] It is important to acknowledge that a person or city may be perceived as not interfering with others, but where "someone has what is not his own . . . another person has been deprived of what is his own."[171]

Given that Plato focuses the *Republic* on the *Kallipolis* (the rehabilitated[172] version of the luxurious city demanded by Glaucon), we must wonder why Plato chooses to include it at all if it is not to be taken seriously, if it is an impossible city. One might wonder why Plato has Socrates defend this city as the healthy, true city, if he barely bothers with that city, concentrating the focus of the *Republic* on the *Kallipolis*, which is the dialogue's third city. Silverman, who also takes the First City seriously, declares, "If we take the city of pigs seriously, then, Plato seems to be saying that there need not be an incompatibility between soul and body such that soul cannot be perfected as long as the soul and body are with one another."[173] I agree, and think the importance of this point has gone unnoticed because scholars are so dismissive of the First City.

For instance, according to Barney, there is something fundamentally wrong with Socrates's sketch of life in the healthy city.[174] In her view, the First City is a "one-dimensional" community "in which only appetitive motivations have any power."[175] She writes:

> This depiction of daily life renders the inhabitants of the First City vivid yet opaque, like figures in an Egyptian tomb painting or on the Shield of Achilles. And what daily life does *not* here include is most striking. There is no military; no constitution, rulers, or political activity; no philosophy or intellectual inquiry. (The absence of these is evident not only *ex silentio* but from the way in which the military and the philosopher-rulers are later introduced, as new classes with distinctive pursuits.)[176]

I disagree with Barney's assumption that there is no political activity happening just because there is no explicit mention of a constitution or rulers. It is certainly true that the *Republic* does not offer as full an account of this city as we would want. Glaucon's interruption and Socrates's acquiescence to Glaucon's demands for luxuries bring an end to its exploration. Still, we should take more seriously the account Plato bothers to give of a place where the conditions for peace are met.

First, I respond with puzzlement to Barney's contention that political activity is not happening in Socrates's city. Although the First City may not have monarchs or elected officials,[177] nearly the entire account of the

First City is focused on the political activity therein, which consists in the citizens' cooperative effort to secure what is required for their survival.[178] Socrates says that cities are founded because people believe that living "together as partners and helpers" is what's best for themselves (R. 369c). From this rational notion springs one of the main political principles of Socrates's city, that each person should work for the common good of all, contributing what each is naturally suited to do (R. 369e–370c). This principle of specialization is one of several principles governing the political activity of the city.[179] In arriving at this principle, the First City demonstrates that some citizens there have inquired into the best approach to survival and have figured out that survival is considerably easier when all work cooperatively (R. 369b-c). I am astonished that Vlastos should call the outcome in the First City, having all the citizens provided for, a "low-grade communal achievement."[180] Perhaps just as perplexing is Vlastos's suggestion that this outcome manages to transpire "without planned foresight of the common good."[181]

Wallach[182] and Reeve also read the First City as one without any rational checks on human desire, but Plato has Socrates expressly indicate that the First City's citizens are careful not to have more children than they are able to provide for (R. 372b-c).[183] This brief comment about procreation in the healthy city is incredibly significant.[184] It insinuates that the citizens are doing more than merely satisfying their appetites using means-ends reasoning, as some scholars suggest.[185] Means-ends reasoning asks how to accomplish a goal, not whether it is good to do so. And Plato has Socrates explicitly indicate that these citizens contemplate not only how to accomplish their goals but, more importantly, whether it would be good to do so (R. 372c-d). They are concerned with their own good, and their behavior demonstrates rational caution (*eulabeia*). It is evident that they are *thinking* about the consequences of their actions in terms of overall goodness.[186] This is something that merely appetitive citizens without reason could not do.

Decisions such as how many children to bear have a tremendous impact on whether and how one's needs can be met. These citizens are acting like people who have contemplated the ways poverty and war threaten health and survival. The citizens enjoy the pleasures of *erôs* but regard health, justice, and peace rather than physical pleasure as their chief concerns. As a result, they need to know how to calculate properly how many children their resources can support. While Plato does not explicitly connect the quest for peace with the art of measurement, we can now see that peace can only occur in an environment where citizens use the art of measurement to calculate the impact of their lifestyle on both the health of oneself as well as of the rest of the world's citizens. Instead of acting like "body-lovers," the citizens of Socrates's healthy city are reflective about the consequences of satisfying their desires. By cautiously avoiding having too many children these citizens are employ rational thought alongside their active appetitive nature. We know this because, as Plato makes explicit later at 431c-d and 439d, it is reason alone (or with the help of the spirit) that makes good calculations about what truly benefits and harms us.

Although Cooper sees the First City as naive, he himself reminds us that on Socrates's account of the First City, "the human individual good—a well-ordered life for each of us individually, which contributes to that larger well-ordering which constitutes our common life together in society—is a fundamentally social achievement, not one that any of us could manage on our own."[187] In my view, the work done to arrange the cooperative survival effort is the quintessential act of political leadership. So, it is a mistake for commentators to contend that no political activity occurs in the First City. In the First City, peace and good health are community projects. As Lenzi writes, "Just as no one can make and wage war without others, so too no one can confront and supersede conflict and war without others."[188]

These citizens use rational caution in pursuit of their own good, but how is this good determined? If any citizens employ rationality to inquire after the nature of Goodness, then philosophy is happening in the First City.[189] When Barney claims that philosophy is not happening in the First City, she notes that her evidence comes from Socrates's silence about philosophy and from the philosopher-ruler being introduced only later in the *Republic*.[190] It is true that the occurrence of philosophy in the healthy city is not explicitly mentioned. Yet, the city is oriented entirely around preventing badness and promoting goodness—particularly good health, good resources (such as food, drink, shelter, clothing), good relations (like peace and companionship), good times, and good prospects. And while a constitution in the First City is not made explicit, the community is unequivocally organized in accord with these principles of avoiding death, disease, poverty, war, and unsustainability, which commits Plato's Socrates to the view that the First City is governed by an unwritten set of constitutional principles oriented toward the Good. Rational leadership must be what facilitates the significant achievements that Socrates attributes to the First City. Perhaps the failure to comprehend this accounts in part for some scholars considering the First City an impossible fantasy.

Given the Platonic notion that moderation stems from rational control, we should suspect that in the healthy city some of the citizens engage in philosophy, think Goodness through, and try as leaders to guide the decisions being made. As we try to make sense of the admirable moderation in the First City we must consider Socrates's subsequent claim that cities can only be happy when philosophers have political power (R. 473c-e). In the account of the First City, Plato has Socrates accentuate that the citizens are happy and that life there is not at all plagued by evils. There is nothing explicit concerning the First City's rulers or whether it even has rulers, but we should infer the contribution of philosophers from the outcome of how well the community lives.[191]

Moreover, philosophical leaders will need the souls of their fellow citizens to be orderly enough to agree to good ideas. So, the philosophical leader must see to it that the community experience includes education guided by reason. In the First City, each individual is able to be healthy on account of being provided for through the principle of specialization, and this health is crucial for the city's stability, especially in terms of the population being educated well enough to accept for themselves the good counsel the city's thinkers recommend. It does not rise above the level of insinuation, but it seems as though Plato is hinting that the First City is a place where the citizens are reflective enough to grasp that health, justice, and peace are manifest when everyone has water, food, shelter, medical care, and education. The First City is a glimpse of such a community "so guided by reason and wisdom, that the usual conflicts, trials and errors by which a measure of wisdom is won in life are absent and unnecessary."[192]

According to Cooper, citizens won't have any chance of achieving their own good without the guidance of philosophical reasoning and philosophical understanding. He argues that in order to pursue its own good successfully a community needs a guarantee that their notion of goodness is true and a way to make sure that their lives are guided by the idea of Goodness.[193] In other words, if a community is concerned with its own good, then it needs philosophy, not just basic goods such as food and shelter. And yet, even though there is no mention of anyone doing philosophy, the citizens of the First City are depicted as having attained their own good. Their good is a prosperity that goes beyond sated bellies and quenched thirsts to health, happiness, and peace that endures generation after generation. As we have already seen, given that Plato repeatedly has Socrates claim that happiness can only be found where philosophers rule as kings and queens (R. 473c-e, 487e, 499a-b, 500e, 521a-b), philosophy is the *sine qua non* of peace for Plato. Thus, the remarkable achievements in the First City, especially the peace and happiness found there, suggest its residents have benefited from philosophical leaders at work in their community, those who have a talent for thinking through what is best now and in the long run. As Meyer writes, "Socrates is deliberately provoking his audience (and Plato his readers) to ask, what is responsible for these good features? This too is a competence that must be present in a properly functioning city."[194] Health, justice, and peace are the demonstrable outcomes of philosophical contemplation and leadership within the simple city.

Why shouldn't philosophers participate in the specialized division of labor, by contributing "their own talents, abilities, and natural dispositions" to "the common store of social good in which all will then share,"[195] especially when their talent for thinking about Goodness is so central to the city's mission? Philosophers contribute something toward the community's benefit, and accordingly they may reap their share of the goods produced for the community's survival, because the point of founding the community was precisely this sharing, to "share things with one another, giving and taking" (R. 369c, 371b). When Socrates proposes the principle of specialization he suggests each of the residents will "contribute his own work for the common use of all" (369e), and he adds, "More plentiful and better-quality goods are more easily produced if each person does one thing for which he is naturally suited, does it at the right time, and is released from having to do any of the others" (R. 370c). If we neglect to recognize the philosopher's work as necessary for the community's flourishing, then philosophers will be forced to spend their time contributing another type of work for which they seem suited. Consequently the contribution they are best suited to make would be impossible; this, of course, violates the principle of specialization (R. 369e–370c). So, for philosophers to make their specialized contributions they will need their acts of questioning, discussing, and thinking things through to be counted as work, so that then they will not have to spend their time on one of the other necessary jobs. If the community adheres to the principle of specialization, then those whose talents, abilities, and natural dispositions are directed toward philosophical inquiry must make their unique contribution just like everyone else in the city's labor market. If Socrates had fully explored his vision of his healthy city (had Glaucon not interrupted him), he may have made the presence of philosophers in his city and the community's need for their specialized contributions explicit.

Perhaps one might hesitate to think philosophers could possibly exist in Socrates's city.[196] We know from Book VI that philosophers do not do well in just any conditions. There, Socrates indicates that it will be difficult for those with a philosophical disposition to grow fully into their philosophical nature if they don't have the good fortune to be raised under a suitable political constitution (*R.* 497a). He goes farther, claiming, "None of our present constitutions is worthy of the philosophic nature, and, as a result, this nature is perverted and altered, for, just as a foreign seed, sown in alien ground, is likely to be overcome by the native species and to fade away among them, so the philosophic nature fails to develop its full power and declines into a different character" (*R.* 497b-c). If the philosophical nature is distorted if reared in the wrong sort of city, then we must wonder, as Adeimantus does, which city would be the sort of place where those with a philosophic nature would be truly free to do philosophy (*R.* 497c). Socrates responds with confidence that the city they have founded together in theory is a fitting place for a philosopher to live. Yet, I see nothing to stop us from concluding that the First City is a place where philosophers *could* do philosophy. It would be a similarly healthy home for a philosopher, and in Socrates's view it may even be more fitting than the *Kallipolis*, given how much more complicated the *Kallipolis* is.

Without philosophers in the city, how could it come about that the way of life is wholly focused on the Good? Socrates's brief account implies that life is so good in the city because the citizens are so moderate. Cooper accounts for this moderation by claiming that the citizens of the First City "are assumed not to be motivated at all by any of that open-ended desire for pleasurable gratification that was the hallmark of human life according to Glaucon's psychological principles."[197] Similarly, Barney calls these citizens "strikingly moderate,"[198] and finds their moderation questionable precisely because she assumes that only the appetite is exercised in the First City.[199] For Barney, this moderation rings false because she rules out the exercise of their rationality. She contends that the First City "embodies the hypothesis that a city without rational rule could be moderate in its appetites, and that hypothesis is false."[200] I agree that without rational leadership a city could not be moderate in its appetites. I would even go as far as to say that this is one of Plato's most fundamental principles. In light of this principle, I argue that the citizens' moderation must be indicative of rationality being actively exercised there. What would it accomplish for Plato's construction of the *Republic* to have Socrates give a brief account of a place where the human beings are not really human? And, as McCoy puts it, what is "inhuman" about a city "that values craft, music, religion, and community"?[201] Rather than assuming the citizens' moderation is inhuman and false, we need to imagine the conditions under which such striking moderation could occur.

By choosing to leave this for the reader to infer, Plato opens the door to interpretations that overlook what is left unspoken about the First City.

Health, Justice, and Peace in the *Republic* and *Gorgias* 163

However, it is well known that in his project of writing dialogues rather than treatises Plato often leaves the reader to interpret something implicit. In that vein, we must do the work of interpreting for ourselves what would have to be the case for the community to achieve the perfect moderation Plato's Socrates describes. In my view, the exercise of rationality in the city is the precondition of their moderation.²⁰² The coherent goodness of their lives must result from thoughtfulness and deliberation.²⁰³ When Plato has Socrates explicitly describe the citizens' moderate appetite, he leaves mostly implicit the roles that our rational and spirited capacities would have to play in order for the citizens to enjoy that outcome.

Is it likely that the spirited aspect of the soul would be active in First City citizens like its rational and appetitive counterparts? Now that we have deduced the role of rationality in the First City, we should anticipate a place for spiritedness, given that the spirited aspect is the natural ally of the rational aspect (*R.* 440b, 440d-e, 441e). The work of reason and spirit are left unspoken in Socrates's account of the First City, but even though Plato does not go out of his way to clarify their status in the healthy city, it is a mistake to assume that the whole soul is not active in Socrates's city where health, justice, and peace are the chosen aims. Notice the divergence of Glaucon's feverish city, which he readily agrees will require warfare and a military operation that remains intact throughout the remainder of the *Republic*, and Socrates's healthy city, which, to use Peterson's words, is a city that "deliberately chose a way of life that would avoid war."²⁰⁴ The account of the First City emphasizes that justice is manifest when everyone is provided for. So, given that the spirited aspect of the soul recoils from injustice, the spirited aspect would be involved in the citizens avoiding poverty and war by choosing not to bear too many children, for instance. These citizens are doing exactly the sort of calculation and engaging in exactly the sort of self-discipline that is called for to prevent war at both *Phd.* 66c-d and *R.* 373e.

Meanwhile, I also wish to challenge Barney on her assumption that the healthy city is austere. Concerning Glaucon's objection that the healthy city is a "city for pigs," Barney claims that "Glaucon's objection is answered by an even stronger insistence on—and endorsement of—the austerity of the First City."²⁰⁵ I disagree with Barney's claim that there is austerity in the First City. She designates an austere city as one focused entirely on "necessary appetitive desires."²⁰⁶ She appeals to the two principles Plato uses in Book 8 to distinguish necessary from unnecessary appetitive desire. Socrates defines necessary desires as those that "we can't desist from and . . . whose satisfaction benefits us" (558d–559a).²⁰⁷ And he asserts that unnecessary desires are those that could be eliminated over time through self-discipline and are "harmful both to the body and to the reason and moderation of the soul" (R. 559b-c). The former are permissible; the latter are prohibited.[208] It has been misleading for scholars to assert that the inhabitants of the healthy city are motivated only by necessary appetitive desires.[209] While I do agree that the First City is mostly focused on satisfying the necessary appetitive desires, Plato is explicit that the pleasures taken by the citizens of the First City are not limited to those that are necessary.

For instance, Plato has Socrates mention that they drink wine. Certainly one could train oneself to desist from drinking wine. The desire to drink wine would have to fall into the category of desires that could be eradicated if one disciplined oneself (R. 559b), which would make it an unnecessary appetitive desire. Additionally, as I have already shown, the First City's citizens enjoy their sexuality, limiting it only to prevent poverty and war (R. 372b-c). While one might see sexual desire as a necessary appetitive desire because it facilitates the continuation of our species, in the life of any particular person it is not strictly necessary.[210] The citizens of the healthy city have some unnecessary desires, and they even satisfy some of them. They are able to do so because of the absence of a single-minded focus on the satisfaction of desire, particularly the desire for things one does not actually need. In contrast with the luxurious city that Glaucon demands, the lifestyle of those in the First City is simple though not austere, severe, harsh, or painful; the citizens do not experience the poverty that tears communities apart. The citizens of such a city do not simply survive but even flourish.[211] As McKeen notices, the passage describing the First City "is particularly rich with allusion to the pleasant and wholesome way of life enjoyed by those in the city of pigs" where they "feast well or entertain sumptuously."[212] Life is good and enjoyable there.

Before I conclude my discussion of the First City, let me explain a disagreement with McKeen. She sees the First City as more ideal in terms of civic unity than Glaucon's luxurious city but as manifesting civic unity to a lesser degree than the Kallipolis.[213] Her reasoning for this claim is focused on the contingency with which the First City's citizens use enlightened self-interest, their lack of formal education outside the family context, and their lack of true appreciation of virtue. McKeen contends that the citizens of the Kallipolis, unlike those of the First City, "follow laws out of a respect for civic unity as such."[214] It strikes me as lacking in textual support to claim as she does that the First City's inhabitants "do not value civic unity, justice, or even the polis itself, for its own sake."[215] My reply has three aspects.

Health, Justice, and Peace in the *Republic* and *Gorgias* 165

First, the *Kallipolis* also depends on contingencies—particularly the contingency of having leadership and philosophy coincide, which Plato views as an unlikely contingency in fact. So, both the First City and the *Kallipolis* are contingent in various ways. Secondly, one could argue that there is less civic unity in the *Kallipolis* than in the First City, given the segmentation into classes, where the two elite classes are quite separate from the producer class. Yet, in the First City there is no indication of or apparent need for any such stratification in location or status. In fact, there is emphasis for civic harmony when at *R.* 372d Plato has Socrates say that the First City enjoys a sustained peace that follows from their view of each other as mutual helpers in a specialized economy (*R.* 369c, 369e–370c).

Third, we must ask if the members of the *Kallipolis*'s producer class have a different education or appreciation of virtue than the citizens of Socrates's healthy city. The text does not suggest any difference, and if the *Kallipolis*'s producers do not have a different education or appreciation of virtue than all the healthy city's citizens, then it doesn't seem appropriate to believe their *Kallipolis* will have greater civic unity than the First City on account of their superior appreciation of civic unity, virtue, and the *polis* itself. Furthermore, Plato does not have Socrates explicitly rule out professional specialization in education in the First City. So, it could very well be the case that the citizens of the First City are educated in a way that is conducive to their appreciation of civic unity, virtue, and the *polis* itself. If that were the case, one could easily find oneself arguing, *pace* McKeen, that the First City would have greater civic unity than the *Kallipolis*. In conclusion, it seems safer to assert that civic unity is valued very highly both in the First City and in the *Kallipolis*.

Was Plato right about what will happen if human beings are provided for in a just and moderate fashion? Would we live in peace and good health? Would we live to a ripe old age and sustainably pass on to the next generation the lifestyle that made health, justice, and peace manifest? If Plato is right that peace will manifest wherever human beings are provided for in a just and moderate fashion, then we must ask what stands in the way of reappropriating the Platonic conception of the healthy and just lifestyle. Why have we been so hesitant to heed Plato's call to eradicate poverty? Is it true that human nature will inevitably find life in the First City inferior to life in Glaucon's feverish city of luxury? It is possible that inheritors of Glaucon's tradition are more inclined to think so than those whose needs have gone unmet. Perhaps a life where everyone has food and shelter and the community enjoys peace, good health, and a sustainable future would sound much better to the ears of individuals living in war zones or in extreme poverty than to Glaucon's.

4.5 Know Justice, Know Peace

At the heart of Plato's political thought is the principle of the interconnectedness of individual souls and political community. If a human being is not properly cared for, then both that individual and the *polis* suffer from the ensuing injustice. For Plato, the *polis* or political community is not some sort of metaphysical entity unto itself; rather, it is the collection of the human beings who are its members.[216] I agree with Vlastos when he explains that the *polis* "can be nothing but the people themselves who are its members—*all of them in all of their institutionalized interrelations*."[217] This implies that if our institutionalized interrelations are not harmonious, then our society cannot be harmonious.

For Plato, there are two different dynamics that can be involved in disrupting the possibility of peace. First, if our society is not harmonious, then that threatens to complicate an individual's personal effort to harmonize the aspects of his/her own soul. So, dysfunctional societies make it more challenging to flourish as individuals trying to be wise and good. Secondly, just as civic disharmony threatens personal harmony so too can an individual's psychic disharmony threaten civic harmony. One of the most fascinating aspects of Plato's social and political thought is that he intimates that individuals who lack peace within, on account of an improperly ordered soul, will jeopardize the *polis*' prospect for harmony and flourishing.[218] This view commits him to being disturbed by any circumstances that disrupt an individual's chance to practice psychic harmony. The well-being of the individual is important not only for individual happiness but more importantly for the flourishing of the entire *polis*.

There is no hope for peace unless political communities govern themselves in a healthy manner, and that can only materialize when individuals' souls are healthy. The virtue of individual justice, which Plato calls internal harmony, is humanity's first step in the quest for peace. Individuals enjoying personal peace are in a position to not unsettle the conditions for others' psychic or physical health. Put differently, justice manifests in political associations because they are inhabited by psychically healthy individuals. Woolf explains this well when he writes:

> [O]ne's good relations with others flow from one's having harmonious internal relations within oneself (one's soul). One's

Health, Justice, and Peace in the *Republic* and *Gorgias* 167

internal relations have primacy for Socrates, so that the possession of harmonious internal relations will be both valuable in itself and a necessary condition of harmonious relations with others. . . . One whose soul is disorderly tends to manifest that disorder in a piratical way of life whose consequence is the impossibility of good social relations with others. So what is explaining, in Socrates' theory, the impossibility of society or good *between* people is lack of order *within* individual souls. . . . This in turn suggests that a harmonious, well-ordered society is (must be) constructed out of harmonious, well-ordered souls, since a disharmonious society will be disharmonious if it should contain disharmonious souls within it. This, then, is a "bottom-up" theory. Conditions at the macro level are to be explained by conditions at the micro level, the level of the individual—thus Socrates' theory is, from this point of view, an individualistic one.[219]

On this account, individual justice is the prerequisite of peace. Complete peace consists, for Plato, of both senses of justice—the psychic harmony of an individual soul and the civic harmony that we colloquially call peace. A collection of just individuals makes the world around them the best it can be, preserving the conditions for peace among them—mainly the absence of poverty.

So, we must also pay attention to the trials embodiment poses for us not only as individuals but as members of a community as well, if we aim for peace. Interpreters have consistently recognized that Plato believes hedonism leads to unjust outcomes, but my project identifies the dangers of even the immoderation that follows from attempting to reject the physical world. For Plato, the *polis* and the individual can only flourish when the extremes of neither hedonistic body-love nor austerity (either on account of body-hatred or poverty) prevail because both impede the psychic harmony Plato calls individual justice, the absence of which, in turn, precludes community peace.

Plato says, know health, know justice, know peace. His philosophers serve their communities by setting the various conditions for peace, and Plato makes clear in the *Republic* that philosophers must prevent or eradicate poverty in their communities in addition to educating citizens about the importance of caring for their souls even more than for their bodies. In these sorts of ways, philosopher-leaders facilitate lives of health and justice for the community. In doing so, the philosopher honors the Good by achieving both psychic harmony as an individual and civic harmony as a leader. Ultimately peace—within the *polis* and among *poleis*—is the yardstick by which we measure how well human beings (with the influence of their leaders) have ordered their souls and maintained good relations with each other. And wherever there is poverty there will not be health, and when that fundamental physical need cannot be met, there is no justice. And as Plato made clear long ago: no justice, no peace.

Chapter 5

Interpretative Possibilities for the Late Dialogues

5.1 Common Themes

How would an exposition of Plato's treatment of the body in the late dialogues look from the position I have elaborated in the previous chapters? It is outside the scope of this work to engage in a thorough study of the late dialogues, but in this short chapter I will offer a sketch of how the *Philebus*, *Timaeus*, and *Laws* might be read in light of my thesis. Plato's positions on various important issues may have developed over the course of his life, as is debated by Developmentalist and Unitarian interpreters, but I will give a brief account of how Plato's attitude toward the body and the physical world in these later works is largely consistent with the interpretation I have offered of the *Phaedo*, *Symposium*, *Phaedrus*, *Gorgias*, and *Republic*.[1]

The typical developmental take on Plato is that earlier in life, while recently influenced by Socrates, he wrote his early "Socratic" dialogues and that as he aged, he wrote his middle dialogues, imbued with his own ideas like a theory of Forms, and that as he neared the end of his life, he wrote the late dialogues that revise earlier views, such as the theory of Forms. This approach tends to dovetail with the austere reading of Plato, especially of the *Phaedo*, the erotic dialogues, and the *Gorgias*. Despite the fact that many scholars do not find sufficient evidence to interpret the late dialogues as revisionist,[2] the revisionist interpretation of the late dialogues is about as dominant as the austere dualist reading of the great middle dialogues.

Does Plato maintain a Developmental view with respect to his position on the physical? Given the argument I have made in the previous chapters against an austere ascetic interpretation of the middle dialogues, I cannot hold the view that Plato revises his earlier austere dualism and becomes a champion of moderation and normative dualism only later. Yet, even with my normative dualist reading of the middle dialogues, we could wonder whether Plato carries forward this normative dualism from the middle dialogues to the later ones or abandons normative dualism in favor of an austere dualism as he aged. Certain passages in the *Laws*, such as the aspersions of homosexuality (636c, 838e–839a, 841d) and sleep (807d–808c) could give one the more austere impression of Plato's thinking that became foremost in Plotinus's mind.

It is not possible here to do justice to the intricacies of the *Philebus*, *Timaeus*, and *Laws*, so I will leave that thorough study for another time. Instead, I will briefly examine these three late dialogues and submit that a study of these dialogues would further develop my thesis. These late dialogues contain themes that are mainly consistent with my reading of the *Phaedo*, *Symposium*, *Phaedrus*, *Gorgias*, and *Republic*. This chapter will point to three themes. First, as we shall see in 5.2, in these late dialogues Plato exhibits a tremendous interest in the physical, both the human and the natural world. There are many instances in these dialogues of Plato making the value of the body explicit. The occasions have a normative dualist tone, ranking the body as less important than the soul but valuable nonetheless. Second, in 5.3 I will examine the case Plato makes in these dialogues for endorsing moderation rather than demonizing pleasure. Finally, the *Laws* echoes many of the political notions of the *Republic* that we saw in chapter 4, such as: reinforcing concepts of proportion, harmony, and unity; dire warnings about wealth inequality; and emphasis on reconciliation and peace. In 5.4, I will investigate the passages in the *Laws* that reiterate the political notions we examined in chapter 4. Let's now explore each of these topics in turn.

5.2 Positive Attention to the Physical

The variety of ways that Plato attends to the physical in these late dialogues is impressive. Observe how Plato draws attention to the body in the dramatic aspects of these dialogues. Think, for example, of his announcing that Socrates got all dressed up (*Ti.* 20c), just like in the *Symposium*, or Plato making the *Laws*' legislative talk a conversation had by three old men taking an extremely long walk that leaves their bodies in need of shade and rest along the way (*L*. 625b-c, 722c). One of the other ways Plato calls attention to the physical world has already been discussed; recall that in chapter 1 most of the evidence of Plato's interlocutors' reverence for nature came from the *Timaeus* and *Laws*. Having already considered those passages in 1.3, I will focus this section on his positive attention to the human body, including his explicit normative dualist ranking of the body's value, his appreciation of sense perception, and his notion of health and his use of medical analogies. For a commentator to draw austere ascetic conclusions about these late dialogues would necessitate finding in them a mainly hostile tone or negative quality where there are references to the physical. But this not what one finds in these dialogues.

Timaeus gives this speech about the universe and the nature of human beings as a gift in exchange for the prior day's conversation that Socrates gave them (the discussion featured in the *Republic*) (*Ti*. 27a). In it, Timaeus investigates the physical components of the world: fire, earth, water, and air (*Ti*. 31b-32c), the varieties therein (*Ti*. 58a-61c), and various properties such as hot, cold, hard, soft, heavy, light, above, below, smooth, rough, and so on (*Ti*. 61d-64a). Plato has Timaeus get into geography, particularly in the famous Atlantis passage (*Ti*. 24e-25a) as well as cosmogony (*Ti*. 28a-34b, 69b-c), zoogony (*Ti*. 91d-92b), the origins and parts of the human body (*Ti*. 43a-47e, 73b-76e, 80d-81b, 83a-85c) and its functions such as sight (*Ti*. 45b-d), sleep (*Ti*. 45d-e), dreaming (*Ti*. 45e-46a), respiration (*Ti*. 78c-79e), health and disease (*Ti*. 82a-86a), and procreation (*Ti*. 91a-d). The fact that Plato has Timaeus venerate the demiurge who created it all makes it impossible to read these references to the physical world and the bodies in it as hostile or negative. Plato goes as far as to have Timaeus say that everything the divine craftsman creates "is beautiful" because it is crafted in the image of "what is always changeless" in order to reproduce "its form and character" (*Ti*. 28a-b). He also adds that the demiurge's creations are good because "he wanted everything to become as much like himself as possible" (*Ti*. 29e-30b; see also 38c and 39e). In all these ways, Plato makes clear that his attitude in the late dialogues toward the physical world should not be interpreted as negative or hostile.

Just as in the middle dialogues, Plato makes his normative dualist metaphysical presumptions explicit at various points in the late dialogues. He refers to the soul as the holiest possession (*L*. 726a), as older and in charge of matter (*Ti*. 34c; *L*. 967d), and as absolutely superior to body (*L*. 959a; cf. *Ti*. 37a). However, these passages do not indicate animosity toward the body. Rather, as the *Laws* indicates three separate times, the soul is the highest priority, with the body in second place and wealth ranking third after soul and body (*L.* 697b-c, 743e, 870a-c; see also 728b-e where a moderate body is given a place of honor after the soul). This would be a strange thing to say even once if Plato had an austere dualist position.

Even so, the value ranking holds the divine as higher than all (*L.* 726e–727a), and, keeping with this point of view, the Athenian says, "The union of body and soul, you see, can never be superior to their separation (and I mean that quite seriously)" (*L.* 828d). This echoes the view of soul's kinship with the divine in the *Phaedo* that we considered in chapter 1, as does the remark later in the *Laws* that "my body is just the likeness of myself that I carry round with me" (959a-b). It is on account of this kinship with the divine that the soul is more valuable than the body, but the physical is nevertheless met with positive regard in these late dialogues. Let's now turn to the positive attention paid to sense perception in particular.

Although not a major theme in the *Philebus*, the place for physical sense perception in rational understanding is acknowledged. There, Plato has Socrates describe perception as the motion that occurs when "the soul and body are jointly affected and moved by one and the same affection" (*Phlb.* 34a). He goes on to distinguish memory from recollection by indicating that memory is the "preservation of perception" (*Phlb.* 34a), which still involves both the body and the soul, whereas recollection is said to involve the recall by the soul alone of what the soul perceived and remembered together with the body. The *Timaeus* also pays attention to sense perception's important role in rational pursuits. At 42a, Plato has Timaeus describe sense perception as a necessity.[3] And later, Timaeus explains that lovers of understanding must engage in both rational and empirical inquiry, in that order of priority (*Ti.* 46d-e).

Timaeus adds that having eyesight to observe "any stars, sun or heaven" opens "the path to inquiry into the nature of the universe," the pursuits of which "have given us philosophy" (*Ti.* 47a). As Gordon says, for Plato "[W]ithout the senses (and *nous*), there is no philosophy."[4] Consistent with this, in the *Laws* Plato writes, "Because no matter what else is true of either, the soul is the seat of reason and the head enjoys the faculties of sight and hearing. In short, the combination of reasons with the highest senses constitutes the single faculty that would have every right to be called the salvation of the animal concerned" (961d). He adds that reason and the senses "combine to ensure the safety of a ship" (*L.* 961e). What Plato is acknowledging in these passages is a powerful tribute to the body's sense perception. These aspects of the late dialogues are reminiscent of the role of sensation in the theory of recollection in the *Phaedo* that I discussed in 2.2. As I argued there, for Plato to appreciate the body playing a positive role at the start of the learning process stands at odds with an austere ascetic interpretation.

Beyond the usefulness of physical sense perception for philosophical endeavors, Plato routinely touts the importance of physical education and the virtue of fitness (*L.* 734d-e, 743d-e, 788c, 795d-e, 797e-798a, 961e-962d). This is consistent with what we found at the *Gorgias* 464b-465d. The concept of health features prominently in these late dialogues. Plato knows his era's medical doctrines and integrates them in his thinking about the physical.[5] Moravcsik claims that Plato's dialogues do not contain a theory of health, while others, such as Tracy, have believed that a theory of health comes out of the *Timaeus*.[6] Tracy summarizes his view of Plato's conception of health and disease as follows: "The microcosm, the composite of body and soul which is man, is thought to be in excellent condition when measure, proportion, symmetry, equilibrium, and regularity prevail in each part and in the composite as a whole. This ordered condition is health, and all that disrupts it, disease."[7]

Whether or not one finds this account sufficient as a complete theory of health, the notion of health in the *Timaeus* is well developed. For example, Timaeus discusses physical depletions and restorations (*Ti.* 65a-b) and the importance of proportion and order for health (*Ti.* 82b-83b, 87d, 88e-89a). This resonates with the restitutive picture that comes out of the *Philebus* where Plato utilizes medicine's concepts of filling and emptying (30b, 31c-d, 34e-35e). Plato's Socrates defines desire as follows: "Whoever among us is emptied, it seems, desires the opposite of what he suffers. Being emptied, he desires to be filled" (*Phlb.* 35a). If we recall the position in the *Gorgias* and *Republic* that we considered in chapter 4, we uncover overlap. In the *Gorgias*, Plato has Socrates make regular use of medicine's concepts of filling and emptying (*Grg.* 493a-494a and 505a-c), as we examined in 4.2.1. And the *Republic* also maintains a view of pleasure and pain that relies upon these medical concepts of filling and emptying, as we found in 4.2.2. As Frede has observed, oddly enough Plato does not utilize the medical framework of destruction and restoration in the construction of pleasure and pain in the *Laws*.[8]

Yet, even in the *Laws* Plato utilizes the medical notions to construct analogies that do a lot of work for him, as I introduced in chapter 1. For instance, the central approach to legislation in the *Laws* revolves around a medical analogy. The Athenian compares legislators with doctors insofar as they both should give explanations: just as the doctor should give patients an account that explains what should be done, the legislator ought to give the governed "preludes" to the laws that justify each law (*L.* 719e-720d). More generally, the *Laws* and *Philebus* make use of medical analogies to model Plato's vision of the good life (*L.* 720a, 902d, 962a; *Phlb.* 25e, 30b-32b). The use of medical analogies is in keeping with the *Gorgias* and *Republic*, where Plato's Socrates uses physical health as an analogy for virtue and medicine as an analogy for the corrective care of the soul (*Grg.* 464b-465d; *R.* 372e-373a, 444c-e) in addition to other medical analogies (see 1.4, 4.2.1, 4.2.2, and 4.4.2). Hackforth also connects the medical notions of replenishment and emptying in the *Philebus* with those in the *Gorgias* and *Republic*.[9]

Having considered these instances of positive attention being paid to the physical in these late dialogues, let's turn now to the importance of measured moderation for physical and psychic health.

5.3 Moderation and Measure

In prior chapters, I demonstrated that the moderation Plato has Socrates champion in the middle dialogues is moderation in the conventional sense of nothing in excess. Is that the case in the late dialogues as well? In this section, I will marshal evidence mainly from the *Philebus* and *Laws* that demonstrates the importance of moderation in the conventional sense. The various passages in the late dialogues that advocate for moderation will be a problem for anyone trying to defend an austere dualist interpretation.

Let's begin with the *Philebus*, where Plato has Socrates debate which the best life is for human beings—the life of pleasure, knowledge, or a mixture of the two. Plato depicts Philebus as contending that "what is good for all creatures is to enjoy themselves, to be pleased and delighted, and whatever else goes together with that kind of thing" (*Phlb.* 11b), whereas he has Socrates initially argue that "knowing, understanding, and remembering, and what belongs with them, right opinion and true calculations, are better than pleasure and more agreeable to all who can attain them" (*Phlb.* 11b-c).[10] But Philebus gives up his defense, and Protarchus agrees to take over (*Phlb.* 11c-12b). In that same instance, Socrates begins to suggest that it may be a third way of life that is superior to both the life of pleasure and the life of knowledge (*Phlb.* 11d-12a, 20b-c).

Socrates and Protarchus agree that whatever the good is must be both perfect and sufficient (*Phlb.* 20c-d). As they make use of these principles, they quickly reject the possibility that pleasure alone could be the good (*Phlb.* 21b-d, 22a, 22e-23a). Having concluded that "[e]verybody would certainly prefer this life [a mixture of pleasure with reason and intelligence] to either of the other two, without exception" (*Phlb.* 22a), Protarchus and Socrates set about to uncover which life, reason or pleasure, will come in second place to the mixed life. Socrates has in mind that "reason is more closely related to" "whatever the ingredient in the mixed life may be that makes it choiceworthy and good" (*Phlb.* 22d-e), and this is confirmed at the end of the *Philebus* (65a-b). Even though reason is deemed far superior to pleasure (*Phlb.* 66e) and the neutral state between pleasure and pain (if it exists) is considered "the most godlike" (*Phlb.* 32e-33b), the interlocutors agree that "both reason and pleasure had lost any claim that one or the other would be the good itself" (*Phlb.* 67a). The mixed life wins the day.

In the *Philebus* Socrates's comments concerning moderate pleasure have a normative dualist tone. For instance, he regards as true pleasures the enjoyment of things such as colors, shapes, smells, sounds (*Phlb.* 51b), and learning (*Phlb.* 51e-52b), and he indicates that they aren't even comparable to enjoying things like "rubbing" (*Phlb.* 51c-d). The pleasure of smell is an interesting case to include here; Plato has Socrates admit that the pleasures connected with smells belong to "the less divine tribe of pleasures" (*Phlb.* 51e). Presumably, it is because smell is so connected with sense perception that it is deemed less divine, but in light of the fact that there is no pain mixed in with this experience Plato's Socrates considers them pure. Ogihara also finds it implausible that Socrates ignores the fact that these pleasures involve the body.[11] Plato takes the enjoyment of the eternal and unchanging to be pure pleasure, even when attached to sense perception (*Phlb.* 66c).

Significantly, Socrates tells Protarchus that to these pure pleasures we should add a variety of good pleasures to the rational life because they are befitting companions for knowledge; he names "the pleasure of health and of temperance and all those that commit themselves to virtue as to their deity and follow it around everywhere" (*Phlb.* 63e). This position stands in contrast to austere dualism, which Plato has Socrates reject as the extreme opposed to hedonism. He takes those with an "inordinate hatred" of pleasure to be the "enemies" of hedonism because "they refuse to acknowledge anything healthy in [the power of pleasure]" (*Phlb.* 45c). So, when Plato has Socrates admit some healthy pleasures into the good life, he is opposing those I call austere dualists; Socrates calls them "our harsh friends" (*Phlb.* 46a). Shortly thereafter, Protarchus says, "I quite understand what you are after. . . . The moderate people somehow always stand under the guidance of the proverbial maxim 'nothing too much' and obey it" (*Phlb.* 45d-e). In the mixed life, reason puts limits on pleasure rather than forbidding it, thereby bringing "moderation and harmony" (*Phlb.* 26a). In light of this picture, we should have questions about the ranking with which Plato concludes the *Philebus*. The healthy pleasures, which are not pure, do not appear in the ranking list; the pure pleasures are placed in the fifth and ostensibly final place.[12] Is there a sixth place for the healthy pleasures that are not pure? Socrates refers there to Orpheus saying that a well-ordered song ends with the sixth generation. Is that a hint prompting us to ask what would be in sixth place? If so, surely it is these mixed but healthy pleasures named at *Philebus* 63d.

He makes clear that moderation is crucial for keeping one's focus on virtue and learning the good (*Phlb.* 63e–64a). Here, he characterizes the moderate lifestyle as one protected by measure and proportion (*Phlb.* 26b-c, 64c-e) wherein "an incorporeal order . . . rules harmoniously over a body possessed by a soul" (*Phlb.* 64b). The virtuous soul imposes order by knowing when to welcome pleasure and when to not do so. At 32d, Socrates claims, "Pleasure and pain may turn out to share the predicament of hot and cold and other such things that are welcome at one point but unwelcome at another, because they are not good, but it happens that some of them do occasionally assume a beneficial nature." Toward the end of the *Philebus*, Plato has Socrates return to the importance of that measured judgment. He writes:

> So, let us pray to the gods for assistance when we perform our mixture, Protarchus, whether it be Dionysus or Hephaestus or any other deity who is in charge of presiding over such mixtures. . . . We stand like cup-bearers before the fountains—the fountain of pleasure, comparable to honey, and the sobering fountain of intelligence, free of wine, like sober, healthy water—and we have to see how to make a perfect mixture of the two. (*Phlb.* 61b-c)

This passage is reminiscent of both the moral psychology of the *Republic*, especially in Book 9, and the *Gorgias*, as we examined in chapter 4. Throughout, Plato has in mind that education enables us to best figure out how to make that perfect mixture.

Let's turn now to the *Laws*. where advocacy for moderation in the conventional sense occurs extensively, albeit alongside a small number of passages in tension with that view.[13] First of all, the importance of moderation is emphasized when Plato has the Athenian say, "Pleasure and pain, you see, flow like two springs released by nature. If a man draws the right amount from the right one at the right time, he lives a happy life; but if he draws unintelligently at the wrong time, his life will be rather different. State and individual and every living being are on the same footing here" (*L.* 636d-e). This too echoes *Philebus* 61b-c. And again, here Plato has in mind that education is what guides human beings toward moderation. The comment in the *Laws* is quickly followed up with a scheme that puts "merely drinking wine" in between "totally abstaining" and "*drunkenness*" (637d). He reiterates that again at 666b. The moderation recommended in this part of the *Laws* calls to mind measured pleasure described in the jar passage we considered in chapter 4, where Plato has Socrates advocate for moderate instead of extremes such as abstaining or constant filling (*Grg.* 493d-494a).

The amount of time spent in the *Laws* discussing wine is, as we are beginning to see, surprisingly lengthy. Although the Athenian has been advocating for moderation, at 673e-674a he breaks a bit from this. He says that there should be many restrictions on drinking wine: none during the day; none for slaves, people intending to procreate, those in military service, or anyone involved in important matters, such as magistrates, councilors, and "steersmen and jurymen on duty" (*L.* 674a-b). We see that he is actually not far from endorsing moderation in this passage because he put these regulations in place merely for fear that a state would permit people to drink as much as they please whenever they want (*L.* 673e-674a). His fear of immoderation drives the restrictions, driving the state toward moderation. Furthermore, in the end, the Athenian characterizes the plan with so many restrictions as one that will allow "modest quantities" of wine to be cultivated from the vines on their Cretan hills (*L.* 674c). He could have required the citizens to abstain from wine altogether, and he does not. Instead, he clearly aims for a state where wine is consumed moderately.[14] This conclusion should not surprise us, given that the Athenian tells us what a connoisseur he is of drinking parties (*L.* 639d-e). In contrast, however, he does go so far as to rule out fish eating in Magnesia, but without explaining why (*L.* 842c, 823e).

The Athenian continues to endorse moderation at 711e when he says, "[B]lessed is the life of the man of moderation." Plato continues that theme at 716d, writing, "[T]he moderate man is God's friend, being like him, whereas the immoderate and unjust man is not like him and is his enemy," and again at 906b, where he indicates that "sensible moderation" protects us. Even though Stalley maintains a developmental view of Plato's asceticism (owing to his austere reading of the *Phaedo* and *Gorgias*), he recognizes that the idea of moderation dominates much of the *Laws*.[15]

Although I read the *Laws* as mostly not advocating austere dualism, there are some passages about sexual morality that put a strain on reading the *Laws* that way. Let's now consider those.

The *Laws* admonishes against nonprocreative sexuality (636c-d, 838e-839a, 841d), because the Athenian sees it as caused by the inability to control one's desire for pleasure (636c). And in the twenty-first law, the Athenian holds up sexually "chaste" men and women as respectable (after childbearing is done), the opposite of the promiscuous (*L.* 784e).[16] But before we can rest assured that this law recommends austere asceticism in sexuality we should pause to consider the fact that immediately after this law is announced the Athenian contextualizes it, saying that "when the majority of people conduct themselves with moderation in sexual matters, no such regulations should be mentioned or enacted" (*L.* 785a). In saying this, he sets moderation as the in-between state between being "chaste" and "promiscuous." Similarly, the Athenian suggests to Clinias that the right life is the state in between the extremes hedonism and avoidance of pain, which he describes as a "genial . . . contentment" (*L.* 792d).

What's more, in the other passages concerning sex, Plato takes a tone that recommends moderation. Plato has the Athenian refer to food, drink, and sex as the three "unhealthy instincts" that "must be canalized *away* from what men call supreme pleasure, and *towards* the supreme good" (*L.* 782e-783b). This resonates with the passage in the *Laws* where Plato has the Athenian rank various kinds of love. The lover who fails to care about his lover's character has a poor showing, while the lovers who are virtuous equals have the one kind of love or "mutual affection" that the Athenian wants to allow (*L.* 837a-d). This harkens back to the message of the erotic dialogues concerning avoiding mere lust, as we found in chapter 3.

Plato remains as concerned here in the *Laws* as he was in the rest of the corpus with the potential pitfalls of being unduly influenced by the pleasure, pain, and desire, which are such powerful incitements (*L.* 732e, 836b). But he sees ways for human beings to be moderate in their enjoyment of such pleasures. For instance, when the Athenian tells Clinias that food can be wholesome (*L.* 667b-c), perhaps he is thinking of the First City's "honest cakes" and other wholesome foods that we saw in chapter 4. Also, at 841a, the Athenian insists that "in sexual matters our citizens ought to regard privacy—*though not complete abstinence*—as a decency demanded by usage and unwritten custom, and lack of privacy as disgusting" (emphasis added). He then adds that if men do fall below the ideal sexual standards, such as by being unfaithful to their wives, then they should at least be discreet (*L.* 841d-e). The Athenian is not optimistic that everyone can be perfectly moderate. Resonant with the *Republic*, Plato has the Athenian conclude that only a small percentage of human beings can manage to be moderate in the face of various temptations (*L.* 918c-d).[17] Similarly, the *Timaeus* also suggests that "most of us . . . have lost all sense of measure, and are lacking in grace" (*Ti.* 47d-e). Even though measured moderation is difficult for us, we must try to figure it out, given that taking care of ourselves requires nourishment (*Ti.* 70e, 90c). Fortunately, each of us has been given reason as "our guiding spirit" (*Ti.* 90a).

5.4 Construing the Political

Even though the *Laws* is a very different kind of dialogue from the *Republic*, it is shares important emphases with the *Republic*. Plato has the Athenian stress the desirability of reconciliation and peace, the need for civic unity, and the dangers of allowing poverty in a community. Let's consider each of these motifs in turn.

Plato's Athenian sounds rather pacifist throughout the *Laws*. There is a competition running throughout the dialogue as to whether orientation toward war or peace should guide the city. The Athenian describes it thus:

> The usual view nowadays, I fancy, is that the purpose of serious activity is leisure—that war, for instance, is an important business, and needs to be waged efficiently for the sake of peace. *But in cold fact neither the immediate result nor the eventual consequences of warfare ever turn out to be real leisure or an education that really deserves the name*—and education is in our view just about the most important activity of all. *So each of us should spend the greater part of his life at peace, and that will be the best use of this time.* What, then, will be the right way to live? A man should spend his whole life at "play"—sacrificing, singing, dancing—so that he can win the favor of the gods and protect himself from his enemies and conquer them in battle. (*L.* 803d-e; emphases added)

Those who want to interpret Plato as a body-hater should be surprised that he endorses a lifestyle occupied by playful singing and dancing. Moreover, if Plato were the austere dualist he is made out to be, intent on ignoring or abhorring the body, then why be concerned with wars that kill and injure bodies? But this powerful indictment of war at 803d-e shows how deeply concerned Plato is about avoiding war.

The Athenian confirms this again at 816c-d; there too, singing, dancing, and sacrifice play a vital role in a good life. The Athenian describes "the dances performed by those who enjoy prosperity and seek only moderate pleasures" (*L.* 816b), of which there are two categories: "the 'war-dance' (which he called 'Pyrrhic') and 'dance of peace' (*emmeleiai*)" (*L.* 816b-c). With a tone reminiscent of the *Republic*'s emphasis on civic unity, he declares, "[T]he same state and the same citizens (who should all be the same sort of people, as far as possible), should enjoy the same pleasures in the same fashion: that is the secret of a happy and a blessed life" (*L.* 816b-d). So, moderate people and cities steer clear of war, and singing, dancing, and sacrifice are a part of that effort.

But virtue is foremost in the pursuit of peace, just as we saw in 4.4.2. Plato has the Athenian say that if a state is virtuous "it can live in peace" if not, then "war and civil war will plague it" (*L.* 829a). The Athenian goes over various circumstances that can lead to enmity—from the petty squabbles between neighbors (*L.* 843b-c) to the injuries done to victims of serious crimes (*L.* 862c). The antiwar point of view is imbued in the Athenian's comments about reconciliation in the wake of injury. He indicates that it is the lawgiver's responsibility to

> use the law to exact damages for damage done, as far as he can; he must restore losses, and if anyone has knocked something down, put it back upright again; in place of anything killed or wounded, he must substitute something in a sound condition. And when atonement has been made by compensation, he must try by his laws to make the criminal and the victim in each separate case of injury, friends instead of enemies. (*L.* 862b-c; cf. *L.* 693b, 743c, 837a)[18]

In these passages, we see Plato aspiring to peace and knowing that that civic unity is integral to it, as we already found at 816d. The Athenian returns to the theme of civic unity again at 875a-b, when he says that "the proper object of political skill is not the interest of private individuals but the common good. This is *what knits a state together*, whereas private interests make it disintegrate. If the public interest is well served, rather than the private, then the individual and the community alike are benefitted" (emphasis added). And again, later, he speaks of the importance of law reinforcing "the cohesion of the state" (*L.* 921c). In these ways, the *Laws* carries forward the *Republic*'s unremitting emphasis on civic unity.[19]

The measures Plato has the Athenian use to ensure civic harmony are numerous and are consistently focused on the physical. They include: soil quality equity (*L.* 745c); sharing water access (*L.* 844b-c); communal meals (*L.* 762b-c); all households having equal proximity to the city center (*L.* 745e); citizens splitting up two-thirds of the agricultural produce without paying for it as foreign residents must pay for the remaining third (*L.* 847e-849d). These requirements are all grounded in the notion of a communal good and cognizance of its material conditions.

After admiring the simple life of the primitive community laid out at the start of Book 3 as "more restrained and upright in every way" (*L.* 679e), Plato has the Athenian say that it would be ideal to combine the rule of law with that simple way of life. The Athenian claims that two circumstances caused the primitive society to be peaceful: they had enough land and food (*L.* 677e-678a, 679a-b), and after so much isolation they cherished and loved one another (*L.* 678e-679a). So, the laws they develop are meant to maintain civic harmony found where people have their basic needs met and where they feel unifying love.

To guarantee this, there is a commitment to control the size of the population, keeping the number of households to five thousand and forty households (*L.* 737e, 740d), so that the land will be sufficient "to support a given number of people in modest comfort, and not a foot more is needed" (*L.* 737d). To maintain this population size, there is even mention of "measures to check propagation" (*L.* 740d), which sounds akin to the birth control mentioned at *Republic* 372b-c. The *Laws*' focus on bodies having enough food, water, and land and avoiding war presents a serious challenge to anyone who would try to read this late dialogue as one in which Plato ignores or abhors bodies.[20]

Let's now concentrate on the *Laws*' commentary on poverty. Similar to the *Republic*, "the distress of grinding poverty" and disease are listed among the possible calamities that beset a city (*L.* 709a). Worrying about this, the Athenian makes a bold pronouncement about redistributing wealth. He indicates that progress cannot be made in a community plagued by "vicious and dangerous disputes about land and cancellations of debts and distribution of property" (*L.* 736d). So, he recommends that "from time to time" the wealthier should be "reformers" who are "prepared, in a philanthropic spirit, to share their prosperity with those debtors who are in distress, partly by remitting debts and partly by making land available for distribution. Their policy will be a policy of moderation" (*L.* 736d-e).

The Athenian portrays this wealth sharing as an act of generosity toward the state more so than to the poor (*L.* 736e–737a), because the state benefits from harmony and is done in by "longstanding complaints against each other" and "mutual malice" (*L.* 737b). Put differently, a harmonious community will be guided by "a sense of justice combined with an indifference to wealth" (*L.* 737a-b). This passage is shot through with echoes of the *Republic*'s notions of being moderate, indifferent to wealth, civically minded, as well as of the resentment caused by stark wealth inequality.

Moments later, the Athenian reminds us of "the ideal society . . . where the old saying 'friends' property is genuinely shared' is put into practice as widely as possible throughout the entire state" (*L.* 739c). I agree with Bobonich that it is a misreading of this passage to take it as an endorsement of all the *Republic*'s political parameters. Instead, *Laws* 739c-d merely endorses the *Republic*'s notions of communal property and city-as-family and its aim at true civic cohesion.[21] In deference to these principles, the Athenian declares that, in order to avoid "civil war" and "civil disintegration," "extreme poverty and wealth must not be allowed to arise in any section of the citizen-body, because both lead to both these disasters" (*L.* 744d). This, again, echoes the *Republic*'s positions on poverty and its threat to civic cohesion.

Magnesia turns out to have four property classes and a scheme in which individuals may transfer to a different wealth class should their wealth levels change (*L.* 744b-d). Morrow notes that the point of these property classes is to prevent the dissolution of civic unity.[22] The Athenian stresses the importance of everyone in the state not going "without the necessities of life" (*L.* 774c; see also 806d). While other cities have a custom of moving the poor to a colony during food shortages, the Athenian says they do not need to do that in their theoretical colony (735e–736b). His concern about the least affluent citizens is substantial enough to write laws forbidding large, costly weddings (*L.* 775a-b) and any dowries at all in order to keep the pressure off poorer families to give a dowry beyond their means (*L.* 742c, 774c). The mention of discrepancies in wealth being problematic in marriage matches (*L.* 773c) could perhaps be interpreted as a microcosm of the problems caused by substantial wealth inequality at the macro level of the city. Plato also has the Athenian explain how extremes of wealth and poverty are not good for molding virtuous character in children (*L.* 791d). Despite the existence of the wealth discrepancies that differentiate the four property classes, the *Laws* has a mechanism for returning excess wealth to the state (*L.* 744d–745a) in order that most affluent citizens should maintain "a moderate and fixed level of wealth throughout their lives" (*L.*

746a).²³ The affluent are permitted to grow two, three, or four times more wealthy than the least affluent but no more than that (*L.* 744e).²⁴ This suggests that wherever wealth inequality grows more disproportionate than four to one, serious civic strife will follow. The community seeking peace, of course, should not allow that.

In conclusion, while I have focused this book on Plato's great middle dialogues, this brief sketch of some themes in the *Philebus*, *Timaeus*, and *Laws* shows how they might be read in light of my normative dualist interpretation. In light of the passages I have considered here, there is reason to envisage the consistency of the late dialogues with the normative dualism I have uncovered in the previous chapters. Given the late dialogues' positive attention to the body and the natural world and the emphasis on the importance for civic unity of meeting individuals' survival needs, it would not be prudent to read Plato's late philosophy as one predicated upon neglect of the body and material realities.

Epilogue

At the start of chapter 1, I observed that philosophy and philosophers such as Plato's Socrates are not easy to understand. Philosophers enjoy thinking things through and conversing the way Plato's Socrates does, but there has been confusion about the role of the human body in this effort. Throughout this project, I have demonstrated that Plato believes withdrawal from the physical is not required or recommended for one trying to be wise and good. The philosophical life instead demands a particular kind of self-discipline, which is exemplified by Socrates. Having considered Plato's notions of training for death, erotic ascent, and medicine for souls and cities, a refined conception of Socratic *askesis* that flies in the face of the orthodox view of Platonism has emerged.

In chapter 2, we saw that human beings who philosophize begin with the body, using sense perception of the physical world to initiate their inquiries. In this way, the body does play an important role in the process of recollection so central to Plato's conception of the contemplative life. Plato's philosophers ultimately use abstract reasoning, but they still need the body to trigger the epistemological process of recollecting nonphysical Being. Put differently, the human body engaging the physical world is the starting point of philosophers doing what they love. In chapter 2 we also saw Plato defend moderation rather than austerity as what facilitates the harmony between the body and the soul. If Plato wants to distance himself from the conventional understanding of moderation, then we should expect a consistent defense of austerity to follow, and we certainly do not get this from Plato's dialogues, not even the *Phaedo*. Plato even hints at this by comparing philosophers to Bacchants, who are most definitely not practicing austere asceticism.

In chapter 3, we examined Plato's understanding of erotic ascent and came to understand the conditions under which erotic desire could be an impetus to inquiry rather than a distraction from it. Despite the fact that Plato's Socrates is abstinent with the beautiful boys of the erotic dialogues, even his beloved Alcibiades, I showed that a philosopher such as Socrates can include the enjoyment of erotic pleasures and could even marry and procreate, because the philosophical way of life does not require sexual abstinence, according to Plato. My study revealed that in the right circumstances erotic desire can facilitate knowledge of the Forms. We saw that Plato does not go as far as to necessitate sexual consummation for the philosopher, but he does accept it as potentially compatible with the life dedicated to philosophy. In the past, most commentators have not recognized this.

Finally, in chapter 4 we examined Plato's use of physical health as an analogical image for both the harmonious soul and the peaceful city. First, I demonstrated that the moral psychology of the *Republic* and *Gorgias* endorses moderation rather than austere asceticism as conducive to harmony within the soul. From this examination we ought to take away the conclusion that, for Plato, the rational aspect should not rule by acting despotically toward the appetite. Inquirers with properly ordered souls are able to nourish the body in a way that does not put either psychic or physical health in jeopardy.

Furthermore, in chapter 4 we also came to understand why philosophers can still be leaders in this world, focused on the pursuit of health, justice, and peace, *because of* their erotic love of the Forms rather than in spite of it. Real philosophers do not disdain human affairs; they prefer, where possible, to try to make this messy world as orderly and good as they can. What's more, Plato's political philosophy calls for leaders who understand why they cannot ignore their own or others' bodies. If leaders were to despise the physical world, then they would ignore the needs of bodies. Loathing the body and withdrawal from the physical world is not compatible with leaders fulfilling their obligation to enable survival. In fact, Plato asks leaders to regard the presence of poverty in the community as the chief threat to civic harmony. For Plato, the elimination of poverty is essential if a community is to enjoy the unity that only justice ensures. Where poverty is eradicated, health is possible. The harmony that ensues from all being provided for is what Plato calls peace.

Some commentators may well remain unconvinced of the view I have defended here. On one hand, I urge scholars to take seriously the possibility that much of what we have traditionally been taught about Plato is not actually an accurate reflection of his dialogues. And on the other hand, I take it as a tribute to the complex beauty of Plato's dialogues that so many different understandings of his ideas are possible. One possibility is that

Plato's own thinking was muddled and that he sends us mixed messages about a variety of issues, including his attitude toward asceticism and the physical. Yet, I find it much more plausible that his dialogues are complicated both because life in our world is bewildering and because he wants us to do the work of thinking for ourselves when perplexed. Comparing Plato's elusiveness to that of Shakespeare, Goldstein writes:

> It has been claimed that Plato was an egalitarian; it has been claimed that he was a totalitarian. It has been claimed that he was a utopian, proposing a universal blueprint for the ideal state; it has been claimed he was an anti-utopian, demonstrating that all political idealism is folly. It has been claimed he was a populist, concerned with the best interests of all citizens; it has been claimed he was an elitist with disturbing eugenicist tendencies. It has been claimed he was other-worldly; it has been claimed he was this-worldly. It has been claimed he was a romantic; it has been claimed he was a prig. It has been claimed that he was a theorizer, with sweeping metaphysical doctrines; it has been claimed he was an anti-theorizing skeptic, always intent on unsettling convictions. It has been claimed he was full of humor and play; it has been claimed he was as solemn as a sermon limning the torments of the damned. It has been claimed he loved his fellow man; it has been claimed he loathed his fellow man. It has been claimed he was a philosopher who used his artistic gifts in the service of philosophy; it has been claimed he was an artist who used philosophy in the service of his art.
> Isn't it curious that a figure can exert so much influence throughout the course of Western civilization and escape consensus as to what he was all about?[1]

As I suggested in chapter 1, in my discussion of pedagogical irony, Plato's style of writing encourages readers to think for themselves, and when we think about his dialogues for ourselves we get the diverse array of readings highlighted by Goldstein. These ambiguities are usually rather uncomfortable for scholars. However, when we read Plato's dialogues (and love them, as some of us do), by virtue of being dialogues not treatises they present us with fascinating ideas and then leave us to think them through for ourselves. So, Plato's invitation to philosophize requires us to work among these ambiguities and the concomitant diversity among readers' points of view. If Plato's Socrates is correct, and I think he is, that dialogue about disagreements is an act of friendship rather than antagonism, then scholars will do well if we can maintain friendliness and cooperation as we work out our disagreements about how to interpret Plato's dialogues.

Having said that, I still hope we can stop blaming Plato for the world's shame surrounding embodiment because it is not a good reading of his dialogues. The austere dualist version of asceticism has nonetheless been incredibly influential. And now we are left to wonder how the world might be different if Socratic asceticism had not been interpreted that way. Perhaps civilization would have a healthier attitude toward women, people of color, nature, the other animals, sexuality and embodiment generally; maybe peace would not be so elusive.

Notes

Chapter 1. Interpreting Asceticism in Plato

1. Spelman 1982 and Spelman 1994, 99. See also Brown 1990, 480, Plumwood 1993, Tuana 1994, 3, and Sandford 2012, 30.
2. Strauss 1964, 64, 138.
3. All references are to the Socrates of Plato's dialogues.
4. Methodologically I proceed from the view that we have access to Plato's ideas through his dialogues; that each dialogue need not be interpreted in complete isolation from the others; and that Plato revised his ideas over the course of his life but that they hang together with a great deal of continuity. Not all interpreters agree with these tenets, but many work from this position as well.
5. By "psychic" care I am referring to the care of the soul (*psychê*) here and in all subsequent uses.
6. Roochnik 2008, 179.
7. In addition to Roochnik, see also Peterson 2011, 30, 85, 89, 123, 166–68, 171–73, 176, 181, 184, 187, 191–92, 194, 217–18; Russell 2005, 162, 164; Carone 1998; and Mahoney 1997.
8. See, for example, *Prt.* 313a-b, *Phd.* 65c, 67a, 115c-d, *R.* 469d, *L.* 959a-b, and the possibly spurious *Alc. I* 130c.
9. *Ennead* I.8.
10. *Ennead* I.4.14.21–26. It should be noted that even Plotinus is not negative about the material world through and through, partly on account of disagreements with the gnostic dualists. See, for instance, *Ennead* V.8.8 where Plotinus intimates a normative dualist view. See Dodds 1965, 24–26, for an account of Plotinus's view.
11. Porphyry 1966, 7.39–47.
12. Ibid., 8.19–25.
13. Ibid., 1.5–10.
14. Ibid., 2.37–45.
15. Ibid., 2.2–6.
16. Ibid., 2.5–6.
17. Ibid., 7.40, 8.20–25.
18. Ibid., 2.1.

19. Ibid., 8.1–4, 8.16–18.
20. Ibid., 3.2–7.
21. Ibid., 1.1–2.
22. Cf. *Ennead* V.I.8.10–14. See also Yount (2014, x), who contends that "Plotinus is the best interpreter of Plato" and that "Plotinus' view does not essentially differ from Plato's view in the areas of mysticism, epistemology, ethics, or metaphysics" (ix).
23. See Friedländer 1958, 56.
24. Trans. Rosamond Kent Sprague in Cooper 1997.
25. Trans. Donald J. Zeyl in ibid.
26. Trans. G. M. A. Grube, rev. C. D. C. Reeve in ibid.
27. Peterson 2011, 30.
28. Woolf (2004, 98–100), observes a similar distinction in how Plato is interpreted, but he describes the contrasting views as an "ascetic reading" and an "evaluative reading."
29. Nietzsche 1967, 97.
30. Ibid.
31. It would be an interesting project, beyond the scope of this one, to explore how the Neoplatonic misunderstanding of Plato's view of the physical was adopted and adapted by Christian philosophers in the Middle Ages, producing a long-standing bias in philosophy against the body and its desires. Adam (1911, 3), remarks on the Christian reception of Plato.
32. Jowett n.d., 162–65, 170; Archer-Hind 1894, reprint 1973, xiii–xiv; Stewart 1915; Zeller 1931, 141; Grube 1935, 63; Collingwood 1945, 59; Hackforth 1955, 49; Bluck 1955, 1, 3, 5, 9, 34; Taylor 1956, 181–82; Dodds 1959, 299; Friedländer 1964, 54; 1969, 42; Gosling 1973, 40, 69–70; Guthrie 1975, 331; Gallop 1975; Elshtain 1981, 21; Gosling and Taylor 1982, 4, 11, 46, 79–80, 83–84; Hartsock 1983, 199–201; Dover 1984, 154; Bostock 1986, 30; Vernant 1991; Rowe 1993, 9–10; Plumwood 1993, 45, 69–103; Frede 1993, 398, 400, 402, 409, 411, 416; 1999, 173; Kahn 1996, 384–85; Nehamas 1998, 161; Lear 1998, 163–64; Robinson 2000, 43–44; Hadot 2002, 67–68, 159; Griswold 2003, 103, 119, 121–23, 128–29; Pakaluk 2003, 104–107; Barney 2008, 8. Cf. Sedley 1999, 326–28. However, although Hackforth, Robinson, and Frede read the *Phaedo* in the tradition of austere dualist interpretation, they do not believe that position outlives the *Phaedo*. As for Griswold, despite his tendency to read Plato as an austere dualist, his earlier work on the *Phaedrus* acknowledges some of the value of the body for Plato. Finally, later Dodds (1990, 13, 30) interprets Plato's dualism in line with what I call normative dualism, rejecting the austere dualist interpretation of asceticism.
33. Roochnik 2008, 184. Roochnik includes among such interpreters both Cornford 1941 and Crombie 1962.
34. Pakaluk 2003, 107.
35. Griswold 2003, 119.
36. Sedley 2007, 263. See also Ste. Croix 1981, 70.
37. Jaggar 1983, 28.
38. Nehamas 2007, 116, 124.

39. Hargrove (1989, 20–21, 75) and Attfield (1994, 78–80, 85) interpret Plato's metaphysical dualism as implying that for Plato the physical world is merely illusory such that appreciation of and concern for the natural world is incompatible with philosophy.
40. Plumwood 1993, 80.
41. Trans. Trevor Saunders in Cooper 1997.
42. Cf. *L.* 903c.
43. Carone 1998, 128.
44. Ibid., 119.
45. See also Carpenter 2008, 49, 51, 56.
46. Plumwood 1993, 4, 6; Shiva 1989. See also Spelman 1982, 128.
47. Ehrenreich 1989.
48. Collins 2004, 100. Cf. hooks's (1992) thesis that black sexuality has been constructed as deviant sexuality where the black female lover is depicted as a wild woman. See also Gilman 1985. Additionally, Washington (1995) observes that the enforced filthiness of slaves was used to link slaves with animals.
49. Bordo 2003, 9.
50. Ibid., 5. See also Spelman 1982, 110, 119–21, 125.
51. See also West 2005, 9–18.
52. See, for example, North 1966, 1.
53. Muscio 2002, 102.
54. See, for example, Plumwood 1993, 33–40, 42–43; Carson 1990, 143–54, 159, 162, especially 143–44; and King 1989.
55. Warren 1991, 110–11.
56. Trans. G. M. A. Grube in Cooper 1997. Cf. Patterson 1986, 56–57.
57. See Brill 2015.
58. Tong 2014, 256.
59. Roochnik 2003, 59. See Rowett (2016, 78), for other birth-related motifs.
60. Annas 1981, 9–10.
61. Ibid., 8, 48; and Ferrari 2005, 15.
62. Trans. Donald J. Zeyl 1997.
63. Zoller 2009.
64. Thagard 1996, 78.
65. Analogical reasoning can be useless if one bases the analogy on superficial similarities, which disbelievers in the existence of souls might say Plato is doing here. In this case, Plato would argue that the body and the soul have a relevant similarity.
66. Blössner 2007, 347. Meanwhile, Bernard Williams (1973, 199, 200) censures "evasion" and "the ineliminable tension in Plato's use of his analogy," but he still indicates that at some points Plato wants us to take the analogy between the city and soul seriously (198–99).
67. Blössner 2007, 347–49. Ferrari (2005, 40–41) makes a similar point.
68. Ferrari 2005, 41.
69. Cooper 2007, 24.
70. Moravcsik 2001, 44, and 2000, 16.

71. Ruttenberg 1986, 153, also makes this observation.

72. See *Cri.* 47d-48b; *Chrm.* 156b–157e; *L.Hp.* 373a; *Grg.* 465c-d.

73. Hobbs (2007, 179–80) draws attention to another example: Plato uses military metaphors, which "extend *andreia* into non-martial spheres, such as philosophy." And Peterson (2011, 127–29) acknowledges that some of the key terms in Platonic metaphysics (such as *form, share, approach,* and *see*) did not inevitably have the technical meanings Plato develops for them. Here too, Plato transforms literal vocabulary into something metaphorical in order to compensate for his lack of the vocabulary needed to express his ideas. Interestingly, Barker (2007, 9) notes that harmonic theory was another intellectual enterprise that was also challenged by the lack of a vocabulary fit for the descriptions theorists were newly attempting.

74. See '*suneinai*' at *Smp.* 176e; '*aspazetai*' at *Smp.* 209b and '*aspazomenous*' at *R.* 480a; '*migeis*' at *R.* 490b; '*erastos*' at *R.* 501d; '*homilôsi*' at *R.* 496a, '*homilei*' at *R.* 500c, and '*homiliôn*' at *R.* 611e.

75. See *R.* 401c, 498b; *Prt.* 313c-d, 320a; *Sph.* 223e; *Phdr.* 246e, 248b-c, 251b-c; *Ti.* 17b.

76. Blössner 2007, 382. See also Blössner 1997, 258–61 and 288 n. 822.

77. Similarly Annas (1981, 112) contends that Plato somewhat revises the vocabulary used for the city's virtues in a way that in part maintains the original connotation and to some extent innovates a new meaning.

78. For instance, Vlastos 1981, 22–23; Nussbaum 1986, 217, 219–20; Griswold 1986, 31, 48, 67, 123, 126, 130, 133, 135; Sinaiko 1965, 54.

79. See Classen 1959, 19, and Brill 2013, 102–104.

80. Hobbs (2007, 179–80) also notices the difficulty concerning the ambiguity between the original meaning and the transformed meaning.

81. Cf. Sorabji 2000 on Plato's position about the possible extirpation of the emotions. Sorabji (2000, 201) refers to "shifting emphases in Plato" and says, "Plato did not give a firm decision in favour of one ideal rather than the other" (concerning whether the emotions should be moderated or extirpated).

82. Zoller 2007; 2010a.

83. Translation by G. M. A. Grube 1997.

84. Rowe 1993, 2–3.

85. Saxonhouse 1999, 123.

86. *Ennead* I.2.7. See O'Meara 2003 for a defense of the view that, even for the Neoplatonists, becoming as much as possible like the divine does not require the exclusion of political life.

Chapter 2. Moderation and Training for Death in the *Phaedo*

1. See, for example, Gallop (1975, 88), who claims that "[n]owhere else in Plato is asceticism so uncompromisingly extolled." See also Frede (1993), who contends that the *Symposium*'s lesson from Diotima revises Plato's earlier rejection of earthly life in the *Phaedo*.

2. Broadie 2001, 304–305.
3. Archer-Hind 1894, reprint 1973; Carafides 1971, 230; Jackson 1971, 18; Nehamas 1998; Buchan 1999, 97; Stephen White 2000, 158–59.
4. Nietzsche 1974, 272. In sweeping contrast, Keuls (1985, 79, 82) reads the last line of the *Phaedo* as a bawdy joke, where Socrates shows off his tumescent penis "whether from the poison or from the jailor's touch" and thanks the god of health with a roster ("a conventional homosexual love gift") as a "tribute to his humorously pretended last moment of sexual excitement." Despite how unusual Keuls's interpretation is, it is interesting, especially in light of her observation (1985, 79) that this joke is "understandable only against the background of the consistent portrayal of Socrates as satyr-like in appearance and perpetually randy." See Peterson 2003 for an account of the various other interpretations.
5. Olympiodorus 1976, 3.5.1–13; and Damascius 1977, I.69.6–9.
6. Roochnik 2008; Woolf 2004; Russell 2005, 11, 77–92, 101, 204; Peterson 2003, 37–39; Saxonhouse 1999; Williams 1999, 38–39; Weiss 1987, 58–59; Burger 1984, 40; Spitzer 1976; Tenkku 1956, 102–104, 111, 118.
7. Roochnik 2008, 187.
8. Russell (2005, 85–87) also makes this argument. He notes that, according to Hackforth (1955, 49), it is Plato rather than Socrates who is the ascetic, and Russell (85, n. 22) comments on what a strange thing that is to say, "given the enthusiasm with which Plato himself celebrates Socrates' joyful life in the *Phaedo*."
9. Davis (1980, 72) and Ahrensdorf (1995, 201) suggest that the idea of soul separation might have been a gift from Socrates to his friends in order to comfort them in their grief.
10. Taylor 1956, 181.
11. My translation.
12. See also Hackforth 1955, 57.
13. Zoller 2007.
14. See Bluck 1955, 9, and Dorter 1982, 28.
15. See, for instance, Vlastos 1975, 53.
16. Anderson 2014, 133.
17. Prior 1985, 35.
18. Frede 2001, 246.
19. Woolf 2004, 101.
20. Cf. *R.* 523a–524b where sense perceptions awaken thought when the senses alone cannot grasp why one finger is both small and big in relation to two other fingers.
21. Gordon (2012, 26) makes a similar point.
22. Woolf 2004, 102–103.
23. Dorter (1982, 28) is in agreement, noting that "[b]ecause detachment from the body comes about by means of our perceiving the permanent within the transitory, it is a process arising out of sensory experience, not out of an immediate, abrupt, and total withdrawal from the world."
24. Cf. *Phd.* 67d; *Grg.* 524b; *L.* 828e, 927a.
25. McKeen (2010, 202) also makes this point.

26. See, for example, Pakaluk 2003, 101-102, 104. Pakaluk distinguishes four possible senses of practicing for death by making use of the examples of four different senses of practicing for spending time in Paris. The first sense is that of "a realization of the definition *in intention*, merely" (2003, 99). In the context of the example this amounts to wishing to visit Paris and thinking of it constantly, but never getting any closer to Paris than this yearning. The second is "an *analogical* realization of the definition" wherein because of limited means one travels to Montreal due to its similar character but never Paris (2003, 99). The third sense is "a *strict* realization of the definition, differing from other such realizations only in degree" (2003, 100). The example here is one who has a brief layover in Paris who "truly is in Paris and would eagerly be there longer for more of the same" (2003, 100). The final sense is that of "a *substantial* realization of the definition" (2003, 100). He uses the example of one who "stayed long enough in Paris to see all the principal sites but would love to go back and live there for a year. He's gotten most of what he wants to get out of Paris, but of course there's always more to see" (2003, 100). Pakaluk rules out the first two possibilities, observing, "If no more than that were meant, then, for all his asceticism, a philosopher would not be one jot closer to the condition of being dead than anyone else" (2003, 100). Pakaluk (2003, 101-102, 104) takes Socrates's definition to be the third—the sense of strict realization achieved to a certain minimal degree. On this view, as far as philosophers avoid bodily activities, the more undistracted by physical images their thinking is, and in turn, the greater the degree of realization of death.

27. Woolf 2004, 106.
28. Cf. *R*. 558d-e.
29. Dorter 1982, 28.
30. Peterson 2003, 37.
31. Peterson 2011, 191.
32. See also Brill 2013, 22.
33. See also Gordon 2012, 189-90. She notes the consistent use here of cognates of *luô* to convey the sense of loosening the grip of sensory input.
34. Harte (1999, 132, 142) makes the same observation.
35. Edmonds (2004, 176) discusses the term *phroura*, which can mean either prison or garrison post. If a translator chooses the latter, then "the soul's sojourn in the body would be regarded as a kind of civic obligation in the service of the gods, a frontier tour of duty from which it would be wrong to go AWOL. Such a sense presents a more positive image of the body than the idea of the body as a prison, which carries the connotation of a punishment for wrongdoing rather than simply an obligation that must be fulfilled." He (2004, 177) concludes that Plato probably intends *phroura* to mean prison here, given the abundance of prison references in the *Phaedo*. See *desmôtêrion* at 57a, 58c, 59d-e, 114c and compare to 60c and 67d. However, not dissimilar to my interpretation of pedagogical irony in chapter 1, Edmonds (2004, 177) adds, "It is quite likely, of course, that Plato chose the word φρουρά precisely because of its ambiguity, because it enabled him

to convey the message of imprisonment of the soul in the body while tempering it with the more positive connotations of garrison duty that is owed to the gods."

36. Linforth 1944, 296.

37. Linforth (1944, 296) notes that the conception of the soul as tomb "is barren and irrational. If the body is a tomb, the soul within it must be dead,— and nothing can be made of that." He adds that there may have been a (perhaps Pythagorean) tendency to blur the distinction between tomb and prison, but Plato keeps prison and tomb distinct.

38. Saxonhouse 1999, 125. Brill (2013, 38, 40–41, 216 n. 6) accuses Plato of a complete lack of consideration of the body.

39. Saxonhouse 1999, 123.

40. Ibid., 126.

41. Ibid., 128. Peterson (2011) has a similar position.

42. Davis 1980, 71, n. 15.

43. See also Sedley 1995, 9.

44. Nails 2002, 138; Diogenes Laertius, *Lives of Eminent Philosophers*, VIII, 46.

45. Peterson 2011, 166.

46. Nails 2002, 82, 260; Peterson 2011, 167. See also Burnet 1911, xix, 9, 19.

47. Rowe (1993, 6-7) opposes the notion that Plato intends to highlight the "Pythagorean credentials" of Echecrates, Simmias, and Cebes. He does not doubt that Echecrates at least was a Pythagorean, but he notes that belief in the soul-as-harmony theory would make Echecrates "somewhat unorthodox, and a rather odd choice if Plato's aim was to introduce us to an ambience of (orthodox) Pythagoreanism."

48. Roochnik 2008, 182.

49. See *Phd.* 88d.

50. Bluck 1955, 3. For a similar point of view, see Melissa Lane's (2007) discussion of the "hydraulic effect" in the *Symposium* and *Republic*.

51. Miller (1991, 8) and Roochnik (2008, 182) observe something similar.

52. Goldstein 2014, 303.

53. Bluck 1955, 34. See also Weiss 1987, 58–59. Weiss (1987, 59) also describes the philosopher as having a "detachment" from the passions.

54. Trans. Alexander Nehamas and Paul Woodruff in Cooper 1997.

55. Dorter 1982, 27.

56. See also Weiss 1987, 58–59, 62.

57. Cf. *Phd.* 79d6-7 and 114c7-8. Dorter (1982, 29) agrees that "the radically ascetic view" is incompatible with Socrates's allowance here for the presence of pleasures, pains, etc. alongside wisdom in the life of philosophical moderation.

58. North 1966, 9.

59. Cf. *R.* 608c.

60. Hackforth (1955, 91) notes that this is the only occurrence in the Platonic corpus outside of the myths where transmigration into animal bodies arises. He takes the passage to be speculative rather than assertive of anything considered an

established truth. Rowe (1993, 196) also sees a "lightness of tone" that characterizes this passage. Gallop (1975, 144) also contends that here Plato is approaching the Pythagorean notion of reincarnation as animals with "savage irony."

61. Cf. *Phd.* 111b.

62. Other commentators join Grube in interpreting Plato as an austere dualist. Archer-Hind (1973, 23), Bostock, Hackforth, and Jowett emphasize the comparison of the two different kinds of moderation under discussion, namely, one that describes the moderation of the many and a different kind that applies only to philosophers. Bostock (1986, 30) asserts that "the philosopher, it seems, is a single-minded ascetic who suppresses all his bodily desires, and this is not what is ordinarily called temperance (or moderation, or self-control) at all." Hackforth (1955, 57) adds that the philosopher "despises the body." And Jowett (n.d., 162) goes as far as to say that the philosopher "wants to get rid of eyes and ears, and with the light of the mind only to behold the light of truth. All the evils and impurities and necessities of men come from the body."

63. Russell (2005, 88) makes a similar point.

64. Weiss (1987, 64, n. 15) agrees.

65. Rowe 1993, 196; Gallop 1993, 35; Gallop 1975, 32. See also North Fowler (1995, 287), who translates *chairein eipontes* as "turn their backs upon."

66. Grube 1997, 73.

67. See also Burnet 1911, 75.

68. Gallop 1975, 145.

69. This analogy is not at all commented upon by prominent commentators, such as Hackforth (1955), Gallop (1975), Dorter (1982), and Bostock (1986). Some commentators, such as Olympiodorus (1976, 8.7), Archer-Hind (1894, reprint, 1973, 25–26), Taylor (1956, 183), Burger (1984, 49–50), and Rowe (1993, 151) go so far as to allude to or summarize the analogy, but they have not focused in particular on Plato's choice to link philosophy with Bacchants. Damascius (1977, I.170–72) comes closest to a substantial comment on this analogy. However, his reading of why Plato chooses to have the analogy revolve around Bacchants differs from mine insofar as he contends that, although Plato "intends to honor the philosopher by the title of Bacchus," the Bacchus is honorable for having "detached himself from genesis as an intermediate term" (I.172). Damascius's is an austere dualist reading of the Bacchants. His reading misses something important about the spirit of a Bacchant that Plato means to capture in this analogy.

70. Cf. *Phdr.* 253a-b where Plato draws another Bacchant parallel.

71. Cf. the language of initiation at *Symposium* 210a, e, 211b-c, and 218b.

72. Morrow 1960, 315.

73. Kingsley 1995, 253, 269.

74. Ibid., 262. Kahn (2001, 53) also sees no fundamental incompatibility between the Pythagoreans and the Bacchants.

75. Kingsley 1995, 264.

76. Ibid., 269.

77. Translation by M. J. Levett, revised by Myles Burnyeat. By suggesting that human beings ought to avoid behaving like animals, which results in being incarnated as animals, the comments at *Phaedo* 81e–82b (the second of the five passages I have examined concerning moderation) foreshadow the *Theaetetus*'s emphasis on becoming like god.
78. Annas 2003, 58.
79. See also Plumwood 1993, 92–93, 97, 100, 102.
80. McPherran 1996, 292–97.
81. See also *R.* 611e.
82. Mahoney 1997, 36.
83. Armstrong (2004) has a similar interpretation of becoming like the divine that does not involve escapism or devaluation of Earth and the body.
84. Note the stark contrast between this image of the body and, for example, the image of the body used by Archer-Hind (1894, xiv), who thinks of the body as the soul's "harassing companion."
85. See also Mahoney 1997, 35–36.
86. Dorter (2003, 11) writes, "Philosophy, as the practicing of death, is not a withdrawal from the world, for then we would be depriving the gods of our service as surely as if we killed ourselves. Rather, it is a way of life that recognizes the primacy of selfless (because universal) reason over the self-centeredness of bodily passions." But Woolf (2004, 104, n. 10) is critical of Dorter for attributing "moderate asceticism" to Socrates; Woolf describes that way of expressing the idea as "an unfortunate phrase." I agree with Woolf that difficulty arises from using the term *asceticism* as Dorter does. As I noted already in n. 26 of chapter 1, Woolf (2004, 98–100) distinguishes between an "ascetic reading" and an "evaluative reading" of the philosophical lifestyle. And although he explicitly indicates that the "ascetic reading" should not be ruled out (2004, 98, 123), Woolf offers condemnation of it that is not surpassed in the literature. Woolf's support for the "ascetic reading" consists entirely of the way in which he takes it to resonate with the *Phaedo*'s affinity argument. His compelling case for the "evaluative reading" resonates with my view, which describes Plato as a "normative dualist." Given that Dorter does in fact read Plato as what I call a "normative dualist," Woolf's issue with Dorter on this point would be resolved if they were both using the phrasing I have adopted, which succeeds in distinguishing between two distinct notions of asceticism. I compare an *austere* view of asceticism with a *normative* view. It is austere asceticism that Woolf, Dorter, and I all want to reject as attributable to the Socratic lifestyle. Despite the differences in terminology, the categories being separated out here are essentially the same for Woolf and me. The problem with his phrasing is that, as his argument pushes the "ascetic reading" away, we are left without a way to represent the sense of practice or discipline that Plato's Socrates indeed wants to emphasize, which is best put across in the term *asceticism*, so long as it is properly qualified. Furthermore, Woolf takes the "evaluative reading" to concern only the philosopher's "attitude, not behavior" (2004, 119), whereas my

reading of Plato's normative dualism accounts for how the philosophical lifestyle concerns both one's attitude and behavior.
 87. Gordon 2012, 213.
 88. Cf. *meletê* at *Phd.* 81a1.
 89. Cf. *Alc.* 129e and *Tht.* 186c.

Chapter 3. Beauty, Education, and Erotic Ascent in the *Symposium* and *Phaedrus*

 1. See, for example, Wender 1973, 79; Okin 1979, 23;, Elshtain 1981, 24, 35, 38; Buchan 1999, 53–57, 68–74; and Waterfield 2002, xxix.
 2. Gordon 2012, 6.
 3. Trans. Alexander Nehamas and Paul Woodruff in Cooper 1997.
 4. Bloom (2001, 57) considers Socrates "the most erotic of philosophers." See also Keuls 1985, 79, 82 and n. 4 in chapter 2.
 5. Murdoch 1970, 85.
 6. Osborne (1994, 96–100) discusses this uncharacteristic act.
 7. See, for example, Taylor 1956, 209, 300, 309, and Rowe 1998, 6–7, 191, 193.
 8. Nussbaum 1986, 198.
 9. See, for instance, Vlastos 1981, 22, n. 65, and Wender 1973, 79, 89.
 10. See also Nehamas 2007, 115–16.
 11. Nails 2006, 198. McKeen (2010, 202) notes something similar.
 12. Burger 1980, 14.
 13. Davidson 1997, 80.
 14. de Vries 1969, 5.
 15. See also Griswold 1986, 28–29.
 16. Burger 1980, 9.
 17. Griswold 1986, 21.
 18. Griswold (23) disagrees, believing Phaedrus is more philosophical than Alcibiades. Yet, he also notes that "Phaedrus is a laughable imitation of the Zeus-like" (130).
 19. See, e.g., Taylor 1956, 233.
 20. Porphyry 1966, 15.7–13.
 21. Davidson (1997, 99, 163) outlines Alcibiades's infamous sexual exploits.
 22. Carone (2006, 223–24; 2001, 82) has a similar outlook. See Scott and Welton (2008, 156–57) for a good account of the historical Alcibiades's notorious treason of Athens and the controversy that surrounded his relationship with Socrates as a result.
 23. See also Kraut 2011, 305.
 24. Nails 2002, 17.
 25. Trans. Stanley Lombardo and Karen Bell in Cooper 1997. Davidson (1997, 82, 92) examines the place of flute-girls in the landscape of prostitution.
 26. See also Saxonhouse 1984, 11.

27. Nussbaum 1986, 171.
28. Plato may or may not be the author of *Alcibiades*.
29. Cf. *Tht.* 150e.
30. Gordon 2012, 182.
31. *Pace* Nightingale (1993, 120, n. 28) and Lane (2007, 47), I do not believe that Plato invites his readers to see Alcibiades's speech about Socrates as a misinterpretation. Scott and Welton (2008, 158, 164) also credit Alcibiades with "a glimpse of Socrates' goodness that eluded the perception of most people" and with "an uncommon insight into the unique virtue of Socrates."
32. Kraut (2011, 306) agrees.
33. Nussbaum (1986, 191) observes something similar.
34. Dover (1980, 166) reports that no examples of these statues survive and that no references to them exist (other than references to this passage in Plato).
35. Nussbaum 1986, 171.
36. duBois 1994, 154–55.
37. See Reeve 2006 for a full investigation of Plato's use of *agalmata*.
38. Nussbaum (1986, 189) also notes the sexual spirit of Alcibiades's recurring use of "the image of *opening up* the other."
39. In contrast, Scott and Welton (2008, 174), Lear (1998, 159, 163–64), and Nussbaum (1986, 195) take it to be easy for Socrates to resist Alcibiades's seduction, not even being sexually aroused by Alcibiades. In particular, Lear accounts for this by seeing Socrates as indifferent to Alcibiades. I see no evidence for this indifference. I agree with Nails (2006, 195) who indicates that Socrates is very much concerned with Alcibiades. Not only does Socrates risk his life to save Alcibiades (*Smp.* 220d-e), but he repeatedly indicates his love for Alcibiades (*Grg.* 481d and *Smp.* 213d). Furthermore, Socrates is hardly indifferent toward any human being. He is so committed to guiding the souls of human beings that it is hard to imagine Socrates being truly indifferent to even a stranger.
40. See also Aristophanes, *Clouds*, 963–83, as well as *Symposium* 183d–184a.
41. See also Belfiore 1980, 136–37 and Anton 1962, 51–52.
42. *Pace* Lear 1998, 164.
43. Von Blanckenhagen 1992, 67. This is in contrast with Scott (2000, 25), who claims that Socrates is not at fault for Alcibiades's shortcomings as well as with Scott and Welton (2008, 172) who indicate that if Socrates had let himself be seduced, it would only have inflated Alcibiades's self-confidence, giving him the kind of power manipulative people use with those who care for them.
44. Reeve (2006, 141) agrees that "the idea that Socrates' love could be won only through joining him in leading the philosophically examined life seems hopelessly far away" from what is on Alcibiades's mind.
45. Cf. Taylor 1956, 227–28.
46. See Danzig (2010, esp. 151–70) for an account of Xenophon's Socrates, who, according to Danzig, thought that one who cares for the soul should avoid any erotic consummation. Nevertheless, Danzig notes that there were suspicions that Socrates did not always live by the advice he gave to others (2010, 151–64).

While Hindley (1999 and 2004) and Dorion (2000, 96–97, n. 114) read Xenophon's Socrates as celibate with young men, Danzig (2010, 164) thinks that "in Xenophon's view Socrates was not always as celibate as he sometimes pretended."

47. Nails 2002, 137.

48. Saxonhouse (1999, 116), Taylor (1956, 178), and Burnet (1911, 13) take it as certain that Xanthippe and the infant son have spent the night with Socrates in prison.

49. See Sheffield 2006 for a thorough account of the relationship between all the earlier speeches and Socrates's philosophical speech.

50. Brisson (2006, 244) takes the main conclusion of Pausanias's speech to be that *philosophia* justifies *paiderastia* (*Smp.* 184c-e).

51. Many commentators take Eryximachus's speech to be the object of Platonic satire, such as Bury (1909, xxvii–xxix); Dover (1980, 105); Rosen (1987, 119); and Nehamas and Woodruff (1989, xvi). But Edelstein (1945, 91) contends that his speech "is not a caricature but rather an historically correct picture of a medical man of that time. It cannot have been Plato's intention to deride Eryximachus as a pedant, a system-monger, unduly fond of medicine." Believing that Eryximachus's speech has substantive content rather than merely being pastiche, I join Jaeger (1971, 13); Konstan and Young-Bruehl (1982, 41–46); Rowe (1999); Hunter (2004); and McPherran (2006). Like Jaeger, Rosen (1987, 90–101) too interprets Eryximachus's speech as indicative of Plato's analogical use of medicine. Levin (2014, 73–109) is intermediate; she contends that the speech is not merely a parody but is nevertheless not worthy of praise for the rigor of its analysis.

52. Nussbaum (1986, 171–76, 184–95) too suggests that in reading the *Symposium* we should not identify Plato only with his Socrates but with other characters. She specifically recommends Aristophanes, with his myth about the origin of interpersonal love, and Alcibiades, with his account of his attachment to one individual, in order to see how Plato makes room for interpersonal love. Halperin (1985, 183) also reads Plato as attempting to explain rather than eschew personal relationships. Based on *Phdr.* 256a-b, *Smp.* 179b–180a, 181d, 183e, 192b-c, and 208c-d, he writes (1985, 183), "Plato is fully alive to the sense of particularity that informs any passionate erotic attachment between persons." See also Kraut (2011, 301–302) for an account of interpersonal love and commitment that arises from Socrates's relaying Diotima's speech.

53. Sheffield 2006, 37.

54. Cf. *Phdr.* 238c.

55. Roochnik 2003, 55.

56. Cf. Xenophon, *Symposium*, 8.15.

57. On horses, see Dover 1978, 58–59, and Henderson 1991, 126–27; concerning wings, see Gordon 2012, 209–10.

58. Dodds 1951, 218.

59. Frede 1993, 409.

60. Gordon 2012, 103–104). Ferrari (1985, 5) agrees.

61. Cf. Plato's mention of wings used in an ascent at *Phd.* 109e. See also the downward directional language at *R.* 519b.
62. Carson 1998, 152-53.
63. Translation by Rosamond Kent Sprague in Cooper 1997.
64. See also Scruton 2009, 51.
65. Patterson 1991, 199. Nehamas (2007, 129) makes a similar point. Griswold (1986, 125) disagrees.
66. For a summary of the inclusivity-exclusivity debate, see Gill 1990.
67. Moravcsik 1971, 293; Vlastos 1981, 23, 31-32; Nussbaum 1986, 183, 190, 197-98; Lear 1998, 163; Blondell 2006, 172-75; Levin 2014, 99-100, 104. See also Crossman 1939, 199. It should, however, be noted that Nussbaum (1986, 220) does not see this "exclusivity" in the *Phaedrus*. Gould (1963, 120) also observes what he takes to be a shift from the *Symposium* to the *Phaedrus* on this point. On the contrary, Griswold (1986, 20) sees the *Symposium* as more rooted in the "eroticism of the body" than the *Phaedrus*, which he sees as manifesting "a curious detachment from eros (particularly eros that is concerned with bodily satisfaction." Yet, Griswold maintains an inclusive reading of the *Phaedrus* (1986, 129). Scott and Welton (2008, 147) are ambiguous concerning whether they maintain an exclusive reading.
68. Kosman 1976; Irwin 1977, 169, 323 n. 58; Price 1981; Price 1989, 43-45; Patterson 1991, 202-205, especially n. 8, 211; Nye 1994, 199-200; Carone 2006, 219-21; Nehamas 2007, 111-14, 123-24; Kraut 2011, 297-98. See also Bloom 2001, 152-53. Woolf (2000, 10) sees the inclusive view in the *Gorgias* also; he writes, "The suggestion is that Socrates' deepest love is for philosophy. . . . But Socrates does not suggest that this makes love for other people eliminable or (in itself) undesirable." Socrates may love philosophy most, but he loves Alcibiades, and it has not held Socrates back from philosophizing.
69. In contrast, see Nehamas 2007, 114.
70. See, for example, Vlastos 1981, 23.
71. See also Waterfield 1994, xxix-xxx, and Nehamas 2007, 114.
72. Kraut (2011, 297) also makes this point.
73. Waterfield 1994, 54.
74. See also Irwin 1977, 234-35.
75. Lane (2007, 62, n. 28) wonders why Socrates made an effort to save Alcibiades's life at Potidaea. If the exclusive reading of the ascent passage were correct, then, as a result of not thinking human life important, we would expect Socrates not to bother to save a human life. Lane cites Scott (2000, 36 and *passim*) who argues that despite ascending beyond the love of individuals, Socrates is concerned for Alcibiades because he nevertheless feels a "powerful attachment" to him. For me, Alcibiades's story of Socrates saving his life is further evidence that supports the inclusive reading of the ascent passage.
76. Cf. *Rep.* 476c-d.
77. Irwin 1977, 169. See also Heinaman 1998, 32.

78. According to Nye (1994, 198–99), "Far from suggesting that the body is a degraded prison, Diotima sees bodily love as the metaphor and concrete training ground for all creative and knowledge-producing activities. . . . Diotima does not argue that heterosexual intercourse is inferior but urges an expansion of loving intercourse that will bear fruit in new thoughts, new knowledge, and new ways of living with others, as well as in physical children (209a)." However, Nye reads the *Phaedrus* differently—with an austere dualist interpretation. Even though she (1994, 201, 202, 212) advocates for an inclusive reading of Diotima's position in the ascent passage, she concludes more than once that Plato's own view is too "Platonist" to be read in the inclusive spirit. Nye criticizes Irigaray for classifying Plato and his Diotima as dovetailing as austere dualist thinkers, or "Platonists," to use Nye's phrasing. Yet, although Nye sees Diotima's position more clearly than many, her presumption that Plato is an austere dualist causes her to miss that he is on the same page as his Diotima. In her introduction to Nye's essay, Tuana (1994, 136–37) also appears to presume an austere dualist reading of Plato's metaphysics, as both Nye and Tuana take Diotima's inclusive view of loving intercourse to be divergent from Plato's own view. My objection to this is the lack of textual support. Nye's account of Diotima's view of love supports my reading of the *Symposium* and does so with textual evidence, but then Nye simply asserts Plato's divergence from Diotima without any evidence of disavowal at all in Plato's authorial choices. She accepts the long-standing presumption of this austere dualist interpretation of Platonism.

79. Frede (1993, 402) makes the point that "freedom from the body and its encumbrances is not among the conditions for the ascent in the *Symposium*."

80. Nussbaum 1986, 183.

81. Ibid.

82. Ibid. Sheffield (2006, 184) also interprets Plato's Socrates in this austere ascetic fashion.

83. Nussbaum 1986, 184.

84. Ibid. Like me, Sheffield (2006, 184–85, 195–96, 206, 212) disagrees with Nussbaum.

85. Carone (2006, 223).

86. Without any mention in Plato or Xenophon of Myrto, we are also left to wonder about Diogenes Laertius's (II.26) report of Socrates having another wife named Myrto, who may have been a common-law wife, in addition to his first wife, Xanthippe, or a wife prior to Xanthippe. When we think of the age difference between his older adolescent son and his two young sons (*Ap*. 34d) that could be explained by having more than one mother for his children. Pomeroy (1975, 67) declares Myrto the second wife of Socrates and mother to his two young sons. See also Bluestone 1987, 144, and Chroust 1957.

87. Ferrari 1987, 99.

88. Gordon (2012, 6) agrees that Plato does not have a desexualized view of erotic interactions.

89. Ferrari 1987, 99.

90. Nussbaum 1986, 174.
91. Taylor 1956, 216; Bloom 2001, 96, 102–103; Benardete 2001, 184.
92. Rowe (1998, 146) takes it as not merely comedic, although his interpretation is different than my own. For him, the scene reminds us that Aristophanes is mainly concerned with the physical aspects of life. Scott and Welton (2008, 56–57) hold a similar view, imagining that there is something comedic here aimed at Aristophanes (or Eryximachus), but that its seriousness is bolstered by the medical language. And Schultz (2013, 155–56) takes his hiccups as indicative that Aristophanes continued drinking after Eryximachus initially banished excessive drinking.
93. Dover (1980, 112) translates "noises and ticklings."
94. Nussbaum 1986, 214.
95. Russell (2005, 108) balks at the notion of seeing pleasure as a "payoff" for the philosopher living the virtuous life, although he is not writing about the *Phaedrus*'s nectar and ambrosia theme in making this point. Yet, in an argument sympathetic to my normative dualist reading of Plato, Russell insists pleasure will be enjoyed by philosophers as "one of the forms wisdom takes in one's life."
96. According to de Vries (1969, 144), J. C. Vollgraff (1912) takes the Greek here slightly differently than most, transposing *adolôs* and *ê*, reading *tou philosophêsantos ê adolôs paiderastêsantos meta philosophias*, "because he regards *philosophein adolôs* as a senseless combination."
97. My reading of this passage puts it in tension with the agreement at *R*. 403a-b that lovers and beloveds should avoid sexual pleasure. That passage in the *Republic* allows for kissing, touching, and being together like fathers and sons but not going any farther than that.
98. See Hackforth 1952; Rowe 1986; and Cobb 1993. However, Gould (1963), Sinaiko (1965), de Vries (1969), Burger (1980), and Ferrari (1987) are exceptions.
99. Jowett n.d., 253.
100. Rowe 1986, 67.
101. Hackforth 1952, 85.
102. Burger 1980, 59.
103. Although Waterfield (2002) correctly renders the phrasing here, he nevertheless has an austere dualist interpretation of the *Phaedrus*.
104. Ferrari 1987, 140, and Waterfield 2002, 32.
105. Cf. *aspazomenous* at *R*. 480a, *migeis* at *R*. 490b, *homiliôn* at *R*. 611e. Schultz (2013, 149) claims that with these erotic descriptions, "Socrates links the highest level of philosophical activity to the appetitive dimensions of human experience. The pleasure associated with the philosophical life provides a place for the appetites and emotions in philosophical experience."
106. Burger (1980, 61–62) observes the tension between Plato's recurrent use of erotic terminology and the praise of restraint from surrender to pleasure. Yet, in her footnote to this comment, she (1980, 140, n 42) notes that Marsilio Ficino was struck by Nicolfonus's remark about the *Phaedrus* that "A man finds there so much of the *erôn* and the *erômenos*, with such odd allusions to that execrable vice,

that one had need of a very vertuous [sic] thoughts and a very charitable mind to allegorize all the strange metaphors of that discourse into a chaste meaning" (Quoted in Marsilio Ficino, *Platonis philosophi quae exstant*, vol. 10, vii). See also Nussbaum 1986, 167. I agree with Nicolfonus and Nussbaum that it is surprising how many commentators have been intent on drawing such chaste conclusions from such sexual context and vocabulary as we find in Plato's erotic dialogues. Even so, I reiterate my contention that, far from being a problem, the potential for reading the *Phaedrus* with a double meaning signifies Plato's exceptional ability to direct messages to both his body-loving readers as well as his readers who have transcended body-love in favor of the care of the soul. While her reading of the erotic dialogues is not as chaste as Vlastos's, Nussbaum herself is guilty of drawing the austere ascetic conclusion that the philosophical lifestyle is incompatible with sexual consummation (1986, 217, 219-20). Nussbaum concludes that the reader must choose between Alcibiades and Socrates, between poetry and philosophy, between pursuits of personal and objective knowledge. She cannot be right. In contrast, Nails (2006, 191) observes the following: "Nussbaum's Plato's *Symposium* offers the vulnerable, passionate Alcibiades as an alternative to the 'rational stone' Socrates whom she describes as, 'in his ascent toward the form . . . very like a form—hard, indivisible, cold' (1986, 195). Frede (1993, 413) also disagrees with Nussbaum's conception of Socrates as "the beautiful stone."

107. Hackforth 1952, 85, n. 2. Rowe (1986, 182) mentions this comment from Hackforth, and tries to expound upon it by noting that "we can then attach a clear meaning to 'without guile': philosophy means conversation, and the true philosopher's conversation will be without ulterior motive."

108. In fact, what seems most likely is that Hackforth's view is similar to Sinaiko's (1965, 80), which takes this passage to refer not to two different people but to one person. However, Sinaiko (1965, 86, 93, 117-18) concludes explicitly that the relationship between the philosophical lover and the beloved does not include sexual consummation.

109. See, Taylor 1956, 309; Vlastos 1981, 22; and Waterfield 2002, xxiii-xxvi.

110. Hackforth (1952, 98) understands this as a reference to heterosexual relations. Griswold (1986, 269, n. 61) believes this could also refer to homosexual relations.

111. I am grateful to Tony Long for this observation.

112. Cf. *Phdr.* 266b and 276d4-5.

113. Fictional Diotima's name means "Zeus-honor" (Nussbaum 1986, 177) or "honored by Zeus" (Bloom 2001, 129).

114. Rowe (1986), as well as Nehamas and Woodruff (1997), read *teleutê* here, meaning consummation, but others have preferred *teletê*, meaning initiation. Waterfield (2002, 38) also uses "consummation."

115. Sinaiko (1965, 53) mentions that that the charioteer is "betrayed by" the dark horse. This strikes me as unfair, given that the charioteer and white horse have gone back on the promise they made to the dark horse.

116. Nussbaum 1986, 220.
117. Burger 1980, 67.
118. Halperin 1986, 66–67.
119. Griswold (1986, 126) maintains that the beloved does not become "enthusiastic." However, this passage strikes me as indicative that, once "backlove" is established, the beloved shares the lover's enthusiasm for consummation.
120. Sinaiko 1965, 54.
121. Dover 1978, 96. See also Xenophon, *Symposium* 8.21–22.
122. Vlastos 1981, 39.
123. *Pace* Price 1989, 81–82.
124. Vlastos 1981, 22, n. 65. Price (1989, 92) agrees.
125. Vlastos 1981, 22–23. See also Griswold 1986, 67.
126. Nussbaum 1986, 217, 219–20; Griswold 1986, 31, 48, 123, 126, 130, 133, 135.
127. Ferrari 1987, 127.
128. Ferrari 1985, 1.
129. Griswold (1986, 126–27) contends that the beloved remains "remarkably passive" and does not attempt to shape the lover's character. That strikes me as incorrect, given that the lover makes sure to choose only a beloved who "has a talent for philosophy and the guidance of others" (*Phaedrus* 252e). Why would Plato have Socrates say that the beloved should have a talent for guiding others, if the beloved isn't going to share the lover's interest in shaping each other's character?
130. Brisson (2006, 250) does not rule out the existence of sexual relations between philosophical lovers.
131. Kraut (2011, 299) agrees that, for Plato, the ideal relationship between philosophical lovers is *not* one "that must be devoid of sexual allure." He also maintains, "It would be equally absurd to hold that no human being should engage in sexual intercourse or have children, and there is no evidence that Plato disagrees" (303).
132. Sinaiko 1965, 38.
133. Ferrari 1987, 262, n. 1.
134. Miller 1991, 8.
135. Ibid.
136. Other examples of Plato neither ignoring nor despising women, sexuality, and the body include, according to Keuls (1985, 85, 103, 402), Plato's being the only writer of the Classical age to even mention female homosexuality (in Aristophanes's speech in the *Symposium*), one of very few to advocate for an older marriage age for women (about twenty years old at *Republic* 460e) than was conventional in ancient Athens (about fourteen or fifteen years old), the first feminist, and an admirer of Socrates who famously was "a friend of women."
137. Nussbaum (1986, 229–31) makes the case that Dion of Syracuse was the object of Plato's love.

Chapter 4. Health, Justice, and Peace in the *Republic* and *Gorgias*

1. Lenzi (2000, 91) remarks that "Plato was the first Western philosopher to counsel social/political human selves organized in society to make love and music, not war." I agree with this, but *pace* Lenzi (2000, 93), I think for Plato justice is the condition for peace rather than peace being a condition for justice.
2. Cf. *R.* 428c-d.
3. Zoller 2009.
4. Cf. *Cri.* 47a-d.
5. Cf. *Phd.* 82d where Socrates indicates to Cebes that someone who is concerned with the soul will not spend time molding the body (*sôma ti plattontes*), or as we would say today, getting into shape.
6. Dorion 2012, 38.
7. Irwin 1979, 190.
8. See Roochnik 1996 for a defense of the thesis that Plato does not envision a literal "science" of living well.
9. Cf. *R.* 558d-559a.
10. Linforth (1944, 311) argues that the allegorical interpretation of the water-bearers myth was original to Plato, even though some elements employed by the myth predate Plato.
11. Cf. *R.* 586b.
12. Linforth 1944, 301.
13. Irwin 1979, 195. Levin (2014, 27) agrees.
14. Jaeger (1971, 25). See also *Phlb.* 34e-35e. More on this in 4.4.2 and chapter 5.
15. Linforth (1944, 299) presents that "the literal meaning of the word for 'satisfactions' (*plêrôseôn*) recalls the 'filling' of the jars in the *Gorgias*."
16. Sommerville 2014, 248. Sommerville's approach to the jar image is generally different than my own, contending that the image does not pertain to hedonism but to Callicles's antipathy toward satisfaction as a cosmological principle.
17. Cf. *Sph.* 230c-d and *R.* 426a-b.
18. It also suggests that a feverish city deserves a different prescription from a healthy city. Maybe the people in the healthy city would get a different prescription about sex, sleep, Sicilian food, etc. than the people in the feverish city do. Schultz (2013, 146, 160) notes something similar.
19. Schultz (2013, 150) also uses the political term *tyrannical* in application to intrapsychic dynamics that suppress the appetite.
20. See, for instance, Lange 1979, 7-8.
21. See, for example, Rice 1989, 568. Meanwhile, feminists such as Plumwood (1993, 91) recognize the inconsistency between the suppression of the appetite and the quest to harmonize the whole soul, but they read Plato as committed to the appetite's suppression. See, for instance, Plumwood 1993, 80, 90-91. In his response to Plumwood, Mahoney (1997, 32) agrees with my reading that Plato ought not

be critiqued for precluding psychic harmony by advocating utter disdain for the appetitive aspect of the soul.

22. Cf. *Laws* 4, 713b-714a.
23. Schultz 2013, 150.
24. Annas 1981, 117; Rice 1989, 568-76; Russell 2005, 206-13, 218-19.
25. Annas 1981, 117. Russell (2005, 218-19) agrees that a harmony model (what he calls an agreement model) is what "in the *Republic* Plato wants and needs most to develop."
26. Annas 1981, 132.
27. Dodds (1959, 298-99) discusses the use of the sieve motif prior to Plato, noting the association with virginity and nonconsummation. Observe the sharp contrast between that convention and Plato's use of the sieve motif.
28. Klosko (1986, 102) writes, "Thus according to this passage, not only are certain desires of the beastlike part to be tolerated, but they are actually to be supported and promoted. Though nowhere else in the *Republic* does Plato duplicate this degree of approval, it is clear that in it he recognizes that under the control of reason the appetites have a legitimate role."
29. Think also of Annas's (1981, 129) reminder that the appetitive aspect of the soul "cannot be completely unreasoning" because in a just soul the desiring aspect is said to *agree* to being ruled. This has been controversial in the literature. See Lorenz 2006 for the opposing view of a stricter partition of the soul.
30. Patterson 1987, 325. See also Ferrari 1987, 99-100; and Warren 2014, 44.
31. Cf. *R.* 498b where Socrates recommends the care of the body to young people so that they may "acquire a helper for philosophy."
32. Reeve 1988, 136-37.
33. Annas 1981, 316.
34. Lötter (2003, 202) also makes this observation. Cf. Berry 1989.
35. Cf. *L.* 731b-d.
36. See also *R.* 535a-b. Also, think of Theodorus's description of Theaetetus where he emphasizes the remarkable and rare nature of this boy who is exceedingly quick, unusually gentle in temperament, and yet supremely manly (*Tht.* 143e-144b). Interestingly, in an echo of Socrates's comments in the *Republic* about rarity, here Plato has Theodorus say, "I never thought such a combination could exist; I don't see it arising elsewhere." Furthermore, a moment later Socrates indicates that Theaetetus's father is also a man of this rare sort (144c).
37. A third passage is more implicit and indirect. At 523b-525a, Plato describes philosophers as those who respond with puzzlement to "summoners," that is, "those [entities] that strike the relevant sense at the same time as their opposites" (524d), or entities that cause conflicting sense perceptions. With such an experience the philosopher's nature is at once confused but seeking to understand (524e), which can be understood as opposing states.
38. See Weiss 2012 for examples.
39. Lane 2007, 45.
40. Ibid., 50.

41. Scott (2007, 152) goes as far as to say that the hydraulic model makes clear that the philosopher "disdains" the physical objects of desire.

42. Scott (2000, 32, 36) has a different reading of Socrates's indifference, which does demand distance from the physical world but still leaves room for a lingering affection for a former *eromenos*.

43. Waterfield (1993, lxi) and Irwin (1977, 237) make similar observations.

44. Cf. R. 595b.

45. Should we consider the *Seventh Letter* authentic, the same claim is made at 326a-b.

46. See also R. 488e where Plato has Socrates make use of this theme of misunderstanding expert craftsmen when he examines how ignorant sailors mistake the ship's true captain for a babbling stargazer.

47. For a fuller account of sophists being mistaken for philosophers, see Zoller 2010b, 83.

48. Weiss (2012, 40) makes the same observation.

49. Peterson (2011, 201, 245, 256) emphasizes that throughout the corpus Socrates does not attempt to correct or constrain how people use the terms *philosophy* and *philosopher*. He accepts the variety of usages employed by various people. See *Euthd.* 307a-b in particular. Think also of Isocrates's usage of *philosophy*, which differs so greatly from Plato's by aligning with rhetoric (*Against the Sophists*, 14–15).

50. Aronson 1972, 393–96; Gosling 1973, 40; White 1979, 22–23, 170, 189, 190, 192–93; Annas 1981, 260–71; Nussbaum 1986, 138; Reeve 1988, 201–203; Price 1989, 91; Waterfield 1993, lvi; Saxonhouse 1994, 79, 83; Cooper 1999, 145–47; Heinaman 2004, 382–83; Sedley 2004, 67–68; Sedley 2007, 260, 273, 275–76; Scott 2007, 145–49, 151–52; Fine 2011, 29–30; and Warren 2014, 35–36, 49. See also Strauss 1963; Strauss 1964, 124–25; and Bloom 1968, 407–408; Bloom 1977.

51. See, for instance, Woolf 2012, 171. This stands in tension with Woolf 2004.

52. McKeen 2010, 199.

53. Waterfield 1993, xi.

54. See also Carone 1998, 118.

55. Mahoney 1997, 36.

56. Cross and Woozley (1964, 101), Davies (1968), and Reeve (1988, 201–203) espouse the view that ruling is in the best interest of the philosophers insofar as their leadership is a condition for having a city such as the *Kallipolis*, which is the kind of community where they can live happily.

57. Shorey 1933, 235; Foster 1936; Adkins 1960, 290–92; Bloom 1968, 407–12; Prichard 1968, 108; Aronson 1972, 393–96; Kraut 1973, 330–31; White 1979, 22–24, 196; Annas 1981, 266–71; and Heinaman 2004. Heinaman (2004, 379 n. 2, 381, 388) even considers ruling inherently evil, for Plato. In contrast, Kraut (1991, 46–55) does not view ruling as incompatible with the philosopher's self-interest.

58. See, for instance, Aronson 1972, 393–94; Gosling 1973, 40; White 1979, 22–23, 190, 192–93; Annas 1981, 260–71; Nussbaum 1986, 138; Reeve 1988, 201–203; Waterfield 1993, lvi; Cooper 1999, 145, 147; Wallach 2001, 286; Heinaman 2004, 382; Sedley 2007, 260, 273, 275–76; Scott 2007, 145–49, 151–52; and Warren

2014, 49. However, Cooper (1999, 147) does also contend that the mixed political and intellectual life is the happiest for the philosopher. Meanwhile, Reeve (1988, 203) notes that a life of nothing but philosophy is not a practical possibility for a human being.

   59. See, for instance, Aronson 1972, 394–96; White 1979, 170, 189; Price 1989, 91; Saxonhouse 1994, 79, 83; Cooper 1999, 146–47; Heinaman 2004, 383; Sedley 2004, 67–68; Sedley 2007, 260, 273, 275; Fine 2011, 29–30; and Warren 2014, 35–36. See also Strauss 1963; Strauss 1964, 124–25; Bloom 1968, 407–408, Bloom 1977. The Straussian argument is that the *Republic* is a failure because the philosophers need to be compelled rather than being persuaded to rule.

   60. I join Gosling 1973, 71; Irwin 1977, 236–38, 241–43; Kahn 1987, esp. 89, 99–100; Reeve 1988, 202–203, 311 n. 10; Kraut 1991, 51–58; Ferrari 2005, 29; Nehamas 2007, 124; and Weiss 2012.

   61. Mahoney (1992, 271) argues that for philosophers being just and being happy are compatible because when a philosopher chooses a third-class good such as ruling over a first-class good such as the life of (exclusive) contemplation "because they must rule if they are to achieve what they value most of all—what is just (*to diakaion*)." I agree with Mahoney (1992, 269) that Socrates never explicitly weighs in on Glaucon's claim that ruling makes philosophers less happy than the life of exclusive contemplation, even though his lack of a denial has led some interpreters to assume his agreement with Glaucon (519d–520a). Furthermore, I agree with Mahoney (1992, 272) that Plato does not depict the life of exclusive contemplation as the highest human achievement.

   62. Demos 1964; Gosling 1973, 69; Kraut 1973, 342–43; Kraut 1997, 213–14; Brickhouse 1981; Mahoney 1992, 271; Vernezze 1992; Irwin 1995, 299; Cooper 2000, 20–21; Yu 2000, 136–37; Dorter 2006, 218; and Sheilds 2007, 39. Scholars concluding that the philosophers do not wish to rule include Bloom (1968, 407–408); Sallis (1975, 379–80); Brann (2004, 95–96); and Scott (2007, 144–51).

   63. The *Theaetetus* echoes that tone in labeling a thinker who stays aloof from matters of conventional concern because "it is in reality only his body that lives and sleeps in the city. His mind, having come to the conclusion that all these things are of little or no account" (*Tht.* 173e). Peterson (2011, 61–89) argues that Plato's Socrates cannot agree with this conception of the philosophical life and that the conception in the *Theaetetus*'s digression comes from Theodorus rather than from Socrates. Russell (2005, 142–43) also does not read the digression as straightforward; he takes it to be a hyperbole.

   64. Irwin 1977, 237.
   65. Weiss 2012.
   66. Ibid., 27.
   67. Ibid., 111–12.
   68. Ibid., 9–10, 132.
   69. Zoller 2015.
   70. Cooper 2007, 28.
   71. Ibid., 29. This echoes Cooper 1999, 146–47.

72. Cooper 2007, 29.
73. Ibid.
74. On this matter I am in agreement with Reeve 1988, 203, 311, n. 10; and Peters 1989, 173, 175–82, 184–85.
75. Peterson (2011, 123) also makes note of Socrates's interest in such worldly matters as "the new goddess whose honoring events he went to the Piraeus to see." Ferrari (2005, 14), too, makes note of Socrates going down to the Piraeus, which he describes as "first port of call for everything strange and socially unsettling" including "a novel type of torch-race in honour of a goddess newly-imported from Thrace (327a, 328a)."
76. Cooper 2007, 30.
77. Ibid., 32.
78. See, for instance, *Prt.* 348a, *Grg.* 458a, and *Ap.* 38a.
79. Scott and Welton 2008, 91.
80. See A. G. Long 2013, 46, for an account of the various ways that a philosopher can examine ideas without external input.
81. See also Blössner 2007, 365.
82. Silverman (2010, 61) also observes teaching others and Plato's writing of the dialogues as types of engagement appropriate for one who loves and considers the Good and wants to create more goodness in others and therefore in the world.
83. Mahoney 1997, 34–35.
84. Cicero 1913.
85. Reeve (1988, 203) draws a similar conclusion. See n. 111.
86. Brown 2000, 8.
87. Mahoney 1997, 34.
88. See also Brown 1994, 161; Saxonhouse 1984, 13; and Lampert 2010, 312.
89. Ferrari 2005, 27.
90. Ibid., 22.
91. Weiss (2012, 142, 152) and Mara (1997, 58) also discuss the danger Socrates faced as a result of trying to make others wiser and better.
92. Vlastos 1991, 177, 253 n. 62; Goldstein 2014, 11.
93. Russell 2005, 87.
94. Vlastos 1991, 177.
95. Klosko 1986, 47.
96. Bobonich 2011, 316. This would not be unlike the philosopher withdrawing from sexual activity when lacking a proper beloved, as we saw in chapter 3.
97. Miller 1986, 191.
98. Ibid.
99. Cf. *Phdr.* 252d–253b where a lover shapes a beloved's soul according to a divine model. See also *Cra.* 427c.
100. See also Armstrong 2004.
101. Weiss 2012, 31.
102. Irwin 1977, 237, 241.
103. See also *Chrm.* 170b.

104. See also White 1979, 164.
105. Cf. *R.* 412d where Plato has Socrates prioritize the guardians' love of the city.
106. See especially *R.* 595a–598d.
107. See also *R.* 602b, where Socrates declares the important difference between the two types of imitation to be whether one is serious or just playing a kind of game, and *R.* 603b, where he claims that if the source being reproduced through imitation is inferior then an inferior replication is produced.
108. Brill (2013, 5–6) agrees.
109. Morrison 2007, 243, referring to what he calls the "universal benevolence" view held by Hall (1977), Kraut (1991), and Kraut (1992). Morrison (2007, 244) is not convinced of this interpretation.
110. However, such a philosophical utopia (where the community is so well ordered that philosophical leadership isn't necessary) poses a serious problem for the politics of the *Republic*. If the community does not need philosophers to rule, to shape their cities, institutions, and souls, then how exactly would philosophers make a contribution to their community in exchange for their share of the farmers' food, well diggers' water, weavers' clothing, carpenters' housing, etc.? This type of concern leads some scholars to rule out the possibility of an exclusively contemplative life; see Reeve 1988, 203; Murphy 1951, 53–54 n. 2; Davies 1968, 125–26. Eric Brown (2000, 7) is critical of this sort of reasoning, claiming that it "sets up a false dilemma between the life of a philosopher-ruler and the life of pure contemplation; left out of the middle is the active philosophical life outside of political office, which would take full account of our tripartite nature." I question what Brown's concept of "active philosophical life" is if not what Reeve imagines philosophers do for the community in exchange for their share of the goods needed for survival provided by the producers. The divergence between Brown and Reeve here could be accounted for in terms of how narrowly or broadly one construes political leadership. It strikes me that Brown sees philosophers happily participating in the active philosophical life while needing to be compelled to take part in formal political office, while Reeve imagines that the philosophical life could be either formal political office or the informal but still intensely political life. My own construal of the political life includes both formal and informal politicking.
111. In contrast with many commentators, Sedley (2007, 275) describes the envisioned compulsion that brings philosophers out of their reluctance to rule as "not brute force operating against their better judgment, but the force of circumstances that makes the decision to rule, although not their preferred choice, one into which after weighing up their options they enter freely." Sedley's (2007, 281) "more benign" conception of the compulsion is compatible with my view that if philosophers were fortunate enough to find the conditions of the world (cities, institutions, and souls) to be optimal already, there would be less work for the philosopher, just the effort to maintain this share of the Good. Of course, philosophers have not been so lucky as to find themselves in conditions where their aptitude for shaping characters and institutions is not needed. Instead, they

must repair the world using the model of the Forms, to use the language of *R.* 500d–501b and 540a-b.

112. Cf. *Tht.* 174d-e. Following the digression, rulers are said to deal with citizens' bodies like a herder of farm animals.

113. See also Kraut 1991, 53.

114. See Ferrari 2005, 93, 110: he indicates that the philosopher-king does not welcome the task of ordering cities and souls (even his own) but merely submits to it as necessary. Cf. ibid., 115–16).

115. Kraut 1991, 51–53; Irwin 1977, 236–38, 241–43; Peters 1989, 176–83; Mahoney 1997, 26–27, 29–31, 34–37; Mahoney 1992, 280; Silverman 2010, 60–61; Silverman 2007, 42–43, 47–52, 61–67. Peters (1989, 180) notes that Irwin "lapses back into the contemplative vision and thus contradicts the more pervasive view in the *Republic* of reason as creative (242–243)."

116. McKeen (2010) has a different argument for the same conclusion.

117. Kraut 1991, 59.

118. Ibid., 58.

119. Ibid., 53.

120. Reeve (1988, 166) agrees, calling it a "psychological law" that "*if a person admires something, he imitates it*" (500c6-7).

121. Compare it with the compulsion that forces soul, which Plato indicates has a natural kinship with Forms, to "weave" a body for itself, according to the talk in the *Phaedo* (87e) or to crash into one, according to the palinode in the *Phaedrus* (246b-c, 248b-d).

122. For instance, at *Ap.* 31d, Plato has Socrates describe his routine effort to get others to care for their souls as something a father or older brother would do for his loved ones. In this we see what Brown (1994, 175) calls Socrates's "love of city-as-family."

123. See, for example, Nussbaum 1986, 183.

124. Lötter 2003, 204.

125. See, for instance, Hartsock 1983, 167, 199.

126. Lötter (2003) is an exception.

127. Griffin (1995, 14) makes a similar point.

128. See Ferrari 2005, esp. 15–20.

129. Waterfield 1993, xxviii. See also *R.* 519e–520a. I would add that, for Plato, the same holds for the unity of an individual's soul.

130. See, for example, Vlastos 1977, 12; and Barney 2001, 220.

131. See, for instance, Cooper 2000, 10, who writes, "We generally don't need others to come to our aid in pursuit of our own particular gratifications, certainly not in the way we need protection from attacks on our persons and property." From a feminist's perspective, I must suggest that Cooper's concept of human need ought to be broader, acknowledging that in fact we do have regular need of each other, especially, though not only, as infants and children, as students, and when one is elderly and/or ill.

132. Andrew 2006, 16.

133. In Peterson's treatment of the *Phaedo*, she (2011, 194) also pays attention to Socrates's request for free meals in the *Apology* as "ludicrously incongruous with" the austere asceticism extolled by Simmias and Cebes in the *Phaedo*.
134. Griffin (1995, 11) takes this as tongue in cheek.
135. See also Ferrari 2005, 19.
136. Saxonhouse 1984, 20-21.
137. Ferrari 2005, 23-24.
138. Andrew 2006, 16.
139. Seneca, *On Benefits*, I.viii.1.2.
140. See also *Ap.* 23c.
141. Cf. Xenophon, *Memorabilia*, I.6.2.
142. Vlastos (1994, 19-20) makes a similar observation and draws a firm conclusion that the historical Socrates influenced Plato's unconventional attitude toward class and sex. He (1994, 19) writes, "One could scarcely overstress the shattering effect in Plato's mind of Socrates' rejection of the age-old axiom that excellence of character was class-bound and gender-bound." Wender (1973, 84-86) also believes that Plato got a push in the direction of feminism from the historical Socrates and then voluntarily adopted such views for himself. See also Taylor 1956, 278. Furthermore, Saxonhouse (1984, 12) emphasizes that Alcibiades's speech in the *Symposium* accentuates the power of Socrates's words on whomever hears them—men, women, and children. She writes, "The music of Socrates' flute . . . is not limited in its impact by the sex, age, or social position of hearer."
143. Additionally, he understands as well or better than most that virtue does not arise from wealth and possessions, but that only virtue could ever make private wealth good for human beings (*Ap.* 30b).
144. Zoller 2009.
145. See, for instance, Ste. Croix (1981, 70-71), who asserts that Plato has been paid "wildly exaggerated respect" (71) for his political thought, which he thinks has been "largely unconcerned with historical reality" (70) and involves "arrogant contempt for all manual workers" (71). Only someone ignoring Plato's First City could make these claims.
146. Plumwood 1993, 98.
147. Keuls 1985, 395.
148. Annas (1981, 78-79) contends that the First City has not been given "a clear place in the *Republic*'s moral argument" and "adds nothing, except a context in which the Principle of Specialization is introduced in a plausible way."
149. See, for example, Crombie 1962, 89-90; Reeve 1988, 171, 178, 186; and Copper 2000, 13-15.
150. Barney 2001, 216.
151. Ibid., 218. Reeve (1988, 171, 186) and Bloom (1968, 346) also take the First City to be impossible. However, Barney takes Bloom's reasons for this belief to amount to a version of the "naiveté" reading. Hobbs (2007, 185) also denies that the First City is a serious sketch of how real human beings have lived or ever could live in peace. Meanwhile, Reeve (1988, 48-49, 170, 176-78, 285 n. 2) sees the

First City as rather similar to the degenerate oligarchic regime in Book 8, which strikes me as incorrect, given that the First City is not at all characterized by the wealth inequality that causes the oligarchic city to lack unity.

152. Barney 2001, 213, 221. See also Vlastos 1977, 12, and Long 2013, 107–108.

153. Barney 2001, 213. See also Vlastos 1977, 12, n. 40; Devereux 1979, 36–38; Hobbs 2007, 182; and Helmer 2016.

154. Barney 2001, 214.

155. Silverman 2007; McKeen 2004. Carpenter (2008, 56) considers the possibility of taking the First City's vegetarianism seriously.

156. Mahoney 1997, 32–33.

157. Zoller 2009.

158. Annas 1981, 75.

159. Accordingly, Trevor (1978, 22) calls Plato "the first great economic thinker of Greece." Schofield (1993, 191) agrees that Plato invents the concept of an economy. Lötter (2003, 194, 196) also emphasizes the economic rationale Plato uses to discuss the formation of communities and the preclusion of political corruption.

160. McKeen 2004, 85.

161. Davidson (1997, 25) complains that Socrates's randomness in listing *opson* demonstrates that *opson* "is something to be ignored, elided or forgotten, something of no importance." He (1997, 25–26) contends that philosophers are nervous about the whole category of *opson* because it "threatens to divert eating away from sustenance and into pleasure." While I agree that Socrates is focused on sustenance in his description of the First City, I disagree that he is hostile to *opson* as pleasurable. Plato has Socrates make explicit that the citizens of the First City enjoy many pleasures even though physical pleasure is not their guiding principle. If Plato's Socrates speaks in positive terms of the citizens taking pleasure in wine, sex, and singing, why would he be unwelcoming to *opson* so long as they too are enjoyed under the guidance of reason?

Perhaps if Plato had made this sketch of the First City more elaborate, we might have a better sense of Plato's view of *opson*, whether he looks down on them as Davidson suggests, whether they include fish or not. Davidson (1997, 27–35) observes the ambiguity between *opson* as fish specifically and as something eaten with bread generally. But he (1997, 30) concludes that Plato was probably unaware that *opson* could mean fish. Nevertheless, Davidson believes that the citizens of the First City would eat fish. He (1997, 17) considers fish "an appropriate source of protein for the inhabitants of the simple proto-city . . . a providential food . . . found in rivers and along shorelines to go with the collard greens and acorns he allows them." If the eating of fish were made explicit, that would change Davidson's reading of Socrates's view of *opson* as ignorably unimportant. Instead, Davidson (1997, 33) goes as far as to insinuate that, because he does not mention fish, Plato was not crazy about fish and probably disapproved of his peers' passion for fish. It is rather surprising and interesting that Plato does not discuss fish, but that alone is not evidence of disapproval. He does have the Athenian forbid fishing and eating fish in the *Laws*, as we shall see in chapter 5.

162. Ferrari 2005, 39.
163. See McCoy 2015 for an account of the gendered tone of the First City and Glaucon's rejection of it.
164. Ibid., 150, 152.
165. Devereux (1979, 38) maintains that Socrates does not characterize the First City's citizens as just.
166. Peterson (2011) has an excellent account of the way that Socrates is subjected to the views of interlocutors by the dialectical nature of their conversation. She (2011, 103–19) emphasizes that this results at times in Socrates possibly disagreeing with an interlocutor's position but building on that position nonetheless to see the further results of that way of thinking. In my view, Socrates's reaction to Glaucon's interruption of his account of the healthy city and the ensuing lengthy discussion stand as an excellent example of this.
167. Cf. *Stm.* 271e where Plato has the Eleatic Stranger link animals not eating each other with averting conflict and war.
168. Annas 1981, 11.
169. Cooper 2000, 12.
170. Ibid., 11.
171. Heinaman 1998, 37.
172. Silverman (2007, 68) observes that, while there is talk of the purification of Glaucon's feverish city, the city is never said to be fully cleansed.
173. Ibid., 69.
174. Barney 2001, 217.
175. Ibid., 221.
176. Ibid., 213. Cf. Brill (2013, 24), who contends that just because commentary on the political is absent in the *Phaedo* doesn't mean that political concerns are absent from it.
177. Strauss (1964, 95), Reeve (1988, 171), and Ferrari (2005, 39) take the First City to be anarchic.
178. Cf. *L.* 680a.
179. Annas 1981, 73.
180. Vlastos 1977, 13.
181. Vlastos 1977, 12. In contrast, Meyer 2005, 232.
182. Wallach (2001, 251–52) contends that nothing in the First City that prevents these citizens from being excessive and "eventually stumbling into war."
183. Cf. *R.* 460a. McKeen (2004, 79) agrees with my view of *R.* 372c.
184. *Pace* Strauss (1964, 95), who asserts that Plato is silent about procreation.
185. Hobbs 2007, 188.
186. *Pace* Strauss (1964, 94), who claims that this city is just "without anyone concerning himself with justice."
187. Cooper 2000, 24. Weinstein (2009, 441) has a similar position.

188. Lenzi 2000, 101.
189. See also Carpenter 2008, 56; and McCoy 2015, 149, 159 n. 3.
190. Rosen (1965, 464–65), Reeve (1988, 176), Waterfield (1993, 389), McKeen (2004, 73, 86), Hobbs (2007, 184–85, 188–89), and Schultz (2013, 146) also think the inhabitants of the First City do not philosophize.
191. On this point, I am in agreement with Reeve (1988, 178), who considers the First City a place that would only be stable if philosopher-rulers were ensuring the happiness of the community, which Reeve assumes *ex silentio* the First City lacks. I disagree with Reeve and Barney that Socrates's silence about rulers should necessarily be interpreted as indicative that the First City does not have even informal leadership.
192. Ruttenberg 1986, 154.
193. Cooper 2000, 16.
194. Meyer 2005, 232.
195. Cooper 2000, 11.
196. For instance, Reeve (1988, 172, 186) thinks the *Kallipolis* is the only city among the three presented in the *Republic* with the institutions necessary for producing philosopher-kings.
197. Cooper 2000, 14. Kass (1994, 120) similarly suggests that the human beings in Socrates's simple city—where meat is not on the menu—are not really human.
198. Barney 2001, 218.
199. See also Helmer 2016.
200. Barney 2001, 220.
201. McCoy 2015, 149.
202. Silverman (2007, 69) agrees.
203. Williams (1973, 199) notes, "Some minimal exercise of *logistikon* would seem to be involved in bringing it about that each man sticks to his own business, which is the most important manifestation of social *dikaiosunê*."
204. Peterson 2011, 110.
205. Barney 2001, 214.
206. Ibid., 218. Other scholars have also made this claim, including Cooper (2000, 13–14), Devereux (1979, 37), Annas (1981, 77), and Reeve (1988, 176–77). Cf. Arnopoulous's (1998, 143) contention that the description of the First City is a "prehistoric account."
207. White (1979, 215) notices that Plato considers neither the possibility that a desire could be impossible to eradicate and still cause harm nor the possibility that a desire could be eliminable and yet beneficial.
208. White (1979, 219) also argues that Plato is not an "ascetic" (White's term) because he does not call for starving necessary appetites.
209. Vlastos 1977, 12; Cooper 2000, 13–14; Devereux 1979, 37; Annas 1981, 77; Reeve 1988, 176–77; Barney 2001, 218.
210. Cf. *R.* 458d.
211. McCoy (2015, 156) also makes this point.

212. McKeen 2004, 72.
213. Ibid., 71, 87–92; 2006, 546, n. 16.
214. Ibid., 92.
215. Ibid., 90.
216. See Vlastos 1977, 14–15, and Blössner 2007, 346, 369, in contrast with Popper 1945, 169, and Grote 1888, 139.
217. Vlastos 1977, 14; emphasis added.
218. See also Neu 1971, 240.
219. Woolf 2000, 6–7, 12.

Chapter 5. Interpretative Possibilities for the Late Dialogues

1. I follow Bobonich (2010, 3), who reminds us that bringing the *Laws* in conversation with other dialogues does not require "any particular view about the development or unity of Plato's philosophical views. Indeed, one can remain neutral on all issues of chronology."
2. See, for instance, Rowe 2010 and Kraut 2010.
3. Carpenter (2008, 45–46) also pays attention to the capacities that souls come to have because of embodiment, such as percipience.
4. Gordon 2012, 27.
5. Van der Eijk 2005, 12.
6. Moravcsik 1976, 338; Tracy 1969.
7. Tracy 1969, 120.
8. Frede 2010b, 118.
9. Hackforth 1945, 58–59. See also Hampton 1990, 52.
10. Trans. Dorothea Frede in Cooper 1997.
11. Ogihara 2010, 217.
12. Frede 2010a, 14; Bossi 2010, 132; Obdrazalek 2010, 212.
13. Bobonich (2002, 289–90) contends that Plato presents two different accounts of moderation in the *Laws*: one driven by self-restraint and another by consonance.
14. Frede 2010b, 115.
15. Stalley 1983, 55. See also Morrow 1960.
16. Cf. *L.* 840a-c.
17. See Bobonich 2002 for a developmental account of Plato's attitude toward nonphilosophers' capacity for being virtuous.
18. Bobonich 2002, 428 notices distinctions Plato makes between general friendship and friendship that requires virtue.
19. Cf. Timaeus's mention of the most unifying bonds being caused by proportion (*Ti.* 31b-c).
20. Morrow (1960, 95) contends that Plato deliberately chose the region of Crete under discussion as the land for Magnesia because of its physical features.

21. Bobonich 2002, 11.
22. Morrow 1960, 132–33.
23. Brunt (1993, 265) emphasizes the minimal wealth inequality among the four classes.
24. See also Morrow 1960, 131 n. 112; Bobonich 2002, 375–76.

Epilogue

1. Goldstein 2015, 5–6.

Works Cited

Adam, James. 1911. *The Vitality of Platonism*. Cambridge: Cambridge University Press.
Adkins, Arthur W. H. 1960. *Merit and Responsibility: A Study of Greek Values*. New York: Oxford University Press.
Ahrensdorf, Peter. 1995. *The Death of Socrates and the Life of Philosophy*. Albany: State University of New York Press.
Anderson, Mark. 2014. *Plato and Nietzsche: Their Philosophical Art*. London: Bloomsbury.
Andrew, Edward G. 2006. *Patrons of Enlightenment*. Toronto: University of Toronto Press.
Annas, Julia. 1981. *An Introduction to Plato's Republic*. Oxford: Clarendon Press.
———. 2003. *Plato: A Very Short Introduction*. Oxford: Oxford University Press.
Anton, John P. 1962. "Some Dionysian References in the Platonic Dialogues." *Classical Journal* 58: 49–55.
———, and George L. Kustas, eds. 1971. *Essays in Ancient Greek Philosophy*, vol. 1. Albany: State University of New York Press.
Archer-Hind, R. D. 1973. *The Phaedo of Plato*. 2nd ed. London: MacMillan, 1894. Reprint, New York: Arno Press (page references are to the reprint edition).
Aristophanes. 2000. *Clouds*. Translated by Peter Meineck. Indianapolis: Hackett.
Armstrong, John M. 2004. "After the Ascent: Plato on Becoming like God." *Oxford Studies in Ancient Philosophy* 26: 171–83.
Arnopoulos, Paris. 1998. "Plato and Aristotle on War and Peace." *Philosophia* 28: 142–52.
Aronson, Simon H. 1972. "The Happy Philosopher—A Counterexample to Plato's Proof." *Journal of the History of Philosophy* 10 (4): 383–98.
Attfield, Robin. 1994. *Environmental Philosophy: Principles and Prospects*. Aldershot: Avebury.
Barker, Andrew. 2007. *The Science of Harmonics in Classical Greece*. Cambridge: Cambridge University Press.
Barnes, Jonathan, ed. 1984. *The Complete Works of Aristotle*. Vol. 2, translated by W. D. Ross, rev. J. O. Urmson. Princeton: Princeton University Press.

Barney, Rachel. 2001. "Platonism, Moral Nostalgia, and the 'City of Pigs.'" *Proceedings of the Boston Area Colloquium in Ancient Philosophy* 17: 207–27.
———. 2008. "*Eros* and Necessity in the Ascent from the Cave." *Ancient Philosophy* 28: 1–16.
———, Tad Brennan, and Charles Brittain, eds. 2012. *Plato and the Divided Self*. Cambridge: Cambridge University Press.
Belfiore, Elizabeth. 1980. "*Elenchus, Epode,* and Magic: Socrates as Silenus." *Phoenix* 34 (2): 128–37.
Bell, Jeremy, and Michael Naas, eds. 2015. *Plato's Animals: Gadflies, Horses, Swans, and Other Philosophical Beasts*. Bloomington: Indiana University Press.
Benardete, Seth. 2001. "On Plato's *Symposium*." In *Plato's Symposium*, translated by Seth Benardete, 179–99. Chicago: The University of Chicago Press.
Berry, Christopher J. 1989. "Of Pigs and Men: Luxury in Plato's *Republic*." *Polis* 8: 2–24.
Bloom, Allan. 1977. "Response to Hall." *Political Theory* 5: 315–30.
———. 2001. "The Ladder of Love." In *Plato's Symposium*, translated by Seth Benardete, 55–177. Chicago: The University of Chicago Press.
———, trans. 1968. *The Republic of Plato, with Notes and Interpretive Essay*. New York: Basic Books.
Blondell, Ruby. 2006. "Where Is Socrates on the 'Ladder of Love'?" In *Plato's Symposium: Issues in Interpretation and Reception*, edited by James Lesher, Debra Nails, and Frisbee Sheffield, 147–78. Cambridge: Harvard University Press.
Blössner, Norbert. 1997. *Dialogform und Argument: Studien zu Platons "Politeia."* Stuttgart: Franz Steiner Verlag.
———. 2007. "The City-Soul Analogy." In *The Cambridge Companion to Plato's Republic*, edited by G. R. F. Ferrari, 345–85. Cambridge: Cambridge University Press.
Bluck, R. S. 1955. *Plato's Phaedo*. London: Routledge & Kegan Paul.
Bluestone, Natalie Harris. 1994. "Why Women Cannot Rule: Sexism in Plato Scholarship." In *Feminist Interpretations of Plato*, edited by Nancy Tuana, 109–30. University Park: The Pennsylvania State University Press.
Bobonich, Christopher. 2002. *Plato's Utopia Recast: His Later Ethics and Politics*. Oxford: Oxford University Press.
———. 2010. "Introduction." In *Plato's Laws: A Critical Guide*, edited by Christopher Bobonich, 1–11. Cambridge: Cambridge University Press.
———. 2011. "Plato's Politics." In *The Oxford Handbook of Plato*, edited by Gail Fine, 311–35. Oxford: Oxford University Press.
———, ed. 2010. *Plato's Laws: A Critical Guide*. Cambridge: Cambridge University Press.
Bordo, Susan. 2003. *Unbearable Weight: Feminism, Western Culture, and the Body*. Berkeley: University of California Press.
Bossi, Beatriz. 2010. "How Consistent Is Plato with Regard to the 'Unlimited' Character of Pleasure in the *Philebus*?" In *Plato's Philebus: Selected Papers from the Eighth Symposium Platonicum*, edited by John Dillon and Luc Brisson, 123–33. Sankt Augustin: Academia Verlag.

Bostock, David. 1986. *Plato's Phaedo*. Oxford: Clarendon Press.
Brann, Eva. 2004. *The Music of the Republic: Essays on Socrates' Conversations and Plato's Writings*. Philadelphia: Paul Dry Books.
Brickhouse, Thomas C. 1981. "The Paradox of the Philosopher's Rule." *Apeiron* 15: 1–9.
Brill, Sara. 2013. *Plato on the Limits of Human Life*. Bloomington: Indiana University Press.
———. 2015. "Animals and Sexual Difference in the *Timaeus*." In *Plato's Animals: Gadflies, Horses, Swans, and Other Philosophical Beasts*, edited by Jeremy Bell and Michael Naas, 161–75. Bloomington: Indiana University Press.
Brisson, Luc. 2006. "Agathon, Pausanias, and Diotima in Plato's *Symposium*: *Paiderastia* and *Philosophia*." In *Plato's Symposium: Issues in Interpretation and Reception*, edited by James Lesher, Debra Nails, and Frisbee Sheffield, 229–51. Cambridge, Harvard University Press.
Broadie, Sarah. 2001. "Soul and Body in Plato and Descartes." *Proceedings of the Aristotelian Society* 101: 295–308.
Brown, Eric. 2000. "Justice and Compulsion for Plato's Philosopher-Rulers." *Ancient Philosophy* 20: 1–17.
Brown, Peter. 1990. "Bodies and Minds: Sexuality and Renunciation in Early Christianity." In *Before Sexuality: The Construction of Erotic Experience in the Ancient World*, edited by David M. Halperin, John J. Winkler, and Froma I. Zeitlin, 479–93. Princeton: Princeton University Press.
Brown, Wendy. 1994. "'Supposing Truth Were a Woman . . .': Plato's Subversion of Masculine Discourse." In *Feminist Interpretations of Plato*, edited by Nancy Tuana, 157–80. University Park: The Pennsylvania State University Press.
Brunt, P. A. 1993. *Studies in Greek History and Thought*. Oxford: Clarendon Press.
Buchan, Morag. 1999. *Women in Plato's Political Theory*. New York: Routledge.
Burger, Ronna. 1980. *Plato's Phaedrus: A Defense of a Philosophic Art of Writing*. Tuscaloosa: The University of Alabama Press.
———. 1984. *Plato's Phaedo: A Platonic Labyrinth*. New Haven: Yale University Press.
Burnet, John. 1900–1907. *Platonis Opera*. 5 vols. Oxford: Clarendon Press.
Burnet, J. 1911. *Plato's Phaedo*. Oxford: Oxford University Press.
Bury, R. G., ed. 1932. *The Symposium of Plato*. 2nd ed. Cambridge. 1st ed. 1909.
Carafides, J. L. 1971. "The Last Words of Socrates." *Platon* 23: 229–32.
Carone, Gabriela Roxana. 1998. "Plato and the Environment." *Environmental Ethics* 20: 115–33.
———. 2006. "The Virtues of Platonic Love." In *Plato's Symposium: Issues in Interpretation and Reception*, edited by James Lesher, Debra Nails, and Frisbee Sheffield, 208–26. Cambridge: Harvard University Press.
Carpenter, Amber. 2008. "Embodying Intelligence: Animals and Us in Plato's *Timaeus*." In *Platonism and Forms of Intelligence*, edited by John Dillon and Marie-Élise Zovko, 39–58. Berlin: Akademie Verlag.
Carson, Anne. 1990. "Putting Her in Her Place: Woman, Dirt, and Desire." In *Before Sexuality: The Construction of Erotic Experience in the Ancient Greek*

World, edited by David M. Halperin, John J. Winkler, and Froma I. Zeitlin, 135–69. Princeton: Princeton University Press.

———. 1998. *Eros the Bittersweet*. Princeton: Princeton University Press, 1986. Reprint, Normal, IL: Dalkey Archive Press (page references are to the reprint edition).

Chroust, Anton-Hermann. 1957. *Socrates, Man and Myth*. South Bend: University of Notre Dame Press.

Cicero, Marcus Tullius. 1913. *De Officiis* [*On Duties*]. Vol. 21, edited and translated by Walter Miller. Loeb Classical Library no. 30. Cambridge: Harvard University Press.

Clark, Lorenne, and Lynda Lange, eds. 1979. *The Sexism of Social and Political Theory from Plato to Nietzsche*. Toronto: University of Toronto Press.

Classen, C. Joachim. 1959. *Sprachliche Deutung als Triebkraft platonischen und sokratischen Philosophierens*. Munich: C. H. Beck'sche Verlagsbuchhandlung.

Cleary, J. J., ed. 1999. *Traditions of Platonism: Essays in Honour of John Dillon*. Aldershot: Ashgate.

Cobb, William S. 1993. *The Symposium and the Phaedrus: Plato's Erotic Dialogues*. Albany: State University of New York Press.

Collingwood, R. G. 1945. *The Idea of Nature*. Oxford: Clarendon Press.

Collins, Patricia Hill. 2004. *Black Sexual Politics: African Americans, Gender, and the New Racism*. New York: Routledge.

Cooper, John M., 1999. "The Psychology of Justice in Plato." In *Reason and Emotion: Essays on Ancient Moral Psychology and Ethical Theory*, 138–49. Princeton: Princeton University Press.

———. 2000. "Two Theories of Justice." *Proceedings and Addresses of the American Philosophical Association* 74: 5–27.

———. 2007. "Socrates and Philosophy as a Way of Life." In *Maieusis: Essays on Ancient Philosophy in Honour of Myles Burnyeat*, edited by Dominic Scott, 20–43. Oxford: Oxford University Press.

———, ed. 1997. *Plato: Complete Works*. Indianapolis: Hackett.

Cornford, Francis M. 1941. *The Republic of Plato*. London: Oxford University Press.

Crombie, I. M. 1962. *An Examination of Plato's Doctrines*. New York: Humanities Press.

Cross, R. C., and A. D. Woozley. 1964. *Plato's Republic: A Philosophical Commentary*. New York: St. Martin's Press.

Crossman, R. H. S. 1939. *Plato Today*. New York: Oxford University Press.

Damascius. 1977. *Lectures on the Phaedo*. In *The Greek Commentaries on Plato's Phaedo, II Damascius*. Edited and translated by L. G. Westerink. Amsterdam: North Holland.

Danzig, Gabriel. 2010. *Apologizing for Socrates: How Plato and Xenophon Created Our Socrates*. Lanham, MD: Lexington Books.

Davidson, James. 1997. *Courtesans and Fishcakes: Consuming Passions of Classical Athens*. Chicago: The University of Chicago Press.

Davies, J. 1968. "A Note on the Philosopher's Descent into the Cave." *Philologus* 112: 121–26.

Davis, Michael. 1980. "Plato and Nietzsche on Death: An Introduction to Plato's *Phaedo*." *Ancient Philosophy* 1: 69-80.
Demos, Raphael. 1964. "A Fallacy in Plato's *Republic*?" *The Philosophical Review* 73: 395-98.
De Vries, G. J. 1969. *A Commentary on the Phaedrus of Plato*. Amsterdam: A. M. Hakkert.
Devereux, Daniel. 1979. "Socrates' First City in the *Republic*." *Apeiron* 13: 36-40.
Dillon, John, and Luc Brisson, eds. 2010. *Plato's Philebus: Selected Papers from the Eighth Symposium Platonicum*. Sankt Augustin: Academia Verlag.
Diogenes Laertius. 1995. *Lives of Eminent Philosophers*. Vol. 2. Translated by R. D. Hicks. Cambridge: Harvard University Press.
Dodds, E. R. 1951. *The Greeks and the Irrational*. Berkeley: University of California Press.
———. 1959. *Plato, Gorgias: A Revised Text with Introduction and Commentary.* Oxford: Clarendon Press.
———. 1965. *Pagan and Christian in an Age of Anxiety: Some Aspects of Religious Experience from Marcus Aurelius to Constantine*. Cambridge: Cambridge University Press.
Dorion, Louis-André. 2012. "*Enkrateia* and the Partition of the Soul in the *Gorgias*." In *Plato and the Divided Self*, edited by Rachel Barney, Tad Brennan, and Charles Brittain, 33-52. Cambridge: Cambridge University Press.
———, and Michele Bandini, eds. 2000. *Xenophon Memorabilia*. Vol. 1. Paris: Belles Lettres.
Dorter, Kenneth. 1982. *Plato's Phaedo: An Interpretation*. Toronto: Toronto University Press.
———. 2003. "The Soul's Mediation between Corporeality and the Good." In *The Classics of Western Philosophy: A Reader's Guide*, edited by Jorge J. E. Gracia, Gregory M. Reichberg, and Bernard N. Schumacher, 10-19. New York: Blackwell.
———. 2006. *The Transformation of Plato's Republic*. Lanham, MD: Lexington Books.
Dover, K. J. 1978. *Greek Homosexuality*. Cambridge: Harvard University Press.
———. 1984. "Classical Greek Attitudes to Sexual Behaviour." In *Women in the Ancient World: The Arethusa Papers*, edited by John Peradotto and J. P. Sullivan, 143-57. Albany: State University of New York Press.
———, ed. 1980. *Plato: Symposium*. Cambridge: Cambridge University Press.
duBois, Page. 1994. "The Platonic Appropriation of Reproduction." In *Feminist Interpretations of Plato*, edited by Nancy Tuana, 139-56. University Park: The Pennsylvania State University Press.
Edelstein, Ludwig. 1945. "The Role of Eryximachus in Plato's *Symposium*." *Transactions of the American Philological Association* 76: 85-103.
Edmonds, Radcliffe G. III. 2004. *Myths of the Underworld Journey: Plato, Aristophanes, and the 'Orphic' Gold Tablets*. Cambridge: Cambridge University Press.
Ehrenreich, Barbara. 1989. *Fear of Falling: The Inner Life of the Middle Class*. New York: HarperCollins.

Ferrari, G. R. F. 1985. "The Struggle in the Soul: Plato, *Phaedrus* 253c7–255a1." *Ancient Philosophy* 5: 1–10.
———. 1987. *Listening to the Cicadas: A Study of Plato's Phaedrus*. Cambridge: Cambridge University Press.
———. 2005. *City and Soul in Plato's Republic*. Chicago: The University of Chicago Press.
———, ed. 2007. *The Cambridge Companion to Plato's Republic*. Cambridge: Cambridge University Press.
Ferrari, Michel, and George Potworowski, eds. 2008. *Teaching for Wisdom: Cross-Cultural Perspectives on Fostering Wisdom*. Dordrecht: Springer.
Fine, Gail. 2011. "Introduction." In *The Oxford Handbook of Plato*, edited by Gail Fine, 3–35. Oxford: Oxford University Press.
———, ed. 2011. *The Oxford Handbook of Plato*. Oxford: Oxford University Press.
Foster, M. B. 1936. "Some Implications of a Passage in Plato's *Republic*." *Philosophy* 11: 301–308.
Fowler, Harold North, trans. 1995. *Plato Euthyphro Apology Crito Phaedo Phaedrus*. Cambridge: Harvard University Press.
Frede, Dorothea. 1993. "Out of the Cave: What Socrates Learned from Diotima." In *Nomodeiktes: Greek Studies in Honor of Martin Ostwald*, edited by R. M. Rosen and J. Farrell, 397–422. Ann Arbor: University of Michigan Press.
———. 1999. *Platons Phaidon*. Darmstadt: Wissenshaftliche Buchgesellschaft.
———. 2001. "Not in the Book: How Does Recollection Work?" In *Plato's Phaedo: Proceedings of the Second Symposium Platonicum Pragense*, edited by Ales Havlícek and Filip Karfík, 241–65. Prague: Oikoymenh.
———. 2010a. "Life and Its Limitations: The Conception of Happiness in the *Philebus*." In *Plato's Philebus: Selected Papers from the Eighth Symposium Platonicum*, edited by John Dillon and Luc Brisson, 3–16. Sankt Augustin: Academia Verlag.
———. 2010b. "Puppets on a String: Moral Psychology in *Laws* Books 1 and 2." In *Plato's Laws: A Critical Guide*, edited by Christopher Bobonich, 108–26. Cambridge: Cambridge University Press.
———, trans. 1997. *Philebus*. In *Plato: Complete Works*, edited by John M. Cooper, 398–456. Indianapolis: Hackett.
Frendo, Henry, ed. 2010. *The European Mind: Narrative and Identity*, vol. 1. Malta: University of Malta Press.
Friedländer, Paul. 1958. *Plato*. Vol. 1. *An Introduction*. Translated by Hans Meyerhoff. New York: Bollingen Foundation.
———. 1964. *Plato*. Vol. 2. *The Dialogues: First Period*. Translated by Hans Meyerhoff. New York: Bollingen Foundation.
———. 1969. *Plato*. Vol. 3. *The Dialogues: Second and Third Periods*. Translated by Hans Meyerhoff. New York: Bollingen Foundation.
Gallop, David. 1975. *Plato, Phaedo*. Oxford: Oxford University Press.
———. 2001. "Emotions in the *Phaedo*." In *Plato's Phaedo: Proceedings of the Second Symposium Platonicum Pragense*, edited by Ales Havlícek and Filip Karfík, 275–86. Prague: Oikoymenh.

Gentzler, Jyl, ed. 1998. *Method in Ancient Philosophy*. Oxford: Oxford University Press.
Gill, Christopher. 1990. "Platonic Love and Individuality." In *Polis and Politics: Essays in Greek Moral and Political Philosophy*, edited by Andros Loizou and Harry Lesser, 69–88. Aldershot: Avebury.
Gilman, Sander. 1985. "Black Bodies, White Bodies: Toward an Iconography of Female Sexuality in Late Nineteenth-Century Art, Medicine, and Literature." *Critical Inquiry* 12: 204–42.
Goldstein, Rebecca Newberger. 2014. *Plato at the Googleplex: Why Philosophy Won't Go Away*. New York: Pantheon Books.
Gonzalez-Arnal, Stella, Gill Jagger, and Kathleen Lennon, eds. 2012. *Embodied Selves*. London: Palgrave Macmillan.
Gordon, Jill. 2012. *Plato's Erotic World: From Cosmic Origins to Human Death*. Cambridge: Cambridge University Press.
Gosling, J. C. B. 1973. *Plato*. London: Routledge & Kegan Paul.
———, and C. C. W. Taylor. *The Greeks on Pleasure*. Oxford: Clarendon Press.
Gould, Thomas. 1963. *Platonic Love*. New York: The Free Press of Glencoe.
Gracia, Jorge J. E., Gregory M. Reichberg, and Bernard N. Schumacher, eds. 2003. *The Classics of Western Philosophy: A Reader's Guide*. New York: Blackwell.
Griffin, Drew E. 1995. "Socrates' Poverty: Virtue and Money in Plato's *Apology of Socrates*." *Ancient Philosophy* 15: 1–16.
Griswold, Charles L. 1986. *Self-Knowledge in Plato's Phaedrus*. University Park: The Pennsylvania State University.
Griswold, Charles. 2003. "Longing for the Best: Plato on Reconciliation with Imperfection." *Arion* 11: 101–36.
Grote, George. 1888. *Plato and the Other Companions of Socrates*. Vol. 4. London: J. Murray.
Grube, G. M. A. 1935. *Plato's Thought*. London: Methuen.
———, trans. 1997. *Apology*. In *Plato: Complete Works*, edited by John M. Cooper, 17–36. Indianapolis: Hackett.
———, trans. 1997. *Phaedo*. In *Plato: Complete Works*, edited by John M. Cooper, 49–100. Indianapolis: Hackett.
———, trans., and rev. C. D. C. Reeve. 1997. *Republic*. In *Plato: Complete Works*, edited by John M. Cooper, 971–1223. Indianapolis: Hackett.
Guthrie, W. K. C. 1975. *A History of Greek Philosophy*. Vol. 4. *Plato: the Man and His Dialogues Earlier Period*. Cambridge: Cambridge University Press.
Hackforth, R. 1945. *Plato's Examination of Pleasure: A Translation of the Philebus with Introduction and Commentary*. Cambridge: Cambridge University Press.
———. 1952. *Plato's Phaedrus*. Cambridge: Cambridge University Press.
———. 1955. *Plato's Phaedo*. Cambridge: Cambridge University Press.
Hadot, Pierre. 2002. *What Is Ancient Philosophy?* Translated by Michael Chase. Cambridge: Harvard University Press.
Hall, Dale. 1977. "The *Republic* and 'The Limits of Politics.'" *Political Theory* 5: 193–313.

Halperin, David M. 1985. "Platonic *Erôs* and What Men Call Love." *Ancient Philosophy* 5: 161–204.

———. 1986. "Plato and Erotic Reciprocity." *Classical Antiquity* 5: 60–80.

———, John J. Winkler, and Froma I. Zeitlin, eds. 1990. *Before Sexuality: The Construction of Erotic Experience in the Ancient World*. Princeton: Princeton University Press.

Hampton, Cynthia. 1990. *Pleasure, Knowledge, and Being: An Analysis of Plato's Philebus*. Albany: State University of New York Press.

———. 1994. "Overcoming Dualism: The Importance of the Intermediate in Plato's *Philebus*." In *Feminist Interpretations of Plato*, edited by Nancy Tuana, 217–42. University Park: The Pennsylvania State University Press.

Hargrove, Eugene. 1989. *Foundations of Environmental Ethics*. Englewood Cliffs, NJ: Prentice-Hall.

Harte, Verity. 1999. "Conflicting Values in Plato's *Crito*." *Archiv für Geschichte der Philosophie* 81 (1999): 117–47.

Hartsock, Nancy C. M. 1983. *Money, Sex, and Power: Toward a Feminist Historical Materialism*. New York: Longman.

Havlícek, Ales, and Filip Karfík, eds. 2001. *Plato's Phaedo: Proceedings of the Second Symposium Platonicum Pragense*. Prague: Oikoymenh.

Heinaman, Robert. 1998. "Social Justice in Plato's *Republic*." *Polis* 15: 23–43.

———. 2004. "Why Justice Does Not Pay in Plato's *Republic*." *Classical Quarterly* 54: 379–93.

Henderson, Jeffrey. 1991. *The Maculate Muse: Obscene Language in Attic Comedy*. Oxford: Oxford University Press.

Hesiod. 1988. *Theogony and Works and Days*. Translated by M. L. West. Oxford: Oxford University Press.

Hicks, R. D. 1972. *Diogenes Laertius: Lives of Eminent Philosophers with an English Translation*. 2 vols. Cambridge: Harvard University Press.

Hindley, Clifford. 1999. "Xenophon on Male Love." *Classical Quarterly* 49: 74–99.

———. 2004. "Sophron Eros: Xenophon's Ethical Erotics." In *Xenophon and His World*, edited by Christopher Tuplin, 125–46. Stuttgart: Franz Steiner Verlag.

Hobbs, Angela. 2007. "Plato on War." In *Maieusis: Essays in Ancient Philosophy in Honour of Myles Burnyeat*, edited by Dominic Scott, 176–94. Oxford: Oxford University Press.

hooks, bell. 1992. *Black Looks: Race and Representation*. Boston: South End Press.

Hunter, Richard. 2004. *Plato's Symposium*. New York: Oxford University Press.

Irwin, Terence. 1977. *Plato's Moral Theory: The Early and Middle Dialogues*. Oxford: Clarendon Press.

———. 1979. *Plato, Gorgias*. Oxford: Clarendon Press.

———. 1995. *Plato's Ethics*. Oxford: Oxford University Press.

Jackson, B. D. 1971. "The Prayers of Socrates." *Phronesis* 16: 14–37.

Jaeger, Werner. 1971. *Paideia: The Ideals of Greek Culture*. Vol. 3. Translated by Gilbert Highet. Oxford: Oxford University Press. 1st ed. 1943 (page references are to the reprint edition).

Jaggar, Alison. 1983. *Feminist Politics and Human Nature.* Totowa, NJ: Rowman and Allanheld.

Jowett, Benjamin. n.d. *The Works of Plato.* 4 vols. New York: Tudor Publishing.

Kahn, Charles. 1987. "Plato's Theory of Desire." *Review of Metaphysics* 41: 77–103.

———. 1996. *Plato and the Socratic Dialogues: The Philosophical Use of a Literary Form.* Cambridge: Cambridge University Press.

Kahn, Charles H. 2001. *Pythagoras and the Pythagoreans: A Brief History.* Indianapolis: Hackett.

Kass, Leon R. 1994. *The Hungry Soul: Eating and the Perfecting of Our Nature.* Chicago: University of Chicago Press.

Keuls, Eva C. 1985. *The Reign of the Phallus: Sexual Politics in Ancient Athens.* New York: Harper and Row.

King, Ynestra. 1989. "The Ecology of Feminism and the Feminism of Ecology." In *Healing the Wounds,* edited by Judith Plant, 18–28. Philadelphia: New Society Publishers.

Kingsley, Peter. 1995. *Ancient Philosophy, Mystery, and Magic: Empedocles and the Pythagorean Tradition.* Oxford: Oxford University Press.

Klosko, George. 1986. *The Development of Plato's Political Theory.* New York: Methuen.

Konstan, David E., and Elisabeth Young-Bruehl. 1982. "Eryximachus' Speech in the *Symposium.*" *Apeiron* 16: 40–46.

Kosman, L. A. 1976. "Platonic Love." In *Facets of Plato's Philosophy,* edited by W. H. Werkmeister, 53–69. Assen: Van Gorcum.

Kraut, Richard. 1973. "Egoism, Love, and Political Office." *Philosophical Review* 82: 330–44.

———. 1991. "Return to the Cave: *Republic* 519–521." *Proceedings of the Boston Area Colloquium in Ancient Philosophy* 7: 43–62.

———. 1992. "The Defense of Justice in Plato's *Republic.*" In *The Cambridge Companion to Plato,* edited by Richard Kraut, 311–37. Cambridge: Cambridge University Press.

———. 1997. "The Defense of Justice in Plato's *Republic.*" In *Plato's Republic: Critical Essays,* edited by Richard Kraut, 197–221. Lanham, MD: Rowman and Littlefield.

———. 2010. "Ordinary Virtue from the *Phaedo* to the *Laws.*" In *Plato's Laws: A Critical Guide,* 51–70. Cambridge: Cambridge University Press.

———. 2011. "Plato on Love." In *The Oxford Handbook of Plato,* edited by Gail Fine, 286–310. Oxford: Oxford University Press.

———, ed. 1992. *The Cambridge Companion to Plato.* Cambridge: Cambridge University Press.

———, ed. 1997. *Plato's Republic: Critical Essays.* Lanham, MD: Rowman and Littlefield.

Lampert, Laurence. 2010. *How Philosophy Became Socratic: A Study of Plato's Protagoras, Charmides, and Republic.* Chicago: The University of Chicago Press.

Lane, Melissa. 2007. "Virtue as the Love of Knowledge in Plato's *Symposium* and *Republic*." In *Maieusis: Essays on Ancient Philosophy in Honour of Myles Burnyeat*, edited by Dominic Scott, 44–67. Oxford: Oxford University Press.

Lange, Lynda. 1979. "The Function of Equal Education in Plato's *Republic* and *Laws*." In *The Sexism of Social and Political Theory from Plato to Nietzsche*, edited by Lorenne Clark and Lynda Lange, 3–15. Toronto: University of Toronto Press.

Lear, Jonathan. 1998. *Open Minded: Working out the Logic of the Soul*. Cambridge: Harvard University Press.

Lee, E. N., A. P. D. Mourelatos, and R. M. Rorty, eds. 1973. *Exegesis and Argument: Studies in Greek Philosophy Presented to Gregory Vlastos* (*Phronesis* suppl. vol. 1). Assen: Van Gorcum.

Lenzi, Mary. 2000. "Plato and Echo-Feminism: Platonic Psychology and Politics for Peace." In *Peacemaking: Lessons from the Past, Visions for the Future*, edited by Judith Presler and Sally J. Scholz, 91–104. Amsterdam, Rodopi.

Lesher, James, Debra Nails, and Frisbee Sheffield, eds. 2006. *Plato's Symposium: Issues in Interpretation and Reception*. Cambridge: Harvard University Press.

Levett, M. J., trans., and rev. Myles F. Burnyeat. 1997. *Theaetetus*. In *Plato: Complete Works*, edited by John M. Cooper, 157–234. Indianapolis: Hackett.

Levin, Susan B. 2014. *Plato's Rivalry with Medicine: A Struggle and Its Resolution*. Oxford: Oxford University Press.

Linforth, Ivan M. 1944. "Soul and Sieve in Plato's *Gorgias*." In *University of California Publications in Classical Philology*, vol. 12, 295–313. Berkeley: University of California Press.

———. 1946. *The Corybantic Rites in Plato*. Berkeley: University of California Press.

Loizou, Andros, and Harry Lesser, eds. 1990. *Polis and Politics: Essays in Greek Moral and Political Philosophy*. Aldershot: Avebury.

Lombardo, Stanley, and Karen Bell, trans. 1997. *Protagoras*. In *Plato: Complete Works*, edited by John M. Cooper, 746–90. Indianapolis: Hackett.

Long, A. G. 2013. *Conversation and Self-Sufficiency in Plato*. Oxford: Oxford University Press.

Lorenz, Henrik. 2006. *The Brute Within: Appetitive Desire in Plato and Aristotle*. Oxford: Oxford University Press.

Lötter, H. P. P. 2003. "The Significance of Poverty and Wealth in Plato's *Republic*." *South African Journal of Philosophy* 22: 189–206.

MacIntyre, Alasdair. 1999. *Dependent Rational Animals: Why Human Beings Need the Virtues*. Chicago: Open Court.

Mahoney, Timothy. 1992. "Do Plato's Philosopher-Rulers Sacrifice Self-Interest to Justice?" *Phronesis* 37: 265–82.

———. 1997. "Platonic Ecology: A Response to Plumwood's Critique of Plato." *Ethics and the Environment* 2: 25–41.

Mara, Gerald M. 1997. *Socrates' Discursive Democracy: Logos and Ergon in Platonic Political Philosophy*. Albany: State University of New York Press.

McCoy, Marina. 2015. "The City of Sows: Sexual Differentiation in the *Republic*." In *Plato's Animals: Gadflies, Horses, Swans, and Other Philosophical Beasts*, edited by Jeremy Bell and Michael Naas, 149–60. Bloomington: Indiana University Press.

McKeen, Catherine. 2004. "Swillsburg City Limits (The 'City of Pig': *Republic* 370c–372d)." *Polis* 21: 70–92.

———. 2006. "Why Women Must Guard and Rule in Plato's *Kallipolis*." *Pacific Philosophical Quarterly* 87: 527–48.

———. 2010. "'Standing Apart in the Shelter of the City Wall': The Contemplative Ideal vs. the Politically Engaged Philosopher in Plato's Political Theory." *The Southern Journal of Philosophy* 48: 197–216.

McPherran, Mark L. 1996. *The Religion of Socrates*. University Park: The Pennsylvania State University Press.

———. 2006. "Medicine, Magic, and Religion in Plato's *Symposium*." In *Plato's Symposium: Issues in Interpretation and Reception*, edited by James Lesher, Debra Nails, and Frisbee Sheffield, 71–95. Cambridge: Harvard University Press.

Meyer, Susan Suavé. 2005. "Class Assignment and the Principle of Specialization in Plato's *Republic*." *Proceedings of the Boston Area Colloquium in Ancient Philosophy* 20: 229–43.

Miller, Mitchell. 1985. "Platonic Provocations: Reflections on the Soul and the Good in the *Republic*." In *Platonic Investigations*, edited by Dominic O'Meara, 163–93. Washington, DC: Catholic University of America Press.

Miller, Mitchell H. Jr. 1986. *Plato's Parmenides: The Conversion of the Soul*. Princeton: Princeton University Press. Reprint, University Park: The Pennsylvania State University Press, 1991 (page references are to the reprint edition).

Mohr, Richard D., and Barbara M. Sattler, eds. 2010. *One Book, The Whole Universe: Plato's Timaeus Today*. Las Vegas: Parmenides.

Moravcsik, J. M. E. 1971. "Reason and Eros in the 'Ascent' Passage of the *Symposium*." In *Essays in Ancient Greek Philosophy*, vol. 1, edited by John P. Anton and George L. Kustas, 285–302. Albany: State University of New York Press.

Moravcsik, Julius. 1976. "Ancient and Modern Conceptions of Health and Medicine." *The Journal of Medicine and Philosophy* 1: 337–48.

———. 2000. "Health, Healing, and Plato's Ethics." *Journal of Value Inquiry* 34: 7–26.

———. 2001. "Inner Harmony and the Human Ideal in *Republic* IV and IX." *The Journal of Ethics* 5: 39–56.

Morrison, Donald R. 2007. "The Utopia Character of Plato's Ideal City." In *The Cambridge Companion to Plato's Republic*, edited by G. R. F. Ferrari, 232–55. Cambridge: Cambridge University Press.

Morrow, Glenn R. 1960. *Plato's Cretan City: A Historical Interpretation of the* Laws. Princeton: Princeton University Press.

Murdoch, Iris. 1970. *The Sovereignty of Good*. New York: Schocken.

Murphy, N. R. 1951. *The Interpretation of Plato's Republic*. Oxford: Clarendon Press.

Muscio, Inga. 2002. *Cunt: A Declaration of Independence*. 2nd ed. New York: Seal Press.

Nails, Debra. 2002. *The People of Plato: A Prosopography of Plato and Other Socratics*. Indianapolis: Hackett.

———. 2006. "Tragedy Off-Stage." In *Plato's Symposium: Issues in Interpretation and Reception*, edited by James Lesher, Debra Nails, and Frisbee Sheffield, 179–207. Cambridge: Harvard University Press.

Nehamas, Alexander. 1998. *The Art of Living: Socratic Reflections from Plato to Foucault*. Berkeley: University of California Press.

———. 2007. "Beauty of Body, Nobility of Soul: The Pursuit of Love in Plato's *Symposium*." In *Maieusis: Ancient Philosophy in Honor of Myles Burnyeat*, edited by Dominic Scott, 97–135. Oxford: Oxford University Press.

———, and Paul Woodruff, trans. 1989. *Plato, Symposium*. Indianapolis: Hackett.

———, and Paul Woodruff, trans. 1997. *Phaedrus*. In *Plato: Complete Works*, edited by John M. Cooper, 506–56. Indianapolis: Hackett.

Neu, Jerome. 1971. "Plato's Analogy of State and Individual: *The Republic* and the Organic Theory of the State." *Philosophy* 46: 238–54.

Nietzsche, Friedrich. 1967. *The Birth of Tragedy*. Translated by Walter Kaufmann. New York: Vintage Books.

———. 1974. *The Gay Science*. Translated with commentary by Walter Kaufmann. New York: Vintage Books.

———. 1976. *Twilight of the Idols*. Translated by Walter Kaufmann. In *The Portable Nietzsche*, edited by Walter Kaufmann. New York: Penguin Books.

Nightingale, A. W. 1993. "The Folly of Praise: Plato's Critique of Encomiastic Discourse in the *Lysis* and *Symposium*." *Classical Quarterly* 43: 112–30.

———. 1995. *Genres in Dialogue: Plato and the Construct of Philosophy*. Cambridge: Cambridge University Press.

North, Helen. 1966. *Sophrosune: Self-Knowledge and Self-Restraint in Greek Literature*. Ithaca: Cornell University Press.

North, Helen F., ed. 1977. *Interpretations of Plato: A Swarthmore Symposium*, Mnemosyne suppl. vol. 50. Leiden, Netherlands: E. J. Brill.

Nussbaum, Martha C. 1986. *The Fragility of Goodness*. Cambridge: Cambridge University Press.

Nye, Andrea. 1994. "Irigaray and Diotima in Plato's Symposium." In *Feminist Interpretations of Plato*, edited by Nancy Tuana, 197–215. University Park: The Pennsylvania State University Press.

Obdrzalek, Suzanne. 2010. "Fleeing the Divine—Plato's Rejection of the Ahedonic Ideal in the *Philebus*." In *Plato's Philebus: Selected Papers from the Eighth Symposium Platonicum*, edited by John Dillon and Luc Brisson, 209–14. Sankt Augustin: Academia Verlag.

Ogihara, Satoshi. 2010. "The Contrast between Soul and Body in the Analysis of Pleasure in the *Philebus*." In *Plato's Philebus: Selected Papers from the Eighth Symposium Platonicum*, edited by John Dillon and Luc Brisson, 215–20. Sankt Augustin: Academia Verlag.

Okin, Susan Moller. 1979. *Women in Western Political Thought*. Princeton: Princeton University Press.

Olympiodorus. 1976. *Commentary on the Phaedo*. In *The Greek Commentaries on Plato's Phaedo, I Olympiodorus*, edited and translated by L. G. Westerink. Amsterdam: North Holland.

O'Meara, Dominic J. 2003. *Platonopolis: Platonic Political Philosophy in Late Antiquity.* Oxford: Clarendon Press.
———, ed. 1985. *Platonic Investigations.* Washington, DC: Catholic University of America Press.
Osborne, Catherine. 1994. *Eros Unveiled: Plato and the God of Love.* Oxford: Oxford University Press.
Pakaluk, Michael. 2003. "Degrees of Separation in the *Phaedo.*" *Phronesis* 48: 89–115.
Patterson, Cynthia. 1986. "Hai Attikai: The Other Athenians." *Helios* 13 (1986): 49–67.
Patterson, Richard. 1987. "Plato on Philosophic Character." *Journal of the History of Philosophy* 25: 325–50.
———. 1991. "The Ascent in Plato's *Symposium.*" *Proceedings of the Boston Area Colloquium in Ancient Philosophy* 7: 193–214.
Peradotto, John, and J. P. Sullivan, eds. 1984. *Women in the Ancient World: The Arethusa Papers.* Albany: State University of New York Press.
Peters, James Robert. 1989. "Reason and Passion in Plato's *Republic.*" *Ancient Philosophy* 9: 173–87.
Peterson, Sandra. 2003. "An Authentically Socratic Conclusion in Plato's *Phaedo*: Socrates' Debt to Asclepius." In *Desire, Identity, and Existence: Essays in Honor of T. M. Penner,* edited by Naomi Reshotko, 33–52. Kelowna, BC: Academic Printing and Publishing.
———. 2011. *Socrates and Philosophy in the Dialogues of Plato.* Cambridge: Cambridge University Press.
Plant, Judith, ed. 1989. *Healing the Wounds.* Philadelphia: New Society.
Plotinus. 1966–88. *Enneads.* 7 volumes. Translated by A. H. Armstrong. Cambridge, MA: Heinemann.
Plumwood, Val. 1993. *Feminism and the Mastery of Nature.* London: Routledge.
Pomeroy, Sarah B. 1975. *Goddesses, Whores, Wives, and Slaves: Women in Classical Antiquity.* New York: Schocken.
Popper, Karl R. 1945. *The Open Society and Its Enemies.* 2 vols. London: Routledge.
Porphyry. 1966. *On the Life of Plotinus and the Order of His Books.* Translated by A. H. Armstrong. In Plotinus, *Enneads,* vol. 1: 2–87.
Presler, Judith, and Sally J. Scholz, eds. 2000. *Peacemaking: Lessons from the Past, Visions for the Future.* Amsterdam, Rodopi.
Price, A. W. 1981. "Loving Persons Platonically." *Phronesis* 26: 25–34.
———. 1989. *Love and Friendship in Plato and Aristotle.* Oxford: Clarendon Press.
Prichard, H.A. 1968. *Moral Obligation, and Duty and Interest: Essays and Lectures.* London: Oxford University Press.
Prior, William J. 1985. *Unity and Development in Plato's Metaphysics.* Lasalle, IL: Open Court.
Reeve, C. D. C. 1988. *Philosopher-Kings: The Argument of Plato's Republic.* Princeton: Princeton University Press.
———. 2006. "A Study in Violets: Alcibiades in the *Symposium.*" In *Plato's Symposium: Issues in Interpretation and Reception,* edited by James Lesher, Debra Nails, and Frisbee Sheffield, 124–46. Cambridge: Harvard University Press.

Reshotko, Naomi, ed. 2003. *Desire, Identity, and Existence: Essays in Honor of T. M. Penner.* Kelowna, BC: Academic Printing and Publishing.

Rice, Daryl H. 1989. "Plato on Force: The Conflict between His Psychology and Political Sociology and His Definition of Temperance in the *Republic*." *History of Political Thought* 10: 565–76.

Robinson, T. M. 2000. "The Defining Features of Mind-Body Dualism in the Writings of Plato." In *Psyche and Soma: Physicians and Metaphysicians on the Mind-Body Problem from Antiquity to Enlightenment*, edited by John P. Wright and Paul Potter, 37–55. Oxford: Clarendon Press.

Roochnik, David. 1987. "The Erotics of Philosophical Discourse." *History of Philosophy Quarterly* 4: 117–29.

———. 1996. *Of Art and Wisdom: Plato's Understanding of Techne*. University Park: The Pennsylvania State University Press.

———. 2003. *Beautiful City: The Dialectical Character of Plato's Republic*. Ithaca: Cornell University Press.

———. 2008. "The Wisdom of Plato's *Phaedo*." In *Teaching for Wisdom: Cross-Cultural Perspectives on Fostering Wisdom*, edited by Michel Ferrari and George Potworowski, 179–88. Dordrecht: Springer.

Rosen, R. M., and J. Farrell, eds. 1993. *Nomodeiktes: Greek Studies in Honor of Martin Ostwald*. Ann Arbor: University of Michigan Press.

Rosen, Stanley. 1965. "The Role of Eros in Plato's *Republic*." *The Review of Metaphysics* 18: 452–75.

———. 1987. *Plato's Symposium*. New Haven: Yale University Press. 1st ed. 1968 (page references are to the reprint edition).

Rowe, C. J. 1986. *Plato: Phaedrus*. Warminster: Aris and Phillips.

———. 1993. *Plato Phaedo*. Cambridge: Cambridge University Press.

———. 1998. *Plato: Symposium*. Warminster: Aris and Phillips.

———. 1999. "The Speech of Eryximachus in Plato's *Symposium*." In *Traditions of Platonism: Essays in Honour of John Dillon*, edited by J. J. Cleary, 53–64. Aldershot: Ashgate.

———. 2001. "The Concept of Philosophy (*Philosophia*) in Plato's *Phaedo*." In *Plato's Phaedo: Proceedings of the Second Symposium Platonicum Pragense*, edited by Ales Havlícek and Filip Karfík, 34–47. Prague: Oikoymenh.

Rowe, Christopher. 2010. "The Relationship of the *Laws* to Other Dialogues: A Proposal." In *Plato's Laws: A Critical Guide*, 29–50. Cambridge: Cambridge University Press.

Rowett, Catherine. 2016. "Why the Philosopher Kings Will Believe the Noble Lie." *Oxford Studies in Ancient Philosophy* 50: 67–100.

Russell, Daniel C. 2005. *Plato on Pleasure and the Good Life*. Oxford: Oxford University Press.

Ruttenberg, Howard S. 1986. "Plato's Use of the Analogy between Justice and Health." *The Journal of Value Inquiry* 20: 145–56.

Ste. Croix, G. E. M. de. 1981. *The Class Struggle in the Ancient Greek World from the Archaic Age to the Arab Conquests*. Ithaca: Cornell University Press.

Sallis, John D. 1975. *Being and Logos: The Way of the Platonic Dialogue*. Pittsburgh: Duquesne University Press.

Sandford, Stella. 2012. "'All Human Beings Are Pregnant': The Bisexual Imaginary in Plato's *Symposium*." In *Embodied Selves*, edited by Stella Gonzalez-Arnal, Gill Jagger, and Kathleen Lennon, 46–65. London: Palgrave Macmillan.

Saunders, Trevor, trans. 1997. *Laws*. In *Plato: Complete Works*, edited by John M. Cooper, 1318–1616. Indianapolis: Hackett.

Saxonhouse, Arlene. 1984. "Eros and the Female in Greek Political Thought: An Interpretation of Plato's *Symposium*." *Political Theory* 12: 5–27.

———. 1994. "The Philosopher and the Female in the Political Thought of Plato." In *Feminist Interpretations of Plato*, edited by Nancy Tuana, 67–85. University Park: The Pennsylvania State University Press.

———. 1999. "Xanthippe and Philosophy: Who Really Wins?" *Proceedings of the Boston Area Colloquium in Ancient Philosophy* 15: 111–29.

Scaltsas, Patricia Ward. 1992. "Virtue without Gender in Socrates." *Hypatia* 7: 126–37.

Schofield, Malcolm. 1993. "Plato on the Economy." In *The Ancient Greek City-State: Symposium on the Occasion of the 250th Anniversary of the Royal Danish Academy of Sciences and Letters, July, 1–4 1992*, edited by Mogens Herman Hansen, 183–96. Copenhagen: Commissioner Munksgaard.

Schultz, Anne-Marie. 2013. *Plato's Socrates as Narrator: A Philosophical Muse*. Lanham, MD: Lexington Books.

Scott, Dominic. 2000. "Socrates and Alcibiades in the *Symposium*." *Hermathena* 168: 25–37.

———. 2007. "Erôs, Philosophy, and Tyranny." In *Maieusis: Essays on Ancient Philosophy in Honour of Myles Burnyeat*, edited by Dominic Scott, 136–53. Oxford: Oxford University Press.

———, ed. 2007. *Maieusis: Essays on Ancient Philosophy in Honour of Myles Burnyeat*. Oxford: Oxford University Press.

Scott, Gary Alan, and William A. Welton. 2008. *Erotic Wisdom: Philosophy and Intermediacy in Plato's Symposium*. Albany: State University of New York Press.

Scruton, Roger. 2009. *Beauty*. Oxford: Oxford University Press.

Sedley, David. 1995. "The Dramatis Personae of Plato's *Phaedo*." *Proceedings of the British Academy* 85: 3–26.

———. 1999. "The Ideal of Godlikeness." In *Plato 2: Ethics, Politics, Religion, and the Soul*, edited by Gail Fine, 309–28. Oxford: Oxford University Press.

———. 2004. *The Midwife of Platonism: Text and Subtext in Plato's "Theaetetus."* Oxford: Oxford University Press.

———. 2007. "Philosophy, the Forms, and the Art of Ruling." In *The Cambridge Companion to Plato's Republic*, edited by G. R. F. Ferrari, 256–83. Cambridge: Cambridge University Press.

Sheffield, Frisbee C. C. 2006. "The Role of the Earlier Speeches in the *Symposium*: Plato's Endoxic Method?" In *Plato's Symposium: Issues in Interpretation and Reception*, edited by James Lesher, Debra Nails, and Frisbee Sheffield, 23–46. Cambridge: Harvard University Press.

———. 2006. *Plato's Symposium: The Ethics of Desire*. Oxford: Oxford University Press.
Shields, Christopher. 2007. "Forcing Goodness in Plato's *Republic*." *Social Philosophy and Policy* 24: 21–39.
Shorey, Paul. 1933. *What Plato Said*. Chicago: University of Chicago Press.
Shiva, Vandana. 1989. *Staying Alive: Women, Ecology, and Development*. London: Zed Books.
Silverman, Allan. 2007. "Ascent and Descent: The Philosopher's Regret." *Social Philosophy and Policy* 24: 40–69.
———. 2010. "Philosopher-Kings and Craftsman-Gods." In *One Book, The Whole Universe: Plato's Timaeus Today*, edited by Richard D. Mohr and Barbara M. Sattler, 55–67. Las Vegas: Parmenides.
Sinaiko, Herman L. 1965. *Love, Knowledge, and Discourse in Plato: Dialogue and Dialectic in Phaedrus, Republic, Parmenides*. Chicago: The University of Chicago Press.
Smith, Nicholas D., and Paul B. Woodruff, eds. 2000. *Reason and Religion in Socratic Philosophy*. Oxford: Oxford University Press.
Sommerville, Brooks. 2014. "The Image of the Jars in Plato's *Gorgias*." *Ancient Philosophy* 34: 235–54.
Sorabji, Richard. 2000. *Emotion and Peace of Mind: From Stoic Agitation to Christian Temptation*. Oxford: Oxford University Press.
Spelman, Elizabeth V. 1982. "Woman as Body: Ancient and Contemporary Views." *Feminist Studies* 8: 109–31.
Spitzer, Adele. 1976. "Immortality and Virtue in the *Phaedo*: A Non-Ascetic Interpretation." *The Personalist* 57: 113–25.
Sprague, Rosamond Kent, trans. 1997. *Charmides*. In *Plato: Complete Works*, edited by John M. Cooper, 639–63. Indianapolis: Hackett.
Stalley, R. F. 1983. *An Introduction to Plato's Laws*. Indianapolis: Hackett.
Strauss, Leo. 1963. "Plato." In *History of Political Philosophy*, edited by Leo Strauss and Joseph Cropsey, 7–63. Chicago: University of Chicago Press.
———. 1964. *The City and Man*. Chicago: University of Chicago Press.
———, and Joseph Cropsey, eds. 1963. *History of Political Philosophy*. Chicago: University of Chicago Press.
Stewart, Herbert L. 1915. "Was Plato an Ascetic?" *The Philosopical Review* 24: 603–13.
Taylor, A. E. 1956. *Plato: The Man and His Work*. New York: Meridian Books.
Taylor, C. C. W. 1998. *Socrates: A Very Short Introduction*. Oxford: Oxford University Press.
Tenkku, Jussi. 1956. *The Evaluation of Pleasure in Plato's Ethics*. Helsinki: Acta Philosophica Fennica, 11.
Thagard, Paul. 1996. *Mind: Introduction to Cognitive Science*. Cambridge: MIT Press.
Tong, Rosemary. 2014. *Feminist Thought: A More Comprehensive Introduction*. 4th ed. Boulder: Westview.
Tracy, Theodore James. 1969. *Physiological Theory and the Doctrine of the Mean in Plato and Aristotle*. Chicago: Loyola University Press.

Trevor, Albert Augustus. 1978. *A History of Greek Economic Thought.* Chicago: The University of Chicago Press, 1916. Reprint, Philadelphia: Porcupine (page references are to the reprint edition).
Tuana, Nancy. 1994. "Introduction." In *Feminist Interpretations of Plato*, edited by Nancy Tuana, 3–10. University Park: The Pennsylvania State University Press.
———, ed. 1994. *Feminist Interpretations of Plato.* University Park: The Pennsylvania State University Press.
Tuplin, Christopher, ed. 2004. *Xenophon and His World.* Stuttgart: Franz Steiner Verlag.
Van der Eijk, Philip J. 2005. *Medicine and Philosophy: Doctors and Philosophers on Nature, Soul, Health, and Disease.* Cambridge: Cambridge University Press.
Vernant, Jean-Pierre. 1991. *Mortals and Immortals: Collected Essays*, edited by Froma I. Zeitlin. Princeton: Princeton University Press.
Vernezze, Peter. 1992. "The Philosopher's Interest." *Ancient Philosophy* 12: 331–49.
Vlastos, Gregory. 1975. *Plato's Universe.* Seattle: University of Washington Press.
———. 1977. "The Theory of Social Justice in the *Polis* in Plato's *Republic*." In *Interpretations of Plato: A Swarthmore Symposium*, Mnemosyne suppl. vol. 50, edited by Helen F. North, 1–40. Leiden, Netherlands: E. J. Brill.
———. 1981. "The Individual as an Object of Love in Plato." In *Platonic Studies.* 2nd ed., 3–42. Princeton: Princeton University Press. 1st ed. 1973.
———. 1991. *Socrates: Ironist and Moral Philosopher.* Cambridge: Cambridge University Press.
———. 1994. "Was Plato a Feminist?" In *Feminist Interpretations of Plato*, edited by Nancy Tuana, 11–23. University Park: The Pennsylvania State University Press.
Von Blanckenhagen, Peter H. 1992. "Stage and Actors in Plato's *Symposium*." *Greek, Roman, and Byzantine Studies* 33 (1): 51–68.
Wallach, John R. 2001. *The Platonic Political Art: A Study of Critical Reason and Democracy.* University Park: The Pennsylvania State University Press.
Ward, Ann, ed. 2007. *Socrates: Reason or Unreason as the Foundation of European Identity.* Newcastle: Cambridge Scholars Press.
———, ed. 2009. *Matter and Form: From Natural Science to Political Philosophy.* Lanham, MD: Lexington Books.
Warren, James. 2014. *The Pleasures of Reason in Plato, Aristotle, and the Hellenistic Hedonists.* Cambridge: Cambridge University Press.
Warren, Karen J. 1991. "Feminism and the Environment: An Overview of the Issues." *APA Newsletter on Feminism and Philosophy* 90: 108–16.
Washington, Booker T. 1995. *Up from Slavery.* Mineola, NY: Dover Publications.
Waterfield, Robin. 1993. *Plato: Republic.* Oxford: Oxford University Press.
———. 1994. *Plato: Symposium.* Oxford: Oxford University Press.
———. 2002. *Plato: Phaedrus.* Oxford: Oxford University Press.
Weinstein, Joshua I. 2009. "The Market in Plato's *Republic*." *Classical Philology* 104: 439–58.
Weiss, Roslyn. 1987. "The Right Exchange: *Phaedo* 69a6-c3." *Ancient Philosophy* 7: 57–66.

———. 2001. *Virtue in the Cave: Moral Inquiry in Plato's Meno*. Oxford: Oxford University Press.
———. 2006. *The Socratic Paradox and Its Enemies*. Chicago: The University of Chicago Press.
———. 2012. *Philosophers in the Republic: Plato's Two Paradigms*. Ithaca: Cornell University Press.
Wender, Dorothea. 1973. "Plato: Misogynist, Paedophile, and Feminist." *Arethusa* 6: 75–90.
Werkmeister, W. H., ed. 1976. *Facets of Plato's Philosophy*. Assen: Van Gorcum.
West, David. 2005. *Reason and Sexuality in Western Thought*. Cambridge: Polity Press.
White, Nicholas P. 1979. *A Companion to Plato's Republic*. Indianapolis: Hackett.
White, Stephen. 2000. "Socrates at Colonus: A Hero for the Academy." In *Reason and Religion in Socratic Philosophy*, edited by Nicholas D. Smith and Paul B. Woodruff, 151–75. Oxford: Oxford University Press.
Williams, Bernard. 1973. "The Analogy of City and Soul in Plato's *Republic*." In *Exegesis and Argument: Studies in Greek Philosophy Presented to Gregory Vlastos* (*Phronesis* suppl. vol. 1), edited by E. N. Lee, A. P. D. Mourelatos, and R. M. Rorty, 196–206. Assen: Van Gorcum.
———. 1999. *Plato*. New York: Routledge.
Woolf, Raphael. 2000. "Callicles and Socrates: Psychic (Dis)Harmony in the *Gorgias*." *Oxford Studies in Ancient Philosophy* 18: 1–40.
———. 2004. "The Practice of a Philosopher." *Oxford Studies in Ancient Philosophy* 26: 97–129.
———. 2012. "How to See an Encrusted Soul." In *Plato and the Divided Self*, edited by Rachel Barney, Tad Brennan, and Charles Brittain, 150–73. Cambridge: Cambridge University Press.
Wright, John P., and Paul Potter, eds. 2000. *Psyche and Soma: Physicians and Metaphysicians on the Mind-Body Problem from Antiquity to Enlightenment*. Oxford: Clarendon Press.
Yount, David J. 2014. *Plotinus the Platonist: A Comparative Account of Plato and Plotinus' Metaphysics*. London: Bloomsbury.
Yu, Jiyuan. 2000. "Justice in the *Republic*: An Evolving Paradox." *History of Philosophy Quarterly* 17: 121–41.
Zeller, Eduard. 1931. *Outlines of the History of Greek Philosophy*. Cleveland: Meridian Books.
Zeyl, Donald J., trans. 1997. *Gorgias*. In *Plato: Complete Works*, edited by John M. Cooper, 791–869. Indianapolis: Hackett.
———, trans. 1997. *Timaeus*. In *Plato: Complete Works*, edited by John M. Cooper, 1224–91. Indianapolis: Hackett.
Zoller, Coleen. 2007. "Seducing Socrates and Resolving Plato's Separate Soul Paradox." In *Socrates: Reason or Unreason as the Foundation of European Identity*, ed. Ann Ward, 30–44. Newcastle: Cambridge Scholars Press.
———. 2009. "Plato's Science of Living Well." In *Matter and Form: From Natural Science to Political Philosophy*, ed. Ann Ward, 35–44. Lanham, MD: Lexington Books.

———. 2010a. "Plato on Philosophy and the Physical in the *Phaedo* and *Symposium*." In *The European Mind: Narrative and Identity*, vol. 1, ed. Henry Frendo, 483–88. Malta: University of Malta Press.

———. 2010b. "To 'Graze Freely in the Pastures of Philosophy': The Pedagogical Methods and Political Motives of Socrates and the Sophists." *Polis* 27: 80–110.

———. 2015. Review of Roslyn Weiss, *Philosophers in the Republic: Plato's Two Paradigms* (Ithaca: Cornell University Press, 2012). *Philosophy in Review* 35: 50–52.

Index

abstinence, 99–100; from physical pleasures, 45–46, 50; sexual, 89, 93, 178, 186; of Socrates, 22, 60–74, 101, 186
abstract inquiry. *See* rational inquiry
abstract, the, 19, 75
addiction, 75
Adeimantus: appeal of quietism to, 138–39; aristocratic views of, 149; questioning being moral, 13–15; on justice, 110–11, 116; philosophical adeptness of, 131, 154; Socrates's testing of, 124, 127
affluence, 122, 182–83. *See also* wealth
African Americans, 10, 148
afterlife, 49. *See also* underworld
Agathon, 62, 64–67, 73, 76, 86, 88, 140
agora, 2, 67, 140, 151
Alcibiades: debauchery of, 47, 53, 198n21; historical, 69, 198n22; potential of, 65, 68, 82–83; shortcomings of, 199n43; on Socrates, 45, 62, 68–71, 80, 82–83, 126, 139, 199n31; Socrates's abstinence with, 22, 60, 62–63, 65–73, 85, 186; Socrates's love for, 2, 71, 73, 86, 199n39, 199n44, 201n68, 201n75; *Symposium* speech of, 75, 200n52, 213n142

allegory of the cave, 79, 107, 128, 130–31, 137, 139, 143
analogies: definition of, 14; Bacchant, 43, 50–54, 196n69; body-soul, 5, 14–17, 108–10, 114–16, 186, 191n65; city-soul, 15, 115–22; 191n66; craft, 108–11, 141–42; finger, 149; medical, 16, 106, 108–10, 114–15, 171, 173–74, 200n51; Plato's use of, 3, 12–18, 21, 108–109, 191nn65–66. *See also* leaky jar metaphor
Anaxagoras, 37–38, 40
animals, 3; attitudes toward, 188; devaluation of, 8; people of color and, 10; the poor and, 10; reincarnation as, 11, 195n60, 197n77; slaves and, 191n48; war and, 215n167; women and, 11
Annas, Julia: on the harmony model, 118, 207nn25, 207n29; on Plato, 12, 54; on poverty, 122; on the principle of specialization, 213n148; on purity, 55; on self-sufficiency, 154; on the transformation of vernacular, 192n77
Apollo, 52–53
Apology (Plato): on free meals, 147, 151, 213n133; on physical survival, 72; on prioritization of the soul

239

Apology (Plato) *(continued)*
over body, 19–20; on Socrates' political leadership, 132–33, 136–37, 139
aporia, 37
appetite, the. *See* appetitive aspect of the soul
appetites: of First City citizens, 158, 162–63; fulfillment of the, 90, 102, 110, 115; for goodness, 82; of healthy people, 114–15; necessary and unnecessary, 163–64; overindulgence of, 19, 121; of philosophers, 43, 87, 203n105; for pleasure, 87, 106, 117; restriction of the, 113, 114; of the soul, 114; for wealth, 152. *See also* appetitive aspect of the soul; *erôs*
appetitive aspect of the soul: desires of the, 6, 117, 119; in the First City, 154, 157–59, 162–64; function of, 3, 116–17, 119, 120; overindulgence of, 19; of philosophers, 126; pleasures of the, 3, 115; rule of the rational aspect over the, 23, 88, 106, 115, 117–21, 186, 207nn28–29; satisfaction of the, 88; starvation of the, 86, 118, 216n208; suppression of, 87, 117, 119, 206n19, 206n21. *See also* charioteer myth; rational aspect of the soul; spirited aspect of the soul
Archer-Hind, R. D., 6, 190n32, 193n3, 196n62, 196n69, 197n84
Aristophanes: Socrates talking with, 62; and the sneeze treatment, 60, 88–90, 209n92; *Symposium* speech of, 75, 76, 87, 200n52, 205n136
Aristotle, 46
Aristoxenus, 42
art of measurement, 158–59
ascent. *See* ascent passage; erotic ascent

ascent passage, 74, 77, 79; exclusive reading of, 83–84, 201n75; inclusive reading of, 84, 201n75, 202n78. *See also* erotic ascent
ascetic dualism. *See* austere dualism
asceticism: austere (*see* austere dualism); consequences of misinterpreting Socratic, 8–12, 188; developmental view of Plato's, 169, 177; original meaning of, 5–6, 34; Pythagorean, 22; of Socrates, 2–4, 21, 34, 45, 62–64, 193n8, 202n82. *See also askesis*; austere dualism; normative dualism
Asclepius (god of health), 25, 193n4
askesis (practice, training): austere dualist, 55, 106; definition of, 5–6, 24; of Socrates, 1, 2, 185; training for death, 57. *See also* asceticism; austere dualism; normative dualism
Athenian (of the *Laws*), 9, 140, 172–73, 176–82, 214n161
Athens (city), 9; Alcibiades and, 71, 198n22; educational success in, 139; marriage age in, 205n136; Socrates and, 2, 45, 63, 132
austere dualism: account of, 6–7, 34, 43, 44; austere dualist interpreters, 6–7; Bacchant analogy as conflicting with, 50–53, 196n69; consequences of, 8–12, 149, 188; as conventional interpretation of Plato, 6; dangers of, 4, 87, 105–106, 121; emphasis on moderation as conflicting with, 44–46, 47–50, 174–78, 296n62; emphasis on war and poverty as conflicting, 179–80; interpretation of the hydraulic model, 124–25, 139; interpretation of the late dialogues, 169–71; interpretation of the leaky jar metaphor, 113; interpretation of the *Phaedo*, 25–27, 28, 33, 35, 41, 46–47, 50–51, 190n32, 196n62,

197n86, 213n133; interpretation of the *Phaedrus*, 62, 91, 92, 95, 202n78, 203n103; interpretation of the separate soul, 28–30, 32; interpretation of the *Symposium*, 62, 66, 83, 192n1, 202n78, 204n106; interpretation of the *Theaetetus*, 54–55; in the *Laws*, 178; as Neoplatonic interpretation, 3–4, 5, 6, 8, 57, 66; Nietzsche and, 6; political leadership of philosophers and, 128, 139; as prescription for body-love, 41–43, 94, 102, 115; as rejection of the physical, 21, 48, 57, 120; sexual experiences and, 87, 94, 95, 178, 204n106; Socrates's lifestyle as conflicting with, 57–58, 71–73; in training for death, 194n26; tripartite soul and, 86–87, 117–20, 121; theory of recollection as conflicting with, 29–30. *See also* asceticism; normative dualism

Bacchae (Euripedes), 52–53
Bacchants, 27, 50–54, 185, 196nn69–70, 196n74
Barney, Rachel: as austere dualist, 6; on the First City, 154, 157, 159, 162–63, 213n151, 216n191
beauty: appreciation of, 83–85; in ascent toward knowledge and the Forms, 76–78, 80; of the beloved, 21, 62, 64, 95–100; of bodies, 80–82; of the Forms, 8; love of, 62; of lovers, 64; of nature, 2, 8, 9–10, 63; of Socrates, 70, 83; of souls, 62, 80–82; of Xanthippe, 73. *See also* beauty, physical; beauty, psychic
Beauty, Form of: ascent to, 76–78, 83–84; contemplation of, 77; erotic desire for, 22, 98; as goal of love, 76; imitation of, 137, 142–43; philosophers' love of, 8; in the physical world, 84, 171; recollection of, 62, 76–78, 80. *See also* beauty
beauty, physical: in ascent toward knowledge and the Forms, 74, 76–78, 80, 95–96; combination of psychic beauty and, 80–86; despise of, 83; as secondary to psychic beauty, 60, 81, 88; as seduction, 73; Socrates's attitude toward, 45, 80–81, 134. *See also* beauty
beauty, psychic, 60, 71, 80–86, 88. *See also* beauty
beloveds: Alcibiades as unsuitable, 63, 65–71; in ascent to knowledge and the Forms, 21, 61–62, 76–78, 80, 83, 85, 93, 95–100; enthusiasm of, 70, 97, 205n119; *erôs* with, 60; ideal, 87; Phaedrus as unsuitable, 63–65; of philosophers, 21, 96, 101–103, 205n129, 210n99; philosophical inclination of, 75, 81, 96, 101–103; physical beauty of, 21, 62, 64, 78–80, 81, 95–100; psychic beauty of, 83; sexual intercourse with, 21, 87, 97, 100, 203n97, 204n108, 210n96; Socrates and unsuitable, 63–71, 74–75, 86, 101–103; as source analog, 14
birth: before, 55; to children, 11, 72, 81, 134; to ideas, 18, 81–82; in beauty, 81, 134, 146; birth control, 181. *See also* procreation
Bloom, Allan, 198n4, 213n151
Blössner, Norbert, 15
Bluck, R. S., 6, 43, 44
Bobonich, Christopher, 139, 182, 217n1, 217nn17–18
bodily passions, 48–49, 129, 197n86
body: appetitive aspect of the soul as linked to the, 3, 117; as associated with nature, 10–11; austere treatment of the, 4, 25, 26, 32, 44; as cause of war, 33; as disruptive

body *(continued)*
to inquiry, 28, 32–33, 125, 197n84; feminists and, 7–8, 26–27; as life raft, 59–57; necessary needs of the, 59; Neoplatonists on the, 4–5, 190n31; peace and the, 156–57, 167; Plato as denigrating the, 3, 6, 7, 41, 102, 179–80; Plato as valuing the, 12, 19, 40–41, 170; as a prison, 35–36, 194n35, 195n37; positive role in inquiry of the, 20–21, 25, 26, 29–32, 36, 39, 125–26; prioritization of the, 13, 43; as secondary to the soul but not loathsome, 7–8, 17, 20, 26, 39–40, 43–49, 88, 102, 147–48, 171–72; Socrates's involvement with his, 34; as source of shame, 4–5; as symbiotic with the soul, 5, 20, 111, 116, 173, 207n31; transition from reliance on the, 35–36, 41–42, 53–54, 76; Western treatment of the, 8, 190n31. *See also* analogies: body-soul; embodiment; sense perception; separation of the soul from the body

body-love: of Alcibiades, 62, 66, 69; Bacchants and, 53; call to abandon, 20; care of the body and, 110; characteristics of, 13, 19, 49; as concerned only with physical beauty, 82; as opposed to wisdom, 33; prescription for, 94, 102, 114–15, 204n106; transition from, 20–21, 41–42, 43, 76, 94, 111, 115; vulgar love as, 75, 76; wisdom as antidote to, 20

Bordo, Susan, 10
Brisson, Luc, 200n50, 205n130
Brown, Eric, 138, 211n110
Brown, Wendy, 212n122
Burger, Ronna, 26, 93–94, 97, 196n69, 203n106

Callicles: hedonism of, 47, 53; on living justly, 13; on philosophers,

138; on satisfaction, 206n16; and self-rule, 110–14
Carone, Gabriela Roxana, 9, 85, 198n22
Carson, Anne, 80
Cebes: austere asceticism of, 213n133; faculties of sight and speech, 30–31; as a Pythagorean, 42, 195n47; Socrates as representing the concerns of, 25–26; on the soul, 42–43, 47, 206n5
Cephalus, 152
Chaerephon, 81
charioteer myth, 77, 78, 86, 90–101, 204n115
Charmides, 73, 81, 82
Charmides (Plato), 81
chastity, 10. *See also* sexual morality; sexual repression
children: in the First City, 155, 158–59, 163; give birth to, 81, 202n78, 205n131; needs of, 122, 212n131; raising of, 11, 182; of Socrates, 71–74, 81, 86, 95, 134, 202n86; women and, 9, 11
Christianity, medieval, 5, 6, 8, 190n31
city of pigs. *See* First City
civic unity: definition of, 149–50; of the First City, 164–65; importance of, 24, 179, 180–81, 183; preservation of, 182; threats to, 152, 182. *See also under* harmony
Classen, C. Joachim, 18
Clinias, 178
communities: cooperative, 12, 154, 159; duty to, 128; formation of, 214n159; harmony in, 154, 182; health of, 105; individuals and, 14, 22, 106, 166–67, 180; First City as, 12, 157, 159–60, 162–64, 216n191; leaders of, 122, 125; peace in, 24, 156, 159, 167, 183; philosophers in their, 21, 107, 129, 130–31, 137, 141–45, 149, 160–61, 167, 208n56, 211n110, 216n191; primitive, 181;

poverty in, 149–50, 152, 153, 164, 167, 179, 181, 186; socio-political, 14, 106, 140, 149; Socrates and, 2, 137, 151
compulsion: to imitate the Forms, 141–42, 146; of philosophers to lead, 107, 131–32, 137, 146–47, 209n59, 211n111
conflicts, 33, 154, 159, 215n167. See also wars
consummation (erotic, sexual): of the charioteer and beloved, 95, 97–98, 204n108, 205n119; Bacchants and, 51; body-lovers and, 19, 75; children through, 81, 202n78; in the First City, 155, 164; of philosophers and beloved, 21, 62, 66, 87, 89, 102; philosophers with the Forms, 17–18; in the philosophical life, 94, 95, 98, 100, 102, 103, 124, 199n46, 203n105, 204n106, 205n131; as relief to return to rational inquiry, 87–90, 103; as shameful, 64, 66, 71, 72; of Socrates, 2, 34, 40, 44–45, 71–72, 73–74; of unphilosophical souls, 100; with an unsuitable beloved, 62, 66, 74, 210n96. See also *erôs*; "sneeze treatment"
contemplative life: erotic desire and, 78, 86; exclusive, 6, 132, 135, 141, 211n110; philosophers and, 129, 141; physical pleasures in the, 20, 34; Plato's conception of the, 185; role of the body in the, 33. See also philosophers; rational inquiry
Cooper, John M.: on the First City, 159, 160, 162, 216n197; on justice in the *Republic*, 156, 212n131; on the philosophical life, 133–35, 209n58; on Plato's use of analogies, 16
cooperation, 118, 154–56, 158, 188
corruption: philosophers' immunity to, 133; of politics, 129, 132, 214n159; of the soul, 114

courage, 15, 16, 50, 85, 116
crafts, 21; political, 16, 136, 143; of the physical, 16; of medicine, 52, 106; specific, 21, 52; value of, 162. See also under analogies
craftsmen: 108–109, 144, 171, 208n46
Critias, 9
Critias (Plato), 9
Crito, 13, 25, 35–36
Crito (Plato), 13, 72
culture, 11, 73. See also Western culture
Cynics, 149

Damascius, 6, 25, 196n69
Davidson, James, 198n21, 198n25, 214n161
Davis, Michael, 41, 193n9
De Vries, G. J., 63, 203n96
death: after, 29, 55, 56, 147; Bacchants and, 53; as cure to life, 25–26; fear of, 13, 19, 33, 147; First City and, 159; murder, 148; Pythagoreans and, 53; resentment of, 33; as separation of soul from the body, 28, 31, 32; of Socrates, 72–73, 137; as source of life, 40; starvation, 147, 148. See also training for death
debauchery, 51, 53, 71, 75. See also hedonism
debts, 146, 152, 181. See also poverty
deception: cure to, 31–32, 59; as problem of embodiment, 28–29, 36, 105
desires: appetitive, 102, 106, 115, 117; cultivation of, 113; definition of, 173; erotic (see under *erôs*); for the Forms 76, 98; healthy, 115; for learning, 128; necessary and unnecessary, 163–64, 216n208; for pleasure, 13, 124, 126, 162, 178; for wealth, 33
desires of the body: denial of, 32, 57, 102, 117, 122, 196n62; as distraction from inquiry, 28; rejection of, 3–4,

desires of the body *(continued)*
5; satisfaction of, 34, 111, 159;
specific, 59. See also under *erôs*
developmental interpretation (of
Plato), 169, 170, 177
dialectic: passion for, 22; as pedagogy,
41, 215n166; in the philosophical
life, 81, 135; as seduction, 64-65,
71, 74, 100-101
dialogues: as form of inquiry, 21,
42, 135-36, 188; as literary genre,
21, 43, 52, 63, 75, 89, 136, 163,
187, 210n82; Plato's dialogues as
resource, 10, 19
Dionysus (god of wine and fertility),
176; Bacchants as worshippers
of, 27; wine, milk, and honey as
associated with, 113; worship of, 27,
51-53. See also Bacchants
Diophanes, 66
Diotima: on the erotic ascent, 76-77,
77-78, 84-85, 95, 202n78; on
giving birth, 72, 81, 146; origins of
the name, 204n113; as teacher of
Socrates, 12, 69, 73, 74; 77, 200n52;
on wisdom, 145
disease: in analogy, 16-17, 109-10,
115, 116; embodiment as, 4, 25-26,
33; of the soul, 13, 17, 108, 116, 173
disharmony: civic, 166, 183; psychic,
13, 166. See also disorder
disorder: psychic, 100, 167; in politics,
107, 129. See also disharmony
distraction: of the body, 7; cure to,
31-32; of erotic desire, 59-60,
61-62, 78, 87-89, 105; from inquiry,
87-90; as problem of embodiment,
26, 28-29
divine, the, 16; becoming like, 55-58,
141, 192n86, 197n83; soul as, 47,
172; soul of, 91. See also charioteer
myth
doctors, 16, 106, 108, 114-15, 156,
173

doctrine of the mean, 46
Dodds, E. R., 6, 190n32, 207n27
Dog, Form of, 79
domination, 117-20
Dorion, Louis-André, 200n46
Dorter, Kenneth, 45, 50, 193n23,
195n57, 197n86
dualism. See austere dualism;
metaphysical dualism; normative
dualism
duBois, Page, 69

early "Socratic" dialogues, 169
Earth, 9, 11, 197n83
Echecrates, 42, 43, 195n47
Edmonds, Radcliffe, 194n35
education, 125, 152, 160, 164, 177-78
embodied inquiry, 24, 28, 41-42, 56
embodiment, 4; as cause of war,
150, 153; as disease, 26, 33; exile
in, 91, 93; nautical analogy, 57; of
philosophers, 134; problems of, 26,
27, 28, 87, 167; society and, 8, 188.
See also body
emotion, 11, 43, 120, 152, 192n81,
203n105
empirical thought: deficiency in, 36,
37-38; hierarchy of philosophical
and, 39-40, 172; transition from
exclusive, 53-54, 59, 79
empiricism, 37
epistemology, 31, 190n22
epithumia (lust), 75
Equal, Form of, 30, 34
erôs (erotic love): of Alcibiades, 69;
Bacchants and, 51, 53; as blinding,
66, 69; for the body, 75, 77;
common love, 56, 75; as compulsion
for philosophers to rule, 146-47;
conquering of, 59-60; as distraction
to rational inquiry, 4, 59, 60, 61-62,
78, 86-90, 103; epithumetic love,
75; as facilitator of knowledge, 19,
54, 60, 61-62, 74-86, 93, 103, 125;

in the First City, 158, 164; healthy love, 60, 89, 75–77; heavenly love, 75–76, 88, 89–90; origins of, 200n52; Plato as ignoring, 1; erotic love of philosophers for the Forms, 17–18, 59–60, 93, 115; philosophers as prone to, 92–93; philosophy as erotic pursuit, 59, 60, 75, 76; purpose of, 81; ranking of different kinds, 178; of Socrates, 2, 61–62, 63–70, 74–75, 81, 85–86, 100–103, 135, 140; Socrates claims knowledge of, 61; Socrates's definition of in the *Symposium*, 76; for the soul, 75, 77; as undertaken with a proper beloved, 60, 93, 98, 101; vulgar love, 60, 75, 76. *See also* abstinence; charioteer myth; consummation; erotic ascent

Erôs (god), 64, 77, 151

erotic ascent (to knowledge and the Forms), 74, 76–78, 80–86, 95, 202n79

erotic desires. *See* erôs

erotic dialogues, 59–60, 101, 103, 169, 178, 186, 204n106

erotic vocabulary, 17–18, 93–94, 98, 203n106

Eryximachus, 62, 64: medical advice of, 89, 114, 203n92; *Symposium* speech of, 74–75, 76, 88–89, 200n51. *See also* "sneeze treatment"

eulabeia (rational caution), 158

exile, 91, 93, 133, 137, 138

feminists: on the appetitive aspect of the soul, 206n21; as critical of Plato's metaphysical dualism, 1, 7–8, 26–27; Plato as first, 205n136, 213n142; on sexual repression, 10

Ferrari, G. R. F.; on the city-soul analogy, 15; on erotic ascent, 94, 99; on justice, 138; on the philosopher-king, 212n114; on poverty, 151; on Socrates's beloveds, 101; on Socrates's first speech in the *Phaedrus*, 86–87; on Socrates's interest in worldly matters, 210n75; translations of, 93–94

fertility, 27, 53

feverish city, 153, 156, 163, 165, 206n18, 215n172

First City, 12, 150, 153–66, 215n165; as anarchic, 215n177; gendered tone of the, 215n163; as impossible, 213n151; justice of citizens, 215n182; prescriptions for the, 206n18; scholars' disregard for, 213n145, 213n148; vegetarianism of the, 214n161; philosophers in the, 216nn190–91; as "prehistoric account," 216n206; war in the, 216n190

food vocabulary, 18, 94

Forms: beauty of, 8; as cause of all things, 84; directional language about, 78–79; disembodied communion with, 25, 31, 55–56; erotic ascent to (*see* erotic ascent); exclusive contemplation of, 107, 124–25, 130–31, 136; imitation of in physical world, 8, 79, 84–85, 137, 141–46, 211n111; intercourse with, 17–18, 21; knowledge of, 29, 40; lifestyle conducive to inquiring after, 33; philosophers' love for, 8, 21, 76, 128–29, 142, 146–47, 211n111; political leadership and, 133–34, 137, 141–46; prioritization of the, 7–8, 39, 125, 126; recollection of, 14, 30, 62, 78, 80, 84, 143; sense perception in understanding, 29–30, 39–40; soul's reunion with, 31, 56, 93, 94, 100; transition to contemplating, 36; as true reality, 19, 29, 141. *See also* Beauty, Form of; Justice, Form of; *and other specific Forms*

Frede, Dorothea: as austere dualist, 6, 190n32; on erotic desire as educational, 77; on medicine in the *Laws*, 173; on Nussbaum's conception of Socrates, 204n106; on sense perception in the theory of recollection, 30; on the *Symposium*, 192n1, 202n79
freedom, 50, 111, 202n78
friendship, 97, 106, 188, 217n18

Gallop, David, 6, 48, 49, 192n1, 196n60
Glaucon: appeal of quietism to, 138-39; aristocratic views of, 149; on beauty, 82; feverish city of, 109, 136, 153, 155-57, 163, 164, 165-66; questions being moral, 13-15, 116; objection to the First City, 163, 215n163; philosophical adeptness of, 131; psychological principles of, 162; on rule of philosophers, 209n61; Socrates's testing of, 124, 127
glory, 69, 151
Goldstein, Rebecca Newberger, 139, 187
Good, Form of the: exclusive contemplation of the, 130; the First City and, 158-62; imitation of the, 133, 137, 139, 140, 141-45, 146-47; inquiring after, 32, 159, 176; philosophers' honor of, 167-68; philosophers' love of, 8, 128, 129, 133, 138, 143; pursuit of the, 86, 121
good, goodness: austere asceticism as epitome of, 10; common, 158, 180, 181; love of, 4; health as inherently, 16, 17; justice as the greatest, 13; as nourishment for psychic wings, 77; pleasure as identical to, 111; pursuit of, 27, 81, 159
Gordon, Jill: on Alcibiades, 69; on the charioteer myth, 78; on Eros, 60; on erotic interactions, 202n88; on philosophy in the embodied life, 57, 172; on the senses, 194n33
Gorgias (Plato): analogy in the, 16, 108-15, 173-74; care of the soul in the, 108-15, 119; leaky jar metaphor, 111-15, 206n15; philosophers as leaders, 138; on politics, 109, 136-37, 142-43; Socrates' asceticism in the, 2; theory of justice in the, 22-23, 108
Griswold, Charles L.: as austere dualist interpreter, 6, 7, 190n32; on the enthusiasm of the beloved, 205n119, 205n129; on homosexual relations, 204n110; on Phaedrus, 198n18; on the *Phaedrus*, 201n67; on the philosopher's sexual consummation with the beloved, 98
Grube, G. M. A., 6, 28, 46-47, 48-49, 196n62

Hackforth, R.: as austere dualist interpreter, 6, 190n32; on moderation, 196n62; on philosophers and their beloveds, 204nn107-108, 204n110; on replenishment and emptying, 174; translations of 93-94, 94-95; on transmigration, 195n60
Halperin, David M., 97, 200n52
happiness: of cities, 127, 160, 216n191; of individuals, 147, 166; of philosophers, 130, 143; of Socrates, 135
harm, physical. *See* violence
harmonious unanimity, 115, 119
harmony model, 117-18, 207n25
harmony: between body and soul, 20, 82, 185; of the body, 5; community, 24; individual, 24, 108; inner, 106, 108, 117, 121, 166; justice as individual, 108-22; justice as political, 147-66; political, 108;

psychic, 86, 111, 119–20, 122, 154, 166, 167, 206n21; of the soul, 5, 106, 116, 195n47; threats to, 121–22, 152–53, 166. *See also* disharmony

harmony, civic, 153, 167; of the First City, 165; philosophers and, 167–77; preservation of, 181–82; threats to, 166, 186. *See also* civic unity

health: in analogy, 14, 16–17, 21, 116–18, 173–74; of the body (*see* health, physical); of the city, 108, 115; in craft analogy, 109–10; justice as, 108; poverty as threat to, 152, 158, 168; prescriptions for, 114–15; of the soul (*see* health, psychic); theory of, 173; in the *Timaeus* and *Laws*, 173–74

health, physical: body-love and, 19; crafts and knacks of, 109–11; discipline that brings, 5; as inherently good, 16, 17; prescription for, 115

health, psychic: body-love and, 13, 19; crafts and knacks of, 109–11; discipline that brings, 5; as inherently good, 13, 17; justice as, 108, 115–22, 156, 166–67; philosophy as, 24; prescription for, 114–15; pursuit of, 17; virtue as, 54

healthy city. *See* First City

heaven, 54, 78–79, 91, 95, 99

hedonism, 167, 178; advocators of, 13, 53, 86–87; Dionysus and, 53; hedonistic lifestyle, 57, 95, 111–15; hedonistic souls, 112, 119; moderation versus, 111–12, 119, 206n16; rejection of, 24, 175

Heracles, 52

Hesiod, 46

Hobbs, Angela, 192n73, 192n80, 213n151

holistic medicine, 5, 111

homosexuality, 170, 193n4, 204n110, 205n136

honors: attachment to, 121; in the cave, 23; lovers of, 33, 48, 121; white horse and, 78, 96

human flourishing, 19–20, 23, 56, 107

human nature, 27, 54–55, 57

hunger, 28, 122. *See also* appetites; body

hydraulic model, 123–27, 139, 208n41

immoderation, 17, 46, 106, 111, 167, 177

immortality, 26, 43, 53, 54, 72

impiety, 31, 114, 138. *See also* piety; suicide prohibition

incarnation. *See* embodiment

injustice: in cities, 15; consequences of, 16–17, 47, 106, 111, 116, 166; justice and, 13–14, 138, 154, 156; philosophers and, 84, 137; in souls, 120–21; spirited aspect of the soul and, 119, 121–22, 163; victims of, 147–48

inquiry. *See* rational inquiry

intercourse. *See* consummation

interdependence, 137

Iolaus, 52

Irwin, Terence: inclusive interpretation of the ascent passage, 83, 84; on the leaky jar metaphor, 113; on philosophers and the Forms, 131, 142, 145; on reason, 212n115; on self-government, 110–11

isomorphism, 15. *See also* analogies: city-soul

Jaggar, Alison, 7

Jowett, Benjamin, 6, 93, 196n62

justice: Adeimantus's account of, 154; in analogy, 13–16; in city-soul analogy, 116–18, 156; civic, 14, 22–23, 106; cultivation of, 23, 55, 57–58, 120; earthly manifestations of, 84–85; fight for, 132–33, 137–38; the First City and, 158, 160–64,

justice *(continued)*
  215n165, 215n186; food justice, 12; Glaucon's account of, 156–57; importance of, 153; individual, 14, 22–23, 106, 108, 118, 166–67; as individual harmony, 108–22; interdependence and, 137; "know justice, know peace," 24, 166–68, 206n1; as political harmony, 147–66; as psychic health, 108; as psychic medicine, 109–11; purpose of, 13–14, 16; Socrates's account of, 13–14, 15, 86, 116, 156; theory of, 23, 116, 118, 120. *See also* harmony model; health; injustice
Justice, Form of, 84, 137, 141–42, 143

Kahn, Charles H., 6, 196n74
Kallipolis, 154, 157, 162, 164–65, 208n56, 216n196
Keuls, Eva C., 153, 193n4, 205n136
Kingsley, Peter, 52, 53
Klosko, George, 139, 207n28
knowledge, 2, 126, 128, 175
knowledge, pursuit of, 22; the body in, 21, 29–30, 39, 43, 44; dialogue in the, 135–36; erotic desire in the, 61, 74–86, 87; Socrates's, 2, 86. *See also* rational inquiry
Kosman, L. A., 83
kosmos (ordered world), 10
Kraut, Richard, 145–46, 200n52, 205n131, 208n57

labor. *See* birth
Lane, Melissa, 124–25, 139, 201n75
late dialogues, 24, 169–83
Laws (Plato): medical analogy in the, 173–74; moderation in the, 176–79, 217n13; nature in the, 9, 171; normative dualism in the, 171–72; on peace and communities, 179–83; on political activity, 140; on sense perception, 172

leadership: conventional, 132; cooperative harmony and, 118; in the First City, 159–62, 216n191; philosophers and political, 107, 126–34, 137–38, 141–46, 160–62, 208n56, 211n110; rare natures of leaders, 122–25, 136; Socrates and, 133, 136–37, 139
leaky jar metaphor, 106, 109, 112–15, 119, 177, 206nn15–16
legislation, 109–10, 143, 173–74
Lenzi, Mary, 159, 206n1
Linforth, Ivan M., 36, 112, 195n37, 206n10, 206n15
Lötter, H. P. P., 148–49, 214n159
love. *See eros*
love of wisdom: analogy between medicine and, 106, 153; embodiment and, 1, 4, 6, 24, 54, 93; prioritization of, 19; ruling and, 145; Socrates and, 135; transition from body-love to, 20, 33
lovers of wisdom: body-lovers and, 33, 54; disposition of, 2, 4; erotic experiences and, 60, 61, 100, 101; Phaedrus as, 64; philosophers as, 143, 145; political leadership and, 107
lust, 95, 98, 99, 101, 178
Lysias, speech of, 63–64, 86–87

Magnesia (city in the *Laws*), 177, 182, 217n20
Mahoney, Timothy, 128, 138, 206n21, 209n61
marriage, 71, 74, 182, 186, 205n136
McCoy, Marina, 155, 162, 215n163
McKeen, Catherine, 128, 155, 164, 165
means-end reasoning, 158
mêden agan (moderation as nothing in excess), 46, 47
medicine: analogous use of, 16, 21, 173–74, 200n51; physical medicine as analogous to psychic medicine,

109–11; replenishment and emptying, 113, 118–19, 173. *See also* doctors; holistic medicine
memory, 32, 172
meta phrônêseôs (practical wisdom), 54, 55
metaphors: Plato's use of, 16–18, 94; relation between body and soul, 3, 202n78; horse and sex, 77; military, 192n73. *See also* analogies; leaky jar metaphor
metaphysical dualism, 1, 3, 6, 9, 191n39
metaphysics of authenticity, 144
Meyer, Susan Suavé, 161
middle dialogues, 24, 169–70, 171, 174, 183
midwife, 12, 151
Miller, Mitchell H., Jr., 102, 140, 142
moderation: in analogy, 16; as essential to justice, 14, 106; in the First City, 159–60, 162–64; in the late dialogues, 174–79, 181, 217n13; of nonphilosophers, 48–49; as nothing in excess, 46, 47, 49; in the philosophical life, 27, 43, 44–45, 46–50, 57, 195n57, 196n62; physical appearance as expressing, 82; as pleasure, 175; as proper ordering of cities and households, 145; self-rule and, 111–13; and the separate soul, 44–50; in the soul, 118–20, 126; soul-love and, 21; as virtue of cities and souls, 15. *See also* leaky jar metaphor
money-lovers, 48, 123, 153
Moravcsik, J. M. E., 83
Moravcsik, Julius, 173
Morrow, Glenn, 51, 182, 217n20
Myrto, 86, 202n86. *See also* Xanthippe
myths: Boreas and Oreithyia, 63; Plato's use of, 128, 195n60; water-bearers, 106, 109. *See also* charioteer myth

Nails, Debra, 62, 199n39, 204n106
Native Americans, 148
natural world. *See* physical world
nature, 2, 8–12, 63, 188. *See also* physical world
Nehamas, Alexander, 6, 8, 83, 84, 93, 204n114
Neoplatonism, 4–6, 8, 23, 57, 190n31, 192n86
Nietzsche, Frederich, 6, 25
nonviolence, 12
normative dualism: account of, 7–8, 26, 39, 85; Bacchant analogy as supporting, 50–53; bodily pleasure and, 126, 175; emphasis on *erôs* as supporting, 61, 90; emphasis on moderation as supporting, 47; hierarchy of psychic and physical beauty as supporting, 81, 84, 85; interpretation of the leaky jar metaphor, 112, 113; interpretation of the *Phaedo*, 26–27, 41, 46–47, 190n32, 195n57, 197n86; interpretation of the *Phaedrus*, 190n32, 203n95; interpretation of the *Symposium*, 83–84; of the late dialogues, 170, 171–72, 173, 183; as prescription to soul-lovers, 94; political leadership of philosophers and, 143–44; reformation of one's attitude toward the body as part of, 31, 39, 57; in training for death, 57. *See also* asceticism; austere dualism; body; soul
Nussbaum, Martha C.: on Alcibiades, 67, 69, 199nn38–39; on the charioteer myth, 90, 97; on Plato and Dion of Syracuse, 205n137; on sexual satisfaction of philosophers, 88, 97, 204n106; on Socrates as model ascendant, 85; on the *Symposium*, 62, 200n52; on transformation of vernacular, 98

Ogihara, Satoshi, 175
Olympiodorus, 6, 25
oppression, 10
opson (relishes, luxuries), 155, 214n161
oratory, 110. *See also* rhetoric; persuasion; sophists
orgasm, 89, 90. *See also* consummation

paiderastia, 66, 97, 200n50
pain, 175–76; avoidance of, 44, 178; body-lovers and, 49; as distraction to inquiry, 32; in the finger analogy, 149–50; in the hedonistic life, 111–13; of hunger, 122; in the philosophical life, 195n57
Pakaluk, Michael, 6, 7, 194n26
palinode. *See* charioteer myth
Patterson, Richard, 120
Pausanius, speech of, 74–75
peace: conditions for, 153, 156, 157, 165, 180, 206n1; desirability of, 179, 180; elusiveness of, 188; in the First City, 154–61, 163, 165, 213n151; fostering, 147; inner, 121; justice and, 118, 206n1; "know justice, know peace," 24, 166–68
pedagogical irony, 19–21, 41, 102, 106, 187, 194n35
people of color, 3, 8, 10, 188
persuasion, 13, 110, 133. *See also* rhetoric; sophism
Peterson, Sandra: on the care of the soul, 5–6; on the *Phaedo*, 26; on body-love, 33; on Socrates, 34, 210n75, 213n133, 215n166; on the First City, 163; on the transformation of vernacular, 192n73, 208n49
Phaedo, 40, 42, 52
Phaedo (Plato), 25–58; affinity argument in the, 197n86; agenda of the, 43; analogical reasoning in the, 14; austere dualist interpretation of the, 2, 25–27, 29, 169, 177, 190n32; as between austere asceticism and normative asceticism, 41; moderation in the, 44–50; physical desire in the, 51; Plato's authorial choices in the, 40–41; the political in the, 215n176; problems of embodiment in the, 28, 59; Pythagorean and Bacchant overtones of the, 52; theory of recollection in the, 29–31; transformation theme in the, 36–39
Phaedrus, 9, 62, 100, 198n18; Socrates's abstinence with, 63–65, 86; Socrates's physical attraction to, 73
Phaedrus (Plato): austere dualist interpretation of, 202n78, 203n103; double meaning of the, 204n106; emphasis of *erôs*, 60, 102; as highlighting problem of distraction, 59; inclusive reading of the, 201n67; on knowing oneself, 61; tripartite soul and, 86, 108. *See also* charioteer myth
Philebus (Plato), 24, 169, 170, 172–77 183
Philolaus, 42
philosômatos (body-lover), 19, 33
philosophers: attitude toward the physical world, 8, 79, 84–85, 126, 128, 191n39; as Bacchants, 51–53, 196n69; beloveds as, 101–103, 205n129; erotic desire of, 61, 77–79, 85–93, 98–100, 147; in the First City, 157, 159–62, 216nn190–91; genuine, 127, 143; love of the Forms, 8, 17–18, 56, 85, 125–26, 128, 130, 141–47; moderation of, 44–50, 196n62; natural, 36–39; as political rulers, 21, 127–47, 167, 209n58, 209n59, 209n61, 211nn110–11, 212n114;

providing compensation for their contributions, 150–51, 211n110; rare nature of, 1, 122–24, 126, 207n37; sexual activity of, 21, 62, 65–66, 80, 87–90, 94, 210n96; as soul-separators, 29, 52; as training for death, 25; transformation to, 35–37, 39–40, 53–54, 57, 79; Western, 86. *See also* sense perception
philosophical inquiry. *See* rational inquiry
philosophy: as aid to loving one's beloved, 92–96, 99–100; Alcibiades and, 66–67, 71, 83; as care of the soul, 51, 153; as erotic pursuit, 59, 75–77, 92–93; as feminine, 11–12; in the First City, 159–62, 216nn190–91; life-denying, 6; Platonic philosophy as 'otherworldly,' 2–3, 7; political leadership as integral to, 128; as training for death, 25–26, 52, 197n86; vindication of, 2; 'without guile,' 92, 93, 95, 100, 204n107; *See also* austere dualism; body; normative dualism
phronēsis (practical wisdom), 45–46, 55
phroura (prison, garrison post), 194n35
physical world: abhorrence of the, 4, 10, 144; beauty of the, 8; components of the, 171; devaluation of the, 8, 10; disdain for the, 8, 25; imitation of the Forms in the, 8, 79, 107, 137, 141–47, 211n111; philosophers and the, 8, 21, 39, 107, 121, 126, 128–29, 134, 140–41; Plato's feelings toward the, 6–8, 25, 149, 171, 191n39; sense perception of the, 31, 36, 56, 57, 59; separation from the, 32; Socrates's engagement with the, 2, 34, 85–86, 136, 208n42, 210n75; treatment of the, 9–10;

withdrawal from the, 26, 51, 136, 193n23, 197n86
piety, 53, 55, 57–58, 133, 139
Plato: as aristocrat, 152; authorial choices of, 40–41, 42, 52, 63, 75, 217n20; and complexity of his dialogues, 186–87; consequences of misinterpreting, 8–12; Dion of Syracuse as Plato's love, 205n137; financial support of Socrates, 151; as the first feminist, 205n136, 213n142; lack of marriage and children, 74; political activity of, 23; as possessor of a rare soul, 103. *See also Gorgias*; *Phaedo*; *Phaedrus*; *Republic*; *and other works by name*
Platonic dialogues, 2, 4, 10, 66
Platonic love, 22, 59, 85, 98, 107
pleasures: of the appetitive aspect of the soul, 3, 117, 119–20; austere rejection of, 6, 26, 28, 44, 48, 117, 125; Bacchants and, 51–53; bodily pleasures in the philosophical life, 44–50, 54, 86, 120–21, 123–26, 175–76, 195n57, 203n95, 203n105; body-lovers and, 13, 19, 20, 75; civic unity as shared, 149–50; as conducive to inquiry, 57; in the First City, 158, 162, 164, 214n161; hedonism on, 111–14, 119; hostility toward, 86; indifference toward, 125; intellectual, 49, 115, 124, 125, 126; the *Laws* on, 176–79; nonphilosophers and, 95, 136; the *Philebus* on, 174–76; prescriptions for, 114–15; Pythagoreans and, 43; of Socrates, 34, 44–45, 74, 75, 126
pleonexia (having and wanting more), 156
Plotinus, 4–6, 23, 66, 135, 170, 189n10, 190n22
Plumwood, Val, 6, 9, 153, 206n21
polis (city), 17, 139, 164, 165, 166–68
political arena. *See* socio-political arena

political dialogues, 23, 106, 108
politics: Alcibiades and, 68, 71;
  conventional, 129, 132, 133, 136;
  true, 136; craft of, 16; as feminine,
  12; in the First City, 154, 157–59,
  211n110; in the *Phaedo*, 215n176;
  philosophers in, 127–39, 141–47,
  160, 192n86, 209n58, 211n110; as
  psychic care, 109–10, 142–43; true
  politician, 110
Porphyry, 4, 66, 135. *See also* Plotinus
Poverty (god), 151
poverty: call to eradicate, 165, 167;
  dangers of, 122, 148–53, 181–83,
  186; the First City's avoidance of,
  155, 158, 159, 163, 164; peace as
  absence of, 167–68, 186; warnings
  about, 12
power, 20, 68, 69, 129, 152
practicing for death. *See* training for
  death
pregnancy, 12, 69, 81. *See also* birth
Price, A. W., 83
principle of specialization, 158,
  160–61, 165, 213n148
Prior, William J., 29
procreation, 40, 60, 72, 158, 171,
  215n184
proportion, 170, 173, 176, 217n19
prostitution, 63, 198n25
Protagoras, 140
Protarchus, 174–76
psychic care. *See* soul, care of the
psychic training, 5–6, 109–10, 114
puritanism, 86. *See also* chastity
purity, 10, 55
Pythagoreans: Bacchants and,
  196n74; on embodiment, 26; in the
  Phaedo, 40–43, 52–53, 195n47; on
  reincarnation, 196n60; as soul-
  lovers, 27, 42–43

racism, 10
rape, 11, 147

rational aspect of the soul:
  experiencing pleasures under the
  guidance of, 60, 66, 87, 90, 102,
  121, 115, 214n161; in the First City,
  154, 159, 162–63; fitness to rule of
  the, 117, 159; function of the, 117;
  as primary in the philosophical life,
  26; rule of as harmony, 117–21,
  175–76, 207n28; rule of as tyranny,
  23, 88, 90, 106, 117–18, 119–20; use
  of to identify the proper lifestyle,
  57. *See also* appetitive aspect of
  the soul; charioteer myth; spirited
  aspect of the soul
rational inquiry: in analogy, 15; the
  body's role in, 19–20, 21–22, 25–30,
  32, 36, 39–40, 43, 57; erotic desire's
  role in (see under *erôs*); as erotic
  pursuit, 75, 76; in the First City,
  157–58, 159, 161; life of exclusive,
  135; lifestyle conducive to, 1, 33; as
  making embodied experience worth
  living, 56; pleasures conducive to,
  57; problems of embodiment for,
  26, 28, 31, 59–60, 61–62; sense
  perception's role in, 21, 29–31,
  34, 36, 39–40, 172–73; Socrates's
  commitment to, 32; transition to,
  20–21, 35, 37, 39; the soul's role in,
  36. *See also* embodied inquiry
rationality: Apollo as linked to, 52; as
  kinship to the divine, 91; feminist
  philosophers and, 26; as masculine,
  11; physical basis of, 7
rational life, 120, 126, 129, 135, 175
reason. *See* rational aspect of the soul
rebirth, 53. *See also* reincarnation
recollection, 79–80; beauty and, 76,
  78; distinction from memory, 172;
  sense perception and, 29–31, 143,
  185. *See also* charioteer myth;
  theory of recollection
Reeve, C. D. C.: on anger, 122; on the
  First City, 158, 213n151, 216n191;

on imitation, 212n120; on the philosophical life, 209n58, 211n110; on Plato's use of *agalmata*, 199n37; on Socrates and Alcibiades, 199n44
reincarnation, 11, 47, 95, 99, 100, 196n60
Republic (Plato): analogical reasoning in the, 14–15; care of the soul in the, 115–22; on the combination of physical and psychic beauty, 82–83; on justice, 13–14, 17, 86, 111, 117–18, 153; paradoxes of the, 12; on philosophical leaders, 122–47, 209n59, 211n110; physical details in the, 70; on poverty, 12, 149–51, 182; Socratic asceticism in the, 2. *See also* First City
revisionist interpretation (of Plato), 169
revolution, 152
rhetoric, 64, 208n49. *See also* dialectic; persuasion
Rice, Daryl H., 118
Roochnik, David: on austere dualist interpreters, 7; on Eros, 76; on the *Phaedo*, 2–3, 26, 42; on Platonic philosophy, 2–3
Rowe, C. J.: on Aristophanes, 203n92; as austere dualist interpreter, 6; on the *Phaedo*, 195n47; on philosophy, 204n107; translations of, 48, 93, 94, 204n114; on transmigration, 196n60
rulers, 129, 137, 142–43, 157, 160, 216n191. *See also* leadership
Russell, Daniel: on the *Phaedo*, 26; on philosophers, 203n95; on the *Republic*, 118, 207n25; on Socrates, 139, 193n8; on the *Theaetetus*, 209n63

Saxonhouse, Arlene: on the body, 21; on the *Phaedo*, 26, 40, 41; on the *Symposium*, 151, 213n142; on Xanthippe, 40, 200n48

"The School of Athens" (Raphael), 79
Schultz, Anne-Marie: on the First City, 216n190; on the harmony model, 117–18; on the philosophical life, 203n105; on the soul, 206n19; on the *Symposium*, 203n92
Scott, Dominic: on Alcibiades and Socrates, 199n43, 201n75; on the hydraulic model, 208n41; on Socrates, 208n42
Sedley, David, 211n111
seduction, 95; in the *Phaedrus*, 63, 64; of Socrates, 71, 73, 85, 199n39
self-care, 100, 111, 122, 145. *See also* body; soul
self-control, 110, 111, 112, 113, 196n62. *See also* self-discipline
self-cultivation, 62
self-discipline, 6, 34, 109, 113; austere, 4, 23, 44, 113; and desires, 97, 111, 114, 164; in the First City, 163; of the philosopher, 4, 25, 185; of Socrates, 1–2
self-governance. *See* self-discipline
self-indulgence, 72. *See also* bodily indulgence
self-knowledge, 23, 61, 86. *See also* knowledge
self-rule, 110–11, 114. *See also* rational aspect of the soul; self-discipline
self-sufficiency, 111, 113, 154
sense perception: body-lovers and, 19; deception of, 28, 35, 59, 105; detachment from the body and, 193n23; in rational inquiry, 21, 29–31, 34, 36, 39–40, 54, 59, 143, 172–73, 193n20; in theory of recollection, 27, 29–30, 34, 143, 172–73; withdrawal from dependence on, 36, 53–54
separation of the soul from the body: Bacchants and, 52; desirability of, 42; literal interpretation of, 25, 27, 28–32, 34–35; moderation and,

separation of the soul from the body (*continued*)
 44–50; paradox of, 25, 31, 43; philosophers and, 27, 39, 44, 52; as separation from the material world, 32; Socrates and, 36–37, 193n9; as solution to embodiment, 26, 27, 28, 59; suicide as, 31–32; as training for death, 25, 28; as transformation to philosopher, 35–40, 43
sex. *See* consummation
sexism, 10
sexuality, 205; black, 191n48; in the First City, 164; horses as symbols of, 77; love and, 108; as lust, 95; nonprocreative, 178; philosophers and, 66; society's attitude toward, 188
sexual morality, 10–11, 178
sexual repression, 10–11
shame: Alcibiades and, 67, 71; of the body (*see under* body); of sexual experiences, 60, 64, 71, 72, 94, 95; Socrates and, 72, 101; in the soul, 96; vice and, 116
Sheffield, Frisbee C. C., 75, 200n49, 202n82
Silenus, 69–70, 80
Silverman, Allan, 157, 210n82, 215n172
Simmias, 29–31, 42–44, 55, 195n47, 213n133
Sinaiko, Herman L., 97, 204n108, 204n115
slaves, 68, 177: to the body, 19, 20, 33; animals and, 191n48
slavishness, 19
"sneeze treatment," 60, 88–90
social-political arena, 154; philosophers' withdrawal from, 22, 107, 147; value of, 107; participation in, 121, 133; nature of, 108, 129, 133
society, 13, 159, 206n1; disharmony in, 167; harmony in, 166–67; ideal, 102, 153, 182; philosophers' contributions to, 151; primitive, 181; poverty and, 107, 149; unjust, 137; urban, 63; women and, 11
Socrates: abstinence of, 62–71, 101–102; asceticism of, 2, 3–4, 5, 21; bodily pleasures of, 44–45; claims to knowledge, 2, 61; commitment to rational inquiry, 32; as erotic philosopher, 61–62; as exemplar leader, 122, 124, 132–33, 136–37, 139–40; as exemplar philosopher, 1–2, 27, 33–35, 36, 57–58, 61–62, 85–86, 95, 126, 134, 150; historical, 5, 74, 103, 152, 213n142; philosophical transformation of, 36–40; physical appearance of, 82–83; Plato's heroization of, 52; political activity of, 23; pursuit of knowledge, 2; rare philosophical nature of, 126, 136; self-discipline of, 1–2; as Silenus, 80; wealth of, 151; wife and children of, 71–74, 95, 200n48, 202n86
sophists, 110, 127, 208n47
sôphrosunê (moderation), 46–47, 50
soul (*psychê*): after death, 7, 28, 49–50, 55, 92; Alcibiades and his, 66, 69, 71, 83; before birth, 55; compulsion and, 212n121; as divine, 47, 55, 172; feminism and, 26–27; neglect of the, 41–43, 51, 135; as more real than the body, 3, 13, 43; as most valuable, 12, 16–17, 19, 42, 43; prioritization of without denigrating the body, 7–8, 17, 20, 39, 40, 54, 102, 121, 147, 171–72; role in rational inquiry, 36, 40; shaped in imitation of the Forms, 129, 132–33, 134, 135, 139, 141–47, 160, 212n114; symbiotic relationship with the body, 3, 5–6, 20, 57, 111, 157, 172; symbiotic relationship with the political community, 17,

106, 150, 153, 166–68; transition to prioritizing the, 20, 35–36, 39, 41, 53–54, 88, 102, 111; as true self, 3, 36, 147. See also analogy; aspects of the soul; charioteer myth; separation of the soul from the body
soul, care of the, 48–49, 76, 189n5; in the Gorgias, 108–15; healthy love as, 76, 89–90; in the Republic, 115–22; as linked to the care of the body, 3, 5–6; neglect of, 41; politics as, 142–43; prioritization of the, 7, 16–17, 19–20, 22, 41–42, 94, 102, 204n106; transition away from exclusive, 20; without denigrating the body, 20, 22, 102. See also leaky jar metaphor; soul
soul, health of the. See health, psychic
soul-love, 21, 27, 43, 75, 94, 110, 115
spirit, the. See spirited aspect of the soul
spirited aspect of the soul: in the First City, 154, 159, 163; function of the, 116, 119–20, 121; overactivity of, 121–22; as ally of the rational aspect, 119, 121, 163; rule of the rational aspect over, 23, 115, 117, 121. See also appetitive aspect of the soul; rational aspect of the soul
Spitzer, Adele, 26
Stalley, R. F., 177
starvation: of the appetite, 86, 118, 119, 216n208; victims of, 147, 148
Stoics, 149
Strauss, Leo, 1, 209n59, 215n184, 215n186
suicide prohibition, 27, 31–32, 34, 56. See also piety
survival, physical: the First City and, 158–59, 161, 164; creation of conditions for, 186; needs for, 3, 151, 158, 183; physical, 12, 72, 105, 108; threats to, 133, 137, 139, 158
sustainability, 12, 153, 165

Symposium (Plato): Alcibiades in the, 65–71, 80, 204n106, 213n142; on birth, 72; on the combination of physical and psychic beauty, 80–82; as compared to the Phaedrus, 201n67; highlighting problem of distraction, 59, 61–62, 88; identifying Plato with all characters of the, 200n52; Phaedrus in the, 64–65; as revision to Plato's rejection of earthly life, 192n1; role of erôs in inquiry, 60, 62; on self-knowledge, 61; speeches of Pausanius and Eryximachus in the, 74–75; Socrates in the, 61–62, 101, 126, 135, 204n106. See also ascent passage

Taylor, A. E., 6, 28, 200n48
teachers, 125, 210n82; Socrates as, 68, 135–36, 151; Diotima as, 69, 73
temperance. See moderation
temptation, 86, 113, 138, 179
Tenkku, Jussi, 26
Thales, 149
Theaetetus (character), 82, 207n36
Theaetetus (dialectician), 74, 103
Theaetetus (Plato), 54–55, 82, 197n77, 209n63
Theodorus, 82, 207n36, 209n63
theory of interconnectedness, 106, 166
theory of recollection, 21, 27, 29–31, 34, 172. See also recollection
Thrasymachus, 13–14, 40, 153
Timaeus: on health, 9, 173; on the physical world, 9, 171, 172; on proportion and measurement, 173, 217n19; on rare natures, 126; on the relation between the body and the soul, 5
Timaeus (Plato): nature in the, 171; Plato's authorial choices in the, 128; reincarnation in the, 11; sense perception in the, 172; theory of health in the, 173

Tong, Rosemary, 11
Tracy, Theodore James, 173
training for death, 25–58; austere asceticism and, 28–29, 32, 57, 105; Bacchants and, 52, 53; embodied inquiry and, 56; philosophy as, 22, 24, 25–26, 58; soul-separating and, 28, 29, 31–32. *See also* separation of the soul from the body
transformation of vernacular, 16–18, 94–95, 98, 192n73, 192n77, 192n80. *See also* analogy
translations, 7; alternative, 55, 84, 128, 194n35; effects of, 93; of Ferrari, 94; of Grube, 28, 46–49; of Hackforth, 93–94; of Jowett, 93; of Nehamas and Woodruff, 83, 84, 93; of Rowe, 93; of Rowe and Gallop, 48; of Waterfield, 84, 94
transmigration of soul, 42, 195n60
tripartite soul, 86, 108, 116, 211n110. *See also* appetitive aspect of the soul; rational aspect of the soul; spirited aspect of the soul
true reality, 19, 29, 81. *See also* Forms, the
truth, 18, 50, 70, 75, 77, 118; desire for, 33; inquiring after, 28, 31, 32, 196n62; lovers of, 127, 139, 145; plain of, 78–79; pursuit of, 124–26, 136
tyranny, 2, 42, 47, 118–20, 152

underworld, 50, 51. *See also* afterlife
Unitarian interpretation (of Plato), 169
unity, 150, 170, 183; of the city, 149, 150, 155, 214n151; civic (*see* civic unity); of the soul, 150, 212n129
unjust city, 109. *See also* feverish city
unsustainability, 159

vegetarianism, 214n155
vice, 95, 116, 203n106
violence, 11, 47, 67, 99, 148
virginity, 207n27

virtues, 16, 54, 119, 145, 147, 175; appreciation of, 164, 165; arguments about, 81; aspiring to, 13, 176; of fitness, 173; of the city, 15, 180, 192n77; civic, 23, 109; friendship and, 217n18; as fulfilling human nature, 55; as health, 174; human (*see* human virtue); of justice, 23, 107, 117, 120, 166; neglect of, 152; passion for, 2; of the philosopher, 49; social, 47; of Socrates, 199n31; of the soul, 15, 54, 116–17; study of, 66; traditional, 16; wealth and, 213n143
Vlastos, Gregory: on the ascent passage, 83; on the dark horse, 98; on the erotic dialogues, 204n106; on the First City, 158; on the historical Socrates, 213n142; on the polis, 166; on Socrates, 139
Von Blanckenhagen, Peter H., 71, 199n43

Wallach, John R., 158, 215n182
wars, 7, 148, 150, 206n1; avoidance of, 159, 163, 164, 179–81, 215n167; causes of, 33, 153, 156, 163; civil, 106, 180, 182; in the First City, 153, 215n182; masculinity of, 155; poverty and, 149, 155, 158, 163; in the soul, 118; warzones, 166
Warren, Karren J., 11
Waterfield, Robin, 84, 94, 150, 203n103, 204n114
wealth, 16, 19, 132, 172, 213n143; Alcibiades', 67; desire for, 33; disregard for, 149; honor for, 152; love of, 20, 33; Plato's, 150; pursuit of, 120–21, 129; redistribution of, 181–82; Socrates' lack of, 151
wealth inequality, 12, 149, 170, 182–83, 214n151, 218n23
Weiss, Roslyn, 26, 131–33, 142, 195n53, 210n91
Wender, Dorothea, 213n142

Western culture, 8, 10, 12, 187, 206n1
Williams, Bernard, 26
wine, 67, 112, 113, 176; Bacchants and, 53; body-lovers and, 19; in the First City, 155, 164, 214n161; god of (*see* Dionysus); in the *Laws*, 176, 177; Socrates and, 44
wisdom, 77, 80, 121, 145, 160; facilitation of, 74, 75, 90; "human wisdom," 61; love of (*see* love of wisdom); lovers of (*see* lover(s) of wisdom); 'otherworldly,' 2; of philosophers, 195n57, 203n95; practical, 55, 56, 57–58; pursuit of, 23, 27, 58, 90, 135; as virtue, 15; of Socrates, 74
women: animals and, 10–11; black, 10, 191; as caretakers, 11; chastity and, 10, 178; consequences of misinterpreting asceticism and, 3, 8, 10–11, 188; guardian-, 73; nature and, 10–12; oppression of, 10–11; Plato and, 10, 205n136; Socrates and, 12, 73, 40, 148. See also feminists
Woodruff, Paul, 83–84, 93, 204n114
Woolf, Raphael: on the austere dualism in the *Phaedo*, 26; on the *Gorgias*, 201n68; on interpretations of Plato, 190n28, 197n86; on justice, 166–67; on sense perception, 30, 31
working class, 10. See also poverty

Xanthippe, 40, 71–74, 86, 200n48, 202n86

Zeus, 96, 198n18, 204n113

www.ingramcontent.com/pod-product-compliance
Lightning Source LLC
Chambersburg PA
CBHW020328240426
43665CB00044B/892